The Sporting Ori

of

Worcester Park Athletic Club

'founded by ex-Servicemen in 1921'

Back Row: J. Pryor, G. Wilson, A. Davies, W. York, A. Ashby, E. Saitch, H. Walsh

Front Row: H. Watts, T. Lane, T. Mearing, E. Dean, F. Williams, C. Bowry

This photograph, which was taken in 1928, shows several of the founding members of the Athletic Club, such as the landlord of the 'North End Tavern', Harold Watts. The players are sitting in front of the original pavilion that was situated in the corner of the ground close to 'The Huntsman's Hall'. This pavilion had probably belonged initially to Cheam Common Cricket Club before being moved to Skinner's Field in 1925. Eight years later, in 1933, it was physically carried by the players to the site of the current clubhouse.

Autobiographical note

David Stemp was born in Blackburn and educated at Nelson Grammar School and then at the College of St. Mark and St. John, Chelsea. He taught English for eighteen years at Glastonbury High School in Sutton before becoming a Special Needs teacher at Stanley Park High School, Carshalton. He first played cricket for Worcester Park in 1972 after taking a group of schoolchildren to the club's indoor net the previous winter. He is apparently still trying to play.

His main claim to fame is that he appeared on the T.V. programme 'Your Shout' in December 1994 before writing and publishing 'Three Acres and a Cow: The Life and Works of Eli Hamshire'.

The Sporting Origins

of

Worcester Park Athletic Club

'founded by ex-Servicemen in 1921'

Written, Edited & Published

by

David A. Stemp

27, Netley Close,
Cheam, Surrey, SM3 8DN

In Memory of John B. Fox 1933 - 2019
Cricketer, Footballer and Committee Member
of W.P.A.C. for over 70 years

First Published in Great Britain in 2021
by David Stemp, 27, Netley Close, Cheam, Surrey SM3 8DN
Telephone - 0208 641 5765
Email - david.stemp@virgin.net
Copyright © 2020 David Stemp
ISBN: 978-0-9525910-9-2
Printed in Great Britain
by SW19 Design & Print, Wimbletech, Marlborough Hall,
Compton Road, Wimbledon SW19 7QA
Telephone - 0800 599 9597
Email - design@sw19designandprint.co.uk
Website - www.sw19designandprint.co.uk

Contents

Acknowledgements

I would like to thank all the staff who helped me at the following places:

The Surrey History Centre in Woking

The Archive and Local History Section of Sutton Library

The Epsom and Ewell Local and Family History Section at Bourne Hall

The Merton Heritage and Local Studies Centre

The Kingston History Centre in the Guildhall

I would like to single out the following members of staff at the Guildhall:

Amy G. Graham for her exceptional knowledge of the Worcester Park area

Alex Beard for his help with all sporting queries

Helen Swainger for her patience in dealing with my sometimes inane questions.

I would also like to pay tribute to the following individuals for their help:

Robin Fisher, for presenting me with an endless stream of information about the history of W.P.F.C., although he would have preferred for me to have concentrated more upon the Football Club.

John B. Fox (1933 -2020), a fount of knowledge about W.P.A.C.

Dr. Tony Humphreys, who had the unenviable task of trying to proof-read the book, although not all his suggestions were implemented.

Norman Beckwith, for his cheerful encouragement and suggestions.

Cyril Southerby (b. 1911,) who, as the W.P.A.C. President in 1993, wrote a brief history of the club based upon his membership of over 60 years.

David Rymill, for providing me with valuable information and photographs.

Apart from Wikipedia the following books were extremely useful:

'Worcester Park, Old Malden & North Cheam: History at our Feet' by David Rymill
'Worcester Park & Cuddington: A Walk Though the Centuries' by David Rymill
'The History of the Worcester Park and Buckland Beagles' written by Hugh H. Scott-Willey and edited by James Stracey
'Cheam - Past & Present' by Sara Goodwins
'History of Cheam and Sutton' by C. J. Marshall
'Cheam School from 1645' by Edward Peel
'Pubs, Inns and Taverns of Epsom, Ewell and Cheam' by Richard F. Holmes

The O.S. maps were reproduced with the permission of the National Library of Scotland.

The following websites were invaluable: ancestry uk; findmypast uk; and, of course, the British Newspaper Archive with its constantly expanding online library of newspapers from days of yore.

FOREWORD

When I began this book in 2016, the centenary of Worcester Park Cricket Club seemed a long way in the distant future. At that time I had intended to do my research in the winter and spend the summer playing cricket and golf. But of course I procrastinated, as I felt that there was plenty of time left before the centenary celebrations. Like many authors, I enjoyed the research more than the writing and, as a result, only a handful of chapters had been drafted before 2020. Without the straightjacket imposed by the pandemic lockdown, I suspect that this book would have failed to make the self-imposed, but nonetheless apposite, deadline of 2021.

Initially I had intended to write mainly about the cricket club, from its formation in 1921 to the present day. With this aim in mind, I would visit the local history centre at the Guildhall, in Kingston, about four times a week, where I would sit, in studious silence, for several hours at a time, scrolling through old copies of the 'Surrey Comet'. On a couple of occasions, I found myself sitting next to a rather large, pleasant looking, elderly gentleman whom I later discovered was called Robin Fisher, a former Worcester Park footballer, who had played for the club in the 1960s.

Robin and I worked for hours on end without speaking, until I noticed that whilst I was looking for information on W.P.C.C., he was writing copious notes on W.P.F.C. As soon as this link was established the silence was broken, as we discovered that we were often researching the same individuals, although my research began in 1921, while Robin's research dated back to the formation of the Football Club in 1900.

Although I had already drafted a couple of chapters about W.P.C.C. in the interwar period, I thereupon abandoned my intention of writing solely about the Cricket Club, and decided to concentrate upon the sportsmen, such as Frederick Blake and Ernie Styles, and the teams, such as Cheam Common Cricket Club and Worcester Park Football Club, that were the precursors of Worcester Park Athletic Club.

If this book were to be a contestant on the radio quiz show 'Just a Minute' it would comprehensively fail, on the grounds of both repetition and deviation. I make no apology for that, as each chapter within the book can (and perhaps should) be read in isolation and, as many of the characters turned out for several teams, a degree of repetition was inevitable. As for the deviation, if I found an interesting fact or character I could not resist inclusion, even when irrelevance to the general purpose of the text was all too obvious.

Although I eventually decided that the book would be about the origins of sport in the Worcester Park area, it became increasingly more about the people who had lived locally, from the agricultural labourer to the wealthy landowner. Disappointingly, (or perhaps fortunately for the reader), not a lot of information exists about the lives of the farm labourers, apart from that which can be extracted from the various census returns, or, perhaps from a passing mention in the sporting columns of the local press. There is even less information about working class women.

By comparison, however, there was often too much information available online about the lives of some of the gentry who, before the rampant urbanisation of the 1920s and 1930s, lived a life of luxury in the many large mansions that graced Worcester Park and Cuddington. One can often check which schools and university a 'gentleman' had attended, whether that person had served in the military or to what organisations, such as the freemasons, he had belonged. Many of the local gentry were prominent members of Victorian or Edwardian society, and as such some of them made frequent appearances in the press when they attended balls, banquets, weddings and funerals.

As a result of my increased interest in some of these characters who were either directly or indirectly involved with sport locally, I realised that I was often losing the essential sporting thread of a chapter. As a result, I decided, wherever possible to include any interesting biographical material in an appendix at the end of the chapter, which readers can then dip into if they so desire. Personally I find that the appendices are often more interesting than the sport, as some of the characters were rather disreputable. This viewpoint led to occasional disagreements with Robin who felt that I was more interested in the social set-up than the sport.

It was relatively recently that I discovered that Worcester Park had been home to a thriving tennis club that dated from about 1879, with the Reverend William Chetwynd Stapylton as its President. This club attracted all the leading members of Worcester Park society, particularly those of the legal fraternity. The club became so prestigious that it drew the likes of Arthur J. Stanley, an F.A. Cup winner and Wimbledon doubles tennis finalist, to its ranks. Hence a chapter on tennis has had to be added to those on cricket and football.

My favourite chapter, however, concerns another sporting body about which I was blissfully unaware five years ago, the Worcester Park Beagles. It is somewhat mind-boggling to learn that the most famous cricketer of that or any other day, and one of the greatest all-rounders ever, none less than W. G. Grace himself, probably strode over the square of Worcester Park C.C., whilst following the hounds, which were kennelled very close to our present clubhouse.

Although there are very few photographs to break up the text, hopefully the reader will enjoy browsing some of the newspaper extracts from over a century ago, whilst the truly enthusiastic sports' nerd should find some of the match results and statistics endlessly fascinating. A few lucky long-time locals might even find a distant relative hidden within the pages of this book.

David A. Stemp   (February 2021)

Sporting Life in and around Worcester Park
in the Early Victorian Era

Before 1860 there is very little record of sport in the area that we now consider as Cheam, Worcester Park and Old Malden. Much of this, of course, was due to the fact that the region was very sparsely populated. In 1851, for example, the population of Cheam, which stretched from what is now Worcester Park Station, through North Cheam, almost to Banstead Downs, was only 1,137, the size of a modern comprehensive. The total area of Cheam was 1,894 acres, which was slightly larger than the neighbouring parish of Cuddington with its 1,827 acres, which supported a population of only 180. In other words, in Cuddington, there would have been just over ten acres for every person, a situation which probably meant that there were more horses, which were needed to work the land, than people. Much of the area known as Worcester Park, according to 'Kelly's Directory of Surrey' in 1878, was *"principally in Cuddington parish, but small portions are in Malden and Ditton."*

A journalist wrote the following droll account of the area in the 'Surrey Comet' in April 1857: *"Adjoining Merton is the parish of Malden, the extent of this village may be imagined, when it is known that until recently it consisted of one squire, one vicar, one public house, one shop, and one blacksmith, there being neither lawyer or doctor in the village, so that the inhabitants were necessarily in the enjoyment of good tempers and good health; and as there was no butcher within a couple of miles, it is fair to conclude that on bringing their dinner home it was accompanied by a good appetite. Worcester Park, formerly a portion of Nonsuch, is in this parish, where the manufacture of gunpowder has been carried on for some years; but recently this property has changed owners, the mills having been removed. It is expected that in a short time this pretty spot will be covered in villas."*

An Advertisement, on the 19th September, 1837, for the sale of all the stock and implements at Worcester Park Farm, in the rather extravagantly named 'County Chronicle, Surrey Herald and Weekly Advertiser for Kent', reveals the true picture of farming in early Victorian Worcester Park, and emphasised the farmer's reliance upon the humble horse as there were *"three narrow-wheel wagons with iron arms, three broad wheel dung carts, and one narrow wheel ditto, with ladders and copses; a market cart, a water cart, a chaise cart on springs, ploughs, harrows, two horse rollers and a winnowing machine."* The stock consisted of *"six young, powerful and active draught horses, a very fast trotting hackney seven years old, ten superior milch and in-calf cows, a fine young Staffordshire bull, three fat calves, 150 very choice four-tooth Down wethers, 16 store pigs, and 150 head of poultry."*

Nowadays it is difficult to visualise the area as comprising just a few cottages, and isolated farms, surrounded by rolling fields and hedgerows. The marl and clay soil supported abundant crops of wheat, barley and oats in the summer, which helped to feed the locals and the hungry City just a dozen miles away, besides providing additional fodder for the large herds of cows, flocks of sheep and poultry, and sounders of pigs, in the winter.

One only has to consult the 1851 census, with its shepherds, cowmen and agricultural labourers, to see that most of the people were dependent upon the land for their livelihood. Life must have seemed idyllic to the passing stranger, as is shown by the following advertisement for 'The Plough' at Old Malden, which appeared in the 'Morning Advertiser' on May 25th 1852, the day before the Derby: *"Epsom Races - The nearest and most pleasant way from Kensington, Chelsea and all the West-end, avoiding dust and crowd, is across Wimbledon Common, Copse Hill, Coombe Hill and Worcester Park, through avenues of magnificent shady trees, now in full beauty of foliage, and the scenery splendid: by The PLOUGH INN, Malden, Surrey, where every Refreshment, Luncheons, Teas etc., can be procured in that rustic village, and partaken of in the beautiful orchard in the rear of the above Inn, at reasonable prices. Distance from the Downs six miles. Good Stabling and Lock-up Coach-houses."*

This idyll was to change, however, with the construction of Malden railway station, in December, 1846, on the London and South Western Railway line, in what is now called New Malden. Suddenly fresh farm products, such as chickens, eggs and milk could speed their way, in bulk, into the city, rather than being taken there, in laborious fashion by horse and cart. (On a personal note, my great, great grandfather, Eli Hamshire, was a carrier in Surrey at this time, ferrying goods on a regular basis between Ewhurst and Guildford. He was the originator of the phrase 'Three Acres and a Cow'.)

A short article in the 'Morning Chronicle', on the 20th December, 1848, highlighted what the coming of the railway meant for the region, and for the people of London: *"The inhabitants of the great metropolis, since the extension of the railways, have been supplied with pure milk in large quantities, in lieu of the stuff previously sold as such. To show the vast quantity brought even by one line will surprise many of our readers. From Worcester-park, near to Kingston-on-Thames, there are 56 cans, each containing from 14 to 18 gallons, sent every seven days, making at least a total of 850 gallons of pure new milk conveyed in that short period."*

The New Malden station retained the name 'Malden' until 1859 when it was re-named the 'New Malden and Coombe Station'. At the same time, in 1859, a station opened on the line from Waterloo to Epsom, with the name of 'Old Malden', a name which was eventually changed in 1862 to 'Worcester Park'.

Although the coming of the railway benefitted the farming community initially, it was eventually to lead to the demise of agriculture in Cheam Common, Worcester Park and Old Malden, over the next eighty or so years, as the area became a magnet for commuters. In Worcester Park, Longfellow Road, with its proximity to the station, was the first road to be settled in the 1860s and 1870s, as it catered for both railway workers and for the first commuters. The built-up area gradually spread southwards towards St. Philip's Church and Lindsay Road, until the housing explosion of the 1930s finally killed off local agriculture for good when Cheam Common became swamped by the new housing estates.

The growing population also had a dramatic effect upon the sporting activities that took place in Worcester Park. Prior to 1860 there was very little mention in the newspapers of team sports within this area of Surrey, especially in the winter months. The most popular sports were those associated with the countryside such as horse racing and shooting. The 'Lord Nelson Inn' at North Cheam, which was a staging point on the road between London and Epsom, was particularly popular with race-goers, and was also a venue for both steeplechases and hurdle races. One of the earliest accounts of a steeplechase, ending at the 'Lord Nelson', occurred in the 'Morning Post' of December 4th, 1832: *"A match for 50l. a side was run on Thursday between a bay horse belonging to Mr. Sipford, and a black horse the property of Mr. Sewell. They started from a field near Norberton Common, Surrey, and went over a very heavy country to Malden, and thence to the Lord Nelson Inn, at Cheame. The black horse won by about 200 yards. The rider of the bay horse had two heavy falls. The distance was between five and six miles."*

Probably more entertaining than the steeplechases, however, were the race days for which the 'Lord Nelson' was famous. 'Bell's Life in London and Sporting Chronicle', for example, for Sunday 3rd September, 1843, devoted over three column inches to the NORTH CHEAM RACES which were held the preceding Wednesday. The first event, for which the owners, riders and weights were listed, was the Cheam and Sutton Stakes which was a handicap race for 12 sovereigns *'the winner to be sold for 40 sovs.'* The second event was the Hunters' Stakes over six flights of hurdles four feet high, which was won by Mr. Hope's 'Tom Tug', ridden by Matthews. This was followed by the Farmer's Hurdle Race and the Pony Stakes which was won by Mr. Ashby. *"The races, and the race ordinary at the Lord Nelson, were very fully attended, the sport very good, and the decision of Mr. Farrell, who filled the double office of judge and clerk of the course, satisfactory. We understand that the proprietor of the course intends to place the races next year on a very superior footing, and to spare neither trouble nor expense to make them attractive to her Majesty's lieges."*

Hunting of deer, foxes or hares, either on foot or on horseback, was probably the principal means of recreation for both rich and poor alike in the early nineteenth century and small packs of hounds were kept in many of the villages. By the middle of the century, the fields and commons surrounding Cheam and Worcester Park would have resounded to the sound of the hunting horn on a regular basis, as the area was home to a number of hunts, such as the Epsom and Ewell, the Morden Harriers, the Surbiton Beagles and the Surrey Union Foxhounds. Despite the growth of London, the area was still that rural, even in 1886, that the Surrey Union moved its kennels, away from the city, to Green Lane, Worcester Park. On some occasions the local meets were even advertised in the national press. The 'Morning Advertiser' of the 28th February, 1829, for example, was pleased to inform its readers that, *'the Earl of Derby's Stag Hounds meet on Tuesday at Cheam, at ten.'*

Another rural activity closely linked to hunting was, or were, the shooting competitions organised by the 'Friends of the Trigger', often undertaken for large sums of money. In these events, great numbers of pigeons and sparrows would be slaughtered, within an allotted time scale. These days we try to preserve the poor sparrow; in the nineteenth century, however, 'Sparrow Destruction Clubs' were rife. One local event, of many, which made the national press was reported in 'Bell's Life and Sporting Chronicle' on July 22nd, 1838: *"The match between Mr. Allen, of the Plough Inn, Malden, and Mr. Cook, of Epsom-court, for £10 a side, was shot on Tuesday. Mr. Allen was the winner, by killing six out of seven. Mr. Cook brought down eight out of nine, but three of the birds fell dead out of bounds. After the match a sweepstakes at sparrows took place by Messrs. Weeks, Morrison, Haregrave, and Heath, which ended in a tie by the four first gentlemen killing five out of six."*

In the early to mid-nineteenth century football matches tended to be associated with Shrove Tuesday celebrations, and were usually riotous affairs. Vast crowds attended the annual event in Kingston, until it was eventually banned for being too unruly. Where football was played in a more orderly fashion, the rules of the game varied from one area to another. It was not really until 1863 when the Football Association was formed that there was a concerted effort to standardise the rules, leading to the publication in December of that year of the 'Laws of Football'. Fourteen years later the Surrey F.A. was formed which eventually affiliated itself to the F.A. in 1882. Worcester Park Football club joined this august body when it was founded in 1900.

Football was slow to take hold in the Worcester Park area, and the 'Surrey Comet' did not really start to publish reports of matches until about 1892. Upcoming matches, whether rugby or soccer tended to be listed under the general heading of 'Football'. This occasionally led to more than a little confusion when trying to research the local history. At one stage I thought that I had uncovered the first ever game of football played by Worcester Park, in an article in the 'Surrey Advertiser' dated the 6th February, 1875. Instead I had uncovered the only ever mention of a local Rugby team: *"FOOTBALL - Last Saturday, the Kingston Football Club, played two matches one at Wandsworth against the Arabs, and one at Worcester Park against Worcester Park. The former after an exciting game was drawn, neither side obtaining any advantage. The latter, however, the Kingstonians won mainly owing to the good play of Earnshaw, Edwards, Duffell, and Gaydon, by one try and five touches down, against one try and one touch down. For Worcester Park, Bugle and Marshall played well."*

By contrast, most of the villagers living in Worcester Park probably watched a game of cricket at some time during their lives, as Surrey was one of the leading hotspots of the noble game. Cricket, for instance, had been played upon Mitcham Green on a regular basis from 1685, and the London newspapers regularly reported upon matches played at Mitcham, Kingston, Banstead, Beddington Corner, Epsom Downs, and at Ewell during the early years of the nineteenth century.

Cricket also tended to be a game associated with the aristocracy, many of whom would host matches for their friends and workforce, particularly upon public holidays. Occasionally these early matches made it into the sporting columns of the press. One of the first of these matches to be reported in 'Bell's Life and Sporting Chronicle', on September 5th, 1841, was a game between youngsters from Cheam and from the Ewell Academy:- *"The return match between eleven young gents of Cheam and eleven of the Ewell Academy, was played at Cheam, the seat of Sir E. Antrobus, Bart., and terminated in favour of Cheam by three wickets. Both parties then adjourned to the house, where a comfortable repast was provided for them through the kindness and liberality of Sir Edmund and Lady Antrobus."*

The Antrobus family were extremely influential in local cricketing circles in the nineteenth century. Sir Edmund Antrobus (b. 1792), was a Coutts Banker, who had inherited the baronetcy and a large fortune upon the death of his uncle in 1826. He had ten children, one of whom, **Robert Crawfurd Antrobus** (b. 1830) after playing for Eton, played several matches for I. Zingari (The Gypsies), a wandering side formed in 1845, and also for the Gentlemen of England in 1850. Another son, Hugh Lindsay Antrobus, when he inherited the estate, lent part of it to the fledgling Sutton Cricket Club in 1861, before they purchased it outright in 1901 (according to C. J. Marshall's 'History of Cheam and Sutton'). He also provided the land upon which St. Philip's Church, in Worcester Park, was built in 1873.

The family lived on a large estate in East Cheam, based around 'Lower Cheam House'. The 1841 census must have been a nightmare to fill in as the property appeared to have nine male servants, fourteen female servants, six gardeners, one farmer, thirteen agricultural labourers, two laundresses, one groom and a carpenter. It is no wonder, therefore, that Sir

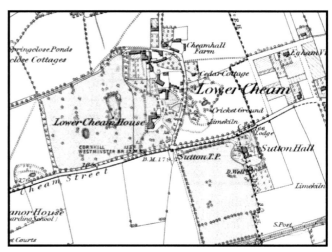

Edmund was able to select two teams from his household and workforce as 'Bell's Life' recorded on August 22nd, 1844: *"A match was played on Tuesday last between two elevens selected from Sir E. Antrobus's establishment at Cheam, of which the following is the score:- One Eleven 28 and 53; the Other Eleven 64 and 18 for seven wickets."* (O.S. map reproduced with the permission of the National Library of Scotland.)

Playing for the Other Eleven was 14 year old Robert Antrobus Esq. and his younger brother, **John Edward Antrobus** (b 1831), who had played as a ten year old against Ewell Academy. Sadly this was his last season playing cricket as he was to die on April 21st the following year. No reason was given for his early demise, although it was reported in all the 'hatched, matched and dispatched' columns throughout the land, with the bland statement, *"April 21st, at Lower Cheam, Surrey, John Edward, fourth son of Sir E. Antrobus Bart., aged 14"* ('Bell's Weekly Messenger').

Those in power such as Lord Morpeth, a Government Minister in the 1840s, realised the benefits to be derived from the 'commingling' of the various classes on the cricket field. *"Lord Morpeth has been constant and unceasing in his efforts to cultivate cricket amongst the social classes of society, but especially amongst those who are engaged in agricultural and industrial pursuits."* ('London Evening Standard' 28th Sept, 1846).

A couple of years prior to this on the 18th August, 1844, Baron Alderson had written the following letter in 'Bell's Life'. *"I went out into the country, and had the pleasure of seeing a match at cricket, in which a noble earl, the lord-lieutenant of his county, was playing with the tradesmen, the labourers, and all around him, and I believe he lost no respect from that course - they loved him better, but they did not respect him less. I believe that if they themselves associated more with the lower classes of society, the kingdom of England would be in a far safer place, and society in a far sounder condition."*

Nowhere were these thoughts more adhered to than in the Cheam/Worcester Park area, where sometimes the lord and the labourer played on the same side, and where sometimes they played against each other. The following scorecard appeared in 'Bell's Life' on September 3rd, 1843.

GENTLEMEN AND PLAYERS OF CHEAM.—This match came off on Monday last on the Cheam ground, and was won by the Players. Score: Players 42 and 70—total 112 ; A. Brook marked 0 and 6, R. Tribe 9 and 1, W. Porter 0 and 11, J. Ordendon 1 and 10, R. Rayner 4 and 16, R. Richardson 0 and 2, H Rayner 3 and 18, T. Constable 4 and 2, W. Thorns 8 and 0, H. Constable 8 (not out) and 1 (not out), Noaks 1 and 0 : byes &c. 4 and 3. Gentlemen 38 and 24 – total 62; R. Antrobus Esq. scored 4 and 3, Andrews 1 and 0, Currie Esq. 14 and 7, F. Smith Esq. 0 and 2, W. Tollner Esq 6 and 0, G. Smith Esq. 2 and 3, C. Smith Esq. 1 and 0, Bushnell 0 and 1, Heaver 5 and 2 &c.; byes &c. 5 and 6.

Most of the Players' team had been born locally and appeared on the 1841 or 1851 censuses as living in Cheam. **Arthur Brooke** (b. 1805) was a wheelwright; **Robert Tribe** junior (b. 1820) became the landlord of 'The Harrow' in Cheam Village between 1849 and 1851, following on from his father who had been the landlord for the previous 35 years; J. Ordendon was probably either **James Ockenden** (b. 1804), a carpenter, or his son **James** (b.1834), who followed the same trade. James junior, along with his brother, John (b. 1842), were to become key players in the Cheam Village side of the 1870s and 80s; **Robert Richardson** lived in the 'Red Lion' pub and was either the landlord's son (b. 1823), who was a smith, or it might have been his cousin, Robert (b. 1828), who lived with the family; **Henry Constable** (b. 1824) was a gardener, whilst his brother **John** (b. 1828) was a tailor; **Robert Rayner** (b. 1815), **Henry Rayner** (b. 1820) and their brother **Frederick** (b. 1819) were all plumbers and decorators in a firm run by their widowed mother; **William Thorns** (b. 1822) was a journeyman butcher; **John Noaks** (b. 1814) was a brewer and maltster; his son **John** (b. 1841) succeeded his father and by 1871 employed five men in the brewery which eventually became Cheam Brewery.

It was difficult to discover much about the nine men listed on the Gentlemen's side, as they tended to be more mobile than the Players who were usually tied to the land. Some of them might have lived in the City and merely visited Cheam, on horseback or by coach, for an afternoon's entertainment. Identifying the Gentlemen was made even more difficult by the fact that three of them embraced the surname 'Smith'. C. Smith was probably **Courtney John Smith** (b. 1828), the son of Robert Vernon Smith, whose occupation was listed as being 'a Gentleman'. Apart from Robert Antrobus, the only other player for whom any information is available was **William M. Tollner**[1] (b. 1802) who lived at 'Sutton Hall', a large mansion to the south of Sutton Cricket Club.

Another cricket match, which was surprisingly played on a Tuesday, occurred between the local Gentlemen and Players, and was reported in 'Bell's Life' on August 22nd, 1847. The paper stated that the match was played at W. M. Tollner's Esq., ground at Cheam, i.e. 'Sutton Hall'. The scorecard showed that the Players were again dominant although it appears that the match was not all that well attended, as there were only seven Gentlemen and eight Players. The Gentlemen scored 29 and 30: J. Aitkin Esq. 4 & 1, H. Aitkin Esq. 4 & 2, Robert Antrobus Esq. 4 & 2, Jones Esq. 4 & 0, Parden Esq. 0 & 8, Harley Esq. 2 & 4, Fontain Esq. 1 & 3*: byes etc 9 & 6. The Players scored 31 and 41: G. Parrot 0 & 6, Robert Tribe 1 & 3, W. Clements 5 & 9*, W. Andrews 5 & 3, H. Rayner 5 & 1, J. Baines 10 & 7, Stephen Smith 2 & 2, John Noaks 1* & 2; byes etc 1 & 8.

Probably the most extraordinary feature of this result was the fact that within the preceding month, **James Aitkin**[2] (b. 1829), **Henry Mortlock Aitkin**[3] (b. 1831) and **Robert Crawfurd Antrobus** (b. 1830) had been members of the Eton side which had comprehensively beaten both Harrow and Winchester at Lords. Either the local Players were much stronger than one might have imagined or else there was no comparison between playing at Mr. Tollner's ground at 'Sutton Hall' and at James Dark's ground at Lords. In the match reports of the time, the Aitkin brothers were referred to simply as Aitkin ma and Aitkin mi, which was short for Aitkin major and minor.

Many of the early cricket matches were often centred around a local inn or beer house. One of these matches was reported in 'Bell's Life', on the 7th September, 1845, as being played *"at the Drill Inn Ground, Cheam, on Tuesday last between eleven players chosen by Mr Madgwick, and eleven chosen by Mr Taylor"*. It was another low scoring two innings' match, which was probably a reflection upon the dubious nature of the wicket. Mr. Taylor's side scored 28 and 37 runs, whilst the team of the very Dickensian sounding character, Mr. Madgwick, won by ten wickets, scoring 50 and 16 without loss. The extremely faint scorecard, which is produced below was obviously submitted to 'Bell's Life' by a member of Mr. Taylor's team, as all of his team have been accorded initials, which are sadly lacking for Mr. Madgwick's side, although most of the surnames can be found in Cheam Village in the 1851 census.

The captain, of what would appear to have been the home team, was **Henry Taylor** (b.1823), a local carpenter. The 1851 census showed him as being a visitor at Weeding's Farm in Malden, the home of his future wife, Ann Clarke, who was the sister of **Thomas Clarke** (b. 1828), a journeyman carpenter. Ann and Thomas were the children of another Thomas Clarke, who farmed 80 acres and employed four men.

F. Boury was probably **Francis Bowry** (b. 1829) a sixteen year old farmer's son from Malden, who, in 1851, was a lodger with the Penningtons at the 'Drill Inn', whilst Robert Tribe had already appeared in the Gentlemen and Players match in 1843. **William Cuff** (b. 1821) and his brother, **James Cuff** (b. 1830), were both bricklayers; James became a founder member of Cheam Common Cricket Club in 1872 and was the Landlord of the 'North End Tavern' from 1871 until his death in 1874.

Three weeks later, on the 28th September, 1845, 'Bell's Life' reported that, *"A match was played at the Red Lion Ground, Cheam, between eleven chosen by Mr. Rayner, and eleven by Mr. Heasman."* Both Henry Rayner and **Henry Heasman** (b. 1806), a carpenter, lived in Cheam Village and probably both drank in the 'Red Lion', which featured as a match venue in several newspaper reports. Looking at the pub today, one wonders exactly where they played cricket. Was it to the North of the 'Red Lion', between St. Dunstan's Church and the pub, where the car park now lies, or was it in the fields behind where Waitrose is now situated?

Wherever the pitch was located, the match was drawn, Mr. Rayner's team scored 48 runs in the first innings and 56 in the second, whilst Mr. Heasman's team notched up 48 and 17 for 6. Two or three of the players from the first game also played in this match including the mysterious Mr. Madgwick who had notched up 10 runs in the first match, and then 11 and 0, plus four wickets, in the second match. The extremely blurry scorecard is included below.

MATCH AT CHEAM.—A match was played at the Red Lion Ground, Cheam, between eleven chosen by Mr Rayner, and eleven by Mr Heasman, when the score terminated thus:—Mr Rayner's side 48 and 54—total 102. Mr Rayner scored (not out) 26 and 11, Knight (c Harles) 2 and 0, Madgwick (b Dicken) 11 and 0, Brooks (b Dicken) 0 and 8, Rayner (c Cheesman) 1 and 0, Thorne (b Peckham) 1 and 0, House (b Dicker) 0 and 15, Barnes (b Dicker) 1 and 0, Richardson (c Lawrence) 1 and 15, Sharp (c Merkett) 0 and 2, Cook (b Dicker) 0 and 1; byes 5 and 2. Mr Heasman's side 48 and 17—total 65, with four wickets to go down. Mr Heasman obtained (b Madgwick) 0 and 5, Hilton (b Madgwick) 0 and 0, Peckham (b Brooks) 4 and 0, Dicker (b Rayner) 5 and 8, Burton (c Knight) 1 and 0, Cheesman (b Madgwick) 21 and 1, Croucher (b Madgwick) 11 and 3, Harles (b Brooks) 0 and 0, Howard (c Knight) 2, Lawrence (st Rayner) 0, Merkett (not out); 0 byes 2 and 0, wide 2 and 0.

Henry Rayner, the plumber and paper hanger, must have been quite a decent batsman as he opened the batting, and carried his bat, in the first innings, scoring 26*, plus a respectable 11 in the second innings. He had also been recorded as opening the batting for Cheam Victoria against the Carshalton Club, four years earlier, in yet another game that was played on a Tuesday. That particular game was another low scoring, two innings' affair which also ended up in the 'Red Lion' - Cheam Victoria scoring 52 and 34, and Carshalton 36 and 36. Rayner top scored in the first innings with 8 runs and followed up with six in the second innings.

The Cheam Victoria team that day was H. Rayner 8 & 6, H. Green 6 & 6, F. Smith Esq. 7 & 2, J. Ockenden 4 & 3, W. Porter 0 & 7, J. Saunders 5 & 0,

J. Goodhugh 5 & 0, G. Smith Esq. 5 & 1*, W. Thorns 1* & 1, A. Brooks 0 & 2, byes etc. 11 & 6.

A much earlier report, featuring the 'Red Lion', had been published previously in 'Bell's Life' on 29th August, 1841: *"The return match was played on Thursday week, on the ground of the former. It was made by the Victoria Club for the purpose of introducing some young players, and in several instances their play was much admired for its steadiness and judgment, never giving a chance away. The game terminated in favour of the Victoria by fourteen runs. The members of both clubs then adjourned to Mr. Richardson's 'Red Lion Inn', where the evening was spent with great conviviality and good feeling."*

No mention was made in that report as to where the game was played or what sort of club Cheam Victoria was. There was, however, a penchant for clubs to attach either 'Victoria' or 'Albert' to club names in the mid-nineteenth century probably as a sign of the players' allegiance to the monarchy. There again the team might have simply been representing the 'Victoria' pub at North Cheam which had opened as a beer house in the 1830s, although on the 1851 census it was simply called 'Queen'. It does, however, seem rather strange that the players returned to the 'Red Lion' if they were representing the 'Queen Victoria.'

The first mention of a cricket match being played in Worcester Park, occurred in 'Bell's Life and Sporting Chronicle', on the 27th July, 1851. The article does tend to suggest that the fixture was an annual event, as it states that Malden were the victors 'as usual'. It had probably originated as rivalry between the owners of two of the largest estates in the area, owned by the Taylors and the Weedings.

> MALDEN v WORCESTER PARK.—This annual match was played in Worcester Park on Wednesday, the 16th inst. There was some good play on both sides. The Malden eleven were, as usual, successful, winning with six wickets to go down. Score : Worcester Park 46 and 68—total 114 ; Martin marked 0 and 7, W. Taylor Esq 2 and 3, C. Abbott Esq 8 and 1, G. Lawrence Esq 4 and 3, F. Taylor jun Esq 11 and 5, F. Abbott Esq 6 and 25, A. Shepherd Esq (not out) 0 and 10, &c ; byes &c 12 and 14. Malden 81 and 36—total 117 ; T. Weeding Esq scored 7 and (not out) 13, R. Alexander Esq 5 and 1, M. Norman Esq 19 and 3, Thorne 9 and (not out) 4, Bowry 13 and 3, Brockwell 4 and 1, &c ; byes &c 19 and 11.

As the report says that the match was played at Worcester Park, it probably took place at 'Worcester Park House' the home of the Taylors. The house had been built in 1797 by one of a long line of William Taylors, the owners of the gunpowder mills on the Hogsmill River. The family tended to live in London most of the time and used the House as a country retreat. In the early years of the century, the society columns, particularly in the 'Morning Post' would regularly list the comings and goings of the Taylor family between the city and the country. It seems that William Taylor was an extremely generous host who could be relied upon to provide visitors with excellent entertainment. *"Worcester-park, near Kingston in Surrey, now inhabited by Mr. Taylor will be the scene of much old English hospitality"* (December 25th, 1813); *"Worcester Park will be rendered very gay by Mr. Taylor, the munificent owner"* (December 8th, 1815); *"Worcester Park has been enlivened this week by an entertainment given by the benevolent owner, Mr. Taylor"* (January 13th, 1816), and *"Mr and Mrs Taylor, for Worcester Park, near Ewell in Surrey"* (November 21st, 1816).

The 'Morning Post' had also reported that William's second son, Charles, tragically died in a horse riding accident on September 13th, 1817, which elevated **Frederick Taylor** (b. 1802) to the rank of second son. As such he had the privilege of running the powder mills for his elder brother, William, from about 1830 until the mills ceased production in the early 1850s. Frederick married Frances Mary Warrington on January 16th, 1830, in Kensington, and they had a son, Frederick James, in 1841.

The fact that 'Bell's Life in London and Sporting Chronicle' had chosen to publish an account of a match between Malden and Worcester Park, which only involved thirteen players, probably indicates the social importance of some of the participants. Of the thirteen players, nine were gentlemen, and as they were probably guests of the landowners it is almost impossible to identify some of them.

The Worcester Park side, however, probably contained the lord of the manor, **William Taylor**, who was aged about fifty, and his ten year old nephew, **Frederick James Taylor** (b. 1841) The Abbotts were probably **Charles James Abbott**[4] (b. 1821) and his brother, **Frederick Jenkins Abbott**[5] (b. 1820), both of whom worked in the City as solicitors, and, in 1851, were to be found living with their parents and sister, at 'Ryden's House' in Walton-on-Thames. This was an ideal place to live for the daily commute to the City, and for occasional visits to Malden. An advert for the sale of the house, forty years later states: *"Ryden's House, Walton-on-Thames (near station); good garden, well-timbered, and attractive grounds, conservatory, vineries, etc., with or without the pleasure farm."*

'Martin' as the only non gentleman in the team could possibly have been a local man in the employ of the Taylors, **Henry Martin** (b.1811), who was a carter at the powder mills.

It was slightly easier to identify the players on the Malden team, as apart from William Thorne, the butcher, Francis Bowry, the farmer, and Thomas Clarke, the carpenter, the Gentlemen, **Thomas Weeding**[6] (b.1831). **Martin Norman**[7] (b.1831) and **Robert Hugh Alexander**[8] (b.1832) were all final year students at the East India College in Hertfordshire. This Thomas Weeding was probably the captain of the Malden team, and shouldn't be confused with his uncle, **Thomas Weeding**[9] (b.1774), who had made a fortune in the City as a merchant and trader. Thomas senior was also a magistrate for the County of Surrey and had used his fortune to purchase large areas of land in the 1830s and 1840s in the Old Malden and Worcester Park area, where he built an impressive house called 'Fullbrooks', although his business commitments meant that he spent most of his time at his Central London address of 47, Mecklenburg Square.

'Fullbrooks' was probably the venue for the return match later that season, on September 7th, 1851, for an eleven aside contest, which the Malden side won in convincing fashion, thanks largely to the fact that they had engaged the services of **Charles Pontifex,[10]** who was already considered to be a cricketing gentleman of some renown, and Martin Norman from the well known Kentish cricketing family. Between them they notched up 66 runs and took thirteen wickets.

MALDEN v WORCESTER PARK.

This return match came off in Worcester Park on Friday week, Malden again winning in a single innings, with 80 runs to spare. Score:

MALDEN first innings 151 ; C. Pontifex marked (run out) 43, M. Norman (b Wood) 23, T. Weeding (b Wood) 11, Underwood (b Northey) 17, Brockwell (hit w, b Osgood) 11, Bowrey (run out) 6, Thorne (c Wood, b Abbot) 11, Harrison (b Abbot) 5, Dabbs (b Abbot) 2, Bartlett (not out) 1, Clarke (b Abbot) 0 ; byes 12, wide balls &c 7.

WORCESTER PARK 41 and 71—total 112 ; C. Abbott obtained (b Norman) 0 and (leg b w, b Pontifex) 5, Northey (run out) 9 and (b Pontifex) 1, C. Shepherd Esq (b Norman) 5 and (b Norman) 0, F. Abbott (b Norman) 0 and (b Norman) 0, Rev G. Lewis (b Norman) 1 and (c Weeding) 3, Millais (b Pontifex) 3 and (not out) 0, F. Taylor (not out) 6 and (b Brockwell) 2, Craddock (b Norman) 2 and (b Norman) 0, Wood (b Norman) 0 and (run out) 1, Martin (c Weeding) 6 and (b Norman) 8, Osgood (c Pontifex) 2 and (c Weeding) 1 ; byes 2 and 7, wide balls &c 5 and 2.

Of the other Malden players, apart from Francis Bowry and William Thorne, the 1851 census tends to suggest that they were as follows: **Philip Underwood** (b. 1825 in Essex), was a farm labourer and tenant of the Weedings, who lived with his wife and four children at 'New Farm Cottage'; **Isaac Dabbs** (b. 1814 in Malden), was an agricultural labourer, lodging near the church with James Eves and his wife, Rachel, who both came from Suffolk; **George Brockwell** (b. 1824 in Ewell), was an agricultural labourer living with his brother-in-law and family at Howell Hill; **Richard Harrison** (b. 1813 in Mickleham), was an agricultural labourer/gardener living in Pond Hill, Cheam; and finally, **Richard Bartlett** (b. 1838 in Dorking), was possibly a 13 year old pupil at the Ewell Academy, the son of an ironmonger.

Of the Worcester Park players, apart from the Abbott brothers who had played in the previous match, and Martin, the carter at the powder mills, three or four appeared to have come from Malden, whilst two or three of the others appear more problematic. Several 'Northeys', for example, were rich landowners in the Cheam and Sutton area, but as this one was missing an initial, or an Esq., it is impossible to tell who he was. In the first match F. Taylor junior played, but on this occasion it could possibly have been his father, Frederick, who ran the powder mills, whilst no Craddocks lived in the immediate vicinity, but could easily have come from Epsom or Kingston.

Of those who lived in Malden and might have played for Worcester Park, **Henry Osgood** (b.1822), was a strong possibility. Henry, who hailed from Eastbourne, was an agricultural labourer, who lived close to 'The Plough' with his wife, Charlotte, and two small children. 'Wood' was probably one of the sons of the sixty six year old widow, Elizabeth Wood, who owned the wheelwright's shop, which was next door to the Vicarage. Her sons were **George Wood** (b. 1828), who was a cooper, and **Thomas Wood** (b. 1818), the wheelwright. Also living in the house was her daughter, Margaret, and a lady of great age, her 91 year old mother, Ann Arbon.

The **Rev. George Bridges Lewis** (b. 1824) definitely lived in Malden, as he was a lodger in the Vicarage, which was the home of the Vicar of Malden cum Chessington, the Rev. William Chetwynd Stapylton (b. 1826 in Edmiston, Notts). Apart from the vicar and curate, the Vicarage also housed three servants, a cook, a maid and a gardener.

Lewis. the curate of the parish, had been born in The Close, Salisbury, where he had been baptised in the Cathedral. His parents, however, lived in Bedford Road, London, where his father was a solicitor. Sadly George's mother died at the age of 33 whilst he was only five. He graduated from Oriel College, Oxford, in 1846, and two years later married Mary Rebecca Madeleine Sutherland in Croydon. The following year a daughter was born, and in November, 1850, his wife died at the age of 23 in Hastings. He did marry again in 1852, Mary Frances Hesketh, from Epsom, who bore him five children. Their marriage lasted for forty years, before she died and he married for a third time.

C. Shepherd Esq. was probably **Charles Shepherd** (b. 1831), who had been born in Scotland, the third son of John Shepherd who became a Director of the East India Company, the Deputy Master of Trinity House and a Member of the Council for India. Charles mother, Anne, had been born in Bombay, whilst his oldest brother, John, had died in 1843, at the age of twenty, in Singapore, whilst probably working for the Company. By 1851 the family were living in relative luxury in Long Ditton, although they owned a house in Portland Square, Marylebone. By this stage both Charles and his younger brother, James, were working for the Home Service of the East India Company. The 1861 census showed him living with his mother in Hove and working at the Office of the Secretary of State for India. Sadly, he died, at the tender age of 32, at his new home on the Island of Madeira on February 14th, 1863. He was merely one of several people, associated with this match and the East India Company, to die at a young age.

The final person in the team, batting at number six, might, or might not be, the most famous person in the team, 'Millais'. For several years I had believed that this player was **John Everett Millais**[11] (b. June 8th, 1829), the famous Pre-Raphaelite painter, who, along with William Holman Hunt, had visited the area on numerous occasions, and spent much of the summer and autumn of 1851 working upon his painting of

'Ophelia' on the banks of the Hogsmead River. Staying with them at that time, however, were fellow artists George Collins, and Millais's brother, **William Henry Millais** (b. 1828).

Little is known of William's life apart from the fact that he was extremely close to his younger brother, and was shown to be part of his brother's sumptuous household, in Kensington, on the 1871 and 1881 censuses, The 1851 census showed that William was living with his mother's relatives, the Hodginson's, in Hampshire, and the census listed his occupation as being a surveyor. He was also an artist, however, whose *"forte was watercolour landscapes, exquisitely drawn"*, and he was known to have exhibited landscape works at the Royal Academy on several occasions. In 1852, whilst the Royal Academy exhibited his brother's 'Ophelia', he had submitted a work entitled 'The Rookery, Worcester Park Farm', which according to 'The Atlas' (May 8th, 1852) was *"A perfect gem of a study. We covet it much."*

As William had completed a painting at Worcester Park Farm in 1851, it certainly made him a contender to have been the 'Millais' in the Worcester Park side. Thanks to an interview that William Holman Hunt gave to 'The Daily Chronicle' in 1896, upon the death of the younger Millais, however, it is possible to infer that John Everett Millais had been a cricket lover from an early age. Hunt recalled the first time that he had met an extremely young Millais and his parents, in about 1844: *"Towards the close of the interview, Millais suddenly turned to his father and mother, in pleading tone saying, 'I've been working now very hard for a long while, and I really feel very tired, and I'm sure it would do me good to have a holiday', ending in almost lachrymose tone. He proceeded -'You know they'll be sure to be playing cricket on Saturday at Holloway, and I should like to go and have a good day at it.' Then he turned to me enquiring, 'Do you play cricket?'*

As further proof that J. E. Millais was the 'Millais' in the Worcester Park team, I managed to find another occasion when he donned the pads, which seems to have gone undetected. On Monday, 5th August, 1854, according to 'The Derby Mercury', J. E. Millais Esq. turned out for the Chatsworth Club versus the Broomhall Club. He batted number nine and scored 2 runs before being run out. It is possible that he might have been staying at Chatsworth House as a guest of the Duke of Devonshire, or he might have been invited there by Sir Joseph Paxton, the Landscape Gardener, whose eighteen year old son, George, had opened the batting for the Chatsworth team.

The only other record of a game of cricket being played in the Worcester Park area, for almost twenty years following the two Malden versus Worcester Park matches of 1851, occurred on the 23rd September, 1856: *"On Tuesday last this village was the scene of much hilarity, to commemorate the recent marriage of T. Weedon, Esq., which occurred about a month since. The proceedings commenced with a game of cricket, with eleven from the sister parish of Chessington. The match was played on the grounds of T. Weedon, Esq., and the game throughout was well contested, and ended in favour of Malden by 12 runs, for which success they were much indebted to the efficient services of the Rev. -- Aitken and Mr. Pontifex, who kindly assisted them with their valuable aid. At the conclusion of the game the whole of the players, and other friends, were sumptuously regaled under one roof, contiguous to the mansion of Mr. Weedon."*

Despite continually getting the name of the bridegroom wrong, the article carried on in similar vein to list the various entertainments such as the triumphal arch, the floral displays, the speeches, songs and toasts which lasted into the night enhanced by *"A graceful diffusion of lights which gave additional splendour to the scene."* Finally the article promised that, *"The score of this match will appear in our next number."*

As no scoresheet appeared the following week, nor the week after that, it is impossible to tell for certain whether the Rev. -- Aitkin was the Rev. James Aitkin, who was the curate at St. Mary's in Beddington, or his younger brother, the Rev. Henry Mortlock Aitkin, both of whom had played cricket for Eton and Oxford University. (More upon these interesting characters can be found in the following Appendix).

Additional Information Upon Characters of Note

[1]**William M. Tollner** (b. 1802). In the early 1820s he worked as an attorney and lived in Sloane Street, Chelsea. On the 27th May 1826, he married Georgiana Frances, the sixteen year old daughter of Count Josh. Mazzinghi, of Cadogan Place, at St. Luke's Church, Chelsea. The newspaper articles of the time show that they lived at 'Stanley House' in the King's Road, Chelsea. This was a large red bricked house, circa 1691 which, from the late nineteenth century until about 1970, was the home of the Principal of the College of St. Mark and St. John. By co-incidence I studied at Marjons between 1964 and 1968 and attended several events in the house.

William stood unsuccessfully in the General Election for Woodstock, in 1830, against the Marquis of Blandford and his brother, Lord Churchill (Woodstock was a pocket borough, under the patronage of the Duke of Marlborough which, despite the fact that it had only 261 houses, and 241 voters, returned two M.P.'s.).

Six years later tragedy struck when his wife died, in Pisa, at the age of only 26. William quickly recovered, however, and married May Hilliard on the 9th October 1837. The record for the birth of his son, who was also called William Michael Tollner (b. 1838), reveals that the family had moved to 'Sutton Hall', a large mansion close to Sutton's cricket ground, on the south side of the Cheam Road, approximately where Landseer Road is now situated. Kelly's Directory for 1867 shows that he was still living there at the time of his death.

William's son, Captain W. M. Tollner, became a career soldier and fought with the Royal Horse Artillery at Sebastopol in the Crimean War, before moving to South Africa in 1860, to re-organise the country's coastal defences for the British Government. Following the disaster at Isandlwana, he was recruited to fight in the Zulu Wars. Whilst there, he captained a side in the first representative rugby match played in South Africa in 1860, when the Gentlemen of the Peninsula played the Cape Garrison. When William died in March 1931, at Port Shepstone, he was the last South African survivor of the Crimean War.

[2]**James Aitkin** (b.1830) and his brother were born at 'The Priory', a large sixteenth century house in Monken Hadley, which straddles the Middlesex/Hertfordshire border. James's father, John, came from a long line of landed gentry in the Hadley Wood area. James appears to have been an exceptional athlete who went on to gain a Double Blue at Oxford in cricket and rowing. Prior to his time at Oxford he had been educated at Eton and represented the school at Lords in the prestigious public school matches, against both Harrow and Winchester. James failed to make the Eton First XI in 1845, but the following year, he and his precociously talented, younger brother, Henry, plus Robert C. Antrobus, all played their part in a rather emphatic victory over Harrow, by an innings and 135 runs. Aitken major, batting at number four, was the third top scorer with 38 (run out) out of a total of 279, whilst Aitken minor took five wickets in the Harrow first innings and six in the second. The following year, the three friends again played pivotal roles in victories over both Harrow, whom they beat by three wickets, and Winchester, whom they thrashed by an innings and 79 runs.

In 1848, James was an undergraduate at Exeter College, Oxford, and was surprisingly selected to play in the varsity match that year. I say 'surprisingly' as, apart from being a 'fresher', his form was not particularly impressive. In a college match against Wadham College, whilst batting at number five, he only scored 2 and 1, out of totals of 141 and 115. He was, however, rather more successful with the ball, taking eight wickets and a catch in the first innings and a further five wickets in the second innings. His dismal batting performance probably accounted for him batting at number eight for Oxford in the victory that year, over Cambridge, at the Magdalene ground. The following year, however, when the match was played at Lords, he was one of the Oxford openers, and top scored with 36 runs in a game that Cambridge won by three wickets. In his final year, batting on this occasion at number three, he top scored for Oxford in the second innings with 31 runs in a winning cause on Cowley Marsh.

According to his obituary in 'The Field' in February, 1908; *"James rowed for his 'Varsity in 1849 in the December race - the second of that year - at No. 5 thwart. The following summer he was one of the Oxford crew who rowed over for the Grand*

Challenge Cup at the Henley Regatta. In 1851 he again rowed for Oxford at Henley, when they beat the Cambridge crew and won the cup for the second year."

James graduated with a B.A. from Exeter College in May, 1851, but remained in the area for some time, as both he and his brother were selected to play for Sixteen of Oxfordshire versus The Eleven of England *"at the Christ Church Ground near the Great Western Railway Station on the 5th, 6th and 7th of June. "A newly invented bat, partly made of cork will be presented by Pilch and Martin to the person obtaining the greatest number of runs." ('Bell's Life').* Although his brother scored 7 runs and took a couple of wickets for the Sixteen of Oxfordshire, James did not play in that match, perhaps because he was in training for the 'Grand Challenge Cup for Eight Oared Boats' versus Cambridge University at the Henley Royal Regatta the following week. At 11st. 9lbs he was one of the heaviest in the winning Oxford boat.

James was ordained in 1852 and two years later received his M.A. from Exeter College, before becoming the Curate at St. Mary's Church in Beddington. This was an area James knew very well as his uncle, another James Aitken (b. 1791) (slight spelling difference), lived in Carshalton Park for over forty years. James seems to have been very close to his uncle, and appears to have stayed there on numerous occasions as the local papers showed that both he and his uncle applied for Game Licences in 1851 in Beddington.

Being ordained virtually signalled the end of James's sporting career, although he did manage to play one final game for Seven Oaks Vine, in August 1854, against Sir John Lubbock's Eleven, at Sir John's country seat of High Elms. Although James acquitted himself with honour, scoring 24 and 10, against the likes of Frederick Norman and Alfred Lubbock, who both played for Kent, the short preamble to the scorecard makes one appreciate how difficult it must have been in the mid-nineteenth century to organise a cricket match: *"At High Elms, on Tuesday, the Vine had recourse to a 'drag' to bring up their team, there being at present no line of rail through about half a score of miles of the most beautiful part of the County of Kent."* (A 'drag' was a gentleman's carriage).

One of James's earliest assignments as a local priest was to officiate at the wedding of his sister, Agnes Maria, to Edward James Daniell at Carshalton Church in January, 1855. Three years later, on Tuesday, the 18th May, James himself was married at St. Mary's Church, Beddington, by the Rev. James Pott, to Ellen Pott, the only daughter of William Pott, of 'Wallington House', Beddington. By this time, James's widowed mother, Harriett, was also living in Carshalton Park with her brother-in-law, James, who had been a witness at his nephew's wedding. This James must have been extremely wealthy as when he died in 1880 he left the two brothers £25,000, which would be approximately three million pounds in 2020.

The newly weds lived in Manor Road, Wallington, close to the 'Duke's Head', until 1867, before moving with their young family to Chorley Wood in Hertfordshire, where James remained as the Vicar for 21 years, before leaving the country to work for several years as the Chaplain of the Royal Memorial Church in Cannes. He spent his final few years as the Canon of Gibraltar, before dying at Hove in January, 1908. The fact that a memorial service was held in Cannes at the same time as his funeral service in Hove, merely shows the esteem with which he was held by all those who met him.

[3]**Henry Mortlock Aitken** (b. 1831), like his brother was born at Hadley Priory and went to school at Eton, where from 1846 to 1849 he played for the First XI and captained them in his final two seasons. His rather fast, round armed style of bowling was so good that he was invited to play for Surrey in 1846, when he was only fifteen. Although he started off as primarily a bowler, he did develop into quite a reasonable mid-order batsman. After being selected for the Oxford team for the varsity match at Lords in June, 1853, he notched up 18 runs at number six, before being dismissed by his friend, Charles Pontifex. He then took three wickets to help the Dark Blues win by an innings and 19 runs.

Henry also played at Lords for the Gentlemen versus the Players in July, 1853, in a match that was long remembered. The ground was crowded with over 5,000 spectators and there were at least 40 carriages lined up, *"filled with female members of the aristocracy, and at least 50 to 60 ladies and gentlemen on horseback."* Henry's contribution to the match was merely nine runs in two innings, batting at number nine, plus a catch, and he was not called upon to bowl. On a lively wicket the Players were skittled out for 42 and 69, which gave the Gentlemen a rare victory, in this event, by 60 runs. Probably the most interesting feature of this victory was the fact that **Sir Frederick Hervey-Bathurst** (b. 1807 Scilly Isles) and **Matthew Kempson** (b. 1831), bowled unchanged throughout both innings. Sir Frederick, who played most of his First Class Cricket for Hampshire, bowled round arm fast, and picked up eleven wickets, whilst Kempson, a Cambridge graduate, who was 24 years Frederick's junior, bowled medium pace roundarm, and picked up the remaining nine wickets.

After Henry was ordained in 1854 he spent the next seventeen years in India, but unlike his brother he continued to play cricket and captained the Calcutta C.C. until he returned to England in 1871, when he became a member of the M.C.C. until his death in Eastbourne in 1915. His obituary in the 'Globe' reminded the reader that Henry had taken part in one of the most famous games of cricket ever, 62 years earlier. Following his death, according to the 'Globe', only two other participants in that match remained alive, Sir Spencer Ponsonby-Fane and William Caffyn, the ex-Surrey professional.

Unlike his brother Henry seems to have renounced the cloth in later life. The 1901 and 1911 censuses failed to indicate that he had been a priest, but showed that he was living on his own means with his wife, née Mary Burrow (b. 1843), whom he had married in 1885. They had no children but lived with a cook and a couple of maids in luxury at 'The Boltons', Kensington.

[4]**Charles James Abbott** (b. 1821) and his brother, [5]**Frederick Jenkins Abbott** (b. 1820), had both been born at 26, Woburn Place, in the heart of London, and their father, Charles Thelwell Abbott, was a partner, in 1821, at Messrs Jenkins, James and Abbott, Solicitors, New Inn, London. Both Charles junior and Frederick qualified as solicitors and by 1843 had joined their father at Messrs. Abbott and Sons at 8, New Inn, The Strand, W.C.

Charles, who was educated at Winchester College, had probably the better cricketing pedigree of the brothers as he was recorded as having played, at Lords, for the Gentlemen of Surrey versus the Marylebone Cricket Club in June 1844, although he hadn't been listed on the team sheet the previous week. He was obviously a late replacement and sadly only batted at number eleven, scoring two runs before being bowled by William Lillywhite, and failed to take a wicket or a catch. Two years later, however, he found himself on the committee of the Surrey C.C. which was formed in 1845. He resigned from that committee the following year, probably because of his limited ability and the pressure of work. By the time of his death in 1889 he had risen to the rank of Under Sheriff for the County of Surrey, and was living with his family at 'Rydens', Walton-on-Thames. His son, William, went on to play for Surrey C.C.

The only sporting information upon Frederick Abbott is that he bought a Game Licence every year from 1839 to 1851 in either Walton or Westminster. Frederick went to Queens College, Cambridge, from where he graduated with an M.A. in 1844, and by 1857 he was a barrister who was called to the bar at the Inner Temple. He married in 1864, and by 1871 he was living in Swanscombe, Kent with his wife and two young sons.

[6]**Thomas Weeding junior** had been born on the 5th of January, 1831, in the village of Oatlands in central Tasmania. His father, James, had been born at Headley, Surrey, in 1791, and married his wife, Frances Lawrence (b.1795), on the 1st September, 1822, at St. Martin's-in-the-Fields. The following year they emigrated to become farmers in Tasmania, on the fast sailing ship 'Mariner'. They arrived in Hobart in September, 1823, and settled in the small village of Oatlands, where there was a military base which helped to control and manage the convicts. (Oatlands still has the greatest number of colonial style sandstone properties of any village in Australia, many of which were built with convict labour.)

Life was not easy for the early colonists in the 1820s as, apart from convicts being foisted onto the farms to act as cheap labour, there was a long running guerrilla war with the local aborigines, which led to the deaths of at least 200 settlers. James died at the early age of 47 in 1838 and was buried at St. David's Anglian Church in Hobart. His epitaph in the 'Hobart Town Gazette' called him *an original pioneer* and mentioned his heroic struggle to survive: *"Mr. Weeding arrived, with property, a free settler, in 1823, with Mrs. Weeding. He was from Dorking in Surry. By honesty and industry, he obtained, and left provision for his family, for which he had to struggle against the attacks of bushrangers, and power. He was a good Christian, an honest man ......"*

Following the death of her husband, Frances continued to run the farm with her four children, Frances (b. 1825), James (b. 1827), Harriett (b. 1828) and Thomas, until her own death in 1853, when she was buried alongside her husband in Hobart. Upon her death the 1,700 acre estate, which was called 'Weedington' passed to her two sons. James, who had to manage the estate for his absentee brother, owned 1,200 acres, whilst Thomas owned 500 acres. James also had a sheep farm of 3,000 acres. According to the 'Hobart Gazette' of 1861, Thomas's 500 acres was valued as being worth £100 per year.

At some stage in the late 1840s young Thomas sailed for England to join his uncle, and, in 1849, applied to join the East India Company College in Hertfordshire. This was a necessary step for anyone who wanted to work as a Civil Servant in India, as the East India Company had a monopoly upon all clerical positions in that country. Thomas wrote a suitably grovelling letter of application to the Court of Directors, part of which read: *"That your Petitioner has received the rudiments of a Classical and Mathematical Education and is desirous of devoting himself to the Civil Service of the Hon Company in India."* It was signed *"Thomas Weeding junior"*. As this was accompanied by a letter of recommendation from his Uncle, who had the power to hire and fire Directors, Thomas was accepted to join the college.

The 1851 census showed that Thomas was one of 83 students, at the East India Company College in Great Amwell, Hailey, Hertfordshire. The majority of the students on this four term course were between 17 and 20 years of age. Thomas qualified with a First Class Pass in December, 1851, and was dispatched the following year to Bombay, to act as the assistant to the Collector.

Thomas returned to England in 1856 and married his uncle's niece, Elizabeth Newberry (b. 1835), at St. John's Church, Malden, on August 30th. Elizabeth's brother, Richard Nicholas Newberry (b. 1838), had also been a student at the East India College in 1854 and, the following year, became a Cornet in the Honorable Company's employ at Nusseerabad, in Bombay. Sadly he died in the Indian Mutiny in May, 1857, at the age of twenty, one of several East India Company employees, associated with the Weedings, who died prematurely. His death was reported in the 'Evening Mail' on the 20th July, 1857, as follows:

"On the 28th May, at Nusseerabad, India, Richard Nicholas Newberry, aged 20 years, Cornet in the 1st Regiment Bombay Cavalry (Lancers), brother by marriage, and all his life as a son to the late Thomas Weeding Esq. of Mecklenburgh-square, London and Fullbrooks, Malden, Surrey. He was shot while assisting to re-capture the guns during the mutiny of the Bengal troops stationed at Nusseerabad."

On the 19th July, 1857, Thomas and Elizabeth had their first child, Mary, who was born in Dhodia, near Bombay. It is not known how much time the family spent together in India, but by the time of the 1861 census, Elizabeth and Mary were staying in Brighton at the home of a wealthy lady friend, Mrs. Bishop. The census stated that Elizabeth was a fundholder, which suggests that she was a lady of private means. By this time Thomas and Elizabeth were exceedingly wealthy as they had the income from the land in Tasmania, plus the estate in Malden as Thomas Weeding Senior had died in 1856, and his wife, Mary, had died on February 29th, 1860, at 28, Portland Place, Marylebone. Both Thomas junior and Elizabeth, Mary's niece, were executors, and beneficiaries, of her will.

By the time that their second child, Thomas Newberry Weeding, was born at 2, Lower Seymour Street in Marylebone, on March 20th, 1865, Thomas junior had committed suicide. He died according to the Bombay Civil Service Deaths and Burial lists, on August 28th, 1864, from a *"wound in the throat self inflicted while labouring under an attack of temporary insanity",* and he was buried at Kurrachee the following day. The 'Bombay Gazette' reported that he was an acting judge at the time, who cut his throat *"while in a fit of delirium from fever."*

Sadly Thomas's only son, who had inherited the property died, *"after a few days' illness",* at Boulogne-sur-Mer, on September 20th, 1865, at the age of only eighteen months, and the estate passed to Thomas Weeding Baggallay (b. June 11th, 1847), in accordance with the will of Thomas Weeding Senior. He, in turn, when he reached the age of twenty one, adopted the name of Thomas Weeding Weeding, and became a vital character in the story of the formation of Worcester Park Athletic Club in 1921.

Elizabeth and Mary continued to live together in comparative luxury until Elizabeth's death in August, 1901, whilst on holiday at Bexhill-on Sea. The census, earlier that year, showed the mother and daughter were living at 10, Kensington Garden's Terrace, in Paddington, with a cook and three maids. Following Elizabeth's death she was buried close to her aunt in the Malden graveyard on September 4th. Five weeks later on October 10th, freed from the responsibility of being her mother's companion, her daughter, Mary, married Shackleton Hallett, a 59 year old Barrister, of 23, The Square, Lincoln's Inn, at St. James's Church, Paddington.

[7]**Martin Norman** (b. 1831) came from a great Kent cricketing family, and was the eldest son of a Kent merchant, Robert Cummins Norman (b.1805), and his wife,

Emily Martin (b. 1810-1842)). His three younger brothers, all born in Chislehurst, had their mother's maiden surname as their middle names. In 1851, Martin had been a fellow student of Thomas Weeding junior, at the East India College in Hailesbury. Whilst Weeding merely graduated with a 'Highly Distinguished Pass' at the end of the Fourth Term, in December 1851, Martin seemed to be the star pupil as he was *"Highly Distinguished, with medal in classics, medal in Sanskrit, and medal in Telogu."* At the graduation ceremony, before his peers and all the assembled dignitaries, he had to read poems which he had translated into both Telogu, a Dravidian language spoken mainly in the Southern states of India, and into Sanskrit. *"The reading of this poem was accompanied by loud cheers."*

It is highly likely that Martin had attended Harrow School, where he would have obtained a sound grounding in the classics and the art of cricket, as the obituary in the 'Newcastle Journal' on October 7th, 1918, for his younger brother, Francis Martin Norman (b. 1833), stated that Francis had attended Harrow before joining the Royal Navy at the age of fifteen. (Brothers often attended the same public schools.)

Apart from being an outstanding student, Martin Norman was also an above average club cricketer and is recorded as playing primarily as a batsman in several games for both the West Kent Cricket Club and Seven Oaks Vine, both before and after his work in Madras for the East India Company. The West Kent C.C. played their first game on Chislehurst Common in 1822. Chislehurst and West Kent still play there today, knowing that their ground is safe from developers, as an Act of Parliament in the 1880s passed the Common over to the people of Chislehurst, with the proviso that cricket should be played there perpetually.

Martin made his first appearance in the press in 1849, in a match against the Carthusians, which West Kent won extremely easily by an innings and 60 runs. As young Martin had only batted at number ten, and had only scored 8 runs before being run out, West Kent allowed him to bat for the opposition, as batsman number 13, and he top scored with eleven runs. The following year in matches against Sydenham and Seven Oaks Vine, which they won again, he had risen to the top of the batting order, scoring 18 and 39 respectively.

The match against Sydenham was particularly interesting as it showed the important role that public school boys played in the development of cricket. The first four batsmen for the West Kent side were Frederick Gosling (Rugby) 43*, Charles Norman (Eton) 40, John Lubbock (Eton) 19, and Martin Norman (Harrow) 18. **John Frederick Gosling** (b. 1833 in North Cray, Kent) had played for Rugby that year and went on to play one first class game for Kent eight years later. **Charles Lloyd Norman** (b 1833 in Bromley) was a first cousin of Martin and had captained Eton in 1850, before going on to play first class cricket for Cambridge, Kent and the M.C.C. **John Lubbock** (b. 1834 Eaton Square) was not really renowned as a player although three of his brothers played first class cricket for Kent. John, however, was a great cricket lover and for several years was the Secretary of the West Kent club. As Sir John Lubbock, in 1871, one of the many social reforms for which he was responsible was the Bank Holiday Act, which allowed the working man more occasions upon which he could play cricket.

It appears as though Martin must have been on a seven years' contract in India, as his next appearance in the cricketing press occurred on July 11th, 1859, when he scored 31 runs out of 87 in the first innings, for the Vine against Westerham, *"of which Mr. M. Norman Esq. obtained 31 in first rate style"*, and ten out of 53 in the second innings. *"The ground was graced by a numerous attendance of ladies, and we trust that they will always be present at the future matches on the truly picturesque ground."*

This might have been Martin's final game as he became yet another premature death connected to both the East India Company and to the Weedings. No cause of death can be found online. The 'South Eastern Gazette' of Tuesday 29th October, 1859, bluntly stated in the 'Deaths' column: *"On the 16th inst., at Camden, Chislehurst, Martin, eldest son of Robert C. Norman, Esq., and the late Deputy Secretary to Government in the Revenue Department, Madras, aged 28."*

It is a great pity that such a brilliant scholar was not able to achieve his full potential. His younger brother, Francis Martin Norman, fought in the trenches at Sebastapol, sailed through the Dardanelles twice under fire, and was wounded in the China Wars. Eventually he rose to the rank of Commander, before settling in Berwick, where he became immersed in all aspects of local life, becoming the Mayor twice, the Sheriff twice, a Justice of the Peace, a Councillor, and eventually a Freeman of the town, before dying in 1918.

[8]**Robert Hugh Alexander** was born on the 13th of November, 1832, in Calcutta, West Bengal, to Nathaniel Alexander (b. 1796) and his wife, Sophia Charlotte Young. He was the second oldest of five sons, and also had four sisters. His grandfather was the Right Reverend Nathaniel Alexander, the extremely powerful and prosperous Bishop of Meath. His father was a wealthy member of the East India Company who by 1848 was living at 'Hylands House' on the Dorking Road, Epsom, with his wife and several members of the family plus numerous servants. Nathaniel lived there until his death in 1880.

Although Robert was born in India, from the age of 11 until he entered the East India College, he was educated by Mr. Day, at Cleveland House, Streatham Hill. Following his graduation from the East India College he returned to India but died at the age of 23 on the 16th of June, 1856, at Noakholly in Bengal. The cause of his death was not recorded, but Bengal was a cauldron of unrest at that time and was the scene of the

Indian Mutiny in 1857. Unlike Thomas Weeding junior, however, his family thought enough of him to have his body returned to England and he was buried in the graveyard at St. Martin of Tours, Epsom.

Although [9]**Thomas Weeding** (b. 1774) was born 147 years before the creation of Worcester Park Athletic Club, his actions had a profound influence upon the Club's formation in 1921. Thomas was an extremely rich and powerful merchant in the City of London, who, between 1830 and 1840, purchased numerous lots of land, for over £10,000, in the Old Malden area, including Skinner's Field. He also managed to acquire the freehold for those fields which were under the manorial jurisdiction of Merton College, by the time of his death in 1858. It was on part of this newly acquired estate in the 1830s that he had built for him 'Fullbrooks', a country retreat, although most indications are that he let the property, choosing instead to live close to his various business ventures in the City. Strangely many of the taxation documents at the time list his home in Malden as being 'Dunford Mill'.

Much of Thomas's wealth was based upon the fact that he was a Proprietor of the East India Company, which was probably the richest company in the world in the early nineteenth century. The Company dominated the cotton, silk and spice trade with the Indian sub-continent, and traded as far afield as China and Hong Kong. Much of this influence was based upon the fact that it had an army of over a quarter of a million solders, which not only gave it enormous power in India but also over the Government of the United Kingdom.

From about 1820, Thomas was regularly recorded as having chaired meetings of the Proprietors of the East India Company, who were basically the owners of the company and held regular meetings to discuss not only the election of directors, but also to discuss any government policies which they felt impinged upon their trade. One such instance occurred in 1840 when Weeding was the lead signature on the following letter, dated June 8th, to the Directors: *"We, the undersigned Proprietors of East India Stock request that you will call a Special General Court of the East India Company, at the earliest convenient opportunity, to take into consideration a Bill which has been introduced into the House of Commons, for permitting and regulating the deportation of Hill Coolies from India to the Mauritius, We have the honour to be, Gentlemen, Your most obedient servants, Thomas Weeding et al."*

Thomas's offices were originally in the 'Old South Sea House' in Threadneedle Street, at the heart of English trade and banking. In about 1824 he moved to 20, Broad Street and a few years later relocated to 6, Great Winchester Street. His office was merely one of at least 20 Offices of Agency in London for the East India Company. At the time he married his first wife, Sarah McCallum of Finsbury Square, on June 29th, 1811, in the Chapel of the Foundling Hospital, his home was at 96, Guildford Street, Russell Square, Bloomsbury. By the time of Sarah's death, however, on New Year's Eve, 1835, the couple had moved to 47, Mecklenburgh Square, a modern development on fields owned by the Foundling Hospital. The Square had been named in honour of George III's wife, Charlotte of Mecklenburg-Strelitz.

Although much of Thomas's work involved the East India Company he had his fingers in numerous other pies which probably restricted his visits to Malden. For many years he was a Director of the Corporation of London Assurance, a company which had been established in 1720 for Marine, Fire and Life Assurance. Adverts in 1839 showed that he was also a Director of the New Zealand Land Company which seemed to be a company devoted to finding settlers for, and arranging passage to, New Zealand. Further adverts in 1840 showed that he was also a Director of the Bank of Asia, whilst in 1846 he appeared on the Committee of the Marine Society Office.

Thomas was also a Director of the St. Katherine's Dock Company, along with William Gladstone. The Dock, which opened in 1828, had been built on 13 acres of land near the Tower of London at the cost, according to 'The Times', of the destruction of over 1,250 dwelling places and the displacement of 11,300 residents. It was here where Thomas was conveniently able to dock his own 480 ton sailing ship 'Sarah', which was on a list of ships trading in India and eastward of the Cape of Good Hope. The adverts showed that the ship *"has superior accommodation for Passengers, and carries an experienced Surgeon. For Freight or Passengers, apply to Mr. Weeding, No. 20, Broad Street."*

As a leading merchant, Thomas was also well aware of the potential benefit to trade of that new invention, the steam locomotive, and, as such, in 1836 he appeared on the Provisional Committee of the New South Durham Railway. Ten years later, in March, 1846, he spoke at a public enquiry in favour of a branch line running through Malden and Worcester Park. Strangely, the journalist of 'The Sun' knighted him: *"Sir Thomas Weeding, a magistrate, residing at Malden, thought this branch line would be of service in bringing lime from Asden for the farmers, a manure of which the ground was much in need. He confirmed the evidence of the previous witnesses as to the probable advantages of the line to the country, and the feelings of the inhabitants respecting it. Maldon is about a mile at present from the main line of the South-Western Railway, but the branch was proposed to run through Malden, and would pass through one of his farms for three quarters of a mile. The parish comprised about 1,250 acres, and this branch was necessary to enable the farmers to keep their heads above water. He made a personal sacrifice to get the railway, because he believed it would be for the advantage of his neighbours generally."* (26th Mar, 1846)

Although being a merchant and a Director of so many companies must have been time consuming, Thomas still found time to involve himself in various charities, education and the church. In the field of education he became a Governor of two important local charitable schools, the Foundling Hospital School and Christ Church Hospital School. As a Governor of the latter body he twice attended 'Drawing Room' events at St. James's Palace, in 1845 and 1849, where he was granted an audience by Queen Victoria and Prince Albert.

Thomas had also been elected on to the Board of Superintendence of the Hall of Commerce in Threadneedle Street in 1843. This Hall had been opened as a meeting point for Merchants, Bankers, Ship Owners, Manufacturers and the General Public, to advertise their wares and to make deals. Apart from this, however, there was a reading room and library where it was possible to read all the latest newspapers from around the world, examine maps and obtain all the latest trading information. There was even a fireproof vault, where valuable documents could be stored.

The 'Morning Post' in 1845, also revealed that Thomas had attended a meeting in Regent's Park, on Saturday February 8th, of the Royal Botanic Society, which was chaired by the Duke of Norfolk. This body had been founded in 1839 in order to promote *"botany in all its branches and applications",* and they leased 18 acres within the Inner Circle in Regent's Park as an experimental garden, which was occasionally opened to the public. Thomas was one of nineteen new members elected to the Society at that meeting.

Thomas was also heavily involved in the church both in the City and in Old Malden, but was not happy to be just an ordinary member of the congregation; he had to take a leading role in proceedings. Apart from his wedding, his first mention, at a church event, occurred on July 1st, 1819, when he was a Churchwarden at St. Pancras Old Church, at a ceremony for the laying of the foundation stone for St. Pancras New Church, by the Duke of York, the second son of King George III. His name, alongside that of the Duke of York, the Vicar, the other Churchwarden and the Architect were inscribed for posterity upon the foundation stone.

Having been a churchwarden, Thomas realised on his occasional visits to St. John's, that the interior of the church in Old Malden was in urgent need of attention. In 1847 he offered to re-pave the church and to replace all the pews, providing that he had overall control over what was done. As the Vicar was absent, the churchwardens of St. John's agreed to this offer, which did not particularly please the Vicar at that time, the Reverend George Trevelyan. Thomas's relationship with the new vicar, the Rev. William Chetwynd Stapylton, in 1850, began in equally stormy fashion when the new vicar removed the locks from some of the pews, but both vicar and landowner eventually reconciled their differences and Thomas became a regular attendee at the church.

Thomas Weeding also tried to stand for parliament at least three times but failed on each occasion, possibly because he was too principled to participate in the cess pool of early nineteenth century politics. On the first occasion in 1827 he paid £1,500 to an election agent to help him obtain a seat at Penryn but withdrew from the contest as, according to 'Bell's Weekly Messenger', May 20th, 1827, *"Several of the voters, he understood, expected money. He retired because he found that unless he had recourse to something like corrupt practices he could not get returned."* He stood again for one of the two seats that Penryn returned in 1831, but came third: *"J. W Freshfield 336; Charles Stewart 242, Thomas Weeding 225: Two first elected."* In 1841, standing as a Conservative candidate he came fractionally closer to success to gaining one of the two seats: *"M. Foster 394; R. Hodgson 343; T. Weeding 335."*

When Sarah, his first wife died, childless, on December 31st, 1835, at the age of 49, Thomas erected a tablet to her memory in St. John's Church "in affectionate remembrance of her virtues." Eighteen months later, however, he had overcome his grief and married twenty-two year old, Mary Newberry (b. 1815) on July 29th, 1837, at Christ Church Hospital in Newgate. The couple lived together happily enough, but still childless, for the next 19 years until his death in 1856. The 'Morning Post' reported the event thus, *"WEEDING - On Sunday, the 5th inst., after a short illness, deeply lamented, Thomas Weeding, Esq., of Mecklenburgh Square, London, and of Fullbrooks, Malden, Surrey, of which County he was for several years a Magistrate."* The Greater London Burial Index merely states that he was *"Magistrate, Merchant and Governor of the Foundling Hospital."*

Thomas was buried in the family vault in Malden Churchyard on October 18th, 1856. In the newspapers of the time, his death passed almost without comment. The only real epitaph seems to be that which can be found on the tablet in the church at St. Johns Church:

> *"He was a Merchant of the City of London,*
> *And a Governor of this and many other Charitable Institutions.*
> *His benevolent and sweet disposition, elegant mind,*
> *Never-failing charity and simple piety, endeared*
> *Him to all classes."*

[10]**Charles Pontifex** was born into a legal and cricketing family, in Holborn, on June 5th, 1831, the son of John Pontifex (b.1796), an attorney at law of 5, St. Andrew's Court, Holborn. His mother, Mary Marshall (b. 1805), whose brother was a solicitor, came from that hotbed of Surrey cricket in the nineteenth century, Godalming, for whom John Pontifex was recorded as having played an occasional game. His great uncle, however, another John Pontifex (b. 1771), was a member of

the Marylebone Cricket Club and played in the first two Gentlemen versus Players matches in 1806, plus several other First Class matches.

Charles, who was considered to be mainly a bowler, attended King's College School, where he represented the school in a victory against Putney College, at Lords, on June 6th, 1850. In that game he batted mid-order and scored 9 and 4, but opened the bowling and took seven out of the 16 wickets to fall. A couple of months later he played for Eleven Gentlemen of Surrey against Twelve Caesars of Godalming, at the ground of his cousin, Alexander Marshall, in Broadwater Park.

The following season saw him playing at Fenners, for Trinity College, Cambridge, on the 26th and 27th of May, 1851, in a trial match for the University team. against a provisional University side. On the first day of the match Charles went in to lunch, not out 14, but after lunch, according to the 'Cambridge Chronicle and Journal', *"when the game was resumed, Mr. Pontifex was unavoidably absent."* The scorecard for that innings merely shows *"C. Pontifex absent after dinner 14."*

The four wickets that he got the following day against the University, however, was not enough to gain him a place in the prestigious Varsity match at Lords that season. He did, however, captain Cambridge against Oxford in June, 1853, in a match that they lost by an innings and 19 runs. Pontifex opened the batting and scored 27 and five runs, but only took one wicket.

Although Charles did not play many First Class games, he did play in 1852, at the age of twenty one, in a six wicket victory for the Gentlemen of the South versus the Gentlemen of the North at Lords. Unfortunately he failed to contribute with either the bat or the ball, although he did pick up a couple of catches. The following week, however, his performance was a little more prominent in a fine eight wicket victory for the Gentlemen of Kent against the Gentlemen of England. In the first innings he bowled Mr. W. Williams and Mr. A. Haygarth, whilst in the second innings he caught Mr. G. Cooke and Lord Guernsey. He also contribute twenty runs out of the 160 run total, whilst batting at number ten.

After he gained his B.A. from Trinity College he followed his father and uncle into a legal career and was called to the bar in 1854. Despite his studies he still continued to play non-First Class games after his graduation, particularly for the Gentlemen of Kent. The 'South Eastern Gazette' of the 24th August, 1858, mentioned his participation in two of the games in the Canterbury 'Grand Cricket Week'. He got a duck against 'I Zingari' and did not take a wicket, and whilst playing for the Gentlemen of Kent against the Gentlemen of England, he failed to take a wicket yet again, but fielded at *'the point'*. Whilst batting he had to retire on 10 *"having been struck in the face by a ball, hit with tremendous force, by his partner, Mr. Watts"*. This set-back did not dampen his enthusiasm for the game as his batting *"excited general admiration"* whilst playing for Godalming against Chiddingfold, the following month, with a couple of his cousins, Alexander and Frederick Marshall.

The 1861 census, which listed him as a barrister, showed that he was staying with his uncle, Henry Marshall, in Godalming. Eventually, however, he gravitated towards the Colonial Service and by 1872 was a Judge in Bengal. When he retired in 1892 he was knighted and went to live in Kensington, where the 1911 census showed him as living with his second wife, Grace (b. 1851), whom he married in 1882, and seven servants, including a butler, footman and a cook. He died the following year on the 27th July.

[11]**John Everett Millais,** who was born in Portland Street, Southampton, on the 8th of June, 1829, was the son of John William Millais, a small landowner on the Island of Jersey, and Mary, the daughter of Richard Evermy. She was also the widow of Enoch Hodgkinson. Much of young John's early years were spent in France and the Channel Islands, where he showed a great aptitude for art. At the age of eleven, his parents took him to London, where his talent was recognised by Sir Martin Archer Shree, the President of the Royal Academy, and he was accepted into the preparatory school for that Academy.

During these early years in London he made the acquaintance of William Holman Hunt, and by 1848, they, and five other like minded artists had formed the Pre-Raphaelite Brotherhood (PRB) at Millais's home at 83, Gower Street. Both Millais and Hunt had strong connections to the Worcester Park area. Holman Hunt had been baptised at St. Mary's Church, Ewell, and his uncle, William Hobman farmed at the nearby 'Rectory Farm', whilst Millais had been known to visit the family of Captain Lempriere, who lived at the 'Manor House', in the Cheam Road, Ewell. On one occasion, in 1846, he went to a dance at Ewell Castle and met the girl who was to be his future wife, Euphemia (Effie) Gray, whom he married in 1855, although she did marry John Ruskin first.

In late June, 1851, Holman Hunt, J. E. Millais, W. H. Millais and Charles Collins came down to the Worcester Park area to look for suitable backgrounds for their latest projects. Both Hunt and Millais stayed painting on the banks of the Hogsmill until mid November, making huts out of hurdles and straw to protect themselves from the weather. Holman Hunt painted 'The Hireling Shepherd' using local girl Emma Watkins as his model, whilst Millais painted 'Ophelia' which he finished off with Lizzie Siddall as his model, freezing in a bath full of cold water, heated by candles.

Millais was an extremely popular and wealthy artist. One only has to look at the size of his household at 2, Kensington Gardens, to realise that this was not a poor artist starving in a garret. In 1885 the Queen bestowed a baronetcy upon him, and in 1896, shortly before his death from throat cancer, he was elected President of the Royal Academy.

****

The Birth of Local Club Cricket

The second half of the nineteenth century saw several cricket teams, such as Cheam Common, Cuddington and Old Malden & Worcester Park emerge in the local area. The first cricket club to be formed locally, however, began in **1864** when a group of residents, who were associated with St. Dunstan's Church in Cheam Village, concluded that there was enough interest locally to form a cricket club. In a way, this could be considered as one small step on the road to the eventual formation of W.P.A.C., as some of the Cheam Cricket Club's early members, who lived at the northern end of the parish, went on to become founder members of Cheam Common C.C. in 1872, and, whilst the latter club provided continual cricket up to and after World War I, Cheam C.C. had a rather chequered existence and slipped into 'abeyance' on at least one occasion and had to be reformed.

Prior to the formation of Cheam Cricket Club in 1864, however, there were isolated examples of matches being played by a team called 'Cheam', which were obviously ad hoc affairs. In September, **1857**, for example, the 'Sussex Agricultural Express' apologised for failing to include the result of the Coulsdon versus Cheam match, as they had only just received an account of the match. Two years later another match between the same opponents was advertised, but again there was no match report. Another interesting advertisement for an intriguing fixture, involving what might be considered a local 'Cheam' club, was one that appeared in the 'Morning Chronicle' of September 9th, **1861**: *"This Day - At Vincent-square, Westminster - Pimlico United versus Cheam Nonsuch Club."*

In **1860**, an account of two games in the 'Surrey Gazette' of August 7th, makes one think that perhaps local cricket matches in Cheam happened more often, and were more popular, than the newspapers suggested, particularly as 36 players took part in a Married versus Singles match, which apparently was an annual event. *"A cricket match was played on the New Cricket Ground, in this village, on Monday last, the 30th July, between eleven players of the Cheam Club and eleven of the Roehampton Club, which after an excellent game, ended in favour of the Cheam Club, by one run and five wickets to spare. The following is the score: Roehampton - first innings, 29 runs. Cheam 18 runs. Roehampton, 2nd innings, 38 runs. Cheam, 40, with five wickets to go down, there being just the time to get the runs before time was called.*

On Tuesday last, the 31st July, the annual match between the married and the single of this village, was played on the Old Cricket Ground, the married again coming off victorious: the village people made quite a holiday of the game: they played 18 of a side. The following is the score. First Innings - Single, 27 runs; Married 77. Second Innings - Single, 51 runs; Married, 2, with 15 wickets to spare."

This article also raises the problem of trying to ascertain the precise location of both the Old and New Cricket Grounds. As the second match was *'a holiday of the game'* it is highly likely that the Old Ground was situated near to the 'Red Lion', where an ample supply of alcohol might have enhanced the joyous occasion. The position of the New Cricket Ground, however, is more problematic, for, as 'The Tatler' claimed in an article about Cheam C.C., in 1953: *"In the first few years of its existence it occupied various fields rented from local landowners."*

A meeting was held on Wednesday, July 4th, **1864**, by various cricketing enthusiasts in Cheam who voted in, by ballot, the following committee, which was to serve until the following April 1st: E. Taylor, W. Thorns, C. Spence, J. Denman, J. Thorns, A. Mack, J. Ockenden, C. Towil. Mr. Kent was to be the Secretary of the club, whilst Mr. A. Shepherd was the Treasurer.

What was probably most remarkable about this elected committee was the fact that there was a noticeable shift away from the Aristocracy, or the Gentlemen, being in charge of proceedings. Most of the committee were ordinary tradesmen, or Players, who had been born in the vicinity. **William Thorns** (b. 1846) and his brother **John Thorns** (b. 1849) were both butchers, who were employed by their father William, who had played several local matches in the 1840s, whilst **James Denman** (b. 1841) was a carpenter. **Edward Taylor** (b.1837) was another carpenter, whilst **Alfred Shepherd** (b. 1839), the Treasurer, was a baker and grocer. **Charles Spence** (b. 1834), who was born in Kibworth, in Leicestershire, and **Thomas Kent** (b.1834) from Uttoxeter, however, were both schoolteachers, and appear to have been the only geographical and social outsiders.

'J. Ockenden' was probably **James Ockenden** (b. 1834), rather than his brother John (b. 1842), who doesn't appear on the 1861 census, but ten years later was working as a postman in Croydon. Although James had been born in Ewell, he lived most of his life in Cheam, where, as the eldest son, he carried on the family business of building and undertaking, with his father. In addition to working in the family business, which dated back to the early eighteenth century, by the time of his death in March 1909, James was recorded as having performed the following roles: Parish Clerk for 37 years; Assistant Overseer for 50 years; in charge of the Cheam sub-post office, with his wife, for 35 years; and a member of the Committee of the Cheam Horticultural Society and Clerk of the Parish Council.

Apart from all these various activities, James also had time to father ten children, five girls and five boys, and apparently found time to play cricket, as according to his epitaph in the 'Surrey Comet': *"Sports in the village always had his support, and in his younger days he was often in the cricket field."*

According to the article in 'The Tatler' magazine, of August 26th, 1953, Cheam's first match was played against Westcott in June, **1865**. As luck would have it, this was one of the few Cheam matches to be recorded in 'Bell's Life in London and Sporting Chronicle' for 1865. Unfortunately the scoresheet is too faded to reproduce, but the following is a brief summary of the club's first victory:

"This match was played on the Cheam Ground on June 13th, and, being a one day match, was decided in favour of Cheam on the first innings by 23 runs."

Batting: C. Spence 0, J. Thorns 47, W. Simmonds 3, J. Denman 2, H. Wherratt 0, J. Ockenden 3, W. Neal 9, A. Shepherd 2, W. Ockenden 3, D. Bassett 0*, W. Thorns 1. (9 byes, 7 wides) - Total 86 runs.

Bowling: first innings H. Wherratt 5 wkts, J. Thorns 4 wkts and J. Denman 1 wicket.

Bowling second innings: H. Wherratt 3 wkts, J. Thorns 3 wkts, J. Denman 1 wkt and W. Neal 1 wicket.

Westcott scored 63 runs in the first innings, and 72 for 8 in the second innings. Cheam scored 86 runs."

The Cheam wicket-keeper was probably Charles Spence, as he caught three victims in each innings.

Life, however, was noteasy for the fledgling club, and their fortunes fluctuated wildly. At times their existence was often perilous as was illustrated by the St. Dunstan's Parish Magazine of June **1874**, which stated that as the Cheam Cricket Club could not find a suitable ground, *"it is desirable that the club remain in abeyance for this season."*

The May edition of the Parish Magazine in **1875**, however, showed that the fortunes of the Cheam Village side were beginning to recover as: *"The Cheam Cricket Club, after being dormant for two years, is showing signs of new life. At a very full meeting at the Parochial Rooms on Wednesday, April 14th, a great number of new members were admitted. The rate of subscription for playing members was reduced from 10s. 6d to five shillings (2s.6d for persons under 16). Mr Hipwell's offer of a portion of his land in Cheam Park for practice was accepted, and officers were chosen for the year."*

Henry Hipwell (b. 1835) was a corn and coal dealer who lived in the High Street, Cheam, in 1871, with his wife, two young children and a servant.

In **1878** the Parish Magazine revealed another hiccup in the progress of the Cheam Village team as, *"the management of the club had not been quite what it ought to have been"*, and some of the members showed a distinct lack of co-operation. They had, however, acquired the lease of five acres of ground in Cheam Park, which was then fenced in with iron railings. This land belonged to a local benefactor, **Mr. Spencer C. Wilde** (b. 1844), an attorney, who lived in 'Cheam House'. Spencer Wilde also gave to the village the land upon which the Parochial Rooms stand, and the ornate lychgate, in front of St. Dunstan's Church, which was built to commemorate his silver wedding.

The ground that Cheam had acquired was probably where Cheam Rec. lies today, as reports appeared in the press in the mid 1880s of children playing in the Village Cricket Pavilion in Cheam Park. In those days Cheam Rec. was part of Cheam Park and the outline of the old pavilion, 20 feet deep by 40 feet long, can still be seen in hot dry weather, when the parch marks are visible, next to the current pavilion.

Harmony seems to have been restored by the end of the following season, however, as the accounts of a couple of social games would appear to indicate. On Saturday August 9th, **1879**, the 'Croydon Advertiser and East Surrey Reporter' reported that a match had been played between the Club and the Secretary's Eleven, which: *"produced the best cricket of the season. The batting of Mr. J. Thorns, Mr. J. Lockwood and Mr. Whiting for their respective sides, and the bowling of Mr. Lockwood for the Club, by his taking three wickets in three successive balls, made it rather an easy victory for the Club."*

J. Thorns, batting at number four scored 61 runs out of 134, and was ably assisted by **J. Lockwood** (b. 1843) who scored 25 runs and took seven wickets. In 1881, John Lockwood was living in the High Street in Sutton, whilst ten years later he was a resident of Cheam. Further information listed on the 1891 census also stated that he was a professional cricketer who was born at Lepton in Yorkshire. As he was not listed as playing for any county in the Victorian era, he might possibly have been employed to teach cricket at a private school.

Seven weeks later, on the 27th September, the 'Croydon Advertiser' reported on a match played between the Married and the Single of the Club that: *"The wind-up match of the season was played on Wednesday last on the Cheam Cricket Ground, between the Married and the Single of the club. They persevered through the rain and played, time resulting in a draw, after which the members sat down, to the number of about 50, to dine at the Red Lion Inn, served in the landlord's usual manner, after which a pleasant evening was spent, one hour extra being granted."* (William Hitchman was the landlord 1866-80)

The 14 Single players were: J. Ockenden jun. 18, J. Earl† 1, R. Stevens 7, H. Keates 5, J. Norrington 3, K. Brown 0*, C. Norrington 0, W. Dudley 0, B. Thorns 4, J. Spencer 2, F. Smart 2, J. Murkitt 1, E. Coleman 0, W. Johnson 0 and extras 1. Total 47. G. Cooper took 7 wickets and W. Thorns 5 wickets.

The 14 Married players were: C. Powell 3, D. Napper 11, T. Connor 0, J. White 5, W. Harrison 1, W. Thorns 8, G. Cooper 3, J. Marley 0, A. Stevens 7*, Alex Stevens 0, J. Chatfield 1, J. Holmes 1, J. Johnson 3*, A. Shepherd DNB, Extras 1, Total 44. R. Stevens took 8 wickets and H. Keates 2 wickets.

On Saturday, February 21st, **1880**, every club in the county was invited to send two representatives to a meeting to be held at 4p.m., in the Pavilion at the Kennington Oval, to discuss arrangements for a Challenge Cup Competition. Although none of the local teams sent representatives to the meeting, it was attended by at least twenty three teams from all parts of the county, some of them still being with us today, and some vanished into obscurity:- Richmond Town, Bagshot, Dulwich Manor, Blenheim, Burlington, Reigate Priory, Manor, Southwark Park, Champion-hill, Melbourne, Columbia, Lennox, One and All, Mitcham, Battersea, Croydon Oakfield, Croydon Victoria, Croydon, Farnham, Vine, South of the Thames, Licensed Victuallers, Kennington and Wandsworth.

The cup was to be called 'The Surrey County Challenge Cup' and was open to any club within Surrey, that was willing to pay the entry fee of one guinea. It was decided that, *"No person shall be allowed to play for any Club, unless he is a member of such club, and was either born in the county of Surrey, or is a bona-fide resident therein."* (Rule 8)

Despite not attending that meeting, Cheam was one of fifteen clubs paying their one guinea entry fee for the competition. They had a bye in the first round, won their second round match, and lost the semi-final against Farnham, in a match that was played on Wednesday 28th July, in Farnham Park.

According to that weekend's 'Surrey Advertiser', *"Farnham gained an unexpectedly easy victory, the majority of the Cheam batsmen being unable to make any stand against the capital bowling of Mr. E. Barrett and George Elliott.*
Score: Farnham 114; of which W. Mason made 18; G. Elliot, jun., 17; S. Marden, 16; R. Bateman, 15; A. J. Nash, 11; and J. Knight 10.
Cheam 54 and 36; of which S. Jones made 11 and 15. Six of the batsmen failed to score in the second innings. R. J. Anson and W. Bradley bowled well for Cheam."
Farnham went on to beat Mitcham in the final.

The Challenge Cup could hardly have been called a roaring success, as Mr. C. W. Alcock, the Secretary of Surrey County Cricket Club admitted, at an end of season dinner at Reigate Priory. In replying to a toast he said, *"It was painful to him to know, as he did, that Surrey cricket was not what it ought to be. He had hoped that the challenge cup that had been offered would have done some good in bringing out good cricketers, but it had not done so well as they could have wished. Hear, hear)."*

He must have been even more disheartened the following year when only ten other teams, apart from Cheam, had entered for the County Challenge Cup by the time of the draw in March, **1881**. (See opposite page)

The draw for the first round, which had to be played by June 1st, was:

> Mitcham v Croydon Amateurs,
> Clapham v Farnham,
> Cheam v Southwark Park,
> Brockwell Park v Richmond Town,
> South Norwood v Esher Village,
> Thornton Heath a bye

The press coverage of the matches in season two of the Challenge Cup was a little more comprehensive than that in season one, and threw up some interesting snippets of information. Cheam's first round tie against Southwark Park, for example, pitted them against one of the giants of Victorian cricket, **Bobby Abel** (b 1857), who played his first game of cricket for Surrey that year. Abel, aka 'The Guv'nor', eventually scored 33,128 first class runs with a top score of 357*.

It is a little awe inspiring to think that someone that famous, who went on to play thirteen test matches for England, had actually played cricket on Cheam Rec. on a rainy day in May, 1881, before his first class career eventually began. It is also extremely sad when one considers that the local council ceased to provide pitches for the public in about 2010, because of financial cuts, after 130 years of cricket on the Recreation Ground. The following account of the match occurred in the 'Sporting Life', Thursday, May 19th, 1881.

"This match, one of the first ties of this cup, was played at Cheam yesterday (Wednesday), and resulted in favour of the latter by five wickets. Rain falling heavily during the morning, a start was not made until half-past twelve. Abel played good cricket for his 28 for Southwark Park, and W. Bradley's 36 was a free-hit innings for the winners. Score:- Southwark Park 97, Cheam 101 for 6 wickets."

Cheam: W. C. Wheeler 7, A. Tabor 1, A. Wheeler 10, W. J. Bradley 36, S. Jones 22*, J. J. Steadman 0, W. Thorns 14*, Tancock, Lockwood and two others did not bat. W. C. Wheeler took 4 wickets, Tancock 2 wickets, Jones 2 wickets, and Lockwood 1 wicket.

The 'Norwood News and Crystal Palace Chronicle', on Saturday 2nd July 1881, reported on their second round tie against the local South Norwood side: *"On Tuesday last, South Norwood played their second round match for the Surrey County Cup on the ground in the Portland-road. They were drawn to play against Cheam, and had amongst their opponents several well-known professionals, including the brothers Wheeler, Lockwood and Ratcliff, and such amateurs as Mr. Bridges, of Beddington Park fame. Against this array of talent, Norwood succumbed, and scored 91 only to their opponents 119, losing the match by 28 runs on the first innings. In the second innings, which was not played out, Cheam made 58, and Norwood 36 for seven wickets. The fielding of Norwood was anything but good in the first innings, the exception being Mr. Leete at deep-long-on, who made some fine catches in spite of the high wind. Mr. W. C. Elborough bowled seven wickets in the first innings, and six in the second. The score was as follows:-"*

W. C. Wheeler 60 & 22, Bridges 9 & 13, A. Wheeler 14 & 8, W. J. Bradley 1 & 6, J. Lockwood 6 & 3, J. Thorns 18 & 1, A. Ratcliff 2 & 0, W. Thorns 4* & 0, D. Napper 2 & 3*, E. Ellis 0 & 1, Steadman, absent 0 & 0, Extras 3 & 1. Wickets: J. Lockwood 6 & 4, W. C. Wheeler 2 & 3, A. Ratcliff 2.

One or two facts in the above report are slightly inaccurate: Alfred Wheeler and Walter Wheeler weren't brothers; one was born in Croydon and one on the Isle of Wight, to different parents; if 'Ratcliff' was a well known professional, it must have been **John Ratcliff** (b. 1848), not A. Ratcliff. John was a butcher from Richmond upon Thames, who had played four first class matches for Surrey in 1876. Although Mr. Bridges was not accorded any initials, it must have been **John Henry Bridges** (b. 1852), a Lieutenant in the Middlesex Yeoman Cavalry, who lived in Avenue House, Kingston Road, Ewell, with his wife, Edith, two young sons and six servants in 1881. He was a nephew of the influential Rector of St. Mary's Church, Beddington, Canon Alexander H. Bridges. John Henry was a founder member of Beddington Cricket Club in 1879, and both he and his wife were noted archers for the Beddington Park Archers. J. H. Bridges had also played two first class matches for Surrey in the 1876 season. (Further information on Page 218).

Having dispensed with Southwark Park in the First Round, and South Norwood in the Second Round, Cheam then received a bye into the final at the Oval, where they met Farnham yet again. The following is a rather insipid report of the game from the 'Aldershot Military Gazette' of 20th August, 1881:

"On Wednesday, at Kennington Oval, Cheam defeated Farnham on the first innings by 35 runs, and thus become holders of the Surrey Challenge Cup of the year 1881. The competition was instituted last year, and Farnham were the winners. Wednesday's cricket was chiefly remarkable by the good batting of Mr. J. Carmichael of the Surrey County Eleven. "

The report in the 'Surrey Comet' was certainly more buoyant in its style, probably because it was aimed more at the people of the Kingston area: *"The final tie for this cup was played at Kennington Oval, on Wednesday, and resulted in a victory for Cheam by 35 runs on the first innings. Farnham, it will be remembered, won the cup last year, and this year their play has been uniformly good through the various ties. In this game their batting went to pieces, and with the exception of J. Carmichael, who made an excellent score of 66, no one could make any lengthy stand against W. C. Wheeler's bowling. For the victors A. S. Tabor, W. Collett, W. C. Wheeler and J. Goodison made 106 runs between them."* (J. Goodison was the keeper)

FARNHAM.		CHEAM.	
1st Innings.		Mr. A. S. Tabor, b Bateman	20
Mr. J. Carmichrel, b Thorn	66	Mr. W. Collett, b Elliott	21
Mr. Barrett, b Wheeler	1	J. Lockwood, b Mason	3
Knight, b Wheeler	0	W. C. Wheeler, c Barrett, b Elliott	41
Elliott, b Wheeler	0	Mr. W. Bradley, l b w, b Carmichael	7
Mr. W. G. Nash, l b w, b Wheeler	3	Mr. J. Goodison, b Elliott	24
Rev. G. J. Thomas, l b w, b Steadman	4	Mr. S. Jones, c Barrett, b Carmichael	8
Mr. W. Mason, l b w, b Thorn	18	A. Wheeler, b Elliott	8
Mr. C. Bateman, b Wheeler	19	Mr. J. J. Steadman, b Elliott	0
Collyer, b Wheeler	0	Mr. W. Thorn, c R. Mason, b Barrett	2
Mr Mason, b Thorn	1	Mr. D. Napper, not out	1
Mr. C. Carmichael, not out	2	Extras	16
Extras	2		
Total	116	Total	151

Unfortunately this victory was Cheam's sole success in the Challenge Cup and they soon lost their crown the following season, on Wednesday 10th May, **1882**, when Mitcham beat them by ten wickets in Cheam Park. Cheam were skittled out for 30 and 73, whilst Mitcham scored 91 and 13 without loss. Mitcham born, **James Caffarey** (b. 1859), who played three matches for Surrey, scored 22 runs and took 5 wickets for 4 runs in the first innings.

The cup competition certainly seemed to have encouraged an influx of new players into the Cheam ranks, several of whom had played first class cricket. Whilst the majority lived outside the parish, all of them seemed to satisfy the residential qualification of Rule 8, by living within the county boundary. Whether they were all paid up members was another question. Out of the twenty eight players who had taken part in the end-of-season game, less than two years previously, only two remained, **William Thorns,** who was by then, a master butcher living in Malden, and **Dendy Napper** (b. 1849), a miller, employing ten men. Dendy also played for Epsom Town and in 1881 was living in Sutton High Street, close to Cheam's professional cricketer from Yorkshire, **John Lockwood**.

Whilst Cheam Common tended to cater for the locals, Cheam C.C. attracted more players from outside the parish. Only two of the players in the team, who played Farnham, resided in Cheam in the 1881 census, **James Snell Goodison** (b. 1852), the team's wicket-keeper, who worked as a coffee broker and lived in the London Road, North Cheam, and **Arthur Tabor** (b. 1852). Arthur was quite a celebrity locally as he had attended Eton, played in the Varsity match, on three occasions, and had taken part in several first class fixtures for Middlesex, and one for Surrey, besides having played tennis in the Men's Singles at Wimbledon. He was also the son of Robert Tabor, the Headmaster of Cheam School, where Arthur taught for most of his life.

Little is known about the background of **S. Jones** and **J. J. Steadman**, as their surnames were too common on the censuses. An S. Jones, however, was recorded as playing as a batsman at that time for both Carshalton and Banstead. 'Jones' must have been a reasonable batsman, however, as he had been the top scorer for Cheam, in both innings, in the 1880 match versus Farnham, whilst Steadman had played for the Surrey Club and Ground in the 1870s and went on to be the captain of the Cheam First XI in 1885.

William Eustace Collett (b. 1839), the veteran of the side, was a solicitor's clerk, who had been born in Lambeth, and was recorded as being a right handed batsman, and a right arm fast roundarm bowler, who played four matches for Surrey. As such, he must have been a more than useful opening batsman for a club side. In 1881, he was still living in Lambeth with his wife, Hannah, his wife's sister, seven sons and the youngest child, a daughter.

Alfred Wheeler (b. 1845), had been born, and lived all his life, in Croydon, the son of a cabman and a charwoman. Alfred had initially worked for a fishmonger before becoming a French Polisher. He must have been a reasonable club cricketer as he was recorded as having played two First Class matches for Surrey in 1872-73. He was a right handed batsman and also a wicket keeper, apparently.

Walter Charles Wheeler (b.1841), had been born the son of a carpenter at Carisbrooke, on the Isle of Wight, where he spent the first twenty years of his life. He was basically a middle order batsman, and right roundarm medium pace bowler, who played at least ten First Class matches for Surrey, Middlesex and Hampshire. In his debut, and only game, for Hampshire against Kent, in 1878, he took 6 for 133. At the time of the 1881 census he was listed as being a carpenter, who lived with his wife, Rosena, and family in Battersea. He top scored for Cheam when they won the Cup, and took six wickets.

Whilst **William Joseph Bradley** (b. 1851), who owned the Messrs. Bradley and Son Brewery in Epsom, lacked the first class credentials of some of the stars of the team, he certainly seemed to be an extremely competent, local, prize winning all rounder who played for a variety of teams in the Epsom area. In 1878, he had played for the Epsom Recreational Ground C.C. which had dismissed the Cheam team for 24 runs on one occasion, William taking 4 for 8 and two 'splendid' one handed catches. At the end of the season the Epsom Recreational Ground C.C. awarded him a new bat for his performances in helping them win four out of the five matches that they had played that season.

The majority of his games, however, were for Epsom Town, who in 1881, awarded him another bat for his performances that season. The 'Surrey Advertiser', whilst commenting upon one match said, *"In style Mr. Bradley was unequalled......Bradley's fast underhand was too good and true to be despised."*

William Bradley seemed to be one of those players who loved to play cricket and would play for anyone. As a brewer, living in Epsom, it is probably not surprising that he also played for the Trainers, Jockeys and Friends XI on more than one occasion, and he was still turning out for Epsom 2nd XI in the Twentieth Century.

For Cheam, however, he tended to play only in Cup matches or on the big occasion. Such an occasion occurred in **1882** when Cheam played the Gentlemen of Middlesex in Cheam Park, which the 'London Evening Standard' reported on Thursday 24th August, 1882: *"This match was played at Cheam Park, Cheam, yesterday, on a good wicket, in the presence of numerous spectators. The visitors went in first and obtained 103. On the home team going in Mr. W. C. Wheeler, who went in first played a very dashing innings of 92. His score included six fours and ten threes, and during his long innings he only gave one chance, a hard one, to long slip. Osborn's bowling was very effective, he taking seven out of the eleven wickets."*

The Cheam side that day was: W. C. Wheeler 92, J. Lockwood 6, A. Wheeler 4, J. Thornes 15, W. J. Bradley 10, J. Constable 9, J. Reeves 2, C. J. Bailey 1, W. Dennis 2, W. Thorns 0, J. Ockenden 0, L. West 4, Extras 9 - Total 154. Bowling: W. Thorns took 4 wickets, W. C. Wheeler took 3 wickets, W. Dennis took 2 wickets, and W. Bradley 1 wicket.

As the decade passed, the Cheam club seemed to be very successful and attracted more and more players, from outside the parish, to their home in Cheam Park. One of them was a visitor from Australia, **Thomas Nunn** (b. 1846), who had been born in Penshurst, Kent. Thomas played just one match for the club, against Claygate, in June, **1885**, before moving on to pastures new. Although his stay was brief he did manage to score the first recorded century, for the club, before returning to Australia, where he went on to play five First Class games for New South Wales. The following match report is taken from 'The Sportsman' of June 27th:-

"This match was played at Cheam on the 24th inst. For the victors Mr. T. Nunn, the Australian inter-colonial cricketer, now on a visit to England, batted in dashing style for a hundred. Upon his return to the pavilion he received quite an ovation. The Australian is just now in excellent form, he having played a grand innings of one hundred and twenty runs at Tunbridge on Saturday last, and in a match at Sutton was credited with seven wickets at a cost of 12 runs."

The Cheam side that day was:- T. Nunn 100, W. C. Wheeler 8, W. Gilbert 0, W. Thorns 8, W. R. Black 9, J.J. Steadman (captain) 6, J. Ockenden 12, J. Hale 0, C. Bailey 1*, W. Cragg 6, H. Wrangham 1, Byes 9.
Bowling:- W. C. Wheeler 7 wickets, T. Nunn 3 wickets.

Although the club had negotiated a fixed rate of £5 per annum for the use of the field and pavilion in Cheam Park, they must have felt a little insecure, when, in **1887**, Messrs Yeates and Fiddyment had obtained permission to turn fifty acres of the Park into an amusement venue, which would be for the benefit of Sunday School children throughout the capital. The venture was an instant success, and as the excursion rate from the City to Cheam station was one shilling for adults and sixpence for each child, it was not overly expensive. In their account of 'A Day at Cheam Park', the 'Croydon Advertiser' wrote a glowing account of the park and its facilities on September 27th, **1887**:

"Cheam Park has recently undergone a very great change in its destiny. From farming to amusement is a great step, but it has been successfully accomplished by Messrs. Fiddyment and Yeates, who during the present summer have received and entertained no less than thirty thousand Sunday School children from all quarters of London. Cheam Park may now veritably be said to be a place at which to spend a happy day. Its beautiful expanse of bright green sward, charmingly enclosed and belted with timber, and ever pleasing variety, form a sylvan retreat of enjoyment. Here throughout the summer thousands of children have enjoyed themselves without fear of molestation to themselves, or apprehension of misadventure to their guardians. Swings and roundabouts have provided them with diversion, and well-conditioned donkeys have carried them on journeys of exploration about the beauties of the park."

The cricketers and the Sunday School children, however, seemed to have co-existed in harmony. Many of the Sunday Schools used the visit to the Park, not only as an opportunity to watch cricket, but as a chance to play cricket matches against local rivals. What is really surprising is the fact that the scoresheets of some of these matches even made the local press. One of these matches occurred on Monday, July 11th, 1887, in the 'Croydon Chronicle' when the George Street S.S. from Croydon beat St. Andrews S.S. of Peckham by 51 runs to 43. As there used to be three squares on Cheam Rec., it seems feasible that there might have been more than one square in the park in Victorian times, to cater for the visitors.

For the day-trippers, therefore, a cricket match became part of the entertainment, whilst for the cricketers, the day-trippers merely added to the number of spectators. An account of a Sunday School outing from Hounslow, in the 'Uxbridge and West Drayton Gazette,' of August 11th, 1894, makes it apparent that many of the visitors considered the cricket match, that was being played, to be one of the highlights of the day. *"The party started from the Bell Road about nine o'clock in nine brakes* (Horse drawn carriages). *Cheam Park, was the place chosen for the outing, and this pleasant resort was reached after a very enjoyable drive through Twickenham,*

Kingston and Ewell. By the time the party arrived the weather had cleared, and the children were able to enjoy the steam roundabouts, swings, donkey rides, switchback railway, and other amusements provided for them, whilst the older members of the party witnessed a brilliant cricket match between the Cheam Park C.C. and the Regent Street Polytechnic C.C.. Tea was served at four o'clock in a large marquee, and after more fun and frolic the homeward journey was commenced at seven o'clock, Hounslow being reached at ten."

Although the club had been very successful on the field, off the field there had been problems with the organisation. Things became so bad by **1888** that, according to 'The Tatler', " a special meeting was called to consider the desirability of winding up the club and the question of the rental of the ground which had been fixed at £5 per annum."

An example of their poor organisation was the fact that the club could only forward their batting statistics to the 'Croydon Advertiser', that October, as, "In a note to the editor the secretary says:- 'We are unable to forward bowling analysis, as a complete record has not been kept on one or two occasions.'"

Cheam Cricket Club Batting Averages for 1888					
13 matches - 7 won; 4 lost; 2 drawn					
Runs for Cheam, 1447; 144 wickets; average 10.7					
Ditto Opponents, 953; 144 wickets; average 6.89					
	Innings	Runs	Not Out	Most	Average
J. Ockenden	14	297	2	86*	24.9
S. Niel	9	149	2	74*	21.2
T. Sillence	8	123	1	52	17.4
F. Hale sen.	11	140	1	34*	14.0
P. Coote	8	96	1	25	13.5
J. Stevens	10	98	0	36	9.8
E. Weston	12	96	1	23*	8.8
C. Sharpe	6	50	0	17	8.2
S. Poffley	4	22	0	10	5.2
W. Stevens	7	29	1	17	4.5
K. Brown	3	13	0	12	4.1
A. Humphreys	4	15	0	7	3.75
G. Jones	7	15	2	8	3.0
F. Hale jun.	5	12	1	7	3.0

By the mid-nineties, Cheam C.C., aka the Cheam Park club, had enough members to turn out a Second Eleven. An advertisement in 'The Sporting Life' of July 20th, **1895**, stated that a match was due to be played that very day between Cheam B and Clinton C.C. in Cheam Park. Although the newspaper listed the Clinton team, no further details were provided, nor did the result feature in the next edition of the newspaper.

Some of the matches that the club played were probably more of a social occasion than a cricket match. One such match occurred in July **1890** at Cheam School, the home of the Tabors, which used to lie where Tabor Court now stands in Cheam Village, between the Ewell/Sutton Road and the railway line.

The prep. school used to boast three or four cricket pitches and was renowned for the First class cricketers that it produced, such as the Studd brothers. The 'Croydon Advertiser' painted an idyllic picture of the occasion, with very little mention of the cricket that occurred: *"The Rev. R. S. Tabor and Mr. Arthur Tabor entertained the Cheam Cricket Club members in the beautiful grounds adjoining the house to a good and enjoyable day's cricket against his own team, which is generally victorious, but on this occasion, through the smartness in the field, the victory was reversed. Cricket commenced at 2 p.m., and some thorough good cricket was witnessed on both sides, especially by some of the scholars at the school, who distinguished themselves with the bat admirably. Tea and other refreshments were provided on the ground during the progress of the match, and after the match a substantial meal was provided for all in a tent erected on the grounds for that purpose, which brought another of the many pleasant and cheerful days similarly spent to a close."*

Another match which was probably a great social occasion occurred on July 1st, **1897** when the Surrey Club and Ground played against Seventeen of Cheam. The 'Sporting Life' recorded the match thus: *"In grand cricketing weather this match was played yesterday (Thursday), in Cheam Park, Surrey. The wicket was decidedly a bowling one, and the local batsmen were dismissed in rapid fashion by Keene and Smith, the former taking ten wickets for 31 runs, and Smith six for 41. Bowling against Surrey (who declared at 202 for six wickets), Hersey took two wickets for 15 runs. Baker played a faultless 37 for Surrey, Webb dismissing him by a very clever catch."*

The Surrey side was: P. L. Holt 31, G. W. Ayres 1, L. Braund 34, T. A. Watson 13, W. J. Baker 37, Smith 50*, E. Hayes 0, Pearce 10, Extras 21, Total 202.

F. Stedman, Hussy and J. W. Keene did not bat.

The Cheam Seventeen were: E. C. Surridge 2, S. C. Williams 6, A. Dudley 24, R. Ockenden 2, F. Neil 10, F. Potter 1, J. H. Laidlaw 0, S. Hersey 5, T. Kidd 4, F. Smith 8, P. Jenner 0, J. Jenner 8, J. Bailey 2, T. S. Webb 0, W. J. Gibbs 0, A. Kelvie 0, E. Potter 1*, Extras 10, Total 82.

About five of the Surrey players were Second XI players who were on the verge of playing, or had just started playing First XI cricket. The most famous of these was **Len Braund** (b. 1875), an all-rounder who began his first class career in 1896, and played 21 matches for Surrey before moving to Somerset. He then went on to play 23 Test Matches for England in the course of a career which spanned World War I.

Ernie Hayes (b. 1876) was another player who had already played for the Surrey First XI by 1897 and went on to play five Tests for England. In total he scored 48 centuries and took 515 wickets with his leg-breaks. The highlight of his career probably came in 1907 when he was named a Wisden Player of the Year. Like Braund his career also continued after the Great War.

John White Ayres (b. 1871) played 25 matches for Surrey, supposedly as a batsman, although he failed to score a single fifty. He did, however, make a top score of 83 when he moved to Essex for a short time in 1899, whilst **John William Keene** (b.1873) only played a couple of matches for Surrey before moving to Worcestershire. In total he played 27 First Class matches and took 66 wickets.

Fred Steadman (b. 1870) stumped three of the Cheam batmen in that 1897 game. As one was off Keene it seems likely that he was standing up to all the bowling. Fred was a tail end batsman and wicketkeeper who in 1897 was still playing for the Surrey Second XI. His first class career for Surrey was basically from 1899 to 1902. In 1901 he got 87 victims that season, a record which stood until Arnold Long beat it in 1962. Eventually he emigrated to Ireland, for whom he played an occasional match. In total he played 140 first class matches, scored five 50's and took 316 victims. His life ended tragically in 1918 when he was knocked down by a train whilst crossing a railway line in Dublin.

The 'Smith' in the team might possibly have been **Charles William 'Razor' Smith** (b. 1877). He was a brilliant off break bowler who was apparently recommended to Surrey by W. G. Grace in the late nineties. Because of his frail constitution, however, Smith was often too weak to play a full season, but when he did play he was a match winner. In 1911 he was one of Wisden's five cricketers of the year. He took 1,077 wickets in 245 First Class appearances.

It was much easier to find out facts about the Surrey team than the Cheam side, as only about three of that team appeared as living in the parish on either the 1891 or 1901 censuses. **Frederick Smith** (b. 1877) was a journeyman butcher who lived in Cheam Village, whilst **Alfred Dudley** (b. 1878) graduated from being a paper boy in 1891 to the landlord of 'The Plough', Sutton Common Road by 1901. The only other possible local player was **John Bailey** (b. 1865) a labourer/gardener who lived in Longfellow Road, Worcester Park in 1901. John had been born in Croydon, but both of his daughters had been born in New South Wales in the mid-nineties, where perhaps John had learnt his cricket.

Of the other players, the only one of note was **Edward Charles Surridge** (b. 1869), a clerk living in Sutton, who seemed to be the Secretary of the club. His name appeared in an interesting advertisement in 'The Sportsman' on February 18th, 1897: *"The Cheam Cricket Club are prepared to receive applications for the post of GROUNDSMAN (preference will be given to a bowler). The salary is £1.1s per week, and the person selected will be expected to commence his duties on Monday, April 19th next. Applications, with testimonials or references, to be addressed to the undersigned not later than Monday, March 1st, 1897, - Edward C. Surridge, Carshalton Road, Sutton, Surrey."* Were the club looking for a groundsman/ professional cricketer for whom they were prepared to pay one guinea per week? Using an inflation calculator, a guinea in 1897 would be worth between £130 and £140 in 2020.

The match against the Surrey Club and Ground might have been one of the final games played by Cheam C.C. in Cheam Park, as at some time in the late nineties it appears as though their lease expired. The 1953 copy of 'The Tatler' is suitably vague as to when this occurred or to where they went: *"After playing at Cheam Park, the club migrated to new pastures."*

From 1897 to 1900 the press coverage of Cheam matches was virtually limited to one line for both the upcoming fixtures, and for the results. On every occasion the home venue was simply recorded as being 'Cheam'. The only scorecard which appeared in the press during this late Victorian era occurred in September **1899** when Cheam played Ashtead. The 'Dorking Advertiser' briefly recorded that the match was, *"Played at Cheam on Saturday, and resulted in a win for Cheam by 68 runs and 1 wicket. Jones for Cheam did the hat trick, and for Ashtead Fernley took 4 for 16."*

Only F. Smith and Edward Surridge survived from the seventeen who had played against the Surrey Club and Ground in 1897: F. Smith 4, H. F. White 11, W. H. Clarke 0, E. Harrison 19, C. Jones 3, E. P. Topping 19, H. Flewkes 5, H. Braithwaite 13*, T. Huddleston 3, J. Daw 0, E. C. Surridge 0*, Extras 3 Total 89 for 9. Ashtead were all out for 12 - C. Jones took five wickets and J. Daw four.

The only other occasion when players were named occurred in the 'Sussex Agricultural Express' from May 9th, **1899**, for the local derby against Sutton. *"At Sutton, Neil scored 44 and Coles 94 (not out) for Cheam, who won easily. Cheam, 162; Sutton, 24."*

After **1900**, however, it became impossible to know who played for the club as there was no mention at all of Cheam Cricket Club in the sporting press. Did it continue to function or was the loss of a permanent ground fatal to its survival? Whilst numerous match reports exist in the press for Cheam Common C.C. and Old Malden and Worcester Park C.C., the only mention of Cheam C.C. was an account of their annual

Christmas party, before a packed audience at the Parochial Rooms, in 1913.'The Tatler' magazine also skipped over the Edwardian and pre-War period completely, and landed at what is now the Cheam Sports and Social Club in Peaches Close: *"but with the outbreak of World War One the club closed down until 1920, when through the efforts of several enthusiastic cricketers, notably the late Lord Ebbisham of Cobham and A. Cobden Soar, it was revived and the present ground of thirteen acres was purchased."*

A couple of scoresheets from that first post-war season made it into the 'Surrey Mirror' and showed a completely new cast of players, one of whom, Canon Wesley Dennis, went on to be their captain.

On July 10th, they played away to Horley and failed to chase down 217. The team that day was: Rev. Wesley Dennis 61*, G. V. Arnold 8, E. Morgan 3, E. Brooks 3, E. Harding 1, J. Booker 22, W. J. Parsons 7, W. Sergeant 8, C. Riddle 7, A. Scar 0, H. G. Laurenburg 20, Extras 20, Total 160. E. Brooks took 6 wickets, A. Soar 2 wickets, G. Riddle and E. Morgan 1 wicket each.

On August 14th the following players avenged an earlier defeat against Tadworth by 19 runs. Tadworth obviously submitted the match report as the Cheam players were initial-less. Lewis 12, Hilton 8, Ockenden 14, Sergeant 4, Duce 3, Morgan 12, Pearson 1, Massey 0, Carter 1, Cooper 1, Whitehead 1*, Extras 11, Total 67. Ockenden and Hilton took 4 wickets each and Duce one wicket.

The new club seemed to be extremely popular as can be deduced from a short article in the 'West Sussex Gazette' on a combined athletics and sports event which was held at Peaches Close in late September, **1920**. The prizes were presented by the local M.P., Sir George Rowland Blades, who was praised for being responsible for the club having 52 Cricket members, 126 Tennis members and 132 honorary members.

In a book entitled 'Cheam Past and Present' by Sara Goodwin, she devotes a chapter, which includes several interesting photographs, to Cheam Cricket and Social Club, through the ages. Whilst writing about the formation of the club she makes an extremely interesting observation:

"It has always been a matter of conjecture as to whether the newly titled club was a reformation of the original club or an entirely new one. Certain it is that on the 9th November, 1921, the decision was taken to purchase the ground which now makes up the sports facilities on the north side of Peaches Close."

In a way the Cheam Village Athletic Club, which was formed at the same time as the Cheam Cricket and Social Club, could also be considered as the true heirs of that original club which had been formed in 1864. They were a club that catered for athletics, cricket and football and they played their cricket on the old cricket ground in the Malden Road, where the original Cheam side had played in the 1870s and 1880s. They were a true village side, who tried to encourage their members to support the local community. Their fixture card boasted that, *"This is purely a local club in every way and every penny spent, whether for Sporting Tackle, Whist drives or Dances is spent in CHEAM."* It was a cricket club for the local community that guaranteed that 75% of its playing membership lived in Cheam.

1 The Club shall be called "The Cheam Village Athletic Club." The colours shall be Royal Blue and White

Handbook
and
Cricket Fixtures

PRICE THREEPENCE

(Courtesy of David Rymill)

Cuddington Cricket Club
aka Worcester Park Cricket Club
1872-1914

The reason for the rather strange title to this chapter is that the distinction between the two areas in the late Victorian era was quite blurred. The newspapers of the time would refer to the same group of players as belonging to either Cuddington C.C. or Worcester Park C.C. Perhaps this ambiguity in the 1870s stemmed from the fact that much of Worcester Park lay in the Parish of Cuddington. Even today when one does a family search on ancestry.co.uk, the search engine will not accept 'Cuddington, Surrey', but it will accept 'Worcester Park', whilst the opposite appears to be true on the findmypast site.

Another reason for believing that the two names referred to the same team is that there is apparently no account in the press of any match between the two hamlets. If there had been, it would obviously have been an important event that would have been reported in the local papers. It is probably best, therefore, to regard any mention of Worcester Park C.C. or Cuddington C.C., particularly in the 1870s, as referring to the same team. After about 1880, however, the team tended to be referred to primarily as Cuddington C.C.

The club, however, does pose a bit of a mystery, as there are no obvious clues as to whom was responsible for its formation, or where precisely they played. There is also an extremely limited amount of information in the 'Comet' and the 'Advertiser' between 1872 and 1888 about any matches that Worcester Park or Cuddington C.C. were involved in, before they merged with the larger Cheam Common C.C. The few newspaper accounts that do exist, however, certainly suggest that there was a properly organised cricket club in Cuddington.

The precise boundaries of Cuddington itself are even a little difficult to ascertain (see David Rymill's marvellous book 'Worcester Park and Cuddington') as the original village, which was situated in Nonsuch Park, was destroyed by Henry VIII in order that Nonsuch Palace could be built. Basically, according to the 1867 O.S. map, Cuddington seemed to lie somewhere to the west of Cheam Common, in the vicinity of what one would now call Stoneleigh and Nonsuch Park. 'The Victoria County History' describes Cuddington as measuring *"nearly 4 miles from north-west to south -east, and is scarcely a mile in breadth. It contains 1,859 acres."* Roughly, it seemed to stretch from Howell Hill, on the south side of Nonsuch Park to Old Malden.

For about three hundred years from the mid sixteenth century, Cuddington appeared to be an area without a church or indeed a village, which was divided into farms and estates, with a few labourers' cottages dotted around. There was, therefore, no apparent nucleus around which a traditional cricket club might form. It seems likely that the formation of the club might have been initially a vanity project for one of the rich landowners, who would occasionally invite his neighbours around to play cricket in his grounds, against teams of gentry from adjoining estates. The numbers could, of course, be made up from the numerous servants that they employed. The arrival of the railway in 1859 had also led to the development of some exclusive housing developments in the Cuddington area, which would have increased the pool of potential players.

Harefield House, a large Regency house, which was situated in the South of the parish, was a possible venue as it definitely had a cricket pitch. In the 1880s the house was owned by Mrs. Sarah Townend, the widow of James Hamilton Townend, a hat manufacturer, who had died of malaria in 1881 as the result of a holiday in Rome and Naples. The house was situated to the North of the Cheam/Ewell Road, beside the Harefield Railway Bridge, which is just along from Nonsuch Girls' School. The actual cricket pitch was probably the same one that is still used as a second ground by Sutton Cricket Club, in Holmwood Close, one hundred and forty years later.

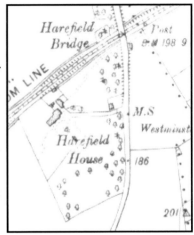

"By kind permission of Mrs. Townend, of Harefield, Cheam, the boys of the Cheam Cricket Club were enabled to enjoy their Bank Holiday. The Cheam Cricket Ground not being available, leave was granted them to play their previously arranged match with Christ Church Choir Club (Sutton) on the ground of the above named lady, who also kindly provided them with refreshment during play. After the first innings had been played both teams sat down to a most substantial tea provided by Mrs. Townend, and eatables by Mrs. Ockenden (Post Office, Cheam), and assisted by Mrs. Spence. After doing justice to the meal play was resumed, and the friends of the players who had assembled to witness the game were regaled in the same bountiful manner, and altogether a most enjoyable time was spent. The game, however, was won by the visitors, they having defeated the home team by five runs." (Croydon Advertiser and East Surrey Reporter August 11th, 1888).

Mrs. Jane Ockenden, the Post Mistress, had two of her brood of ten children playing, 17 year old Edward Thomas, and 14 year old Charles Albert, whilst Mrs. Harriett Spence was the mother of another of the colts, 15 year old Charles Edward Spence. Harriett, née Starr, had been born in Cheam and was recorded on the 1871 census as being a school mistress, who had lived in Church Road with her father, who was a groom, and her mother, who had also been a local infant school teacher. The following year, she had married **Charles Spence**, one of the original committee members of

Cheam C.C., who was a teacher at the Cheam and Cuddington National Boys School, in the Malden Road, before it became Cheam Church of England Boys School. The girls were educated by Miss Phillips in the Parochial Rooms. (As a personal aside, Cheam C. of E. School used to provide Glastonbury High School, where I was the Master i/c Cricket, with some great cricketing talent in the 1960s and 70s).

Charles Spence left the local school in June that year, with his wife, to move *"to a more important sphere"*, as the Headmaster of a school in Tottenham. He was replaced by William Leaver who was a teacher, organist and choir master. When Charles died prematurely in 1886, Harriett and her five children returned to Cheam.

As mentioned in the preceding chapter, Cheam C. C. in the mid 1880s usually played in Cheam Park, in a field which in the 1920s became Cheam Rec. When Mr. Fiddyment turned the Park into an amusement attraction in 1887, Cheam Park began to attract thousands of visitors at weekends and on Bank Holidays, which might have been the reason why the Cheam youngsters had to find another venue for their game.

Another possible venue for a cricket pitch in south Cuddington would have been in Nonsuch Park, between what is now called the Mansion House and Bellgate Lodge, where there is a large flat, treeless area. It would have painted a pretty picture, as one drove up the driveway from the Lodge to the Mansion House, to see the local gentry playing cricket on the manicured lawn.

Nonsuch Park in the nineteenth century was owned by the Farmer family; **William F. G. Farmer** (b. 1812) was the Deputy Lieutenant of the county and **William R. G. Farmer** (b. 1839) was a Magistrate. There is no indication that either of them played cricket but there is a mention of a Mr. Farmer batting at number three for Cheam versus Ewell in August 1889. As all the other players in the team were accorded initials, it suggests that Mr. Farmer, was probably one of the younger members of the Farmer family living in the Mansion House.

Another article which tends to suggest that cricket might have been played in Nonsuch Park had occurred in an advertisement in the 'Sporting Life' of June 23rd, 1860, which stated that Merstham United would play 'Cheam Nonsuch', at Cheam, on the following Monday. As they were called 'Cheam Nonsuch' it seems probable that they played in the grounds of the Mansion House.

As cricket pitches were often associated with public houses in early Victorian times, and, as there are several references to teams playing at the 'Red Lion' ground in Cheam, the 'Drill' ground at Cheam Common and the 'Eight Bells' ground in Ewell, it seems likely that cricket would have been played close to the only two inns in Cuddington; the 'Bell' opposite Nonsuch Park and the 'Plough' at Old Malden.

The first match for a team from the Cuddington/Worcester Park area, which appears in the press, was discovered by accident, as the search engines do not always capture what one hopes to find. Hidden away at the bottom of a column of 'The Sportsman' for July 6th, **1872**, was an account of a match played by The Grange School:-

"This match was played on June 15th, on the Ewell Ground, between the Grange School and the Worcester Park Club. The latter saved a one innings defeat by time being called, Score:-"

GRANGE SCHOOL.		
H. Critchley, l b w, b J. Williamson	7	W. Dewar, b E. Williamson. 5
H. B. Holland, b J. Williamson	0	G. Hill, b Abdy. 0
R. R. Holland, b J. Smith	41	W. Blackford, c E. Williamson, b J. Williamson 0
H. Youldon, b Abdy	27	J. Madden, not out 13
D. Gover, b Abdy	0	G. Paice, run out 0
T. Marshall, c Deare, b J. Smith	19	Extras 50
		Total ...162

WORCESTER PARK CLUB.	1st inn.	2nd inn.
L. Chapman, c Youldon, b Marshall	2	b R. R. Holland 1
Rev. J. Smith, b Marshall	7	b Youldon 0
E. Williamson, b Marshall	3	c Critchley, b Youldon 1
J. Williamson, c and b Youldon	7	not out 14
C. Deare, b Youldon	2	b Youldon 11
H. Horne, b Marshall	0	not out 2
G. Abdy, b Marshall	0	
T. Chancellor, b Marshall	2	
C. Waddilove, b Youldon	3	
W. Smith, not out	0	
Extras	4	Extras 7
(†) Total	—31	Total ...—40

From the information that is available on a handful of the Worcester Park team, it would appear that all the players fall in to the privileged spectrum of Victorian society. **Cyrus Waddilove** (b. 1828) was a solicitor, and tennis player of some renown locally, and was shown, on the Cuddington census of 1871, as living near the Avenue, Worcester Park, with his wife, six children and five servants, whilst 'Abdy' probably referred to another Cuddington resident, **George W. Abdy** (b. 1853) the son of a Lieutenant Colonel in the Indian army, who lived at 'Abdene' in Worcester Park. George had become an articled clerk in a solicitor's office the preceding year.

Henry Warlters Horne (b. 1846) was another member of the legal profession who had graduated from Oxford with a Law degree in 1870 and had been called to the bar in the Inner Temple, the following year. To continue the legal theme, it is also possible that E. and J. Wilkinson were Edward and James, the sons of another London solicitor, James Wilkinson, who also worked in the City.

Although only two of these players definitely lived in Cuddington, Cyrus Waddilove at 'Worcester Park House' and George Abdy at 'Abdene', there are two strong local candidates for 'W. Smith'. William H. Warre Smith was a twenty four year old merchant who lived next door to the Abdys, at 'The Oaks', whilst next door to him lived thirteen year old Wallace Smith, the son of an architect.

The first actual mention of 'Cuddington C.C.' occurred in the 'Surrey Comet' on May 31st, **1873**, when they played a return away match, in Worcester Park, against a team from the medical profession, led by Mr. W. F. Everett, the Hon. Secretary of Merton C.C.: *"Last Saturday an interesting match, return, was played at Worcester Park between 11 gentlemen of the medical profession, selected by Mr. W. F. Everett, and the Cuddington C.C. The result was in favour of the former by six wickets on the first innings. There was some excellent batting on both sides, as the score will show. Mr. Weller's faultless innings of 51 (not out) was much admired, and when he made the winning hit - a beautiful drive for 5 - he was much applauded, and carried off the field by some of his side. After the match the winners, accompanied by some friends, had tea together at the hotel, and spent a very pleasant evening. A vote of thanks was given to Mr. Everett for the able manner in which he had captained the eleven and the proceedings terminated."*

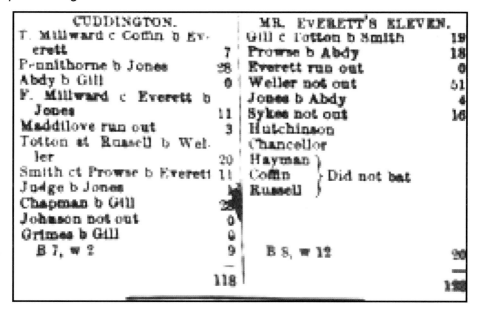

The match report provides one with a fascinating cartoon of cricket 150 years ago. Eleven doctors descended upon Worcester Park station, and were perhaps met by buggies to ferry them to one of the large country houses in the area. The match was won by a 'five' being run and the hero being carried off the field on his companions' shoulders, before the assembled players retired for a meal at a local hostelry. If the match had been played at Worcester Park House, then the hotel could have been either the 'Queen Adelaide', Ewell, or the 'Railway Tavern' near Worcester Park Station, which became the 'Huntsman's Hall' in the 1880s and latterly 'The Brook'.

The lack of initials for most of the players, makes it rather difficult to identify the Cuddington players, in order to ascertain their social status, or to say whether they actually lived in Cuddington. The only two, one can positively identify, however, were the brothers, **Thomas Frith Millward** (b.1844) and **Frank Frith Millward** (b. 1849) who both lived at 'New House Farm', Malden, in 1871. If the match was played at their farm, or 'Manor Farm', then 'The Plough' which was only about 200 yards away would have been the ideal venue for the evening's festivities.

Frank Millward was listed on the census as being a farmer's son, whilst Thomas was an assistant tipstaff and rate collector. By 1881, however, Thomas had graduated to being a station master, whilst by the turn of the century he was an estate agent. Thomas must have been quite well educated for a farmer's son because he was also listed, in the 'Surrey Mirror' of January 4th, 1895, as being both the clerk of Malden Council, and of Cuddington Council. One of the brothers had even played for the Bachelors in the first ever match played by Cheam Common in 1872, as note was made of his *"destructive underhand"*, which skittled out the Married Men.

Four of the other players in the side had probably played for the team that had been called 'Worcester Park' in 1872: i.e. Abdy, Smith, Chapman and Maddilove (an obvious printing error). They were joined by a 'Johnson' who was probably seventeen year old **Henry Elliott Johnson** (b. 1855), who went on to become a prominent local sportsman, and solicitor.

It isinteresting to note that for most of these early matches the team was recorded as playing in Worcester Park rather than Cuddington. They had probably moved to the grounds of one of the large houses in the Avenue, such as 'Worcester Park House', which was recorded as having in its 40 acres, *'pleasure grounds'*. As the nearby station was also called 'Worcester Park', anywhere in the immediate vicinity, therefore, was probably branded with that soubriquet.

On the 6th September, 1873, the 'Surrey Comet' published an amusing apology under the title 'The Cuddington Cricket Club' which tends to suggest that the team must have been quite well known locally and organised to such an extent that they required a secretary: *"On August 23rd we published the score of a match which was said to have been played between the Cuddington and Surbiton clubs. Last week the secretary of the former club wrote to say that it was not the Cuddington club that was engaged. We now find that the match was between the Surbiton and Chessington clubs, and the players of the latter side request us to state that they never wished to identify themselves with the Cuddington C.C."*

The match, on August 16th, 1873, between Chessington and Surbiton United which was played on the grounds of Captain Corkran at Southboro' Park, certainly threw up some interesting characters, none of whom, surprisingly, lived in Cuddington, although they did live within a five mile radius of the parish, in Kingston, Surbiton, Epsom and Chessington. The players tended to be aged between sixteen and twenty-nine, their parents being wealthy farmers, builders or solicitors. The final six players in the team were three sets of brothers, one of whom took his family to Australia on an assisted passage, before dying eventually in Wagga Wagga.

On May 16th, **1874**, 'The Field' produced the following scorecard for a match which had been played on the previous Saturday. Although the report of the match was a little lacking in detail, at least the use of initials looked as though it would allow one to find out a little more about the members of the team. Sadly, the only truly positive identification of a new player was that of the Vicar's son, **Edward Chetwynd Stapylton** (b. 1856), who would become one of the leading figures behind the formation of the local tennis club, along with his good friend, Henry Johnson.

METEORS v. WORCESTER PARK.
PLAYED at Worcester-park on the 9th.   Score:

METEORS.		WORCESTER PARK.	
Mr C. R. Dimond, b Abdy	4	Mr H. Milward, c Leach, b Fox	12
Mr G. P. Leach, run out	5	Mr A. Barrow, b Fox	5
Mr E. A. Parke, c Deare, b Hooper	36	Mr H. Smith, c Leach, b Lodge	1
Mr H. J. Lake, c Deare, b Hooper	47	Mr G. Totton, b Fox	8
Mr S. U. Fox, b Ably	25	Mr R. Hooper, c Tritton, b Lodge	0
Mr S. A. Sampson, b Smith	0	Mr C. R. Deare, b Fox	16
Mr H. Steele, b Abdy	23	Mr O. Abdy, c Leach, b Parke	5
Mr A. H. Tritton, st Totton, b Hooper	0	Mr E. Stapylton, not out	0
Mr G. E. Leke, not out	7	Mr H. Johnson, not out	3
Mr J. A. Burrell, st Totton, b Hooper	2	Mr E. W. Williamson, } reserves	
Mr T. B. Lodge, st Totton, b Hooper	1	Rev. T. Smith, }	
Byes 16, w 10, l-b 2	28	Byes 6, w 3	9
Total	180	Total	68

Of the other players in the team, the wicket-keeper was probably **George Trotton**, a stock jobber, who had been born in 1849 in Bangor, Wales, but was living in 1874 in Kensington, whilst the opening batsman was possibly **Charles Aubrey Barrow** (b.1852), a medical student who would eventually practice in Sutton. The top scorer was possibly **Charles Russell Deare**, who had been born in South Africa in 1852 and was a commercial clerk, living in Cheshunt.

The next mention of Cuddington C.C. occurred in the 'Surrey Comet' on May 8th, **1875**, with a short match report of that season's opening fixture:

"The Cuddington Cricket Club played their opening match at Worcester Park last Saturday, their opponents being eleven gentlemen selected by Mr. Ponsonby. Each side played one innings: the bowling and fielding were excellent. Totals: Mr. Ponsonby's eleven, 54; Cuddington, 72."

Although there were several members of the Ponsonby family who were important figures in the cricketing world in the mid Victorian era, such as Sir Spencer Cecil Ponsonby, who had played for both Surrey and Middlesex, it is highly likely that this Mr. Ponsonby was **Frederick George Brabazon Ponsonby** (b. 1815), who had played First Class cricket for Cambridge University and Surrey, was a founder member of I Zingari and was a permanent Vice-President of Surrey Cricket Club. He must have known the area quite well as twenty years earlier his family had lived at

Hampton Court Palace, and, through his connection with Surrey he must have come into contact with local landowner, Thomas Weeding Bagallay.

Cuddington C.C. received another mention in the press on May 8th, 1875, when 'The Field' listed all the upcoming fixtures for that season for the Putney Club and the Islington Albion Club which played at Alexandra Palace. Putney were due to play Cuddington, away at Worcester Park, on May 17th, and at home on August 2nd, whilst Islington Albion, which was based around a Georgian pub, which still exists today, were due to play away at Worcester Park on May 22nd and, at home, for the penultimate game of the season, on the 11th of September.

If Cuddington had a fixture list which equalled those of Putney and Islington Albion, it appears as though they might have had between twenty and thirty fixtures per season, which would have entailed a good secretary, a considerable amount of organisation and plenty of travel. They would also have had to provide opponents with a reasonable ground upon which to play, if they were to keep the fixtures.

Cuddington must have been reasonable opponents, therefore, as they remained on the fixture list of Islington Albion, the following year. The Islington Albion was an extremely famous cricket team in the 1870s, but like many of the small clubs their mere existence could be problematic. In the pre-amble to their fixtures, 'The Field' wrote in May, 1876: *"There is a great power in a good name. Years ago the Albion Club was, by force of circumstances, all but extinguished, but it lives still, and thirty matches, are announced to be played this season, most of which will be played at the Alexandra Palace ground."*

Cuddington C.C., not only played enough fixtures to warrant a Secretary but an article in the 'Surrey Comet' of 15th July, 1876, even described their ground as being 'beautiful.' The match featured 16 gardeners of the area against 14 coachmen. These encounters were often advertised in the press as being 'Whips' versus 'Spades'.

"Gardeners v Coachmen. - On Wednesday last a match of considerable interest was played by the Gardeners and Coachmen of the neighbourhood. The match was promoted by Mr. Wheir (gardener to H. Jeffrey, Esq., of Worcester-park, and the Cuddington C.C. having placed their ground, &c., at his disposal, circulars were issued which had the effect of securing a holiday for all gardeners and coachmen; and the weather favouring the efforts made for enjoyment, the scene on the beautiful cricket field more closely resembled a village merrymaking than a cricket match.

There was, however, some remarkably good play considering that many of the men were strangers to the game, while others were necessarily out of practice.

Amongst the gardeners the bowling of Cane deserves special mention; straight to the wicket, it told well with opponents eager to make a score, and he succeeded in taking three wickets with three successive balls. His batting was also very good. Beasley and Simmonds did good service to their side at the wickets. For the Coachmen, Bowtel's and Young's bowling was very effective. These two men were also "ties" for the honour of "top score" of the day - 20.

The Gardeners won by 11 runs. The following is the score: -

Gardeners: Luff 3, 1; Cane 19, 0; Beasley 14, 0; Simmonds 10, 3; Farr 1, 3; Goodwright 5, 10; Peats 2, 0; Philbrook 0, 3; Giles 0, 5; Jones 0, 0; Wheir (captain, not out) 1, 2; Tilbury 3, 6; Smith 0, 0; Scraggs 3, 6; Raynor (not out) 1; extras 11, 7 - totals 72, 47.

Coachmen: Healy 9, 0; Froud 5, 2; Foxet 3, 6; Young 20, 3; Mills 9, 1; Bowtel 0, 20; G. Healey 3, 8; Allum (captain) 2, 0; George 2, 0; Shepherd 0, 0; Tibble 0, 0; Musket 0, 3; Vince 0, 0; Harwood (not out) 0, 3; Cook (not out) 1; extras 6, 2 - total 59, 49."

Sadly the records failed to reveal any details about Mr Wheir or his employer, H. Jefferys, although a **Frederick Luff** (b.1846), a **George Simmonds** (b. 1832), a **George Goodwright** (b. 1853) and a **John Philbrook** (b. 1841), were all listed as being gardeners in the area at the time of the 1871 and 1881 censuses. There were, however, far fewer coachmen listed, as there was probably a greater demand for gardeners than coachmen in the vicinity. The only coachmen to appear in the censuses were **Richard Shepherd** (b. 1836) and **John Muskett** (b. 1830).

Any cricketing news emanating from Cuddington dried up after this game until 1888. In fact any mention of Cuddington at all in the local papers during this period was extremely rare, the most newsworthy incident being a case of poaching. Perhaps by the late eighties, it was becoming that difficult for the residents of Cuddington to regularly turn out a team, that they opted to amalgamate with Cheam Common for the majority of their fixtures. Cuddington was, after all, still basically a rural area with large farms and estates with an extremely low population density. Turning out a regular team must have been exceedingly difficult.

The first match for the new alliance to appear in the 'Comet' occurred on 29th September, **1888**, when they lost against Christ Church Choir in a match: *"Played on Saturday, at Surbiton, and won by the choir by 20 runs. This is the last match of the season of the Choir Club. F. Lenham, for the winners, took six wickets for four runs."*

The Cheam Common and Cuddington side that day only managed to amass 23 runs, the top scorers being Lockwood, the professional cricketer who had played cricket for Cheam, and one of the Blake family. This was probably **John Blake** (b. 1871), who went on to play for Old Malden and Worcester Park C.C. for thirteen years, from 1893 until his premature death in 1906. No mention was made of the six wickets that John picked up that day by the reporter, who was obviously a Christ Church player. Whilst all the home side's team were accorded initials, none were furnished for the away team.

The C.C. & C.C.C. team that day was: Westing 0, Powell 1, Venus 1, Connor 0, Cooper 2, Styles 1, Stuttaford 1, Lockwood 7, Blake 7, Wain 0*, Stokes 0.

Two of that team were probably original Cheam Common players from 1872, **Charles Powell** (b. 1844) and **Thomas Connor** (b. 1846). Charles, who had been born in Hardwicke, Gloucestershire, was the landlord of the 'North End Tavern', from 1875 to 1891, and as such was obviously a very popular player, who managed to find time to turn out for both Cheam and Cheam Common. Thomas, who had been born in Bermondsey, was a painter and decorator, who, with his wife and five children, lived next door to the 'North End Tavern', in 1891.

In a way the merger of Cuddington C.C. with Cheam Common did not seem to have been entered into wholeheartedly by the Cuddington players as there were still several instances of them turning out one-off sides during the next ten years. The 'Sporting Life' of 23rd June, 1894, for example, in the list of upcoming fixtures for that day, stated that Cuddington were due to play Cheam at Worcester Park.

By the beginning of the **1898** season, Cuddington C.C. seemed to have broken away from Cheam Common C.C. completely, and were playing most of their home games somewhere in Worcester Park. The following seven fixtures appeared in the 'Surrey Comet' and 'Sporting Life', for the 1898 season:-

May 21st Malden Wanderers v Cuddington at Worcester-park - 'Comet'

May 28th Ashtead v Cuddington at Ashtead - 'Sporting Life'

May 30th B.H. Monday Hampton Wick v Cuddington at Worcester-park - 'Comet'

June 4th Ham & Petersham v Cuddington, at Worcester-park - 'Comet'

July 30th Hampton Wick v Cuddington at Worcester-park - 'Comet'

Aug 1st B.H. Monday Hampton Wick v Cuddington at Worcester-park - 'Comet'

Aug 13th Ham & Petersham v Cuddington at Ham - 'Comet'

They were all against strong, well established teams who, in comparison to the Cuddington team, obviously provided the newspapers with their fixture lists and occasionally furnished them with match reports. From the sparse fixture details furnished above it looks as though Cuddington might have played about 25 matches, per season. It is interesting to note that the four opponents listed above still exist, and provide the modern W.P.C.C. with opposition almost 120 years later.

Of the four scoresheets to appear in the press in 1898, the first was for the Bank Holiday match on Monday, May 30th against Hampton Wick Royal. In a way it probably demonstrated how weak the Cuddington team were, against some of the top clubs, as they lost on the first innings by 86 runs. Hampton Wick batted first and scored 150 runs, the wickets being shared between Barton with four wickets, Shipton with three wickets and Martin with two wickets. The Cuddington response is set out below.

CUDDINGTON.			
Dearman b King	0	not out	11
Barton b Robinson	0	b S. Miles	1
Eades b King	2	b Daniel	2
Drew c Colmer b Robinson	17	b S. Miles	2
H. Martin not out	29	b Daniel	4
Morris b Robinson	0	b Daniel	0
J. Martin c H. Daws b Robinson	0	b Daniel	0
Dare b King		b S. Miles	0
Shipton b King		b Daniel	0
Montgomery b King	8	not out	0
Burke st Miles b King	1	did not bat	
B 2, 1 b 1	3	B 8, w 1	9
Total	64	Total (8 wkts)	29

The Cuddington opener could have been **C.N.G. (Gordon) Dearman** (b. 1867), who had topped the averages for Cheam Common and Cuddington in 1891, whilst the Dare, in the above scoresheet, was probably either **Henry Dare** (b. 1854), a gardener who came from Cambridgeshire, or one of his five sons. The family, who lived close to St. Philip's Church in 1891, were to play a prominent role in the W.P.A.C. story. **Walter, aka Charlie, Dare** (b 1881), a jobbing gardener, tended the pitch at Lindsay Road, whilst his younger brother, **Albert Dare** (b. 1889), another gardener, became the groundsman at Skinner's Field from 1929 to 1959. It is also interesting to note that Dearman, Drew and Dare went on to become founder members of W.P.F.C., in 1900.

At least the use of initials, in the above scoresheet, made it possible to identify **Henry Martin** (b. 1852), as a Coachman, who lived with his wife and daughter at Court Stables, in the hamlet of Worcester Park, and **John H. Martin** (b. 1870), a Groom, who lived in the grounds of the wealthy Charles W. Smith, a retired Fur Merchant, who went on to become the president of the football club. The Martins did not appear to be related.

Although the 'Comet' said that the match against Ham & Petersham, on June 4th, was due to be played at Worcester Park, the scorecard in the paper the following week stated that the game was played at Cheam. This, presumedly, meant that it was played somewhere in Cheam Common, an area which stretched from Worcester Park Station to half way up Pond Hill (the Malden Road, Cheam). They might possibly have played on the Cheam Common ground, opposite the North End Tavern or even on the pitch behind 'The Drill', where Cheam Common had originally played cricket. The fact that one of the Pennington family, whose family owned the pub, was playing, makes that a definite possibility.

In reply to Ham and Petersham's 150 for 3 wickets that day, Cuddington managed 68 for 7 wickets thanks to: Legg 5, C. Montgomery 2, Drew 0, Dearman 20, Martin 0, Morris 8, Montgomery 8, Eccles 20*, Pennington 5*, Barton and Shipton DNB.

On August Bank Holiday Monday, August 1st, 1898, Cuddington entertained Hampton Wick Royal again at Worcester Park and lost by 58 runs on the first innings. No mention was made in the short two line report of the fact that Shipton had taken   nine wickets, eight of them bowled, in the first innings, or that he picked up another three wickets in their second innings when they scored 156 for 6 wickets,

HAMPTON WICK (A) v. CUDDINGTON.
Played at Worcester Park on Monday, and resulted in a win for the Hampton Wick men by 58 runs.
Score :—

HAMPTON WICK.

H. Daws b Shipton	11	not out	7
A. E. Miles b Shipton	11		
S. C. H. Lawrence b Barton	7	b Barton	0
L. C. Moore b Shipton	2	b Shipton	37
A. Lucas b Shipton	0		
W. D. Colmer not out	36		
H. O. Smith b Shipton	0	lbw b Drew	46
E. T. Spearing b Shipton	20	c Holland b Shipton	3
P. Moore b Shipton	3	c and b Eades	5
P. Daws b Shipton	16	not out	34
J. Robinson c Drew b Shipton	0	b Shipton	10
Extras	23	Extras	14
	—		—
Total	129	Total (6 wkts)	156

CUDDINGTON.

Holland b P. Daws	5	Eades b Lucas	2
Morris st L. Moore b P. Daws	4	Barton run out	0
		Montgomery b Lucas	6
Dearman b P. Daws	1	Shipton b Lucas	9
Drews c H. Daws b Lucas	5	Cleary not out	0
H. Martin st L. Moore b P. Daws	24	Extras	11
J. Martin b P. Daws	4		—
		Total	71

The Shipton in this team was probably **Frederick Henry Long Shipton** who was born, the son of an Evangelist, at Knowle in Somerset in 1868. By 1891 he was living in Walton and worked as a journalist, and beside his name on the census is the word 'Author'. He married Kate Ingram, the daughter of the landlord of the 'Anchor Hotel' in Redhill in 1893. and they settled down to raise a family in 'Devonshire Villas', Lime Grove, New Malden, where they stayed until about 1908. By 1911 Frederick and his family had returned to Walton on Thames, where he was listed as being the Secretary of an un-named Public Company. He made the local press as a participant in several angling competitions besides being a leading member of the Walton Conservative Club, where he won both billiard tournaments and rose growing competitions.

As a cricketer Shipton must have been a better than average bowler as he had previously played for Cheam Common C.C. versus the Surrey Club and Ground in 1896. He continued to play cricket even after he left the Worcester Park area and in 1913 was elected as Captain of the Walton Conservatives' Saturday Cricket team.

The 'Holland' who opened the batting, in that match, was probably **John Holland** (b. 1869), a chemist in the gas works, who had relocated with his wife and young family, from Clapham in about 1895. His two sons, **John W. Holland** (b. 1891) and **Frederick C. Holland** (b.1894), became key players for Worcester Park & Old Malden C.C. and W.P.F.C. before the First World War, and for Cheam Common C.C. after the War. After 1921 they also became leading figures in the Athletic Club and featured prominently upon both the sporting and social side of the new club. Frederick became the Chairman of the Bowls Club whilst John spent about fifteen years as wicket keeper and Vice-Captain of the First XI. His brother-in-law, Frederick Blake, who had married Florence Maud Holland in 1908, was the Captain of both the Football and Cricket teams for much of this time.

The only other match to grace the pages of the 'Comet' in 1898 was a defeat in the return match against Ham and Petersham on August 13th, when a ten man Cuddington side were defeated by 50 runs, despite Burke taking five wickets. The team that day was: Martin (8), Holland (0), Austin (0), Drew (19), Eades (0), E. Montgomery (4), Shipton (1), Montgomery (0), Burke (7) and Styles (1*)

It is interesting to note that the top scorer on that occasion was **Frank William Drew (b. 1873)** who became the regular goalkeeper for the W.P.F.C. First XI, when they formed in 1900, whilst 'Styles' was probably either Joseph John Styles (b. 1850), a gardener from Washington Road, who was recorded as playing for Cheam Common in 1891, or one of his boys, Albert, aged 16, or Ernest, aged 13, both of whom went on to play First XI football for W.P.F.C. and became prominent members of W.P.A.C. By 1913 Joseph had hung up his boots and became the umpire for Cheam Common C.C. whilst Albert was the team's Vice Captain.

Albert Styles definitely played in one of the two matches which made the press in **1899,** when the team started with a heavy defeat in an away match against a slightly weakened Ashtead side. The short amusing match report shows that even a century ago, team selection faced the same problems of illness and conflicting interests as today (although many of the interests might be different). *"Played at Ashtead on Saturday, and resulted in a win for Ashtead by 133 runs. Ashtead began their season with a moderate team, the leading members being indisposed or having caught the golf fever."* ('Dorking and Leatherhead Advertiser' - Saturday May 13th)

In response to Ashtead's 156, Cuddington were skittled out for a mere 23 runs, *"Dearman made the highest score for the visitors, but when he had made nine, Mr. Cameron threw his wicket down."*

The team that day was G. Dearman (9), H. Martin (0), F. Drew (0), G. H. Taylor (0), F. Eades (5), F. Shipton (0), M. Eldridge (0), J. Hopkins (0), C. Dare (5), A. Styles (0), D. Hopkins (2), Extras 2. Joseph Hopkins, the future W.P.F.C. First XI Football Captain made a rare cricketing appearance.

Less than a month later Cuddington managed an unlikely win in an away game against Malden, where despite having been bowled out for a mere 49 runs, James Cleary with six wickets and Fred Shipton with four wickets skittled their opponents out for 29 runs. (See faded scorecard below).

MALDEN v. CUDDINGTON.
Played on Saturday at Malden. Score :—

CUDDINGTON.		MALDEN.	
Dearman b Wright	6	Staniland b Cleary	6
H. Martin c & b Baker	18	Wright b Shipton	4
Drew b Burton	5	Oliver c Drew b Cleary	0
Eades run out	8	Evans c Drew b Cleary	1
Knowles b Chalkley	5	Chalkley b Cleary	1
Shipton c Watson b Chalkley	6	Baker b Shipton	1
Stevens b Chalkley	0	Watson b Cleary	11
Dare c Oliver b Chalkley	1	Burton c & b Cleary	0
Cleary b Chalkley	3	Meadows b Shipton	0
Rush not out	3	Lovelace c & b Shipton	0
Turner b Chalkley	0	Larkin not out	0
B 3, l b 1	4	Byes	5
Total	49	Total	29

Three matches made it into the press in **1900**, thanks again to the opposition scribes. In the first match, on May 19th, away to Ashtead, Cuddington were thoroughly trounced by 101 runs. Batting first Cuddington only managed 72 runs, Frank Drew scoring half that total. One might query, however, what regular opener, Gordon Dearman was doing batting at number eight:- A. Mann (0), C. Dare (3), H. P. C. Austin (5), W. Stephens (13), F. F. Eades (8), F. W. Drew (36), H. W. Martin (4), G. Dearman (1*), F. H. L. Shipton (0), H. Burke (0), H. Gilbert (0), Extras 3.

In response Ashtead seemed to follow the custom of the day by batting on, even after victory was achieved, notching up 173 runs by the time stumps were drawn, and the pubs were open, with both Shipton and Austin taking four wickets apiece.

Henry Percy Charles Austin (b.1874), was an assistant school teacher who lived next door to Charles Powell, on Cheam Common Road, close to St. Philip's Church. Henry had been one of Cheam Common and Cuddington's leading bowlers in the 1890s and had played twice against the Surrey Staff and Ground. On the second occasion he had even dismissed the legendary Leonard Braund, L.B.W. for two runs.

Henry Austin was another of the Cuddington players who became involved with W.P.F.C. when it formed in 1900, though perhaps not as a player. The 'Surrey Mirror' of September 23rd, 1902, revealed that he was the referee of a one-all draw between Epsom and Worcester Park that season.

In the return match on June 30th, 1900, the Ashtead players struggled with the vagaries of the Cuddington pitch and failed to chase down a measly 34 runs, which was all the home team could muster despite restoring Gordon Dearman to the top of the order. H. W. Masters was the only person to reach double figures, although Charley Dare, batting at number ten, made an invaluable eight runs. The last man in was 17 year old, William G. Hopkins, another erstwhile W.P.F.C. First XI player, who

also lived in Cheam Common Road. The Ashtead players obviously failed to cope with the pace and accuracy of Fred Shipton on this occasion, who starred yet again with six wickets.

Although most of the games played by Cuddington in 1900 have vanished into the realm of forgotten memories, the third match that made the papers that year almost disappeared as well, thanks to a typographical error, which foiled the search engine. It was by a sheer accident that I discovered the following match in the 'Surrey Mirror' of August 3rd, 1900, a match that Caterham won despite losing ten wickets. It was yet another match in which Shipton succeeded in getting at least five wickets.

The Caterham scribe failed to accord the away team initials, and whether the names were spelt correctly is a matter of conjecture. There were several new players in the team such as Sulley, Niel, Boles and Brind. Niel was probably **Sidney Neil** (b. 1870), who had played both for Cheam, and for Cheam Common in one of the matches that they had played against the Surrey Staff and Ground in the mid-1890s. He worked as a barman at the 'Red Lion' in Cheam Village, where his mother, Clara, was the landlady from 1880-88, and from 1896-1906. It is strange to note that he had an older sister called Sidnetta.

There were also two Drews in the team. The number four batsman was obviously Frank William Drew, whilst the number ten batsman, Drew, was his fourteen year old stepson Charles A. Stone whose mother, Clara, was nine years older than Frank. He was to appear in games for Cheam Common as 'C. Drew'.

The final mention of Cuddington Cricket Club, in the press, occurred in the 'Leatherhead and Dorking Advertiser' of August 10th, 1901, when they were defeated at Ashtead by 73 runs. The team that day was F. Buckridge 0, W. Ridout 31, Hadler 6, B. Garson 0, F. W. Drew 10, W. Stevens 0, H. P. C. Austin 16, P. Pownall 3, J. Tully 4, H. Shipton 1, E. E. Curtis 2*, extras 0, total 73. Stevens took 6 wickets, Shipton 4.

They were obviously, by then, struggling to turn out a team as most of the regulars had disappeared. Only four members of that team, Frank Drew, W. Stevens, H. P. C. Austin and Frederick Shipton had been recorded as having played for the club during the previous three seasons. Of the seven new players, the only one who could positively be identified was **Edwin E. Curtis** (b. 1885) who in 1901 worked on his mother's dairy farm at Horton. Ten years later he was listed as being a florist and poultry farmer.

It seems likely that Cuddington Cricket Club gradually faded into oblivion sometime during the Edwardian era. The formation of the football club, and its link to the Blake family, might have indirectly affected the numbers available to play for Cuddington. Players, such as Charlie Dare and John Holland, seemed to switch their allegiance to the Old Malden and Worcester Park Cricket Club which was captained by John Blake and for whom a young Fred Blake played.

Of those who had remained true to Cuddington C.C., Henry Austin married Lucy Mary Hopkins, a fellow teacher, from Longfellow Road, in 1904, and left the district to teach in Croydon, whilst by 1909 Frederick Shipton had moved to Walton and Frank Drew was the leading batsman for Cheam Common.

****

Tennis in Worcester Park pre-1921

When Worcester Park Athletic Club was formed in 1921 there were four main sections - Cricket, Football, Tennis and Bowls. Whilst cricket and football seemed to appeal to all classes of society and were thriving in the Worcester Park area prior to the First World War, tennis seemed to be the preserve of those from a more privileged background, and bowls tended to appeal to those who had retired from playing either cricket or football.

Whilst there was little mention in the Victorian press of the individual bowls players who lived in the area, (although a team did represent Malden), tennis fared much better as many of the large estates in Worcester Park and Cuddington had their own tennis courts, where the wealthier members of society could entertain their friends on a summer's afternoon. By the late 1870s tennis had become the latest craze amongst the privileged, and the names of those who played the game, the celebrities of the time, became newsworthy.

The popularity of tennis locally was probably heightened in 1877, when the All England Croquet and Lawn Tennis Club decided to institute as a prize, a 25 guinea Challenge Cup, to be open to all amateurs. One of the first local players to enter this competition was the future Headmaster of Cheam School, **Arthur S. Tabor** (b. 1852) who had played cricket (quite successfully) for Eton, Cambridge University, Middlesex and Cheam. His record at tennis, however, was not quite as good: in 1878 he lost to the eventual winner, P. F. Hadow, in the second round; in 1879 he was knocked out in the first round by 3 sets to 1: whilst in 1880 he reached the second round yet again.

In a way it is difficult to appreciate, nowadays, how wealthy parts of Worcester Park were, 140 years ago, until one encounters some of the property advertisements in the national press. The following, rather amazing, advertisement appeared in the 'St. James's Gazette' on June 3rd, 1886, apparently for a bungalow (the room dimensions, which were very generous, have been omitted):-

*"The BUNGALOW, Avenue-road, Worcester Park, in the parishes of Maldon and Cuddington, near to Worcester Park Station, containing 15 bedrooms, 3 dressing rooms, and 2 bathrooms, a suite of 3 lofty rooms, including drawing room, ballroom or Library, and a billiard room; also a noble dining room, opening to a handsome conservatory, a breakfast room, and domestic offices, stabling for two horses, entrance lodge or coachman's house, gardener's cottage, and well timbered pleasure grounds, **tennis lawn**, kitchen garden, glass houses, etc. For sale, with possession, and suitable for a gentleman's occupation or for a public institution, school etc."*

At a little over two acres in size, the Bungalow was quite modest in area when compared to 'Worcester Park House' which, in an advertisement from 1872, was called a *"capital moderate sized mansion, containing about 40 acres, richly timbered, with gardens and pleasure grounds, an ornamental orangery, vinery and training ground, stabling and carriage houses, and a coachman's cottage, also two good cottages for gardeners."*

For a period of six or seven years, **Worcester Park Lawn Tennis Club** became one of the most famous clubs in the south of England which, apart from providing an exclusive setting for all the young athletic gentry of the area to play tennis, also managed to attract one or two other notable players to its ranks. Although no documents exist concerning the club's foundation, it appears to have been founded in about **1879** and featured the **Reverend William Chetwynd Stapylton**[1] (b. 1825), the vicar of St. John the Baptist, Old Malden, as its president, with his sons as the backbone of the club.

Although many of the properties in the locality, such as 'New House Farm', boasted tennis courts, Worcester Park Tennis Club was probably based in the grounds of 'Wighill', the home of the Vicar's recently married son, Edward C. Chetwynd, who was one of the leading players of W.P.L.T.C., and played in virtually every match that was reported in the press. The fact that 'Wighill' actually had more than one tennis court was revealed in an advertisement in the 'Surrey Comet', twenty years later, when the then owner of the property, Mr. Hanning, was looking for an *"Under Gardener, wanted to look after lawn tennis courts - mowing with pony."* Mr. Hanning had also been a member of the club. A Conveyance document for a neighbouring plot of land in 1899, also said that *'it is immediately opposite the Lawn Tennis Club Grounds and a residence known as 'Wighill.'*

The first recorded match of Worcester Park L.T.C. occurred, in May 1879, against the Iceni Club, a team of gentlemen from Norfolk. The 'Comet' described the ground as being *"beautifully situated, which owing to the exertions of the indefatigable secretary was in excellent order. The enclosure surrounding the courts was from an early hour in the afternoon filled with a highly appreciative audience, including the president of the club, the Rev. Canon Chetwynd Stapylton, and most of the aristocracy, and ladies and gentlemen both of the vicinity and adjacent country; and many a bright eye grew still brighter, and rosy cheek flushed still more deeply, as stroke by stroke the rival combatants fought desperately for victory and fame. It had been agreed that the match should consist of three double and three single sets."* ('Surrey Comet' - May 24th, 1879)

The Worcester Park team won the Doubles' competition by two matches to one, thanks to victories from Messrs **Henry Elliott Johnson**[2] (b. 1855) and

Cyrus Waddilove[3] (b. 1827) by three sets to love, and Messrs. **Arthur Pollock**[4] (b. 1850) and **Edward Chetwynd Stapylton**[5] (b. 1855), in a match where *"victory seemed to hang in the balance from moment to moment, until at last the Park men, whose condition was apparently better than that of their opponents, appeared gradually to wear them down, and won an exciting contest by two sets to one, amidst the universal applause of the residents.*

The final pairing of Messrs. **Henry Warlters Horne**[6] (b. 1846) and **Frederick C. Stapylton**[7] (b. 1857) lost a close match by three sets to two.

The Park team was also victorious by the same margin in the singles competition thanks to Mr. Waddilove beating the Rev. Avison Terry Scott, in a three set game, by two sets to one; and Mr. A. Pollock beating Mr. F. Colvin, in a five set match by three sets to nil, whilst Mr. Ed. Stapylton was defeated by Mr. Maule by three sets to nil. *"Worcester Park were thus victors by two to one in both the double and single sets. The return match which is to be played about the end of June is already looked forward to with considerable interest by the home club and their Norfolk friends."*

Unlike the cricket and football teams of the time, which catered for all layers of society, The Worcester Park Tennis Club seemed to be made up almost entirely of young men, in their mid-twenties, who had attended a reputable public school, such as Eton, Harrow, Rugby, Repton or Winchester before completing their education at Oxford or Cambridge. There seemed to be a bond of life-style between all the members, that was strengthened by the fact that many of them were inter-connected either through marriage or through career choice, the majority becoming either solicitors or traders in the City.

Disappointingly the return fixture against the team led by the **Reverend Avison Terry Scott**[8] (b.1848), a former First Class cricketer and a curate, who was working in Wimbledon from 1873 to 1879, and his former friends of the Iceni L.T.C., Norfolk, failed to be reported, although an extremely interesting match against the Revellers Cricket Club did appear in 'The Field' on the 26th July: *"The Revellers sent down a team of five on Wednesday last to try conclusions with the same number of Worcester Park players. It was arranged that three matches should be played - two doubles and one single. After the recent heavy rain the ground was rather soft, but still played better under the circumstances than was expected. As will be seen by the return, the Revellers won two out of three matches."*

As a cricket team the Revellers were a bit of an enigma. In February 1879, the club took the decision to relocate to Yorkshire, and two prominent members of the Committee, Captain Mills and Mr. Vesey, who were both from Sheffield, were to be in charge of proceedings. An article in the 'Sheffield Independent' of Monday

February 10th 1879 stated that the club was about to make Sheffield its headquarters for Yorkshire, although, *"it is not intended that this shall be merely a Sheffield branch, as the matches will be theoretically under the control of the London Committee, though Captain Mills and Mr. Vesey have their full authority to do in all matters as they think proper."*

The tennis team that the Revellers turned out that day was certainly extremely experienced, and included some of the leading exponents of the game in the United Kingdom. For Worcester Park to have been able to come so close to victory was a good indication of the quality of play of the home team. In the first match L. R. Erskine and C. E. Baker for the Revellers defeated Arthur Pollock and Edward Stapylton in a closely fought contest 6-5, 5-6, 3-6, 5-4 (?) and 6-2. **Lestocq Robert Erskine** had been born in Edinburgh in 1857 and played in the inaugural Wimbledon Championship competition in 1877 and won a couple of matches. The following year he was the beaten finalist, whilst in 1879 he was knocked out in the second round.

In the other doubles match Arthur Rokeby Price and Wilfrid Rokeby Price for Worcester Park came back from a love set against A. J. Stanley and W. F. Richmond to win 0-6, 5-4 (?), 6-1 and 6-2. After the first set *"Worcester Park did not allow their opponents a chance. W. R. Price was very deadly at the net."*

Little is known about W. F. Richmond, apart from the facts that he regularly played football and cricket with the Stanley brothers and was a ten-handicap golfer at Guildford Golf Club. **Arthur John Stanley**[9] (b.1853), however, was certainly a talented tennis player, footballer, cricketer and golfer who had played 14 cricket matches for the Revellers, out of a possible 28 the previous season, with a top score of 41. The pinnacle of his tennis career, however, probably came in 1885 and 1886 when he and Claude Farrer, were runners-up, on both occasions, to William and Ernest Renshaw in the Men's Doubles Championship at Wimbledon. William Renshaw also won the Men's Singles on both those occasions.

Following this match both Arthur and his brother, **Charles Herbert Stanley**[10] (b. 1852), seem to have been lured by the beauty of the Worcester Park ground to switch allegiances, as they both appeared in the Worcester Park ranks in 1881. Perhaps playing tennis in Worcester Park was more desirable than playing cricket in Yorkshire. For one tennis competition that Arthur entered, however, his club was listed as being the M.C.C.

Unfortunately, the deciding match against The Revellers, the singles between fifty one year old Cyrus Waddilove for Worcester Park, and **Herbert Fortesque Lawford** (b. 1851), was a bit of a mismatch which he lost 3-6, 1-6, 6-1 and 1-6, although he *"played much better in the third set."* Lawford was already famous in tennis circles for inventing 'top spin' and he was set to become a singles finalist at Wimbledon on six occasions between 1880 and 1888. He actually holds the record for the most defeats in the final, his only victory, coming in 1887. In 1885 he became the inaugural British Covered Court Champion, and is also credited, along with L. R. Erskine in winning the first ever major Men's Doubles Championship when they won the Oxford University Men's Double Championship in May 1879. They beat a pair of players from Cheam, **George E. Tabor** (b. 1855) and **Francis Durant**[11] (b. 1857), who was one of the stars of the Worcester Park Club. In 2006, H. F. Lawford was inducted into the International Tennis Hall of Fame.

The Revellers weren't the only cricket team against whom the Tennis Club played over the following five or six years, as they played regular fixtures against Surbiton, Hampstead and Richmond Cricket Clubs.

The fact that many Cricket Clubs turned out tennis teams is not perhaps that surprising when one remembers that the Laws of Tennis were drawn up in part by the M.C.C. in 1875. Even today clubs such as Cranleigh Cricket Club still have Tennis Weeks, when the outfield becomes a patchwork quilt of grass tennis courts.

The match against The Revellers C.C. had introduced the Rokeby Price family, who like the Chetwynd Stapyltons hailed initially from Yorkshire and were distantly related by marriage. **Arthur R. Price**[12] (b.1854) and **Wilfrid Thomas R. Price**[13] (b. 1856), both lived at Pitt Place, Epsom, with their mother, Fanny, and their father, Hall Rokeby Price who, apart from being the Master of the Ironmonger's Society, sat on the Board of the London Stock Exchange for 32 years; the final seven as Chairman. Hall R. Price was also a leading figure in society locally as, apart from being a churchwarden in Epsom, he organised several fund raising events for his favourite charity, of which he was the Treasurer, the Yorkshire Society's School in Westminster Bridge Road. This was a school *"for Boarding, Clothing, and Educating Boys born in Yorkshire, or one of whose parents was born there. The parents of all such boys must have been in a respectable line of life, and now reduced by misfortune or dead."* The charity tried to provide an education for about a dozen boys, between the ages of nine and twelve, each year.

Much of the information in this chapter about Worcester Park L.T.C. appeared initially in 'The Field, The Country Gentleman's Newspaper' which was published every Saturday and often contained up to 100 pages of advertisements, upcoming sports fixtures and results. Mention of the Worcester Park Tennis Club was, however, very sporadic in the early days, and next appeared in June **1881** when the results of two fixtures were reported on consecutive weekends, against Surbiton C.C. and Esher L.T.C .

W.P.L.T.C. won the home match against Surbiton on Saturday, June 18th, by seven rubbers to two *"the rubber being the best of three sets, each of the three pairs to meet each of their opponents three pairs once."* Nearly all the matches that they played followed this format. Singles matches were a rarity.

The result of the Surbiton match was as follows:

A. J. Stanley & F. C. Stapylton beat R. B. Perkin & R. K. Perkin (6-4, 6-4)

W. R. Price & F. Durant beat F. A. Deare & E. Wight (3-6, 6-2, 6-1)

E. C. Stapylton & H. E. Johnson lost to P. C. Bates & G. A. Bolton (3-6, 5-6)

W. R. Price & F. Durant beat R. B. Perkin & R. K. Perkin (6-2. 6-2)

A. J. Stanley & F. C. Stapylton lost to P. C. Bates & G. A. Bolton (4-6, 6-2, 3-6)

E. C. Stapylton & H. E. Johnson beat F. A. Deare & E. Wight (6-2, 6-3)

W. R. Price & F. Durant beat P. C. Bates & G. A. Bolton (6-1, 6-2)

E. C. Stapylton & H. E. Johnson beat R. B. Perkin & R. K. Perkin (4-6, 6-1, 6-3)

A. J. Stanley & F. C. Stapylton beat F. A. Deare & E. Wight (6-5, 6-3)

The following weekend, with young **Alfred Waddilove**[14] (b.1862), in the team, in place of Francis Durant, W.P.L.T.C. were beaten comprehensively by eight matches to one by Esher L.T.C. *"although the very adverse circumstances of wind and rain would have necessitated a postponement with less determined players. For the visitors, Mr. W. Price's services were noticeable and Messrs. A. Stanley's and Mr. F. Stapylton's were well sustained though somewhat unlucky throughout."*

A fortnight later three of the team, Henry E. Johnson and the Stapylton brothers scored an emphatic seven matches to two victory over Weybridge in a singles competition. There were three rounds played, each match being the best of three sets. Weybridge's best player, Mr. Madison, who had picked up both of their points was unable to stay for the final round. As a result Edward C. Stapylton scored a comfortable victory over the substitute, Mr. Hawes, 6-0, 6-3.

Some of the best players in the Tennis Club were also members of other clubs, which precluded their being available for selection every week. Messrs. Arthur J. Stanley and Arthur Pollock, for example, were both members of the London Athletic Club, which was based at Stamford Bridge. On Monday 27th June 1881, the L.A.C.

arranged a lawn-tennis tournament amongst it members, and succeeded in obtaining a splendid entry of sixty-two players. The majority of these competitors probably were not up to the standard of the Worcester Park pair, however, as is evidenced by the fact that Arthur Pollock managed to win his second round match *"rather easily"* despite being handicapped by *"a bad wrist, which prevented him returning many back-handers,"* and he also managed to win both his fourth round sets to love.

The semi-final match between A. J. Stanley and Arthur Pollock *"was a very close one, and the play was very good on both sides. The latter won by three sets to two."* In a way this must have been a bitter-sweet victory for Arthur as the final against H. Berkeley was due to be played at 3.30 p.m. on Saturday July 2nd, the very day that he was due to play Mr. H. C. Jenkins of the M.C.C., in the first round, at Wimbledon. As a consolation prize A. J. Stanley (M.C.C.) was one of 48 players taking part that day in the first round at Wimbledon, where he lost to Mr. T. J. Gallway of the Emeriti C.C., by three sets to one.

Mr. Pollock, however, won the Final of the L.A.C. Tournament with ridiculous ease, winning 6-0, 6-1, 6-1, with only the final game of the match reaching deuce. At least it was a beautiful day and there was a large number of spectators, who were also assembling to watch the Americans from the Manhattan A.C., of New York, take on the L.A.C. at the Three Miles Open Scratch Walking Race and the Half Mile Open Running Scratch Race. A crowd of over 1,500 saw the Americans E. E. Merrill and L. E. Myers win their respective events.

The early 1880s appeared to have been the heyday of the Tennis Club, and they were blessed with good coverage in the press. The first match that appeared in June **1882**, showed little change in the personnel of the six man squad apart from the addition of Mr. T. P. Sainsbury, who was paired with E. C. Stapylton. The other two pairs were F. Durant & W. R. Price and F. C. Stapylton & H. E. Johnson.

"On Saturday last, the 27th ult., at Richmond, a match was played between the L.T. team of Richmond C.C. and the Worcester Park L.T.C. The day was windy and unfavourable, and the result a victory for the visitors by nine matches to love."

The highlight of the 1882 season was probably the Worcester Park Challenge Cup which brought out all the star players of the Club, who were competing to find a worthy challenger to Francis Durant, who had won the cup for the preceding two years. This was the same format as that embraced by the All England Club at Wimbledon, whereby everyone competed to challenge the previous year's winner. At Wimbledon, however, all the preceding rounds were in the previous week, whereas the whole competition, at Worcester Park, took place on the same day, which seemed to give the defending champion an unfair advantage. One can not help but feel sorry for the losing finalist, who had already played nine sets before the final started.

On June 17th, 'The Field' provided the following exceedingly full account of the whole draw and the final between Francis Durant and Arthur Pollock:

"At Worcester Park, on Saturday last, the 10th inst., the challenge cup, presented to the W.P.T.L.C. by Mr. Arthur Pollock in 1879, was finally won for the third consecutive season by Mr. F. Durant, who is thus entitled to keep the trophy. This match was played with Mr. Pollock, the winner of the final tie, on a heavy ground, during a high wind and occasional showers. Mr. Durant won the toss, and elected to play with the wind, but lost the set after a hard-fought struggle, at 5-7, deuce being called once. On changing over, Mr. Pollock lost a set in the same court at 4-6. The third set was comparatively easily won by Mr. Pollock at 6-3, when victory for him seemed more than probable. At this point Mr. Durant played up remarkably well, and the fourth set was very evenly contested, the games being called five all. Mr. Durant, however, managed to win the eleventh and twelfth games, bringing the sets to two all. In consequence of the wind the players now changed courts after each game, but Mr. Pollock fell off in his play, and was beaten rather easily at 6-2.

The following is the result of the play throughout, best of five sets to win:

FIRST ROUND

Mr. A. R. Price scratched to Mr. A. J. Stanley

Mr. A. Pollock beat Mr. H. E. Johnson (6-3, 6-1, 6-1)

Mr. W. R. Price scratched to Mr. E. C. Stapylton

Mr. F. C. Stapylton beat Mr. C. H. Stanley (6-0, 6-1, 6-1)

SECOND ROUND

Mr. A. Pollock beat Mr. A. J. Stanley (6-3, 6-1, 6-3)

Mr. F. C. Stapylton beat Mr. E. C. Stapylton (6-5, 6-3, 6-5)

FINAL ROUND

Mr. A. Pollock beat E. C. Stapylton (7-5, 6-1, 6-2)

FINAL MATCH

Mr. F. Durant (holder) beat Mr. A. Pollock (5-7, 6-3, 3-6, 7-5, 6-2)"

From the rather sporadic tennis fixtures that were reported in the press, it appeared as though the Club probably had regular home and away fixtures against the likes of Surbiton, Esher and Weybridge. The results of these fixtures were often prefaced by a short paragraph which, on occasions, revealed a snippet of information that was not available elsewhere such as the weather conditions, and the names of players who had performed with distinction. In the following report for a match against Weybridge, which appeared in 'The Field' in July 1882, the article even provided the name of the hon. sec., Mr. Thomas, a gentleman who never appeared in any of the teams, but was obviously a valued member of the Club.

"A match between these clubs was played on June 24th, on the excellent grounds of the Worcester Park Club. The day was fortunately fine, but there was a good deal of wind in the early part of the afternoon. The result of the match was a very easy victory for the Weybridge team, whose severe volleying seemed too much for their opponents: but the Worcester Park Club were not quite playing up to their usual strength. For the home team Messrs. Johnson and F. and E. Stapylton played very well. The Worcester Park Club showed their usual hospitality, and Mr. Thomas, their hon.sec., most kindly placed his house at the disposal of the visitors."

The Worcester Park team, which did appear to be much weaker that day, only managed to win two sets that afternoon and lost by nine matches to love. The team was:- Messrs. F. C. Stapylton & H. E. Johnson; Messrs. H. S. Hanning & A. R. Price; Messrs. E. C. Stapylton & E. Sainsbury (in the third round E. Sainsbury was replaced by N. C. Sainsbury).

Although the three members of the Sainsbury family who were mentioned that year, proved to be very elusive, and were perhaps visitors from abroad, the hon. sec., of the Club, **John Alick Thomas**[15] (b. 1854) was living with his widowed mother, in 1881, at 'Abberley House', whilst **James Henry Skrine Hanning**[16] (b. 1854) lived a couple of houses away at 'Hartlands' with his father, a retired J.P., from County Cork.

It is surprising to note that, on the evening of the 1881 census, Charles Herbert Stanley was listed as being a visitor at 'Abberley House,' despite also being at home at 9, Lancaster Gate, Kensington, with his parents, brother and six sisters on the same evening. One possible reason for Charles being at 'Abberley House' that day might have been Annie Louisa Thomas, the 22 year old niece of John A. Thomas. If he were there trying to woo her, he certainly failed, as, two years later, on October 11th, 1883), she married her neighbour, James H. S. Hanning, at Old Malden Church.

The **1883** tennis fixture list in 'The Field', on April 27th, only records two matches for Worcester Park that season, both against Surbiton, away on May 12th, and at home, on June 9th. It was a little surprising, therefore, to see a full report, in 'The Field' of a nine game to love drubbing of Richmond C.C. on May 19th, at Worcester Park. Although it was a Doubles competition, W.P.L.T.C. obviously wanted to get as many players involved as possible and added a seventh player to the squad. The Park squad that day was Messrs. H. E. Johnson & W. R. Price, H. H. Playford & F. C. Stapylton, E. C. Stapylton & F. C. Evill and Arthur Pollock, who played in the final two rounds in place of F. C. Evill, who managed to play for Richmond in the final round.

The two new faces in the team were relatively recent arrivals in the Old Malden area. **Frederick Claude Evill**[17] (b. 1861) was studying medicine at London University and lived with his parents at 'Worcester Court House', whilst **Herbert H. Playford**[18] (b. 1858) was a Commercial Clerk who lived with his parents and rather large family at 'Radnor House', Motspur Park.

Although 'The Field' only revealed a couple of upcoming fixtures for 1883, if one scoured the vast array of newspapers of the time, one becomes aware that the club had quite a comprehensive fixture list and were engaged in matches most weekends. 'The Sporting Gazette', for example, which could not compete with 'The Field' in writing match reports, merely revealed that Worcester Park L.T.C. had lost against the Vandals three rubbers to one on June 9th. 'The Globe', in their turn, briefly reported that the Club were due to play away at Weybridge, on July 7th, whilst the 'Morning Post' simply stated that they were going to play against Esher on June 16th.

As Francis Durant had won the Challenge Cup outright the previous season, a new Challenge Cup competition was instituted in 1883. The name of the donor of the trophy was unfortunately omitted from the report of the competition which occurred, not on a Saturday, which seemed to be the preferred day for most of their matches, but on Friday the thirteenth. 'The Field' again provided the event with a comprehensive coverage, although the customary pre-amble was a little less detailed: *"the play for this cup has resulted in a victory for Mr. A. J. Stanley, who met Mr. H. H. Playford in the final tie on Friday, July 13th, and secured a somewhat easy win against him by three sets to love (6-3, 6-1, and 6-1). Mr. Playford did not seem to be quite in his usual form. The following shows the results of the various ties:*

FIRST ROUND
Mr. F. C. Evill scratched to Mr. W. R. Price

Mr. F. C. Stapylton beat Mr. C. H. Stanley (6-4, 4-6, 6-2, 6-5)

Mr. A. J. Stanley beat Mr. F. Durant (6-5, 2-6, 4-6, 6-3, 6-2)

Mr. E. C. Stapylton beat Mr. H. E. Johnson (6-1, 6-5, 6-4)

Mr. H. H. Playford beat Mr. A. Pollock (2-6, 6-1, 6-4, 6-2)

SECOND ROUND
Mr. F. C. Stapylton beat Mr. W. R. Price (6-3, 6-2, 6-4)

Mr. A. J. Stanley beat Mr. E. C. Stapylton (5-6, 6-3, 6-3, 3-6, 6-4)

Mr. H. H. Playford (a bye)

THIRD ROUND
Mr. H. H. Playford beat Mr. F. C. Stapylton (6-1, 6-5, 2-6, 6-5)

FINAL ROUND
Mr. A. J. Stanley beat Mr. H. H. Playford (6-3, 6-1, 6-1)

It is rather surprising that Arthur Stanley ever found time to pursue his career as a stockbroker as he appeared to be a full time, amateur sportsman, who spent the whole of his summer playing either cricket or tennis, whilst in the winter he played football for Clapham Rovers. Although he rarely won events in the early days, he usually survived the first round and was often complimented, in the press, on the quality of his play. Apart from playing tennis at Worcester Park, Wimbledon and for the London Athletic Club at Stamford Bridge, in 1883, Arthur also seemed to find plenty of time to take part in tournaments as far afield as the Prince's Club at Oxford, the Devonshire Club at Eastbourne and at the Exmouth L.T.C.

Whilst on a tennis tour of the West Country, in mid-August, 1883, following a third round defeat at Exmouth, he moved on to the Teignmouth Tournament, where he won the 10 guinea first prize in the Gentlemen's Singles Competition. **William Edward Martyn** [19] (b. 1856), of Exeter L.T.C., whom he had defeated in the second round of the Singles, became his partner in the Doubles, where they were defeated in the third round (3-6, 4-6), by the rather strangely named pair, Mr. E. C. Pine-Coffin and P. G. Von Donop. Arthur was less successful in the Mixed Doubles where he partnered twenty year old Alice G. Tickell, the youngest daughter of the president of the club, Colonel James Tickell. The pair lost by two sets to one (4-1, 1-4, 2-4). As a consolation prize, both Martyn and Stanley managed to be selected for Twelve Men of South Devon in the Torquay Cricket Week, where Arthur performed with distinction.

The first match of the **1884** season for the Worcester Park L.T.C., on April 26th, which featured the new pairing of W. E. Martyn and A. J. Stanley, must have been a bit of an eye opener for some of the members of the Tennis Club, who were used to playing on the pristine lawns of Worcester Park, as they found themselves playing on cinders in Harrow. This gripping encounter slipped under the radar of the Tennis Editor of 'The Field' on this occasion, but was thankfully caught by the 'Sporting Gazette', which gave an extremely full and comprehensive account of the encounter: *"Played at Harrow, on the cinders on Saturday last, and resulted in a narrow victory for the visitors by five rubbers to four. When eight matches had been played the score was four all, so considerable excitement centred on the last match. This was exceedingly well contested, Harrow winning the first set. The next two, however, fell to Worcester Park, who thus secured victory. A. J. Stanley and Martyn, as will be seen, won all their rubbers."* (A precis of the nine matches is below)

H. E. Johnson & H. T. Greenwell lost the first round (2-6, 4-6), won the second round (6-3, 6-3) and lost the third round (4-6, 4-6).

W. E. Martyn & A. J. Stanley won the first round (6-3, 6-0); won the second round (6-3, 8-6) and won the third round 6-1,6-2).

E. C. Stapylton & C. H. Stanley lost the first round (2-6, 4-6); lost the second round (6-1, 0-6, 3-6) and won the third round, and the match, (3-6, 6-3, 6-4).

Apart from W. E. Martyn, the only other newcomer in the team was **H. T. Greenwell**, a rather elusive character, who probably hailed from the North East of England, where on the 10th of January, 1857, the wife, of the Rev. William Greenwell, was reported in the press as having had a son, who was not named. Rather unhelpfully, when the 1861 census was filled in, the Vicar merely provided initials for his children, the son in question being H.T. This could possibly have been the same H. T. Greenwell, who partnered H. E. Johnson, as a player of that name took part in several tennis tournaments in Scarborough in the mid-80s. Whoever he was, H. T. Greenwell was certainly an enthusiastic member of the Club, whose light shone for an extremely short period of time, as he proudly entered at least three tournaments, in the space of a couple of months. as a member of the prestigious W.P.L.T.C., unlike the Stanley brothers who often played under the flag of the L.A.C. (the London Athletic Club).

The first tournament in which H. T. Greenwell appeared was the Lawn Tennis Championship of Ireland, which commenced in Fitzwilliam Square, Dublin, on a rather showery Monday, 19th May. He appeared to have travelled there in a small party, from Worcester Park, that included Charles Stanley, Arthur Pollock Miss A. Tabor and Miss Hallam. It was not a really successful venture, as both Greenwell and Stanley perished in the first round of the Singles, whilst Arthur Pollock only entered the Mixed Doubles with Miss Hallam, who had to retire in the First Round against Charles Stanley and Miss A. Tabor, who in their turn fell at the next hurdle.

The following week H. T. Greenwell travelled to Bath where he was eliminated by three sets to two, in the first round of the Gentlemen's Single-Handed Championship of the West of England, where the first prize was a *"challenge cup, value £52 10s., and silver tea and coffee service value £30,"* before he, at last, achieved a modicum of success in Worcester Park colours, when he beat W. Aldridge in the first round of the London Athletic Club tournament on June 17th. With that he disappeared from the ranks of Worcester Park tennis for that season, and returned to the North East.

Two further new players, F. Milne and F. G. Pierce, appeared in the Worcester Park L.T.C. ranks in the three additional match reports that were recorded in the press that season. Although there is no trace of F. Milne living locally, **Thomas William Pierce** (b. 1865) and his brother, **Frederick George Pierce** (b. 1867), both of whom had been born in India were living, at the time of the 1881 census, with their mother in Hampstead. By the mid-1880s their father, Colonel Thomas William West Pierce, who later became a Major General, had returned to England and the family were residing at 'Arundel House', Worcester Park. Thomas jun. also played cricket for Cheam Common in the 1880s.

There did, however, seem to be an element of consistency in the team, which revolved around the Stanley and Stapylton brothers, and Henry Johnson, which might have been slightly intimidating for newcomers. There again, in a six man team, there probably was not a lot of scope to introduce new players.

On June 14th, W.P.L.T.C. recorded an easy victory at home against Hampstead by seven matches to two. 'The Sportsman' only mentioned two of the pairs - E. C. Stapylton and A. J. Stanley who won all their matches and C. H. Stanley and H. E. Johnson, who had provided their opponents with a 'hard tussle'. The following week the team travelled to Hammersmith where they lost nine/love to the West Middlesex L.T.C. The team that day was:- F. C. Stapylton & F. Milne; H. E. Johnson & H. H. Playford; E. C. Stapylton & A. J. Stanley.

The team certainly seemed to prosper more at home than they did away, although the match at Worcester Park on July 19th proved to be a close-run event, when they scraped a victory over a team from Blackheath L.T.C by five matches to four. Much of the team's success that day was down to Edward Stapylton and A. J. Stanley who won all three matches. New boy Frederick George Pierce had, (as had F. Milne in the previous match), to partner Frederick Stapylton, and met with the same degree of success.
A. J. Stanley & E. C. Stapylton won the first round (6-4, 6-0), won the second round (6-1, 6-3), and won the third round (6-1, 6-3).
H. E. Johnson & C. H. Stanley lost the first round (1-6, 4-6), lost the second round (5-6, 6-4, 5-7) and won the third round (6-1, 3-6, 6-2).
F. C. Stapylton & F. G. Pierce won the first round (6-2, 6-4), lost the second round (1-6, 0-6) and lost the third round (2-6, 6-4, 5-7)

In hindsight the 1884 season seemed to have been the heyday of the Worcester Park Tennis Club and although a handful of the forthcoming fixtures for each season cropped up in the press, over the next three years, only three further match results were reported. The first report occurred in 'The Field' on June 13th, **1885**, when the team entertained the 'Anonymi' at Worcester Park:

"The above match was played on Saturday, June 6th, at Worcester Park, and resulted in a win for the latter club by six rubbers to three, thirteen sets to eight, 108 games to 80. The Anonymi had to play a substitute, as one of their men did not turn up."
A. J. Stanley and W. Milne won the first round (6-1, 6-3), won the second round (6-3, 6-5 (sub)) and the third round (6-2, 6-2).
E. C. Stapylton & H. E. Johnson lost the first round (4-6, 2-6), won the second round (6-3, 4-6, 6-2) and won the third round (6-4, 5-6, 6-2 (sub))
H. Greenwell & C. Stanley lost the first round (6-4, 3-6, 7-9 (sub)), lost the second round (5-6, 0-6), and won the final round (6-2, 6-5).

The Tennis Club had managed to attract another class player to its ranks to play against the Anonymi, **William Reginald Milne** (b. 1865) who lived with his parents and three brothers in Chelsea in 1881. Both William and his older brother, Oswald, had played at Wimbledon the previous year, as members of Weybridge L.T.A. Nineteen year old William had beaten his brother in a close match (9-7, 8-6, 1-6, 6-3) in the second round only to lose against E. Renshaw in the next round. Arthur Stanley, whom William partnered so successfully against the Anonymi, had also been eliminated in the second round that day at Wimbledon, where it is interesting to observe that he chose to enter the tournament as a member of the more exclusive Worcester Park L.T.A., rather than as a London Athletic Club player.

It is also interesting to note that H. Greenwell made a re-appearance for the team although most of his appearances in the press that year occurred as a tennis player in Scarborough and Whitby. It might have been that he was allowed to play against the Anonymi as a warm up for the London Athletic Club tournament, which he and the two Stanley brothers entered the following week.

Apart from the game against the Anonymi, only four other fixtures were listed for the Worcester Park team that season: home against Richmond on May 16th; away against Blackheath on June 27th; away against L.A.C. on July 4th; and home against Hampstead C. C. on July 18th. The match at Blackheath is a good example of one of the perennial problems faced by any sport's team, the occasion when someone lets the team down, by failing to turn up. 'The Field' presented the following account of the match :-*"Played at Blackheath, resulting in a victory to the home team of five rubbers to four. Worcester Park coming down a man short, W. F. Currey, of the B. L. T. C., kindly played as a substitute"*.

F. C. Stapylton & H. E. Johnson lost the first round (3-6, 6-5, 6-8), won the second round (6-1, 6-2) and won the third round (4-6, 6-2, 6-2).

E. C. Stapylton & H. W. Horne won the first round (6-3, 6-1), won the second round (6-1, 6-1), and lost the third round (6-4, 3-6, 2-6).

C. H. Stanley & W. F. Currey lost the first round (4-6, 2-6), lost the second round (1-6, 4-6), and lost the third round (6-1, 1-6, 4-6).

Five further fixtures were advertised in **1886**: away against Harrow on May 22nd; home against Richmond on May 29th; home against L.A.C. on June 19th; home against Harrow on June 26th; and home against the Anonymi on July 17th; whilst in **1887** only four fixtures were noted: away against Richmond on May 29th; home against the Anonymi on June 25th; home against Richmond on July 2nd; and finally away against Weybridge on July 9th.

These fixtures obviously were not the only matches that the Club played in 1886 and 1887, as they usually played the same teams on a home and away basis, each season, but the lack of press coverage seemed to indicate that there was no longer a person within the Club who was prepared to send a fixture list or match report to the local or national newspapers. The final match report for the Worcester Park Lawn Tennis Club, occurred for a match played on June 18th, 1887, again against the Anonymi, which they lost on that occasion quite comprehensively. It is highly likely that the match report was submitted by their opponents, as 'The Field' seemed to feature matches by the Anonymi on a regular basis. The match report briefly informed the reader that, *"This match resulted in a win for the Anonymi by six rubbers to three, thirteen sets to six, 95 games to 66."*

H. Foster & H. Bonsor lost the first round (1-6, 1-6), lost the second round (3-6, 1-6), and lost the third round (2-6, 3-6)

F. C. Stapylton & H. E. Johnson won the first round (6-3, 2-6, 6-4), lost the second round (6-8, 3-6), and won the third round (6-0, 6-1)

E. C. Stapylton & C. H. Stanley won the first round (6-4, 6-3), lost the second round (3-6, 4-6) and lost the third round (0-6, 1-6)

The top pairing of **Herbert Webb Bonsor** (b. 1856) and **Henry Foster** (b. 1846) might have had great social standing locally, but their skill on the tennis court seemed a little limited as they only managed to win 11 games in three matches. H. W. Bonsor was the son of Joseph Bonsor of Polesden Lacey and the brother of a wealthy brewer, Sir Henry Cosmos Orme Bonsor, the M.P. for Wimbledon (1885-1900). Herbert worked for his brother, Cosmos, whilst his wife, two sons and a daughter lived at 'Chessington Cottage', Cuddington. Henry Foster, who was a partner in a leather company, also lived locally at 'Tolworth Hall' with his wife, a son, three daughters and six servants.

All publicity for the Tennis Club, in the national press, appeared to have ceased completely by **1888**, although certain individuals, such as A. J. Stanley and his brother, still made the tennis columns of 'The Field' and the 'Sporting Life'. On May 5th, 1888, A. J. Stanley's team, for example, which did not include any Worcester Park players, beat Cambridge University, in a tight contest, five rubbers to four.

By 1886 the writing had seemed to be on the wall for this once popular Tennis Club. The founder members of the club, Henry Johnson and the Stapylton brothers, were no longer in their early to mid twenties. All three of them had successful careers, whilst Edward Stapylton also had a wife and three children to look after. Perhaps they were beginning to feel the need of a new, slightly more sedate activity to occupy their leisure time. As luck would have it, 1886 was the very year that the Worcester Park Beagles arrived on the scene, based at 'The Huntsman's Hall' with kennels in Green Lane. According to 'A History of the Worcester Park Beagles' by Hugh H. Scott-Willey, (edited by James Stracey) Herbert Webb Bonsor, who had turned out for the tennis team the following year, *"was the moving spirit in forming the Worcester Park and it was due to his influence and energy that the Hunt was able to make a place for itself so quickly in the country it had come into being to hunt."*

All three of the friends became founder members of the Beagles, with Herbert W. Bonsor, whilst the Rev. William Chetwynd Stapylton was elected an Honorary member. When **Mr. A. A. H. Auriol Barker**[20] [b. 1854) chaired the first general meeting of the Worcester Park Beagles, on October 11th, 1886, Herbert W. Bonsor took on the role of Master of the Hunt, whilst Frederick Chetwynd Stapylton was elected the Hon. Sec. and Treasurer, and, his brother, Edward, and Henry E. Johnson became committee members. Three years later, in 1889, when H. W. Bonsor retired, Frederick was promoted to the post of joint master of the pack, whilst Henry Johnson took on the role of Secretary and Treasurer.

Being a member of the Beagles was certainly a great career move for any ambitious, social climbing gentleman, as, in the words of James Stracey, it *"had the reputation of being a rather exclusive affair and one to which it was an honour to belong. Every aspirant to membership was scrutinised with care, proposed, seconded and then balloted for - 'one black ball in three to exclude'."* It also attracted those who had nothing left to prove, such as W. G. Grace, from about 1900 to 1910.

Although the Tennis Club no longer attracted the quality of player to grab the attention of the national newspapers, there were one or two mentions in the local press which indicated that the club survived, after a fashion, for several years. On May 3rd, **1890**, the 'Surrey Comet', whilst reporting on the A.G.M. of the Berrylands Lawn Tennis Club, mentioned that Berrylands had fixtures arranged for the following season against *"Richmond, Harrow, Guy's Hospital, Southgate, Chiswick, **Worcester Park**, and Weybridge."* As three of those teams had been regular opponents of Worcester Park in the past, it is quite likely that they were still on the Worcester Park fixture list in the 1890s.

The next mention of the club occurred eight years later when a short article, in the 'Surrey Comet' of November 12th, **1898**, revealed that the club appeared to have a thriving social section, and that the ladies of the club were an integral part of the social scene:- *"On Saturday evening an entertainment was given in Miss Page's schoolroom by the members of the Worcester Park Tennis Club and their friends, in aid of the North-Eastern Hospital for Children, Hackney. There was a good attendance, and a series of tableaux vivants were successfully performed under the direction of Miss Nicholette, and were loudly applauded by an appreciative audience. ......Miss Absolon sang 'I love you my love, I do,' and Mr. Boylan gave 'The Scientific Man,' while Miss Hearsum was encored for her banjo solo. Miss Lawrence, Miss Violet Absolon, Miss Barton and Mr. Absolon also contributed to the success of the evening."*

The **Miss Nicholette**, who was in charge of the performance, must have been either Olivia Nicholette, a fifty eight year old widow, or one of her two daughters, who had all been born in India and lived at 'Oakdene', Cheam Common, whilst the equally exotically named **Arthur de Mansfield Absolon** was a widowed bank clerk who lived in Epsom with his son John, and daughters Mabel and Violet (b. 1881). Violet, who lost her mother at the age of two, seemed to be drawn towards the performing arts. She was herself widowed at the age of 28 and, with a young daughter to look after, she obtained a position as a maternity nurse. Violet eventually emigrated to New York in 1924, so that her daughter, Dorothy Violet Wisbey, could fulfil her dream of becoming an actress.

It is probably fitting that the last mention of the Worcester Park Lawn Tennis Club which occurred in the 'Comet', twelve years later, on July 4th, **1910**, featured a Ladies team, when the Ladies of W.P.L.T.C. played Mrs. Mould's team:- *"Played on the ground of the Thames Ditton L.T.C. on Monday, and won by Mrs. Mould's team by six matches to three, 110 games to 92. After the game, Mrs. Mould entertained the players and a number of friends with her customary hospitality."*

It was a little more challenging to find details of the Worcester Park team on this occasion, partly because women usually change their surnames when they marry, and partly because few of them appear on the electoral roll, as it was not until 1918 that women, over the age of 30, achieved the vote. From the 1911 census, however, it is possible to deduce a little about most of the Worcester Park team that played that day, which was:- Mrs. G. Reade & Miss D. Highmore (they won all three matches); Miss M. Flores and Miss L. Stuttaford; Miss L. Smith & Miss M. Wright.

Although it is effectively impossible to trace the final pairing of the Misses Smith and Wright in the existing records of Births, Marriages, Deaths and Censuses, because of the preponderance of young ladies with those surnames, one can make reasonable guesses as to the identities of the other four ladies.

Mrs. G. Reade was probably the wife of George Reade who appears on the 1911 electoral roll as living in Worcester Park, whilst Miss D. Highmore was undoubtedly **Dorothy Rivers Highmore** (b. 1884), who lived with her father, a solicitor and barrister, Sir Nathaniel J. Highmore K.C.B., who worked for His Majesty's Customs and Excise. The family had lived at 'Henley Lodge' in 1901, between the homes of Herbert Bonsor and Allan Henry Auriol Barker, whilst in 1911 they were living at 'Haileybrowe', Worcester Park. Both her brothers died in their early thirties, unmarried, Joseph of an illness in early 1914 and Charles from Spanish Flu, contracted whilst serving as a Second Lieutenant in the Machine Gun Corps, in 1919. 'Dossity', the last remaining child of Sir Nathaniel, remained a spinster and died in 1958 at Chalford, Wistbury, Wiltshire. Four years before her death she had presented the Highmore Collection of medical books to the Library of the Royal College of Surgeons.

Of the second pairing, Miss M. Flores was probably **Mabel Flores** (b. 1878), the daughter of a retired art dealer, and publican, George P. Flores, who lived at

Blenheim House, Grand Drive, Morden, with his three daughters. Her tennis partner was **Louise Stuttaford** (b. 1871), who in 1891 had been living with her parents, four sisters and two brothers at 'Oaklands', Worcester Park. All seven of the children had been born in Port Elizabeth, the Cape Colony, although her father William, a retired merchant, was a Cornishman, and her mother Anna, came from North Devon. It seems to have been quite a sporting family as her brother, Frank Rowland, had played both cricket and rugby at the Naval College in Greenwich, where he captained his fellow officers on the rugby field. Frank is also recorded as having played cricket for Cheam Common on an odd occasion. Although it is possible to discover quite a lot of information about her brother's life, the records provide little information about Louise's life, apart from the fact that she played tennis and remained a spinster for the rest of her life. She must have had quite a comfortable existence, however, as, by the time of her death in 1933, at Anglesey House, Chesterfield, Derbyshire, she left £22, 919.

Although there is no further information concerning Worcester Park Lawn Tennis Club after 1910, there is no reason not to presume that the tennis club continued to flourish at least until the First World War, and perhaps some of their members actually played at Skinner's Field from 1922 when tennis became one of the main sections of the Athletic Club, which had initially three courts and fifty tennis members.

By 1910, tennis was no longer just a game enjoyed by the elite of society. That was certainly true in what one might consider to be the working class area of Worcester Park, aka Cheam Common where, in 1910, sporting innovation in the community was again led by the Church, as another tennis club was formed, 'The Cheam Common (St. Philip's) Lawn Tennis Club', *"which was inaugurated some two years ago, and provided a need in the district, will at the coming annual meeting consider a proposal to establish a junior section. This should meet with general approval, and should be a means of training some good young players for the senior section."* (Surrey Comet, Jan 13th, 1912)

Where they played is a bit of a mystery, but a Six Inch Ordnance Survey map of the area, from 1933, shows that there was a Pavilion half way down St. Philip's Road, and that there was a small open space between it and Brinkley Road, where the tennis courts were probably situated. The same map also shows that tennis courts existed on the site of the current Cheam Leisure Centre, which was built in 1938, and which technically was part of Cheam Common, although it is about a mile from the church. An article in 'The Comet' of 1934, mentions that there were nine hard courts on the site of the proposed Cheam Baths, although disappointingly there was no indication as to when they had been laid down.

Information about the new tennis club comes basically from tiny tantalising snippets provided by the 'Surrey Comet', which seemed to alternate between referring to the club as 'St. Philip's Tennis Club' and 'Cheam Common Tennis Club,' which was very confusing initially as it seemed as though there were two

St. Philip's Church, Worcester Park.

clubs. Although no results for the new club were forthcoming in the 'Comet', the newspaper does provide an insight into the organisation of the club, an aspect that was sadly missing for the Worcester Park L.T.C. (postcard courtesy of John Fox)

On January 20th, 1912, the 'Comet' gave quite a detailed account of an E.G.M. under the heading 'St. Philip's Lawn Tennis Club', which listed most of the relevant officers and the subscriptions that the players had to pay. It is interesting to note that at this time of Women's Suffrage the club made a point of emphasising that two of the committee should be female :-

An extraordinary general meeting of the St. Philip's Tennis Club was held at the Café Royal on Friday last week, when the principal point round which discussion centred was the question of the preparation of courts for next year and whether the club should be content with having one court properly laid out or prepare two courts. After consideration it was decided to adopt the latter course. It was decided to raise the subscription to 15s. for gentlemen and 12s. 6d. for ladies. Other business transacted at the meeting included the election of four committeemen to fill vacancies. It was decided that two of the committee should be ladies, and the choice of the meeting fell upon Miss Woolcott and Mrs. Stammers. The Rev. L. N. Woolley and Messrs. Pollard, Robinson and Moulton were elected to the remaining places. The resignation of Mr. W. J. Grinham was recorded with regret, and a hearty vote of thanks for his past services was passed unanimously. It was arranged that for the present Messrs. J. K. Allen and A. E. Marshall should add the duties of hon. treasurer to their existing ones of hon. secretaries."

Despite the fact that initials are absent from several of the committee members in the above account, and despite the fact that the characters obviously attracted a smaller amount of press interest than the members of the Worcester Park L.T.C., it soon became apparent that the less wealthy Cheam Common Tennis Club had drawn some highly respectable and interesting members of the local community into its fold, such as the ex-committee member, **William John Grinham** (b. 1874), who had to retire from the committee when he and his wife, Bonella, and their daughter, moved from 'Wapella', St. Philip's Avenue, to Coulsdon. Like his father, William was a master gold and silver engraver, and as such, was able to afford the luxury of a servant.

The driving force behind this new tennis club was probably the **Reverend Leonard Napier Woolley,** who spent about eight years from 1907 to 1915 as the vicar of St. Philip's. Leonard had been born in London and had attended Regent's Park College, where he had obtained his M. A., and was ordained in 1897. He married a local girl in 1910, Kathleen Mary Hanbury, from Ewell, and they had two children whilst at Cheam, and another boy when they moved to Lambeth in 1915. Although he was not as wealthy as many of the clergy, Leonard also managed to afford a servant to help his wife with looking after the children and the rectory. One of his main concerns as vicar of the parish, which appeared in the 'Comet' on several occasions, seems to have been the spiralling cost of funerals.

The only other member of the committee who seemed wealthy enough to warrant a servant was **Arthur Edward Marshall** (b. 1876), a civil service clerk, 2nd division, higher grade. Arthur had been born in Barton-on-Irwell, Manchester, the son of a schoolteacher. Arthur lived at 'Tacoma', St. Philip's Avenue, for three or four years before 1911, but by the time of the census he was living with his wife, three young children and a sixteen year old servant, at 'The Cottage', Oatlands Avenue, Weybridge. He must have made some good friends among the members of the church, during his stay in the parish of St. Philip's for him to take on the role of secretary and treasurer, despite living so far away.

George Moulton (b. 1859) was probably the oldest person on the committee and, along with A. E. Marshall, was another Mancunian. He and his wife Emily, in 1911, were living at 'Cheviot', St. Philip's Avenue. The census reveals that George was retired and living off his own means. There is no clue online as to what business George had been engaged in.

It is interesting to note that the Cheam Common Tennis Club had shown their support of the Women's Suffrage Movement by electing two ladies to their committee, although at first glance these did appear to be two extremely safe choices. Both were in their early 40s and lived locally. **Amy Stammers** (b 1871) lived at 'The Limes' Cheam Hill with her husband, William Archer Stammers, a building surveyor and their two young children, whilst **Mary Judith Woolcott**[21] (b. 1872) was a spinster, who lived in the School House of St. Philip's School with her father. Mary, however, was not a typical reserved, prim and proper Edwardian spinster. Throughout her whole life she displayed an independent and adventurous streak which must have been an example to all those who espoused the cause of Women's Suffrage.

Whether the subscription charges proved too much, or the club failed to provide two courts to play on, for some reason the tennis club failed to prosper in 1912, and by the end of the year there were fears that the club might have to close. On January 25th, 1913, under the striking heading '*CHEAM COMMON LAWN TENNIS CLUB*', the 'Comet' reported that: *"It is understood that the Cheam Common Lawn Tennis Club is not to be allowed to become defunct, as was once feared, without a determined effort to revive it. Local influence is being brought to bear on the club guarantors, and a few friends of the club are promoting a social evening at the Malden and Cuddington Institute on Friday. There is every reason to believe that the club will be re-opened, if a membership of forty can be guaranteed. This should not be found impossible in a residential district of the character of Worcester Park, the inhabitants of which have such a reputation for sportsmanship. The names of intending members will be gladly received by Mr. A. E. Marshall, The Cottage, Oatlands Avenue, Weybridge, who will willingly furnish any information desired."*

In a way this desperate cry for help, by a local sports club, to the people of Worcester Park, was a precursor of a situation that would occur on several occasions in the following thirty years for the Athletic Club. Whist drives and dances, especially at the Institute, were to become a tried and tested format for fund raising. The following, however, is the first account to appear in the 'Comet' of one of these events: *Cheam Common Tennis Club - Under the auspices of the Cheam Common Tennis Club a whist drive and dance was held at the Malden and Cuddington Club on Friday in last week. There were about 60 ladies and gentlemen present. The first half of the evening was occupied by the drive. Mr. W. Marshall acting as driver. The prize winners were Mrs. Robins and Mr. Dawes. After refreshments, served under the superintendence of Mrs. Creed, the company spent the remainder of the time in dancing, the music being provided by Mrs. Lavell and Miss Carter."*

Whether the club managed to acquire the requisite number of members to continue is not recorded, but all play would have had to cease the following year to make way for the conflict in Europe. Although there is no indication as to whether the Cheam Common Tennis Club was resurrected in 1919, tennis still appeared to remain a highly popular sport in the Cheam area. Tennis was no longer just the purview of only the privileged of society, as it had been in 1879, but in post war Britain was available to most people, as can be seen by the fact that the newly created Cheam Cricket and Sports Club, at the far end of the parish, had 126 tennis members in 1920 ('West Sussex Gazette', 23rd September, 1920), whilst even at the poorer end of the borough the newly formed Worcester Park Athletic Club had had to limit the number of tennis members to sixty by 1923, and increase the number of courts to twelve.

Appendix of Tennis Players

[1]**Reverend William Chetwynd Stapylton,** the President of the Tennis Club, was born on the 15th May, 1825, at Cockglode, Nottinghamshire, the third son of Henry Richard Chetwynd Stapylton, a Major in the 10th Hussars, and Margaret Hammond. As with many of his family he was educated at Eton, where he went in 1837. There he proved to be a remarkable, all-round oarsman by winning the sculling, double sculling and the pair oared races. The last event he won on three successive occasions, thereby creating a record which was not equalled for over 60 years.

William also rowed at bow in the Eton Eight against Westminster in 1842 and in 1843. besides featuring as the Second Captain of the Boats in the Regatta in 1843. Following Eton, he went to Merton College to study Classics and rowed for the University Eight in 1844, 1845 and 1846. In 1847 he obtained his B.A., and became a Fellow of Merton College from 1847 to 1851. He was ordained into the Clergy in 1849 and received his Master's degree in 1853.

Following the death of the Rev. George Trevelyan at Old Malden in 1850, Merton College found it difficult to find an incumbent for such a dilapidated church, until William volunteered to occupy the position for two years. As his long time friend, Archdeacon Avison T. Scott wrote in the 'Kent & Sussex Courier' in April 1919, *"He accepted in 1850 the living of Old Malden, in Surrey. 'Muddy Malden', as the village was often called, was then a very out-of-the way place, with shockingly bad roads, and Church life was at a very low ebb. The Holy Communion was celebrated but three times in a year. And not only were there the old fashioned high pews in the Church, but these high pews were locked. With characteristic vigour the new Vicar knocked off those locks, only to find them replaced by the Secular power."* This was a reference to William's initial conflict with Thomas Weeding, who eventually gave the new Vicar his grudging support.

Being the Vicar of St. John the Baptist, Old Malden, was a post that he was to hold for forty four years, during which time he became an extremely important and respected member of the local community. He was also appointed in 1878 as a Hon. Canon of the Rochester Diocese.

On the 26th October, 1852, William married Elizabeth Biscoe Tritton, the daughter of the Rev. Robert Tritton and Mary Biscoe, and they had four children, Ella (b. 1854), Edward (b.1855), Frederick (b. 1857) and Granville (b.1858). William continued to live at the Rectory until the death of his wife in 1893, when he decided to leave the area and move to Hallaton in Leicestershire, where he was the Rector until 1907, and where he married Mary Elizabeth Johnson (b. 1851) in 1895. Mary was one of William's old parishioners from Worcester Park, who, in 1891, was still living at home with her younger brother, Henry Elliott Johnson, who had played tennis in the club's first match against the Iceni in 1879.

For the final few years of his life, William, who still maintained a *"fine athletic figure and upright carriage",* moved to Tunbridge Wells where he continued to work in the local parish of St. James's. When he died on March 4th 1919, in Tunbridge Wells, at the age of 93, he was buried at St. John's Church, Old Malden, whilst his long time friend Archdeacon Avison T. Scott conducted a memorial service at St. James's. For a clergyman he must have been quite wealthy as he left an estate of £9,458 to his two surviving sons, Edward and Frederick.

[2]**Henry Elliott Johnson** (b.1855, Pimlico) undoubtedly seemed to have been an extremely popular character and was one of the central characters in the story of the Worcester Park Tennis Club, where his life certainly seemed to connect in one way or another with most of the other members. Henry played tennis, golf and hunted with several of the members; he formed a legal partnership with Cyrus Waddilove and one of his sisters married the widowed vicar, Canon William C. Stapylton.

Henry was another solicitor associated with the club, and lived most of his life in Cuddington, although the 1871 census showed that he was a boarder at the Royal Grammar School, Guildford. At the time of the 1881 census, he was living with his mother, various aunts, two sisters and step father in part of 'Abberley House', which they shared with the family of John Alick Thomas. Life must have been quite hard for the family as there was only a cook and a housemaid to cater for their needs.

Henry remained a bachelor until he married Edith Caroline McKenzie Merriman, the daughter of Septimus Merriman from Old Malden, in 1907, when he was fifty-two and she was thirty four. They were married by the Rev. William C. Stapylton at St. John's Church, Old Malden, with Arthur J. Stanley as one of the witnesses. They lived at 'Copsemead'. Worcester Park, until Edith died in 1914. Henry died on July 3rd, 1925, when he left about £25,000. One of Edith's brothers, Hugh Maskelyne Merriman, an underwriter, was an executor of the will.

[3]**Cyrus Waddilove** (b. 1827) had been the veteran of the Worcester Park tennis team, when they played the Iceni in 1879. He had been born at 13, Welbeck Street, Marylebone, the son of Edward, a gentleman bootmaker, who worked in Montague Place and who later became the J.P. for Southampton.

It is probable that Cyrus studied law at King's College, which had a prominent Law Department, as he was recorded as having played cricket for the college on several occasions in 1850 and 1851. Cyrus followed in the steps of his brother, Edward, and qualified as a solicitor in 1858, and appeared to specialise in church affairs.

In the 1870s Cyrus became the Registrar for the Archdeaconry of Middlesex, and following that he became the Registrar for the Archdeaconry of London. In the mid-1880s he formed a legal partnership with Henry E. Johnson, and their office was at the delightfully named 28, Night Rider Street, Doctors' Commons E.C. Cyrus was also one of the proctors of the Doctors' Commons and towards the end of his career he became the Deputy Registrar for the Arches Court of Canterbury.

In 1859, Cyrus had married Louisa Shepherd in Shirley, and at some point in the following decade they moved to 'Worcester Park House' with their three sons and three daughters, where they were looked after by five servants. Cyrus had first appeared upon the local sporting scene in 1872 when he played in one of the first ever recorded cricket matches for Worcester Park, and the following year turned out for Cuddington C.C.

Despite being over fifty when the W.P.L.T.C. played the Iceni in 1879, and despite being much older than his team mates, Cyrus was singled out by the 'Comet' for his fine play: *"Mr. Waddilove's admirable judgement and marvellous power of placing his ball in the place where his opponent was not, were once more prominently conspicuous. We sincerely trust that this year we may see this undoubtedly fine player enter for the Wimbledon Cup, and we should be much surprised if his generalship and sang froid, combined with the natural advantage which he possesses in his enormous reach, did not give him 'advantage' over most of his more youthful competitors."*

It appears that Cyrus, apart from playing for Worcester Park L.T.C., was also a member of the All England L.T.C. as he took part in their members' handicap competition, at Wimbledon, that year, which was the best of five sets. He succeed in winning his first round match against Mr. W. M. Bird (6-2, 6-4, 6-4), but then succumbed to Mr. A. Eveleigh, in a tight match, three sets to two.

Cyrus died at 13, The Drive, Hove, on the 27th February, 1904, with his old tennis and business partner, Henry E. Johnson, being named as the executor of the £28,000 that he left. The majority of his money was left in trust to his widow to provide her with an income until either she died or re-married.

[4]**Arthur Pollock** (b. 1849) had been born in Plymouth to Selina Mary Eccles, from Lancashire, and Arthur Becher Pollock. Although his parents had been married in the Church of England, Arthur was baptised, in 1851, in a Non-Conformist ceremony in Regent's Square.

It is probably not surprising that Arthur, like several of the players associated with the Tennis Club, was a solicitor, as he came from a legal family. His grand-father, Sir David Pollock, had been the Master of the Bench in the Middle Temple, and sometime Chief Justice of Bombay, whilst his father, after being educated at Westminster School and Trinity Hall, Cambridge, had been called to the bar in 1846. Like his father before him, Arthur's office was based in Lincoln's Inn Fields.

Although there is no record of Arthur's education, the sports papers of the time show that he became heavily involved with Athletics in his late teens and participated primarily in sprint and hurdle events, often with great success. Initially he competed for both the South Norwood A. C. and the Brixton Amateur A. C., and then for the London Athletic Club. Whilst at the L.A.C. he also took part in a 150 yard swimming race in the Thames at Teddington in 1872. By the mid to late 1870s, Arthur became more of an official at events and was often called upon to act as either a judge or a starter.

Arthur was also singled out for his skilful play in a football match, in 1869, in which he played for Brixton versus Crystal Palace. He did not, however, have an extensive career as a footballer, although he was also recorded in 1876 and 1877 as playing a couple of rugby matches for Wasps, as a forward, versus Harlequins and Richmond.

In July 1877, Arthur married the sister of a fellow athlete, Marion Cockerell, at St. George's, Hanover Square. It would appear that the newly married couple must have settled in Worcester Park for a couple of years following their marriage, as their son, Vivian Arthur, was born there in 1879, which was also the year that Arthur presented the Tennis Club with a Challenge trophy. Two years later, however, the family had re-located to 'Ashleigh', Arthur Road, Wimbledon, which needed six servants for it to operate to their satisfaction.

No mention of Arthur as a tennis player occurs in the sporting press until after his arrival in Worcester Park. It is highly probable that he really honed his tennis skills at 'Wighill', and very quickly became one of the best players in the club. His career as a player, however, did not seem to last long, although he did make a couple of appearances at Wimbledon, his second appearance being in 1883 as a line-judge. Six years later, he was also listed as one of the committee members of the All England Lawn Tennis Club that staged the 1889 Championship, along with Henry W. Horne and Arthur J. Stanley.

Arthur and Marion were clearly one of the leading couples in Wimbledon society in the late Victorian era, and were regularly recorded at the top of guest lists for various events, such as weddings, funerals and balls. Their social status must have received a boost when they moved to 'Somerset Lodge', at the end of the century with a staff of seven servants, including a butler and groom.

As he drifted towards middle age, the sports that he favoured reflected his social standing. Foremost amongst his sporting activities was grouse shooting, from the Glorious 12th of August to the 10th of December each year, in Scotland, where he would rent a shooting lodge for his friends and clients for a complete season. His friends must have been very impressed in 1886, when *"The mansion-house of 'Noranside' with the shootings of Noranside and Coul have been let for the season to Mr. Arthur Pollock, solicitor, London."* ('Dundee Evening Telegraph' Thursday 29th July, 1886.)

His visits to the Highlands perhaps fostered his love of golf, which was to remain a passion of his for over forty years. In 1889 he joined the Royal Wimbledon G.C., and, in February, playing off a handicap of 14, won the first medal that he entered. By the following February, whilst playing off a handicap of 12, he repeated the feat, which warranted the following comment in 'The Field':- *"The medal was won by Mr. Arthur Pollock, whose allowance of 12 odds will doubtless be attended to by the handicapping committee."*

Four months later, in June 1890, despite having had his handicap reduced to nine he won yet another medal for a competition between the Royal Wimbledon and the London Scottish G. C. His victory fostered the following comment in 'The Field' of June 21st:- *"As will be seen by the scores appended, the medal, which becomes the absolute property of the winner, was carried off by Mr. Arthur Pollock, of the Royal Wimbledon G.C. A most popular win, and that with a score that would have contented a scratch player."* (Gross 88 - Net 79)

Whilst Arthur played at some prestigious clubs such as St. George's, Sandwich, and the Royal and Ancient G. C., his wife, Marion, seemed almost as competitive. She joined the Wimbledon Ladies G.C. and often figured amongst the best players in their medal competitions. Perhaps her competitive streak made her a hard task master to work for as a servant, as advertisements seemed to recur in the press on a regular basis for maids to work at 'Somerset Lodge'.

Apart from being an excellent sportsman, Arthur appears to have been quite successful and popular as a solicitor, if the will of one of his old tennis and golfing opponents is to be believed. When Herbert Fortesque Lawford, of the Conservative Club, St. James's, died in 1925, he left £3,000 to Arthur, out of a total of £86, 221 *"in grateful recognition of skilful advice,"* and a request that he act as solicitor to the trust. To his servant he left his knickerbocker suits and motoring coats.

As fate would have it, when Arthur Pollock died on November 4th, 1931, aged 82, he was living at the Golf Hotel, Woodhall Spa, Lincolnshire. Despite his lavish lifestyle, according to the 'Lincolnshire Standard and Boston Guardian' he left almost £52,000. The main bequest was £1,000 a year to his wife, £2,000 to his daughter and £200 to John Oliver Foster, the cashier of Pollock and Co., Lincoln's Inn Fields. The remainder was to be put in trust for his son and daughter.

[5]**Edward Chetwynd Stapylton** (b. 1855) was the eldest son of the Reverend W. C. Stapylton and had been born and brought up in the Vicarage in Old Malden. Neither he nor his brothers followed their father to Eton and then to University, but entered the world of commerce. In September 1879, Edward was married by his father, at St. John's Church, to Mary Beatrice Cowie. The 1881 census revealed that Edward was a wine merchant, who lived with his wife and nine month old son,

Richard, and a couple of servants at 'Henley Lodge'. By the time of the 1891 census, however, four young daughters had appeared on the scene, plus a nurse, and they lived at 'Wighill', with a couple of gardeners' cottages nearby, so that the tennis courts could be kept in pristine condition. Wighill is a small village in Yorkshire from where part of the family hailed. In 1895, his first son, William Eric, was born.

Apart from tennis, Edward had played cricket for Worcester Park, with Henry Johnson, against the Meteors in May 1874, when he scored 9* and Henry 3*, and in 1875 and 1876, at an age where many of his contemporaries were at University, he spent the winter playing rugby, at half-back, for Ravenscourt Park.

His main form of recreation, as he grew older, however, was hunting with the Worcester Park Beagles and playing golf. He might possibly have been one of the original members of Epsom Golf Club, which had been founded in 1889. He was certainly a member there in 1891 as, playing off a handicap of 20, he came second in the September medal competition.

As Epsom was only a nine hole course in the early days, and as the annual subscription was only 10s. 6d. in 1890, it is not surprising that Edward and his friends sought longer and more interesting clubs at which to play. By 1894, while still remaining an Epsom member, Edward had also become a member of the Royal Wimbledon Golf Course, where his handicap had improved to twelve, and at about the same time he appears to have joined Littlestone Golf Club, a links course on the Kent coast.

Edward did not seem to figure in the golfing press as often as Henry Johnson or the Stanley brothers, possibly because he had three sons and four daughters at home. By the turn of the century he was still living at 'Wighill' and his golf handicap had only crept up to eleven. By the time of the 1911 census, Edward, his wife, and only one son and daughter, were living at 'Larchfield' which was quite a modest ten roomed house in Weybridge, where they were waited upon by only a cook and parlour maid. Mary Beatrice died in 1923 and Edward passed away in 1938, at Hove.

[6]**Henry Warlters Horne** (b. 1846) was the eldest son of a barrister and was born at 26, Montague Square, Marylebone. He was educated at Rugby and New College, Oxford, from where he graduated with a B.A. in 1870, and was surprisingly listed as still being a law student, living in Kingston on the 1871 census. That, however, was also the year that he was called to the bar at the Inner Temple.

Cricket appears to have been Henry's main sporting interest as a youngster, although all the signs are that his enthusiasm for the sport greatly exceeded his ability. His name crops up on cricket score sheets on at least a dozen occasions in either 'Bell's Life', 'The Sporting Gazette' or 'The Field', during his final year at Rugby, although he never played for the First XI. He tended to play either for the Second XI or the

'Next XI', or in intra-school matches and, on most of those occasions, he was usually not out, batting at number ten or eleven, and never appeared to bowl. On one glorious occasion, however, on April 29th, 1865, whilst playing for the 'Next XI - with Humphrey and Diver' versus the First XI, he scored 62 runs, out of a total of 125, whilst batting at number eight.

Henry did not let his lack of success at Rugby dampen his love of the game, and over the next four years he played numerous matches for New College, The Butterflies and the Conservatives. Although he never bowled, at least he rose to the top of the batting order on the odd occasion, and once, against Worcester College, he managed to score an undefeated 31 runs.

After being awarded a third class degree in classics in 1870, he continued to play cricket for a couple of years. In 1871 he is recorded as scoring a duck whilst batting at number five, for Hampton Wick versus Dulwich, in Bushey Park, and 37 runs in his only innings for the Butterflies. His main claim to fame on the local cricketing scene, however, was that he featured in the first ever recorded match by a Cuddington/Worcester Park side in July 1872, alongside Cyrus Waddilove.

On the 8th of April, 1874, Henry married Harriett Elizabeth Pollock, at Christ Church, Islington. Harriett was the younger sister of Arthur Pollock, who was also a witness at their wedding. Henry and Harriett were to have six children, all of whom were given the middle name of 'Pollock', just as Henry had inherited his mother's surname as part of his given name. Following the wedding the happy couple moved to 'Heston Lodge', Thornton Hill, Wimbledon and spent the remainder of their lives living in various pleasant homes in and around Wimbledon Village, where Henry was to become a much valued member of society. For several years, for example, he was the Chairman of the Free Library, and, more importantly, he was also one of the eight Conservators of Wimbledon Common, who had great power over the local bye-laws and any development on the Common.

Although Henry did not appear to be a particularly gifted tennis player, he certainly seemed to love the game, as he appeared in 1888, at the age of 42, taking part in a Veteran's event at the South of England Tournament in Devonshire Park, Eastbourne. He was also a committee member, in the late eighties, of the All England L.T.C., alongside his brother-in-law, Arthur Pollock, and A. J. Stanley.

Henry's main passion, once he turned forty, however, seemed to be golf and, along with H. H. Playford, was one of the first members of the Tennis Club to turn to golf as their main sport of choice. By 1887 he was already a member of the Royal Wimbledon G. C., and played off eighteen until March, 1889, when he won a silver salver for the four best monthly medal cards of the previous year, and his handicap was cut to thirteen. By 1895 his handicap had risen to about eight, before gradually falling back to ten, where it seemed to stay for the remainder of his playing career.

Although Henry's name does crop up as having played at both Warlingham G. C. and at the Hastings & St. Leonards Golf Club, the majority of his golf was played at the Royal Wimbledon G. C., where, as one of the Conservators of the Common, for over ten years, he was an exceedingly valued member, as feelings between the golfers and the locals weren't always amicable. Five of the Conservators had to be elected, for a term of three years, by the ratepayers living within three-quarters of a mile of the Common, and three were nominated by the War Office, the Board of Works and the Home Office respectively.

On March 20th, 1905, the 'Westminster Gazette' commented on the conflict, between the residents and the golfers in the following paragraph:- *"The golfers have of late become so prominent - if not, indeed, so aggressive - upon Wimbledon Common and Putney Heath that the privileges which they claim as against the rights of the general public form the burning topic at the approaching election of the Conservators of Wimbledon and Putney Commons."*

Fortunately for the future of the Royal Wimbledon G. C., Henry, and the other pro-Golf Club candidates were elected and the golf club survived. By this stage in his life, Henry, however, seemed to reduce his appearances upon the golf course, and by 1911, the only information available on him is that he and Harriett were living in a 17 room house at 38, East Hill House, Church Road, Wimbledon, with just two of their children and five servants. When he died there in 1918, he had spent at least half of his life serving the people of Wimbledon, and left a modest £22,000 to Harriett.

[7]**Frederick Stapylton** (b. 1857) was the second son of the Rev. William C. Stapleton, and like his elder brother, Edward, was one of the rocks upon which the Worcester Park L.T.C. was founded, and, like his elder brother, he did not appear to have attended a recognised public school or University. By the age of twenty three, in 1880, however, Frederick had already become a broker at the London Stock Exchange. One of his three guarantors for that post was the father of two other members of the club, Hall Rokeby Price, who was on the Board of the Stock Exchange for 32 years, and was to become its Chairman for the final seven years of his life, was a useful guarantor.

One of Frederick's main sporting interests in the 1880s, apart from tennis, was the thrill of the hunt, and he quickly volunteered to be the Secretary and Treasurer of the newly formed Worcester Park Beagles in 1886, before taking on the prestigious role of joint Master of the Hunt in 1889. It was not merely the local wildlife that was in danger when he was around, however, as a snippet in 'The Field' of October 1st, 1887, placed him, and Charles Stanley, at Noranside and Coul, in Forfarshire, where they were the guests of Arthur Pollock. On the first day of a week-long killing spree, they accounted for 33 partridges, 29 hares, 47 rabbits, and 1 capercaillie.

In the 1890s, like most of the other tennis players, Frederick also became addicted to golf and played at Epsom, Littlestone and the Royal Wimbledon Golf Club. He had a reasonable handicap, which seemed to hover between ten and twelve, and he was usually quite highly placed in the monthly medal competitions. On one occasion, in 1896, 'The Globe' recorded that Frederick was one of five members, who tied for the Littlestone Club's Denge Trophy.

Although Frederick's office was at first in the Cornhill Chambers and then at 24, Lombard Street, he remained living at the Old Malden Rectory until he married Maud Morrison, the only daughter of a banker, William Hiram Morrison (b.1844) of Hudson City, New York, on the 27th June 1891. The marriage was performed by his father at St. John's Church, Old Malden. William was assisted in performing the ceremony by his brother-in-law, the Rev. Robert Tritton, from Bognor, .

Following their marriage, Frederick and Maud went to live at 'Park View', Leopold Road, Wimbledon, in a house next door but one to Arthur Pollock, where they had two children, Alan and Helen Maud. Following the death of Alan, aged five, the couple moved to 'Englefield Lodge,' Englefield Green, in 1898. They remained there until they moved to Hatton Hill House, Farnham, in 1923, where Frederick lived until his death in 1942. He left £29,096 to his wife, as sadly both his children were already dead.

[8]**Reverend Avison Terry Scott** (b. 1848) was born in Cambridge and was the son of the Rev. John Scott, the Vicar of Wisbech. He went to school at Brighton College, and from there went to Trinity College, Cambridge, in 1867, and gained his 'Blue' for cricket in 1870 and 1871. In total he played 11 first class matches as a top order batsman for Cambridge. He also played for Cambridge Town, Gunton, the Iceni and Wimbledon, for whom he turned out, on an occasional basis, for six seasons.

Avison gained his B.A. and was ordained as a deacon in 1871, and moved to Swaffham, in Norfolk, where he worked as a curate for a couple of years, before a six year stint in Wimbledon, where he was to become a lifelong friend of William Chetwynd Stapylton. In 1874, he gained his Master's degree and married Dora, the daughter of the Rev. R. H. Tillard, at Blakeney in Norfolk. In total they had seven children, two girls and five boys, the eldest of whom, Charles Tillard Scott, played rugby for Cambridge and for England from 1899-1901.

For the final 35 years of his life the Rev. Scott lived in Tunbridge Wells where he became the Vicar of St. James's Church and an Archdeacon. When he died in 1925, he left £17,589 to his widow and eldest son.

[9]**Arthur John Stanley** (b. 1853) had been born on June 26th, in Kensington, to a wealthy stockbroker father, Charles, and his wife, Annie, who both hailed from Yorkshire. As a child, Arthur was educated at Repton, in Derbyshire, at the same time as his cousin, Auriol A. H. Barker, and, despite being three years younger,

played in the same cricket team. In February, 1872, Arthur gained admittance to Trinity College, Cambridge, where, although being recorded as playing cricket for his college against Clare College in 1873, his main sport appeared to be athletics, primarily sprint events. He was also recorded in 1873 as taking part in a 200 yard swimming handicap in a local river.

After Cambridge he became a serious competitor for the London Athletic Club and entered events as far afield as Littlehampton. Some of his performances were quite respectable, as he was recorded as winning the hundred yards on one occasion in a time of 11.5 seconds, and, on another occasion he won the wide jump with a jump of 17 foot 3 inches.

Although Arthur had played occasional games of cricket for the 'Old Reptonians' in the early 1870s, he seemed to take it up more seriously in the middle of the decade when he began to play cricket on a regular basis for several teams including Kensington Park, the 'Nondescripts', and the London branch of 'The Revellers', for whom he became a committee member, and a tourist to Cambridge in 1883.

Arthur's most surprising appearance on the cricket field, however, occurred, whilst on his tennis tour of the West Country in 1883, when he turned out for twelve men of South Devon against a similar number from Torquay. A. J. Stanley was to play a prominent role in the South Devon team's performance that day, as was recorded in a rather quaint and amusing short article which appeared in 'The East and South Devon Advertiser' on August 25th:-

"SOUTH DEVON V TORQUAY. This twelve a side match was played at Torquay, on the 23rd inst., on the most perfect cricket day of the season. The home team commenced the batting, and as the names of the eleven are well known in Devonshire, little need be said as to its strength. Lieut. Thomas and Mr. Rigby both played well for their runs, but Mr. Stanley's bowling was too much for the twelve, and their expectations of reaching 200 were cut short by his difficult 'breakers'. Captain Stiles of South Devon knew the strength of his men and 'placed' them accordingly. Mr. Mapleton again showed true county form for his 28, while Mr. Stanley played an admirable innings of 44. Mr. Patterson (an Uppingham Rover), hit clean and hard for his 21. Finally the South Devon closed for 142, or 35 runs on. When time was called Torquay in their second innings had lost their three best wickets for 62 runs. Thus the visitors scored another victory."

A. J. Stanley picked up eight of the eleven wickets to fall in the Torquay first innings, and batted at number five. At number four in the South Devon batting order was William Edward Martyn, who had partnered Arthur in the Doubles competition at Teignmouth, and who turned up the following year playing tennis for Worcester Park.

While Arthur entered the singles at Wimbledon from 1881 to 1885, without notable success, and was a losing finalist in the doubles in 1885 and 1886, the major sporting success in his life had to be on the football field where he was recorded as playing from 1874, either on the right wing or at right half for Clapham Rovers, often as captain. Although his team lost 1- 0 to the Old Etonians in the Cup Final of 1879, they beat Oxford University 1- 0, to win the F.A. Cup, at The Oval, in 1880.

In 1879, he was also recorded as having played, in the month before the Cup Final, for both 'The Remnants' in the semi-final of the Berkshire and Buckinghamshire Challenge Cup, and for 'The Casuals', whom he often captained. (This was four years before the formation of 'Corinthian Casuals'). Apart from these clubs he also regularly figured in the sports pages of the press, as appearing for Hendon, Hertfordshire Rangers and the Wednesday Club, and, after his career in football ended he tried his hand at hockey for Molesey, for a few games with his brother, Charles, and William E. Martyn of the Tennis Club.

Arthur was recorded on the 1881 census as living in the family home at 9, Lancaster Gate with his parents, his brother, Charles, and six sisters and six servants, whilst in 1901 he appeared as a visitor at the home of Henry E. Johnson in Cuddington. Perhaps he returned to Cuddington to brush up his tennis as he was to enter the doubles at Wimbledon again that year, at the age of 47, partnering H. Wilson, over a decade after his last entry in the event.

Not content with excelling at Athletics, Swimming, Cricket, Tennis and Football, Arthur was also a good golfer and played with his friends Henry Johnson and Edward Stapylton at the Littlestone Golf Club, where he had a handicap of 3, (in August 1901). The following month he was even selected to play golf for England in a three way Open Championship with the Irish and Scots at Dollymount, Dublin, His name seems to have appeared, in the sporting press, as playing at most of the top courses in the country such as the Royal Lytham and the Royal Liverpool, whilst in 1906, playing off a handicap of two, he came second in a competition in Cannes.

Unlike most of his team mates at the Worcester Park Tennis Club Arthur had no need for a large country house as he had no wife and family. His home, when he was not travelling around the country playing sport, was a fourth floor flat at the top of 5, Gray's Inn Square, Gray's Inn Road, W.C.1. It was a building of considerable historical interest as Sir Francis Romilly had lived there, and was about a mile away from the office that he shared with his brother, and other family members at 29, Cornhill E.C. 3. As much of the lower floors were occupied by solicitor's offices, the building would have been quite a quiet retreat during the evening.

On Wednesday, 27th February, 1929, at 4.30 a.m., a fire broke out on the first floor of the building and quickly spread along the ancient timbers to the fourth floor, where, the only resident in the building, a 76 year old Arthur J. Stanley lay asleep. A bitterly cold wind fanned the flames and extensive damage was done to the third and fourth floors, and part of the roof caved in. When the fire brigade arrived, the cold wind apparently froze the water from their hoses and icicles formed on their ladders

The fact that Arthur managed to survive was probably a tribute to his overall fitness and composure, despite his age. His account of the incident to a reporter from the 'Daily Echo', was reported in nearly all the major newspapers: *"I was sleeping on the top floor," he said, "I then realised that I was coughing. I roused myself properly to find the room full of smoke. I slung on an overcoat, and made for the door, but here the smoke was very dense and choking. I grabbed a sponge, soaked it in water, and put it into my mouth. I then managed to make my way downstairs through the thick smoke. It was very fortunate for me that the smoke aroused me, because the top of the building was soon well alight."*

By the time of his death, at the age of 82, on 16th July, 1935, Arthur was living within a stone's throw of where he had lived over 50 years before, in the ground floor apartment of 53, Lancaster Gate. Despite having spent a considerable amount of his life playing a variety of sports, he still managed to leave £18,000 in his will, a third of which went to his nephew, Evelyn Charles Stanley.

[10]**Charles Herbert Stanley** (b. 1852) had been born, at The Terrace, Hyde Park, barely a year before the birth of his more talented younger brother, Arthur, under whose shadow he must have lived all his life and, like his brother, he seemed to be obsessed with competing in as many sports as possible. There must have been not only a great sense of rivalry between the brothers on the athletic track and the tennis court, but also a great sense of camaraderie, as they often tended to play for the same teams at both football and tennis.

Like his brother, Charles was probably educated at Repton School in Derbyshire, as he was recorded as playing football for the Old Reptonians, alongside his brother, in December, 1872, against the Wanderers at the Oval, in a match that they lost 3-1, as apparently their team was not used to playing under Association rules.

Unlike his brother, however, his parents did not bother to send him to University, and the 1871 census saw him living at home with his parents and numerous sisters. His occupation at that time was listed as being 'a clerk', although by 1881 he had graduated to working at the Stock Exchange as a Broker.

Whilst Arthur was away at University, Charles took to the Thames and joined the Grove Park Rowing Club where he competed in events such as the coxed fours. It seems to have been a hobby that he maintained into his fifties, as in 1907, he was listed as being a competitor in the double sculls at the Datchet Regatta, although his team did not fare very well.

Like his brother, Charles was also quite an enthusiastic Athlete and tended to compete primarily in sprint events, often in the colours of Clapham Rovers F.C., for whom he played at football on numerous occasions, at either back or half back, and often with his brother from about 1877. Charles actually kept goal for Clapham Rovers, the F.A. Cup Holders, in October 1880, at Charterhouse School *"when the boys secured an easy victory by thee goals to 'love'."* His brother was the captain for what must have been an ignominious defeat.

Charles also played football in the late seventies and early eighties for the Casuals, Hendon and the Old Foresters, but towards the end of the eighties seemed to have moved his affection more towards hockey, where he played as a half back, for Molesey and Putney. Hockey was probably the one area where he excelled over his brother.

On the cricket field and the golf course there was no real comparison between the two brothers. Charles's only appearances on the cricket field tended to be as a non-bowling tail-ender. He was basically there to make the numbers up, whilst his brother was an extremely competent all-rounder.

On the golf course, although his handicap never rose above 12, he was a member of at least three quite prestigious golf courses: Southdown G.C., Sunningdale G.C. and Littlestone G.C. The difference in the play between the two brothers was highlighted quite strikingly in the following excerpts from an account of a Christmas meeting at the Littlestone Golf Club, which occurred in the 'Illustrated Sporting and Dramatic News' of December 29th, 1894, whilst one brother won his match by seven and six, the other lost by the same score. *"there was no mistaking the character of the defeat which Mr. A. J. Stanley inflicted on Mr. J. Fleming, as seven up with six to play gives no room for flukiness.......In the match between Mr. Gibbins and Mr. C. H. Stanley the former had a very easy task indeed as when twelve holes had been played he was the large number of seven holes to the good.."*

Unlike his brother, Charles certainly had a life outside sport, and, on 22nd August, 1889, he married Evelyn Gertrude Turing Lawford, the sister of Herbert Fortescue Lawford, the 1887 Wimbledon Champion, at Christ Church, Lancaster Gate. The newly married couple moved to 'Littlecroft' Datchet, before relocating to the much larger thirteen roomed mansion 'Holmwood', Eton Road, Datchet, where by 1901, the couple already had three children, Ronald Bruce, Evelyn Charles and Gertude Joan, and as a symbol of his wealth, Charles and the family were looked after by a cook, a house maid, a parlour maid, a kitchen maid, a nurse maid and a domestic nurse. An elderly gardener also lived in a small cottage in the grounds.

Apart from playing a variety of sports, Charles also seemed to find some time to pursue his career as a stockbroker, and in March, 1900, he was appointed Secretary of the Institute of London Underwriters. He shared an office at 29, Cornhill E.C.

with his brother, Arthur, where they were joined after the First World War, by his second son, Evelyn Charles. His eldest son, Ronald Bruce, a Captain in the R.A.F., had survived the War, only to die in the Military Hospital, in Sunderland, in March, 1919. When Charles, himself, died in 1931, his sporting and opulent lifestyle meant that his widow, Evelyn, only received a rather modest £4,044.

[11]**Francis Durant** (b. 1856) had been born at 26, Park Street, St. George's, Hanover Square, to Eva Dora Ann Vardon and Charles James Durant, an exceedingly wealthy silk broker. In 1861, Francis and his twin sister, Mabel Elizabeth, were being brought up in a household which was looked after by a butler, a governess and five servants. Francis was probably educated at Eton as he cropped up as playing for a joint Eton and Winchester cricket team versus the Rev. Gepp's XI in 1871.

As a tennis player, Francis really sprang to prominence in 1879 when he was a losing double's finalist, alongside, yet another solicitor, George E. Tabor, in the Oxford University Lawn Tennis Challenge Cup, in May, and the Wimbledon Gentlemen's Doubles in July. On both occasions, the pair, who represented Cheam, were beaten by L. R. Erskine and H. F. Lawford (Carlton LTC). In June of 1879 he represented the All England Tennis Club against Oxford University, at Wimbledon, in an easy 8-1 victory. The following month, despite having been eliminated in the first round of the Singles at Wimbledon, by the highly fancied Mr. V. St. Leger, the winner of the Irish Championship, he did win his first round of the All England L.T.C. handicap for members, and perhaps more importantly he did succeed in winning the Worcester Park Challenge Cup for the first time.

In 1880 his father, who had been a member of the Company of Fishmongers for almost thirty years, managed to get his son enrolled in that ancient body and with it he gained the Freedom of the City of London. Francis was by this stage a silk merchant like his father, and the family were living at Cheam House, in what is now Cheam Park, with only a small retinue of servants: a butler, a cook, a house maid and a kitchen maid. The House was destroyed by a flying bomb in 1944, although the old Stable Block, which has been converted into a nursery, still remains.

Although he continued to play tennis throughout the 1880s, he disappeared from the sports pages in about 1890 and his only mention thereafter was either work related or as a society figure. In 1907 he married Dulce Ada Nina Baddeley, the daughter of a stockbroker, who was 27 years his junior. They had one son, Bryan Cecil Durant, who went on to become a Rear Admiral, and the three of them lived in a 14 room mansion in Hanover Square, where they were waited upon by six maidservants. They also had a chauffeur, who sadly wrote off their car in 1909 on what is now the Kingston Bye-Pass, close to the Robin Hood Inn. He crashed into the back of a large wagon and horses, and received head injuries when he was hurled out of the vehicle. The horses bolted and were eventually halted by a witness to the crash.

Francis and Dulce certainly became leading society figures in Edwardian London and regularly made the gossip columns. For Xmas 1909, for example, they stayed at the Hotel Gassion at Pau, whilst the following Christmas they were guests at the Hotel Cap Martin, along with Mr. and Mrs. David Lloyd George. They were also able to travel to exotic places, such as Buenos Aires and Marseilles, as Francis pursued his work both as the Official Silk Broker of the Kashmir State and a board member of the Silk Association of Great Britain.

When Francis died in 1921, at his Devonshire Square home, he left over seventeen thousand pounds to his still elegant and vivacious, thirty eight year old widow, Dulce. Her period of mourning was definitely brief as a few months later, in May 1922, a full length portrait of her, by F. Cadogan Cowper, was one of the leading exhibits at the Royal Academy. She was hardly painted in widow's weeds but in *"a white satin dress, gracefully draped with lace and festooned with ropes of pearl; the train is of lace, while the corsage is almost composed of it; telling touches are the large magnolia at the waist and the white feather fan with mother of pearl sticks."* ('The Sphere')

[12]**Arthur Rokeby Price** (b. 1854) was the eldest son of Hall R. Price, and although he attended Rugby until the age of eighteen there is no record of him going to university. In fact, in February 1874, when he might have been at university, he was playing Rugby, as a forward, for Sutton versus Hendon. In 1881 he was still living at home in Pitt Place, Epsom, and worked as a stockbroker in the City. That year, thanks to his father, and the Guild of Ironmongers, he received the Freedom of the City of London.

Unlike most of his fellow Tennis Club members, he did not become a golfer, or follow the hounds, but seemed to devote himself to work, and in 1905 was elected to the Committee of the Stock Exchange. By the time of his death in October, 1912, he was still working as a stockbroker and living the life of a wealthy bachelor at 'High Housen' in Woking. In a way the household was quite modest as it only had eight rooms, a butler, a housekeeper and a parlour maid. As a result of his frugal lifestyle, he managed to leave almost £110,000, which would equate to over eight million pounds today.

[13]**Wilfrid Thomas Rokeby Price** (b. 1856), the second of the two sons of Hall Rokeby Price, did not follow his brother to Rugby but went to Winchester College, from where he won a place at New College, Oxford, to study Modern History. Wilfrid was the more athletic of the two brothers, and the newspapers of the time show that he was a regular competitor in the College Sports Days, taking part in several events, over the course of four years, ranging from the hundred yards to the half mile, plus the hurdles and putting the shot.

Wilfrid played in several tennis competitions whilst at New College, and also took part in an eliminator to see who should represent Oxford at tennis. Although he won the first round of the competition he failed to get his 'Blue' for tennis. He did, however, prove to be quite successful at cricket in June 1878 , by scoring 54 runs, out of a total of 158, for New College, in a losing cause, against his old school, Winchester College. Winchester scored 211 for eight, whilst one of their players, A. H. Rooper, had his one moment of fame, which the paper failed to mention, as he picked up all ten New College wickets.

After finishing university Wilfrid became an assistant solicitor and continued to live at the family home in Epsom. Apart from being a member of the Worcester Park L.T.C. he became a committee member of the Epsom Athletic Club in their inaugural season of 1884. In November of that year, he also captained a team from Epsom against the Chamois (Carshalton) at Association Football. He played on the right wing and scored the opening goal in a five - nil victory.

Following his marriage in 1888 to Emily Catherine Murray, the daughter of a solicitor, of 'Woodcote Hall', Epsom, the family moved to Watford, where he became yet another of the Tennis Club members to work as a solicitor. The couple had two sons and three daughters, before they returned to Surrey in the early years of the Twentieth Century, to live at 'Eddlewood', Weybridge, . At about the same time, in 1904, Wilfrid's father, Hall Rokeby Price, who had been a member of the Company of Ironmongers for fifty seven years, managed to get his son the Freedom of the City of London through his membership of that august body.

When Wilfrid died in August, 1926, at the Cottage Hospital in Tenby, he left what might be considered to be a rather modest sum of £9,589 in his will, in comparison to his brother's fortune. He had, however, had a wife and five children, plus the mandatory servants to support.

[14]**Alfred Charles Waddilove** (b. 1862), the eldest son of Cyrus and Louisa Waddilove, was born on February 27th at Devonshire Terrace, Marylebone, and was about seven years old when the family moved to Cuddington. He was a boarder at Tonbridge School where he proved to be a good all round sportsman. He was recorded in 1880 as playing for the Rugby team, as a three quarter back, and for the Cricket XI he opened the bowling and batted mid-order. Alfred also took part in the School Swimming contest, which was held in the River Medway, where he entered the diving contests. His best performances in sport, however, occurred on the athletics' track. In the Tonbridge Sports' Day of 1880 he won both the half-mile and the mile races. He certainly seemed to possess stamina, as is shown by this short description of the mile race in 'The Field':- *"Leggat made the running for the first two laps, and then retired. Hamilton then led till the last lap, when Waddilove passed him after a hard struggle, and kept his place to the end."*

In 1881, Alfred went to Trinity Hall, Cambridge where he continued to perform as an athlete, by coming second in the half mile handicap in the College Sports' Day. Although there was no mention of his playing tennis, at either Tonbridge or Trinity, he was obviously an enthusiastic player, as, apart from playing for Worcester Park L.T.C., he was recorded as travelling to Eggesford to enter the Mid-Devon Tennis Tournament, in 1882, where he reached the Second Round in the Singles and the Third Round in the Doubles.

On the 1st of July, 1891 Alfred married Edith Adella Newson, the youngest of six daughters of an architect who lived in Molesey. The marriage, which occurred at All Saints Church, Kingston, lasted less than a year as Alfred died at Canada de Gomez, Santa Fe, Argentina, on June 4th, 1892. Whether he was working there, or on holiday, or whether he was buried there is a mystery, as there is no mention of his death in any of the newspapers. What is more surprising is the fact that it took a further seven years for probate to be passed on the £115 6s. 6d. that he left to his widow, who, by that stage had married Algernon Boardman Dickson, a wealthy underwriter, in 1895, and lived at Shanklin on the Isle of Wight.

[15]**John Alick Thomas** (b. 1854), had been born at Stansted Abbotts, Hertfordshire, one of six children of a clergyman, who had married, Louisa Ann, a lady from Jamaica. Apart from a brief mention in a match report that he was the Hon. Sec. of W.P.L.T.C., the fact that he was an important member of the club might have been missed. He was probably a keen social player who was not quite talented enough to make the team, or none of the matches, that he played in, were reported. There is certainly no mention of him appearing for any sport in 'Bell's Life' or 'The Field' before about 1893, when he turned up as yet another member of Littlestone Golf Club with the likes of Henry Johnson, the Stapyltons and the Stanleys. His greatest golfing achievement, however, probably came when playing in the Hunstanton Resident's Cup, in August 1901, when he won the cup by two shots, playing off a handicap of eleven.

After leaving school John Alick trained as an architect at the practice of William Slater and Richard Carpenter, between 1871 and 1874. Following a stint sketching in Normandy, he set up the practice of Whitfield and Thomas, in 1878, with Richard Osborne Whitfield. Over the next thirty years, or so, he was responsible for designing many of the new houses in the Worcester Park area, including 'The Croft', which became his own home. Apart from houses, his main talent seemed to be in designing churches, of which St. Mary's, Cuddington, is probably the best example. He also designed the new clubhouse at Littlestone Golf Club, which presumably made him one of the most valuable members of the club.

Following the death of his mother in 1888, John Alick married Kate Edith Florence Fairbank, the daughter of a Yorkshire landowner, on May 13th, 1890, at St. John's

Church, Old Malden, with the Reverend, William C. Stapylton officiating. One of the witnesses to the wedding, yet again, was the popular Arthur John Stanley, who seemed to be intrinsically linked to so many of the Worcester Park Club members.

The happy couple lived initially at 'Elm House' before moving in to the newly built 'The Croft'. They had three children, a daughter and two sons. Tragically both sons were to die in the Great War. His eldest son, twenty three year old, Captain Alick Vaughan Thomas, died attacking the Turkish trenches at Gallipoli in 1915, whilst twenty two year old Lieutenant Maurice Wotton Thomas died, as a member of the Royal Flying Corps, in 1916, at the Somme.

John Alick Thomas continued his love affair with golf, however, after the Great War, and, according to David Rymill was still playing golf at the age of eighty at the prestigious Coombe Hill Golf Club. He died on the 12th of February, 1940, at the age of 86, leaving his widow, Kate, at 'The Croft', with just one parlour maid as the cook had been called up for war work.

[16]**James Henry Skrine Hanning** (b. 1854) had been born in Park Lane, Marylebone, the eldest son of Frances Catherine Skrine and James Hanning, who was a landowner and Justice of the Peace for County Cork. Not a lot is known about the younger James's sporting prowess apart from the fact that he did play at least one match for W.P.L.T.C., on a day when the team failed to perform well.

The family had lived in Berkshire and Sussex prior to their arrival at 'Hartlands' in Worcester Park, in the late 1870s, following the death of their mother in Dieppe, in 1878. The 1881 census showed that the household, at that time, appeared to be comprised of the widowed James, the younger James, four of his siblings, a cook, a house maid, a parlour maid, and a 14 year old local girl, who was an under housemaid.

When his father died in 1881, James, a young Chartered Accountant, must have assumed the role of Head of the family, and two years later, on the 11th of October, 1883, he married his next door neighbour, Annie Louisa Thomas, of 'Abberley House'. The wedding, at St. John's Church, Old Malden, turned out to be quite a family affair, as the happy couple were married by James's younger brother, Clement Hugh Hanning, a curate at Brenchley in Kent, and the witnesses were John Alick Thomas, the bride's uncle, Herbert H. Skrine, the groom's uncle, and James's sister Frances C. Hanning.

By 1899 James, Annie and their three children were living at 'Wighill', where James appeared to have taken on the responsibility of running the Tennis Club. The family stayed there until about 1911 before they moved to Oxted. By this stage James was a stockbroker. At the time of his death in 1930, however, the family were living at 'Hill Crest', Tadworth, and James left over £14,000 to be shared between his son, John Rowland, who was another solicitor, and his daughter Agnes Annie, a spinster.

[17]**Frederick Claude Evill** (b. 1861) was the sixth child, out of a total of ten, who were born at 'Lyncombe House,' St. John's Hill, Battersea, to Fanny and William Evill, a starch manufacturer from Bath. The 1881 census revealed that the family had moved to 'Worcester Park House', where William, apart from being listed as a Company Director, had also become a Justice of the Peace.

Frederick had been educated at Clifton College, in Somerset, and, by 1881, was a student at St. Bartholomew's Hospital in the City of London, where five years later he qualified as both a physician and a surgeon. He then continued to work as a House Surgeon at St. Barts and as a House Physician at the Brompton Hospital for another three of four years. During this time, apart from the occasional game of tennis for Worcester Park, Frederick did not seem to have any interest in sport, although his many performances for the St. Bart's Amateur Dramatic Society met with rave reviews in several of the national newspapers. His best review probably occurred for his role in 'Garrick' in 1888:- *"This old city worthy was personified by Mr. F. C. Evill, whose gifts as an actor I have often before recognised. He did not seem to be acting at all. He was the old man himself, and he never forgot the part he had to play. In voice, gesture and feeling he was the worried and much exercised but wealthy and well-meaning city magnate, whose only 'company', unlike Garrick's was the old East India Company"*.

In about 1890 Frederick obtained a post as a surgeon aboard a Peninsular and Oriental Company (P.&O.) ship bound for Australia, where, in April 1891, he became registered as a doctor in Broken Hill, New South Wales. Later that year, Frederick travelled to Victoria where he married Sybella Stratherne Murray, a wealthy farmer's daughter, who came from Kingsclere in Hampshire. In October, the following year, their only child, Douglas, who was to become quite famous, was born in Broken Hill. Douglas was to gain his pilot's licence in 1913, and then served in two World Wars before retiring, in 1946, as Air Chief Marshall Sir Douglas Claude Stratherne Evill.

By 1895 the family had returned to England and were living at 10, Hillside, Wimbledon, before they relocated to a modest nine roomed house, 'The Lodge', Manor Road, in Chipping Barnet, Hertfordshire, where they only needed a cook and a parlour maid to tend to their needs. After a pretty anonymous life in Barnet, the couple eventually retired to 18, Warwick Gardens in Worthing, where Frederick died in March 1929, leaving £12, 246 to Sybella and Douglas.

[18]**Herbert Henley Playford** (b. 1857) was born in Putney, the eldest son of Herbert Harvee Playford, who, apart from being a shipping merchant, was also a legendary oarsman and sculler in the rowing fraternity. The father's obsession with water sports had probably led to him naming his son 'Henley'. Apart from winning numerous prestigious events, the father had been one of the founders of the London Rowing

Club, and was still a Vice-President of that club when he died prematurely, on New Year's Day, 1883, as a result of respiratory problems, which had been aggravated by years of standing on damp tow paths in all weathers. If the 2,000 word tribute, in 'The Field' of January 6th, can be believed, the younger Herbert certainly had a lot to live up to, and, in many respects, he failed:-

"Herbert Henley Playford was a faithful husband, an indulgent father, a sincere friend, and the most accomplished oarsman and sculler that we have ever seen. His form was perfection, his pluck indomitable, and his back-work was a source of admiration and wonder among all his contemporaries. As a finished and elegant sculler he had no superior."

Young Herbert was brought up in a rather strange, and perhaps disfunctional household. His mother had died when he was five, leaving the father to bring up two young sons. When Herbert was fifteen his father re-married Selina Boydell and had another son the following year. Selina, however, brought five further children to the marriage. The 1881 census revealed that Herbert and Selina were living at 'Radnor Hall', Motspur Park, with eight children who ranged in age from six to twenty three, with only a Cook and a Maid to help. They were still living there at the time of the father's death, and he is buried at St. John's, Old Malden.

By the time young Herbert was nineteen, he was already an exceptional athlete, whose name occurred with great frequency in the rowing columns of the sporting press, as he tried to live up to his father's reputation. In comparison to his father he certainly had a weight advantage, as when the senior Playford was at his prime he stood 5 foot 10 inches tall and weighed in at just under ten stones. His son, however, had a sturdier physique and, although his height was not recorded, for one of the races Herbert junior was listed as being 11 stones 11 pounds.

In 1877, the twenty year old was part of a four man crew that won the Thames Cup, and then at Henley that year he was in the London Rowing Club eight man team that won the Thames Challenge Cup. His greatest victory, however occurred in 1881, when he and his cousin, Frank L. Playford, rowed at No. 7 and Stroke respectively, in the Grand Challenge Cup at Henley, after what was *"a memorable race with the Leander and Hertford College crews."*

Herbert's competitive rowing career seemed to grind to a halt after the death of his father in 1883, and he suddenly burst on to the tennis scene. He must have had some exposure to the sport before then, however, as his father had been a judge at Wimbledon the previous year. Apart from reaching the final of the Worcester Park Challenge Cup that season, he also reached the sixth round of the London Athletic Cup, before losing to the eventual winner in the semi-final. He also won his first round match at Prince's that year but lost against C. Montgomery at Wimbledon.

By 1886 Herbert junior seemed to have abandoned tennis for marriage and golf, as in July that year he married Florence Alice Boydell, his step sister, at St. Mark's, Surbiton. The 'happy' couple moved in to a house, initially, in Crescent Road, Wimbledon, for three years, and followed that with a move to Beaufort Road, Surbiton. It is interesting to note that Herbert had named both houses 'Harvee', presumably as a tribute to his late father, a man whose reputation he constantly strove to emulate.

In the meantime the couple must have been very worried by the behaviour of Charles Herbert Boydell, who was one of Florence's brothers, and a half brother of Herbert, when in August, 1885, the 'Surrey Advertiser' reported that *"The Englishman, Charles Henry Boydell, who wrote threatening letters to Mr. Gladstone and several English ladies from Vienna, was tried in that capital on Saturday, and sentenced to six months' imprisonment, with hard labour."*

Further imprisonment followed for Charles, when presumably he went to Australia to start a new life, and he ran in to a spot of trouble with the law, as was reported in 'The South Australian Police Gazette', of March 7th 1888:- *"Charles Henry Boydell, alias Playford, clerk, England, age 25, height 5ft. 8in., light-brown hair, light blue eyes, scar under left ear, mole under left arm, larceny, Adelaide; six months."*

Herbert was one of the first members of the Tennis Club to espouse Golf, and he was probably one of the most successful. By November, 1887, he was already playing off a handicap of sixteen at the Royal St. George's Golf Club, Sandwich. Membership at Guildford and the Royal Wimbledon followed and Herbert's handicap plummeted to seven by 1890, and by that time he was a member at Home Park, where, in 1898, he was playing off scratch.

H. H. Playford might have been a good all-round sportsman, but there were certain flaws in his character, which would have embarrassed his father. At the time of his marriage Herbert was listed as being a stockbroker in the City. In October of that year, however, the Stock Exchange issued the following notice:-

"It is notified by the secretary of the Stock Exchange that Mr. Herbert Henley Playford has been declared a defaulter today."

This blot upon his character did not stop him being initiated into the United Grand Lodge of England in December 1894, although for some undisclosed reason they excluded him from the Freemasons in November, 1899. This might have been for some serious infringement of their rules, or it might have been that he had left the country for good, as he was recorded as taking a ship to Canada in July, 1898, after which all further trace of him vanished.

Herbert and Florence had a son, Anthony Boydell, in 1889, and a daughter, Phyllis Marion, on the third of October, 1891. It was shortly after the birth of Phyllis that serious cracks began to emerge in the marriage, which led to Florence suing for divorce in 1903 on the grounds of *"adultery coupled with cruelty".* The court heard that *"subsequent to the birth of the said Phyllis Marion on divers dates between the 6th October, 1891 and the month of June 1898, at various places within the Administrative County of London, the said Herbert Henley Playford committed adultery with various persons whose names are unknown to your petitioner and which she has been unable to ascertain....That in the years 1897 and 1898 he committed adultery with one Winifred Dare then residing in or about Bloomsbury.... That since the celebration of the said marriage the said Herbert Henley Playford committed adultery with some woman or women unknown and thereby contracted venereal disease, and that in or about the month of August 1892 he wilfully and recklessly communicated such venereal disease to your petitioner....That in June 1898....left and has ever since lived apart from her and deserted her without reasonable cause for two years and upwards."*

The fact that Herbert failed to turned up to the court proceedings, and the fact that he had deserted Florence since June, 1898, lends credence to the idea that he had basically failed to live up to the high standards set by his father, and had simply walked away from his children, his friends, his brothers and sisters, and his golf to restart his life in Canada, never to be heard of again.

As soon as Florence had received the decree absolute and custody of the children, in 1904, she married Sidney Hearne in Kingston. Their son Anthony was sent to a private school at Sutton Valence in Kent, and the 1911 census recorded that he was lodging with a family in Surbiton and that he was apparently an under-graduate at Keble College, Oxford. There is, however, no record of him attending Oxford. Whether he attended Oxford or not, Anthony joined the South Wales Borderers at the start of the First World War, as a Second Lieutenant, and was reported 'Killed in Action' in September 1915 at the Battle of Loos, in the Pas-de-Calais.

[19]**William Edward Martyn** (b. 1856) was born at 14, Brompton Row, Kensington, the son of a Cornish Doctor. By 1861, the family had moved to Trevor Terrace, Westminster, where William lived with his elder brother, Orlando Bridgman Martyn, three younger sisters, an older step sister, plus three servants. In 1875, the family moved to the more luxurious 'Westmoreland Lodge', Inner Park Road, Wimbledon.

William and Orlando were educated at a very minor private school at Cowbridge, Glamorganshire, from where they both graduated with scholarships to study Mathematics at Oxford. Orlando, who was a year older than William seemed to be the better athlete at Cowbridge, as in the school's Sports Day, whilst Orlando was winning sprints, all William managed to achieve was second place in the sack race.

William did, however, have a penchant for cricket, and was recorded as scoring 54 runs, on May 30th, 1874, against Swansea Grammar School, whilst his brother managed twenty five.

Orlando went to Merton College in October, 1874, and William followed him to Oxford the following year. The school proudly reported in the 'Cardiff Times' that *"Mr. W. E. Martyn, second scholar of Cowbridge School, has been elected to an open studentship at Christ Church, Oxford, of the annual value of £100, and tenable for five years."*

Although William played a considerable amount of cricket at Oxford, he never quite impressed the selectors enough to make the University First XI. Perhaps, having attended Cowbridge rather than Eton, dealt a detrimental blow to his aspirations, although he did play for the 'Next Sixteen' against the University XI, and also became the Treasurer of the Christ Church Cricket Club. During the long summer vacations, however, apart from returning to Wales to play the occasional cricket match, he frequently turned out for Wimbledon C. C., where in 1876, in a match against Upper Tooting, he scored 81 runs, in a productive partnership with the Reverend Avison T. Scott, who scored 95.

Following University, in 1880, Orlando went off to become a barrister at the Inner Temple, whilst William became a trainee solicitor and returned to the family home at 'Westmoreland Lodge'. It was there that he embarked on a short, but undistinguished tennis career, when he became a member of the Wimbledon Lawn Tennis Club. William also tried his hand at rugby in 1880, and appeared, in the press, playing as a forward for Wimbledon versus Blackheath and St. Thomas's. The following season, playing for the Nomads, he scored a try, as a three quarter back, by *'cleverly eluding his opponents and scoring beneath the posts'.*

William's main sporting love, however, for at least thirty years, seemed to have been cricket, and in the early part of his career he notched up several half centuries. Besides playing quite regularly for Wimbledon over the years he also played for Chiswick Park C.C. and Richmond, and it was whilst playing for the latter that he probably played one of the best innings of his career, when, on May 13th, 1882, he was the top scorer with 41 runs, in a match that Richmond won by an innings and three runs. The opponents that day had recruited three 'colonists' from the Australian touring team, Billy Murdoch, Hugh Massie, and 'The Demon' Frederick R. Spofforth, the fastest bowler of the nineteenth century, who took four wickets but was apparently quite expensive.

In 1882, William went on a long August tennis and cricket tour of the West Country, which was to become a regular event. He entered the Singles tournament at the Victoria Club, Exeter, where 'The Field' described him as *"the most brilliant player to be entered"*, but sadly he was apparently very unlucky to lose in the first round, which gave him more time to turn out for Exmouth C.C., against 'I. Zingari', 'The Ishmaelites' and Hampstead C.C. William also managed to lose in the first round of the Teignmouth Tournament, although he did reach the second round in the Mixed Doubles.

For the next three or four years August became a month of Tennis and Cricket in the West Country, until Tennis fell by the wayside, and August became solely a month devoted to Cricket. Although William had played initially for Exmouth, as the years rolled on, he became a regular tourist for teams like 'Incogniti' and the M.C.C., and was often joined by Orlando. On Wednesday, 20th August, 1884, he recorded his first 'ton' whilst playing for Exmouth versus Mid Devon. He scored 125, which included 14 fours, whilst Orlando was out, leg before, shortly thereafter for 97, which included a six, a five and twelve fours. The brothers must have been quite fit as they also ran 15 threes.

In a two day match in 'The Exmouth Week', in early August, 1887, whilst playing for 'The Incogniti' versus 'The Ishmaelites', William notched up his top career score of 141, out of a total of 355, which included one 6 (over the boundary) and 20 fours. That was also the year that he seemed to switch to Hockey as his winter sport, playing on the left wing for both Wimbledon and for Putney .

William's batting seemed to improve in the early nineties, and he notched up another ton (118) for Wimbledon versus Chiswick Park, in June, 1892, whilst in the following season, during a two day match at the Sussex County Ground, against the Gentlemen of Sussex, he scored a *"meritorious"* 129* out a total of 235 for 3 in the second innings, to secure a draw for the 'Incogniti'.

Although Tennis was no longer a serious sport for William by the end of the 1880s, it still remained an opportunity to socialise. Instead of playing at the All England Club, he played for Wimbledon Park, and it might have been in this social setting that he met his future wife, Eleanor Elizabeth Muir, who lived at 'Heathlands' on Wimbledon Common. 'The Field' of June 4th, 1892, showed William and Miss Muir, whilst playing for Wimbledon Park, beat a pair from the East Sheen L.T.C. (6-0, 6-5). Eleanor was definitely a fine catch, as she was a four handicap golfer, and the happy couple married in the parish Church in Wimbledon on December 18th, 1895, with Orlando as one of the witnesses.

William and Eleanor went to live at 'Gladswood', 9, Southside, a 17 room house close to Wimbledon Common where they were to live for over forty years, with their four children. The 1901 census showed that they had four servants, one of whom, Mary Godby Pinchen (b. 1876) was listed as being a nurse, who presumably had to look after their three year old daughter, Margaret Jean. It is strange to note, however, that Mary was still living with the family ten years later, and apart from the four servants, was listed as being one of the two nurses, who had to look after the three younger children. What is more strange, however, is that the census listed Mary as being the daughter of William. Could she have been the result of an indiscreet romantic dalliance that William became involved in, whilst at Oxford, with Mary's mother, who had been the wife of a sailor from Clay, Norfolk? Or was it merely a mistake filling in the form? Whatever the reason, when Mary died in 1960, she left over £7,500, which was a fortune for a servant to leave.

It might have been William's wife, Eleanor, who played both at Littlestone-on-Sea and Wimbledon Ladies G.C,, who sparked his interest in golf. She might actually have coached him as his first appearance in 'The Field', in October, 1897, showed him playing off a remarkably low 10 handicap. Surprisingly, over the next fifteen years, however, this handicap remained extremely constant, which led the golf reporter of 'The Illustrated Sporting and Dramatic News' on the 5th of February, 1910, to remark, after William won the Senior monthly medal at the Royal Wimbledon:- *"I do know that Mr. Martyn hit the big ball for many years before he attempted to strike the small one. Having regard to the normal progress which cricketers make at golf, I was surprised to find Mr. Martyn still playing with a double figure handicap."*

William, however, did not play as much golf as some of the other members of the Tennis Club as he continued to play cricket into his fifties. His final century, 102 out of a total of 201, occurred in July 1904 whilst playing for Wimbledon versus the Horton Asylum. His appearances, however, diminished quite markedly as he grew older, and his last major innings was probably the 75 runs that he scored for the 'Incogniti' in a match against Wimbledon in 1906. He still managed, however, to open the batting for Wimbledon, against Ealing as late as 1911, which was the fifth decade of his cricketing career.

Old age seemed to have advanced upon William at a great pace, however, and shortly after he finished playing cricket, he also ceased to play golf. He did, however, manage to win the putting competition at the Royal Wimbledon G. C. in October, 1913, which elicited his admirer at the 'Illustrated Sporting News' to write: *"The putting competition was won by a man, who, I think, was a cricketer long before he became a golfer, but I suppose advancing age has caused Mr. W. E. Martyn to turn to the game which does not demand such fast work. Mr. Martyn seems to be a putter of more than ordinary ability, as he claimed a total of 35."*

William still remained active as a solicitor and shared an office in the City, at 2, Temple Gardens, E.C., with his brother Orlando, and his son, Graham. Instead of sport, however, travel, particularly to Genoa, with either Eleanor or one of his children tended to fill the void, and he eventually died at 'Gladswood' on

August 28th, 1937, aged 81. The probate declaration showed that he left slightly over £13,000 to his wife Eleanor, and his solicitor son, Graham Reed Martyn.

[21]**Auriol Allan Henry Auriol-Barker** was born at Baslow, Derbyshire, in 1849, the middle son of the Reverend Anthony Auriol Barker and his second wife Agnes. The Vicar's first wife, an aunt of the Stanley brothers, Sophia Stanley had died in 1840, by which time two of her three children were also dead.

Much of Auriol's early life was devoted to hunting and steeple chasing, and, as a boy, when living at Bolton Hall, in Cumberland, he kept a rough pack of foxhounds, which, with his brothers, he hunted on foot.

The 1861 census recorded that the eleven year old Auriol A. H. Barker (he did not alter his surname to Auriol-Barker until much later), was one of 13 pupils at the Reverend Edward Roberts' Vicarage and Boarding School at Harborne near Birmingham. Following this he attended Repton, where, although he played a little cricket, his main sport was Athletics, and, on going up to Trinity College, Cambridge, in 1870, he was unlucky in his final year to miss his 'Blue' as a sprinter when he dislocated his foot.

After University Auriol became a solicitor, with chambers at 13, South Square, Gray's Inn, for numerous years, and at some stage he changed his surname by deed poll to the hyphenated 'Auriol-Barker'. When he moved to Surrey he became a familiar figure with the Surrey Staghounds, and also used to hunt with the Whaddon Chase. Auriol was also one of the key figures in the formation of the Worcester Park Beagles and was on that Hunt's first committee.

Auriol moved to 'Longfield', Worcester Park, soon after his marriage to Isabella Cockerton, in 1881. The lavish nature of the wedding is apparent from the size of the bridal bouquet and the description of the bridesmaids' dresses, as was furnished by the following account in 'Vanity Fair' on October 22nd, 1881:- *"at a recent wedding in London, of Mr. Auriol Barker and Miss Cockerton, the bride carried a bouquet more that two feet in diameter. The seven bridesmaids completed a colour-harmony in rich material, the first bridesmaid wearing the palest shade of old gold, and the tint deepening, until it became a bronze in the seventh lady"*

Isabella and Auriol had two daughters, Clementina and Agnes, and a son, Digby, who died in 1921. By 1911, the family had moved to an eleven roomed house, which he named 'Barrow Hill' in memory of his grandmother's house in Derbyshire. The house lay in Royal Avenue, Worcester Park, where the family were served by a cook and four maids. They remained there until Auriol's death in 1938.

As an intrepid horseman, Auriol became an extremely keen steeple chaser at Lingfield and the neighbouring courses, and had numerous victories on his famous steeplechaser 'Best Man'. Then in about 1902 he turned his attentions to polo, and was one of the founders of the original Worcester Park Polo Club, at Motspur Park, and its first honorary secretary. He continued to take an active part in polo, and won several Gymkhana events at Ranelagh, until he was over eighty years of age. At 82 it was reported that he was still a most active follower of the Mid Surrey Drag-hounds.

In later years, although no longer taking part in competitive polo, Auriol continued to play in practice games on his own ground (Auriol Park). He was also on the Council of the National Pony Society, until a month before his death, at the age of eighty-nine, in April, 1938, when he left just over £23,700 to his son-in-law and fellow polo enthusiast, Herbert Stephen Gaselee, a tug boat owner, who lived in Worcester Park with Auriol's daughter, Clementina, and his grand children.

[21]**Mary Judith Woolcott** had been born in Peckham, on December 17th, 1871, to Francis Woolcott, the son of a brick and tile maker from Uffculme, Devon. In 1869 Francis had managed to acquire a job, initially as a clerk and then as a railway porter at London Bridge Station, where he probably met his future wife, Ruth Roffey, from Kent. In May 1873, whilst on a holiday in Devon, Ruth died, at the age of 27, and was buried in Uffculme. As there was no way that Francis could look after his eighteen month old daughter, he left Mary with his family, and five years later married, Annie, an illiterate Irish widow.

In a way the premature death of her mother probably gave Mary a streak of independence, and a better education than she would have had, which served her well throughout her life. She was never afraid to try something new. The 1881 census showed that she was living in Uffculme with Francis's eldest brother, Samuel, and his wife, Elizabeth, where she must have been virtually an elder sister to three year old, Alice, and one year old, Annie. The fact that her uncle, a journeyman carpenter, set a great store by education can be seen by the fact that three year old Alice had been listed on the census as being a 'Scholar'.

Mary attended the Ayshford Grammar School, Uffculme, which was a 'free school', first as a student and then as a pupil teacher. In March, 1887, the 'Western Times' recorded that she had passed the Cambridge University Certificates in English and Religious Knowledge. She must have impressed the school authorities with her work as a pupil teacher as they enrolled her at the Diocesan Training College in Salisbury, which had been founded in 1841 to supply women teachers to Church of England schools in the Salisbury and Winchester Dioceses. This was one of the first teacher training colleges in the country to be formed after Sir James Kay Shuttleworth had founded St. John's, Battersea, the preceding year, which was part of the College of St. Mark and St. John's, Chelsea, (that this author attended over fifty years ago).

About 60 girls attended the King's House, which is now a Museum, where they were instructed in all the subjects that one would expect them to teach. Mary proved to be an exceptional student as was evidenced by a short report of an Ayshford governors' meeting in the 'Exeter and Plymouth Gazette' on the 14th October, 1890, which stated that: *"The Chairman said no doubt they would be pleased to hear that Miss Mary*

Woolcott has gained a first-class scholarship at her recent examination at Salisbury; in fact, the best any teacher sent by the school had done, (Hear, hear.) She had gone back that day to see if she was able to stay on."

Mary must have been successful in her endeavour to remain at the college as a further report in the 'Western Advertiser' revealed that *"Miss Mary Woolcott, formerly pupil teacher in the Uffculme Board School, and now in Salisbury College, has been appointed schoolmistress at Madish, in Sussex." (November 10th, 1892)*

By 1901, Mary was living in Station Road, Cheam, as a lodger of Emma and Charlotte Starr who were both seamstresses, and in their fifties. According to the census the property that they lived in was close to Cheam Rectory where the Reverend Charles H. Rice lived. Mary was listed on that census as being a Headmistress, although no indication was given as to where she taught. By 1905, however, the electoral rolls reveal that she was living in the School House at St. Philip's, Cheam Common, and six years later she had been joined by her father Francis, a retired railway pensioner, who apparently rented an unfurnished bedroom and living room from Mary for five shillings a week.

Following the death of Francis in 1915, Mary really displayed her true independent and adventurous nature when she resigned from her post at St. Philip's and, on October 14th, 1916, boarded the 'Orita' at Southampton, to travel to Coronel, Chile, where she became the Principal of a school. She remained there for nineteen years, before, at the age of 64, she returned, via Bueno Aires, to stay with her relatives at 'Linden House', Uffculme. After that she disappears from the pages of History.

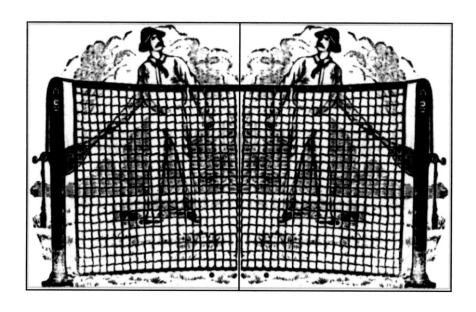

Old Malden and Worcester Park Cricket Club

Although matches had been played between the hamlets of Old Malden and Worcester Park from before 1851, they did not appear as a combined cricket club until **1892**. They were the youngest of the teams to have any influence upon the development of Worcester Park A.C., and yet it was an important influence, as it was where Frederick Blake honed his cricketing skills.

The 1867 six inch O.S. map shows Worcester Park as lying mainly to the west of the London and South Western Railway line, stretching from Worcester Park Station and the main Kingston-Cheam road, up the Great Avenue, to 'Worcester Park House' and the Hogsmill River. Several of the houses in the Avenue were large villas that had been constructed as a result of the coming of the railway to Worcester Park in 1859, whilst some of the smaller cottages were much older and housed the families of men who worked in the powder mills which were situated along the Hogsmill.

Malden, or 'Old Malden' as it became known, was situated almost parallel and slightly to the north of Worcester Park on the 1867 map, stretching from 'The Plough' to St. John's Church and the Hogsmill.

Whereas the Cuddington/Worcester Park C.C. team of the 1870s was made up predominantly of the privileged who lived in the mansions within the Worcester Park area, the Old Malden & Worcester Park C.C. team of the 1890s was comprised basically of working class men who lived in the terraced houses of Cheam Common and Old Malden.

Three or four matches are recorded as being played by a Worcester Park C.C. side in 1879 and 1880, but, judging from the working-class composition of the team, it obviously had no connection to the team of the early 1870s. As the majority of the players lived in Cheam Common, the match reports were probably submitted by opponents, who presumed that they had been playing against a team from Worcester Park, whilst in reality they had been playing against Cheam Common C.C.

Although Old Malden C.C. is not mentioned in the sporting press, following their success against Worcester Park in 1851, they definitely had a cricket ground by the end of the century. This ground, or 'cricket meadow' as it was referred to in 'The Surrey Comet', was generously lent by Mr. Madge to the Old Malden Jubilee Committee to use for their Sports Day for several years from 1899. As Mr. Madge farmed at 'New House Farm' and 'Manor Farm', it looks as though their ground was probably on the site of Manor Park. This supposition is supported by the fact that the 'Comet' of June 24th, 1899, stated that:-*"Village Sports will be held at Old Malden this afternoon in a field opposite the Plough Inn. Mr. Justice Bucknill will present the prizes at the termination of the sports, about 5.30. Mr. Keswick M.P., and Major Coates are also expected to be present."*

The club also appears to have been financially sound, as can be seen from the fact that the Club's Treasurer, Mr. Streeter, generously donated £11-15s.-7d. to New Malden Cricket Club in November, 1890, at their end of season celebration, thus turning a loss for that year into a profit. Using the Bank of England inflation calculator that seemingly trivial looking sum is the equivalent of £1,500 in 2020.

The decision to call the team 'Old Malden and Worcester Park', in **1892,** led to a little confusion amongst their opponents, and in the press, as can be seen from the following short report of a match which appeared in the 'Sporting Life', on May 22nd, 1893, for a match played against a rather mysterious team called 'Social':-

"Social beat Worcester and Malden, at Worcester Park, by 2 runs and three wickets. Score - Social, 62 (for seven wickets); Worcester, 60."

Apart from this snippet of information, very few results exist for matches played by this new conflation, and it seems obvious from the couple of scorecards which were submitted to 'The Comet', in **1893**, by Hook and Southborough, that their opponents still referred to the team as 'Old Malden'.

Despite the addition of about three players from the south side of Worcester Park Station, the results of those two matches against Hook show that the 'Old Malden' team was still extremely weak, as the top score in those matches was only seven, and there were eight ducks. It is rather surprising, therefore, to note that their Secretary, Mr. Hann, in an advertisement for fixtures in the 'Sporting Life', in August, considered their strength to be 'weak medium'.

On July 15th, at home, chasing a score of fifty, after Biggs and Blake had taken five wickets apiece, Old Malden managed only 15 runs off the bat. The team that day was: Gaskin (0), Birch (2), Powell (1), Biggs (3), Blake (1), Kempshall (0), Peters (2), J. Lock (6), Hann (0), Hide (0), Lock (0*), Extras 8. Total 23.

Five weeks later, on August 26th, in the return match at Hook, after dismissing the home side for 76 runs, thanks to six wickets from J. Cuff, the batsmen failed again. The side was virtually the same, and were thankfully accorded initials in 'The Comet', which made identification a little easier:- J. Birch (0), R. Gaskin (0), C. Powell (6), J. Lock (0), T. Biggs (4), J. Cuff (4), P. Peters (7), W. Lock (3), A. Hyde (6), A. Hann (0), Poffley (0*), Extras 1, Total 31.

Of those players mentioned in those two matches, a surprising number came from the small area around Idmiston Road, and most of them were involved in manual work. **Joseph Cuff** (b.1865) was a bricklayer, who lived at 22, Idmiston Square, with his brother-in-law, Thomas Connor, a decorator, who had played for Cheam Common. His uncle, James Cuff, had been one of the original members of Cheam Common and was the landlord of the 'North End Tavern'; **Henry G. Kempshall** (b. 1860) was a carpenter, who lived at 20, Idmiston Square; **Owen Dunsford Poffley** (b. 1875) was a G.P.O. sorter, who lived at 5, Idmiston Square, **Richard W. T. Gaskin** (b.1861) was a foreman at the Gas Works and lived at 21, Idmiston Square; **William Lock** (b. 1863) was a railway plate layer, who lived in Old Malden, **Alfred Hyde** (b. 1870) was a gardener in 1891 but, by 1901, was a grocer in Old Malden; **Thomas Biggs** (b.1869) was a gardener who lived at 1, Fullbrooks Cottages; **Thomas Lock** (b. 1863), was initially a gardener who also lived at 5, Idmiston Square, before becoming the Steward of the Institute in 1901; **Arthur Hann** (b. 1858), seems to have been the exception as he was a schoolmaster and organist, who lived at 6, Idmiston Road in 1891, and was also the club's first Hon. Secretary.

At least three of the team who played in those two matches against Hook, lived on the south side of the railway tracks, in the Malden Road, Cheam Common. In 1891, **John Blake**[1] (b. 1870) was listed as a farmer's assistant who lived in the Coke shop, which was next door but one to the 'Huntsman's Hall'. A couple of houses along from the Blake household lived **Philip Peters** (b. 1862), a builder, who had played for Cheam Common on several occasions, whilst at the top of Cheam Common Road, virtually next door to the 'North End Tavern' lived the ex-landlord of that hostelry, **Charles Powell** (b. 1843), who had reverted to his former occupation of being a builder. Although Charles Powell was a little long in the tooth by 1893, he was surely one of the keenest cricketers in the area, having played for both Cheam and Cheam Common, for whom he had been a founder member.

The only entry in the local press that accorded the new team the correct name appeared in the 'Surrey Comet' of September 23rd, 1893. The result, however, was much the same, with only the veteran Charles Powell managing double figures.

CHESSINGTON v. OLD MALDEN AND WORCESTER PARK.

Played at Chessington-park on Saturday, and won by the home team by 57 runs. Score :—

CHESSINGTON.		OLD MALDEN.	
M. Bowyer lbw b Cuff	7	F. Watson b Napper	0
H. Moore b Cuff	0	H. Batt b Napper	2
E Taylor c Powell b Watson	8	J. Birch b Napper	7
F. Napper b Batt	25	C. Powell not out	10
G. Kelsey b Biggs	11	J. Blake run out	0
T. Browning c Watson b Birch	14	J. Gaskin b Napper	2
G. Bird c Watson b Biggs	1	F. Cuff b Napper	0
G. Newton b Batt	1	T. Biggs c Browning b Napper	0
W. Kelsey not out	6	W. Lock b Napper	4
R. Humphrey c & b Birch	5	A. Hyde absent	0
H. Ede b Batt	6	T. Tozer c G. Kelsey b Napper	3
Byes	1	Byes	9
Total	94	Total	37

If the plan of adding 'Worcester Park' to the club's name had been to attract more players from the Worcester Park area, then that plan appeared to be a failure, as two of the three new players in the team were from Malden. The most promising of these players was probably the opening batsman **Harry W. Batt** (b. 1867) who, in 1891, was a draper's assistant from Idmiston Road. He had also been the top scorer for Malden Village C.C. versus Kingston Rovers in May that year, and was to go on to be a prominent batsman for Old Malden and Worcester Park.

The most interesting recruit to the team, however, appeared to be the number eleven batsman for Old Malden, who was either **Thomas R. K. Tozer** (b. 1864), a teacher with a reputation for the excessive use of corporal punishment, or his brother **Theodore John Tozer** (b.1873), an engineer. Thomas, who had taught in Ewell, as an assistant teacher in 1884, had been reprimanded for his excessive use of punishment and for *"neglecting his duties of supervising their work."*

The Tozer brothers, whose family hailed from Devon, lived in the School House, Old Malden, with their father, Thomas, who was a carpenter, and their mother Selina, who was a school mistress in the village school. The 1881 census also shows that Arthur Hann, a fellow teacher and cricketer, had been a lodger with the family before his marriage, and presumably worked in the village school.

As a cricketer, Arthur Hann does not appear to have been that competent, as he batted down the order and rarely bowled but, as the Hon. Sec. of the Old Malden & Worcester Park Cricket Club he was certainly impressive for the short time that he did the job, as can be seen by the number of results that he managed to get printed in 'The Comet' in **1894**. Looking at the table on the following page makes one wonder if they had become a really good team in the space of a year, or whether he only informed the papers if they had won.

Although only the result of the game was given for three of their matches, the full score card was reproduced in the paper for the other eight fixtures, and there was often a sentence or two to complete the picture of the game. John Blake's 8 wickets for 9 runs against Hook and Southborough, for example, apparently included a 'hat trick', whilst the victory over Lydford was *"owing to the splendid bowling of Shipton and Blake"*. The match report for the game against St. Michael was hardly in the league of Cardus or Atherton but it did contain a couple of interesting facts which were not apparent from the scoresheet: *"Played at Raynes Park on Saturday, an exciting game ending in favour of Malden by six runs five minutes before time."*

Probably the most striking fact shown by the table was the shortage of runs in an afternoon's cricket. Only twice did the team score more than a hundred runs and they won half their matches with scores of less than fifty. This makes the Bank Holiday innings of Harry Batt, against Pelham, all that more surprising and outstanding, *"his 92 being without a chance."*

Old Malden & Worcester Park - Results 1894					
Date	Opponents	Venue	Result	Scores	Individual Performances
April 28	Hook & S.*	Away	Won	26 v 17	A. Duck 10. J. Blake 8 wkts for 9 runs.
May 5	Lydford	Home	Won	32 v 28	J. Blake 8. F. Shipton 6 wkts, J. Blake 4 wkts.
May 19	Hook & C**	Away	Won	18 v 17	
June 2	Cheam Common	Home	Won	94 v 49	A. Duck 24, H. Fairminer 22, J. Blake 22. H. Batt 18 runs and four wickets.
June 9	St. Michael	Away	Won	52 v 46	H. York 26, J. Blake 8 runs and 5 wkts.
June 23	Mutual	Home	Won	29 v 24	
July 21	Chessington	Home	Won	59 v 20	H. York 16, T. Watts 10, C. Banks 8, J. Blake 7 wickets
July 28	Ganden	Home	Won		No Scores given
Aug 4	St. John's	Home	Won	123 -6 v 53	A. Duck 38, C. Powell 29, G. Aspin 15, H. Fairminer 13 and 7 wkts, G. Cooper 11.
Aug 6	Pembroke	Home	Won	125 v 36	H. Batt 92, H. York 22. J. Blake 7 wkts for 13 runs
Aug 11	Chessington	Away	Won	28 v 20	H. Fairminer 9 runs and 6 wkts. J. Blake 4 wkts.
*Hook & Southborough ** Hook and Chessington					

Most of the players from the previous season had continued to play for the team in 1894, although, as can be seen from the table, there were a few useful additions to the squad, all of whom tended to be manual workers who lived mainly in the vicinity of lower Cheam Common Road. Probably the most capable player was twenty year old, **Herbert Fairminer** (b. 1874), who was a labourer, who had been born in Cheam and lived in Longfellow Road. **Henry York** (b. 1865) was another local lad, who was a carpenter and lived with his wife, two daughters and a son at 2, St. John's Cottages in the Malden Road, Cheam. **Thomas Watts** (b.1859) had been born in Pond Hill, Cheam, the son of an agricultural labourer, but lived most of his life in Longfellow Road, where he was employed as a general labourer. **Arthur Henry Duck** (b.1859) was another carpenter who lived with his wife and daughter in Lincoln Road, Cheam Common, whilst **Charles Henry Banks** (b.1873) was a painter and decorator, like his father, and lived at Hope Cottage, 11, Longfellow Road.

The only other new players, about whom there is a degree of uncertainty as to their occupation or residence, were G. Cooper and G. Aspin, who both played in several matches. On the 1891 census there were two George Coopers, both of whom were in their early twenties, and both of whom lived in Tolworth. One of the G. Coopers was a general labourer and the other was a labourer on the railway. There again, as a G. Cooper had played for Cheam Common on June 2nd against the Old Malden men, he could possibly have been the same George Cooper, a general labourer, who was living in Longfellow Road at the time of the 1911 census.

As for G. Aspin, there was no-one of that name within 200 miles of Cheam on the 1891 census, although there were about ten George Aspins in Lancashire and one in Yorkshire. Initially I had presumed that this 'G. Aspin' was a young labourer who had come to chance his luck in the prosperous South. I then discovered an account of a suicide inquest, in April 1894, which stated that the body of the victim had been pulled out of the Hogsmill by George Aspin, a school teacher.

It is uncertain whether Arthur Hann was still the Hon. Sec. for the **1895** season, for although about 15 fixtures were listed in the local paper, only five scorecards were published by 'The Comet', but at least three defeats were mentioned. Only about five new players made an appearance in the scorecards; **William Blake** (b. 1867), a farmer and John Blake's eldest brother; **Henry Harrison** (b. 1863), a tailor who lived in Cheam Village; Preston, S. Parsons and **Charles Farr** (b. 1844), a gardener, who lived with his wife and family at 'Hunters Cottage', Worcester Park in 1891. None of these new players played a prominent role in any of the matches, as the strength of the team still seemed to revolve around the bowling of John Blake and Herbert Fairminer.

Old Malden & Worcester Park - Results 1895					
Date	Opponents	Venue	Result	Scores	Individual Performances
May 4	Mitre	Home	Won	33 v 11	A. Duck 9. J. Blake 5 for 3, H. Fairminer 5 for 4.
May 11	Malden Village	Home	Won	87 - 25	H. Batt 31, H. York 16, T. Watts 13. J. Blake 8 wickets
May 18	Cheam Common	Away	Lost	39 v 44	No scorecard.
May 25	Hook & Southboro	Home	Won	112 v 26	C. Banks 24, H. Fairminer 23, H. York 13, T. Biggs 12. H. Fairminer 7 wkts, J. Blake 3 wkts.
June 8	Archibald*	Home	Lost	47 v 66	
July 6	Chessington	Away	Lost	67 v 91	H. York 15, T. Watts 11. G. Cooper 3 wkts.
July 13	Cheam Common	Away	Won	71 v 34	No score card. "Blake took six wickets for ten runs, four with successive balls."
July 20	Mutual	Home	Lost	40 v 43	P. Peters 11. H. Fairminer 7 runs & 6 wkts.

*The result against Archibald was published in a paragraph in the 'East London Observer'. Apparently Archibald won the toss and batted first, but *"fared badly, losing 4 wickets for ten runs"*. In return, *"Worcester Park did very badly against the bowling of T. M. Weaver, who took 7 wickets for 15 runs."*

The 'East London Observer' then presented the staggering information that, although the season was only about a third of the way through, *"Weaver is bowling in good form this season, having taken already 120 wickets at a cost of less then 4 runs each."*

By **1896** the role of Hon. Sec. seemed to have passed from the competent hands of a local teacher into those of Richard Gaskin who, although he came from a sporting family, was basically a manual worker and might not have realised the amount of work that being a secretary entailed.

There must have been an element of doubt among the members as to whether he was up for the job. This feeling can not have been helped by an advert that appeared in the 'Sporting Life' on April 4th, which indicated that there were still numerous vacancies in that season's fixture list:- *"Malden and Worcester Park (medium) have dates open in May, June, August and September, also Whit Monday and August Bank Holiday: private ground. - R. Gaskin, 51, Idmiston Square, Worcester Park, Surrey."*

The element of doubt can't have been lessened by the fact that the address was wrong, as he lived at number 21 As it transpired, 19 fixtures were listed in the press in 1896, and the results of six of them made the sports pages, although two or three of them had probably been submitted by their opponents, and two of the others were lacking in detail. What is obvious, however, is that the opening bowling combination of Fairminer and Blake was still a potent force.

Old Malden & Worcester Park - Results 1896					
Date	Opponents	Venue	Result	Scores	Individual Performances
May 9	Hook & S*	Home	Lost	20 v 26	H. Geary 7. H. Fairminer 5 wkts. J. Blake 5 wkts
May 16	Mutual	Home	Won	93 v 55	A. Duck 25, G. Cooper 16, T. Hillman 13, H. Fairminer 11. No bowling figures.
May 30	Gordon W.M.C.C.	Home	Won	83 v 43	J. Blake 27, H. Harrison 14, H. York 10*. J. Blake 5 wkts, H. Fairminer 4 wkts.
June 6	Sutton Guild Rovers	Away	Won	74 v 56	T. Hillman 24, C. Banks 18, J. Blake 14. H. Geary 9. H. Fairminer 6 wkts, T. Hillman 2 wkts
June 13	Clapham Liberals	Home	Won	100 for 4 v 24	No scorecard. Clapham Liberals and Radicals were two men short.
June 20	Cheam Common	Away	Won	65 v 46	H. Geary 17, A. Duck 16, G. Cooper 10. J. Blake 7 wkts, H. Fairminer 3 wkts.

Despite the paucity of information, however, a couple of new players with some semblance of quality appeared the scene. **Herbert Geary** (b. 1871), was a schoolmaster who lived in the Schoolhouse in Old Malden with his wife and two daughters, whilst **Harry Thomas Hillman** (b. 1865) was a postman who lived in Knowle Cottages, Longfellow Road, with his wife Rhobina, a son, and four daughters. On one side of their house lived his parents and some of his siblings, whilst on the other side lived his brother Herbert, and his family. In total 20 Hillmans lived in those three houses in Longfellow Road in 1901, and they proved to be extremely important in the foundation of the local football club.

Richard Gaskin remained the Hon. Sec. for the **1897** season, which started in a promising fashion in the press, with a full and complete scorecard on May 1st, for the match against Hook and Southborough, at Old Malden. It seems likely that the match report was submitted to the 'Comet' by the Old Malden scribe, as no mention was made of S. Parson's five wickets for Hook. Was this the same S. Parsons who had played for O.M.&W.P. two years previously and, perhaps being frustrated watching Blake and Fairminer taking all the wickets, week after week, had gone to ply his trade elsewhere? The scorecard was prefaced by this short summary:-

"Played at Old Malden on Saturday, an exciting match ending in a tie, each side having scored 30. For Malden J. Blake took six wickets for 11 runs, and Fairminer three for 11."

The team that day, which showed four newcomers, was: H. Fairminer 4, G. Burrows 1, T. Hillman 1, A. Duck 10, J. Blake 5, R. Gaskin 0, C. Banks 0, T. Watts 1, H. Hague 4, T. Farr 3*, H. Farr 1.

Although there is no trace of H. Hague, the two Farrs were probably the sons of Charles Farr of 'Hunter's Cottage', Worcester Park. **Harry Farr** (b. 1880) and **Charles Edward (Ted) Farr** (b. 1882), who like their father, were both gardeners and tail end batsmen.

George Alexander Burrows (b.1876) was the most competent player to appear on the scene in the Hook match. He was the adopted son of Henry Aspin, the landlord of 'The Plough'. On August 14th, 1897 he married a local school teacher from Cheam, Louisa Saitch (b. 1873), at the parish church of St. John the Baptist, Old Malden. Louisa was the daughter of William Saitch, a greengrocer from Green Lane, Cheam Common, whose sons delivered fruit and vegetables by horse and cart throughout the district. The parish register for the wedding describes George as a 'cycle salesman', but by 1911 he was selling typewriters. George was a reasonable batsman who stayed with the club for several years and even captained the team in 1901, when John Blake was injured. (Could George Aspin have been George Burrows?)

Match reports were apparently submitted to 'The Comet' for the next three matches following the Hook game, but the 'Comet' chose only to provide a four or five line account of each match, which obviously led to the Malden scribe throwing in the towel, as the club did not report another result after May 22nd. There is nothing more disappointing than spending an hour or two copying out the scoresheet, and writing a summary of the match, than to have it ignored by the editor.

The three short summaries that did appear, however, showed that Blake and Fairminer were still a deadly opening duo:-

May 8th - M. & W. P. v Despard - *"Played at Old Malden on Saturday, and won by the home team, for whom J. Blake took seven wickets for 11 runs, and H. Fairminer three for 13. Despard 27; Malden 43."*

May 15th - M. & W. P. v Wellington - *"Played on Saturday at Old Malden and won by Wellington by 23 runs. H. Fairminer, for the losers, bowled exceedingly well, taking seven wickets for 15 runs, five with six balls. Malden 38 (H. Fairminer 13), Wellington 61 (Ellis 20*)."*

May 22nd - M. & W. P. v Mutual- *"Played at Old Malden on Saturday and won by the home team by 16 runs. H. Fairminer for the winners took seven wickets for three runs, and J. Blake two for 10. Malden 35 (J. Blake 16); Mutual 19."*

The 'Sporting Life' gave an even briefer account of the return match against Despard which was played on July 3rd, again at Old Malden:- *"Worcester Park beat Despard, at Worcester. Score - Worcester Park, 75 (for six wickets): Despard, 65."*

The 'Surrey Comet' of July 3rd, under the title of 'Jubilations at Old Malden', gave a comprehensive account of the festivities enjoyed by the people of Old Malden and Worcester Park when they celebrated the Queen's Diamond Jubilee on the preceding Saturday. All the local dignitaries were there, and three of the cricketers, John Blake, J. Lock and Herbert Geary acted as stewards, besides taking part in the customary cricket match which seemed to be associated with that sort of festivity. It was basically a match between the working class and the privileged of the Tennis Club.

"The proceedings commenced at two thirty, when a cricket match, Malden and Worcester Park C.C. versus Mr. E. C. Stapylton's XI, took place at the former's ground. An interesting game ensued, each team batting once. Mr. Stapylton's XI subsequently won by 66 runs to 59. The teams were as follows:- The Club: T. Biggs, J. Blake, G. Burrows, G. Cooper, H. Fairminer, R. Gaskin, H. Geary, T. Hillman, J. Lock, C. Mansell and F. Nicholls; the XI: E. Chetwynd Stapylton, B. Dover, H. Gaselee, A. Hanbury, J. H. S. Hanning, S. Harris, H. E. Johnson, E. Miller, A. Smith, W. J. Stuttaford and W. Trubshaw."

The **1898** season began with the following plea, by Richard Gaskin, in the 'Sporting Life' of April 23rd, for five opponents for that coming season. It is so much easier

---

Malden and Worcester Park (medium) have open May 14, June 25, September 3, 17, 24 (private ground).—R. Gaskin, Idmiston-square, Worcester Park, Surrey.

these days obtaining fixtures online, rather than having to write to the paper, and then wait for teams to respond. (This system in essence lasted until the beginning of this century, as I had the dubious honour of being the Worcester Park Fixture Secretary at that time.) Richard Gaskin would then, of course, have to confirm the fixtures. Numerous letters must have passed back and forth before he could eventually finalise his fixture card, and forward it to the 'Surrey Comet'. It is not surprising, therefore, that the first 'forthcoming match' that was listed in the 'Comet' was for June 4th, as the paper probably did not receive the fixture card until the end of May.

Although the fixture card was perhaps late in arriving, the 'Surrey Comet' did list the majority of that season's fixtures, which can be seen in the following table. When one

Part of the 1898 Fixture List						
May 14	Battersea Rose	Home		July 30	Despard	Home
June 4	Despard	Home		Aug 6	Battersea Park Staff	Home
June 11	Melton	Home		Aug 13	Old St. Mary's	Home
June 18	Stamford Green	Home		Aug 15	Fillebrooke	Home
June 25	Mr. C. A. Madge XI	Home		Aug 20	Melton	Home
July 2	Ewell 2's	Home		Aug 27	Battersea Park	Home
July 9	Old St. Mary's	Home		Sept 10	Mutual	Home
July 16	Hook & S*	Away		Sept 17	Atlas	Home
July 23	Mutual	Home				

takes into account the missing May and September matches, the Old Malden and Worcester Park team probably played about 24 matches that season. Their 'private ground' must have been a very popular place to play as their opponents seemed quite content to play two away matches, rather than the more conventional home and away set-up. Their only away game, apparently was against Hook and Southborough.

Only three results for these matches appeared in the press in 1898, however, for a season which saw John Blake start his eight year stint as captain of the team. The first one was a three line report of a victory versus 'Rose' on May 14th *"Played at Old Malden on Saturday. Malden 68 (J. Blake 23*, P. M. Walters 20); Rose 52."*

Despite this being such a short report it did mention a player who was possibly the first person of privilege to play for the club, **Percy Melmoth Walters** (b. 1864), a barrister, who had been born in Ewell, and in 1901 was living in 'Malden House' with just his wife, a cook and a maid.

John Blake was missing for the team's match against Hook, which ended as a narrow three run defeat. Herbert Fairminer again notched up five wickets, and newcomer,

F. J. Healey chipped in with three more. With the bat: G. Cooper 8, G. Burrows 5, H. Geary 20, A. Duck 13, C. Banks 4, F. Healey 0, H. Fairminer 3, J. Lock 3, W. Farr 7, P. Peters 3, T. Biggs 3, Extras 11, Total 80.

Frederick John Healey (b. 1880) had been born the son of a gardener in Longfellow Road, and was baptised at St. Philip's Church. He was the sixth child of William and Mary Healey, but was the eldest son. Nine years after his birth, a second son, George, was born. By the time of the 1901 census, his father had become a groom and coachman, whilst Frederick had become a coach painter.

The most interesting match of the season took place on the August Bank Holiday Monday, when they played Fillebrook in a two innings' match, which they won on the first innings by 87 runs to 75. Like many a good captain, John Blake put the enjoyment of the others before his own and chose to bat at number eleven. The team that day was: G. Burrows 0, H. Geary 10, R. Stapylton 34, A. Duck 15, H. Fairminer 4, G. Cooper 12, T. Biggs 2, E. J. Skinner 5*, T. Hillman 0, H. Harrison 0, J. Blake 0.   For the bowlers Fairminer took four wickets, Blake 2, Skinner 1, Stapylton 1 and Duck 1.

Ernest John Skinner (b. 1875) was the son of a wealthy tailor who lived in Portland Place, Marylebone. Ernest was a tailor's cutter who was living in New Malden in 1901. The other new player was one of the Worcester Park elite, **Richard Chetwynd Stapylton** (b.1880), the eldest son of Edward Chetwynd Stapylton, who had captained a team against Old Malden the year before. Richard was still a student at Malvern College, and had obviously been well coached. This was especially apparent in the second innings when he hit a splendid 64 runs, out of 148 for four.

John Blake made one of his highest career scores in the second innings, when he made 53 not out. Perhaps he delayed the declaration until he got his fifty, and in so doing forfeited the chance of getting an overall victory, as Fillebrook ended the day on 60 for 5 in the second innings, the wickets being taken by Fairminer (2), Burrows, Biggs and Skinner.

Richard Gaskin remained the Hon. Sec. in **1899** and again seemed to struggle to get a fixture list to the 'Comet' before the end of May, as no upcoming matches for the Old Malden team were listed before June 3rd. Among the new opponents to appear were Sutton Guild Rovers, University and Clapham Cleveland. Out of the 15 matches listed in the 'Comet' the only away matches were against Despard and Hook.

Although the year hadn't exactly begun in an auspicious manner for John Blake, in January, when he was fined ten shillings for having *"a horse and cart at such a distance as to be beyond his control,"* he certainly seemed on song with the ball in the couple of matches that were recorded in the 'Comet'.

In the first match, on May 27th, against Clapham Cleveland, they won quite convincingly by 96 runs versus 49, *"For the winners G. Burrows batted well for 49, and J. Blake took six for 12 runs."* In the second match, at Hook, on July 15th, Blake's eight wicket haul helped to skittle the home side out for 62 runs. The M. & W. P. side was:- G. Burrows 20, J. Blake 4, A. Duck 7, C. Banks 3, E. J. Skinner 40, H. Merriman 0, H. Fairminer 5, G. Cooper 8, F. Farmer 9, H. Hillman 1, A. Farmer 2, Extras 9, Total 109

Of the new players: **Herbert Hillman** (b. 1867) was a builder's labourer, who lived in Longfellow Road with his wife and children; **Albert Charles Farmer** (b. 1874) was a gardener who lived with his wife, Louisa, and two daughters at 'Hermitage Cottage', Cuddington; **William Frederick Farmer** (b. 1866) was a wood cutter, who like his brother, Albert, had been born in Surbiton; **Hugh Maskelyne Merriman** (b. 1882), in contrast, was the son of a wealthy, retired insurance underwriter, Septimus Merriman, who lived with his family and servants at 'Whitcombe', Cuddington. Although Hugh failed to score in this match, he had represented Berkhampstead School, an ancient private school, the previous year. Hugh followed in his father's footsteps and became an insurance underwriter.

Whether G. Aspin was still playing for O.M.&W.P. in 1899 is unknown, but the idea that he was a labourer was probably erroneous, as a press report in the 'Comet' of September 9th showed him opening the batting for 'Twelve Gentlemen of Surrey' versus 'Seventeen of Surbiton and District' at Surbiton. Aspin made eight runs out of a total of 191 for seven declared, and the opponents made 107 for thirteen wickets when bad light stopped play at 6.30 p.m. Batting at number three for the Gentlemen was Bernard James Tindal (B.J.T.) Bosanquet, the inventor of the 'googly'.

The year **1900** not only heralded in a new century but seemed to indicate a period of change in the fortune of the club. It is not known whether Richard Gaskin was still the Secretary, but whoever was entrusted with that task failed to provide the 'Comet' with a single fixture or scorecard. Fortunately, two of the stronger clubs that the team played against were regular contributors to the local paper and provided three scoresheets which show several new members. With three or four new players in each

Old Malden & Worcester Park - Results 1900					
Date	Opponents	Venue	Result	Scores	Individual Performances
June 23	Wimbledon Spencer	Home	Lost	74 v 88	G. Burrows 35, A. Hillman 10. J. Blake 4 wkts, C. Banks 2 wkts, E. Skinner 2 wkts, H. Skinner 2 wkts.
Aug 11	Wimbledon Spencer	Away	Lost	65 v 97	H. E. S. Skinner 24, A. Duck 12. C. Banks 5 wkts, H. Fairminer 3 wkts, J. Blake 2 wkts.
Sept 1	Roehampton	Home	Lost	21 & 89 -3	O.M.&W.P. ten men and no J. Blake. H. Fairminer 6 runs & 2 wkts. G. Cooper 1 wkt

team, and with Fairminer and Blake not showing their previous potency, it is perhaps not surprising that they lost all three matches.

Of the seven new players who appeared in these three matches, nothing can be found on W. Searle, A. Mansfield or Randall. Of the others, both **Alfred Butcher** (b. 1882) and **Henry Reeve** (b 1884) lived in Idmiston Square. Henry was a groom and Alfred was a cattleman. Two of Alfred's brothers were members of the fledgling football club, as was **Walter Charlie Dare** (b. 1881), a gardener, who lived close to St. Philip's Church. Charlie seemed to show no particular loyalty to any team, but turned out for Cuddington, Cheam Common and Old Malden and Worcester Park.

On the strength of him getting the top score in the first match against Spencer, **Harold Edward Shiell Skinner** (b. 1884) seemed to have been the most competent of the new comers, and, as he hailed from a more privileged background, he had probably been educated at a private school, where he would undoubtedly have been coached in the art of cricket. Harold played in both the Spencer matches with his brother, Ernest John, and scored 24 and a duck.

By 1898 Harold's father had retired and the family moved from Portland Place to New Malden, where both parents died within a couple of years. In 1901 Harold was lodging with his brothers, Robert and Ernest, at 'The Orchard', New Malden, in the home of an Indian ruby merchant. His occupation was listed as being a clerk first class in insurance. Ten years later he had graduated to being an insurance inspector and played his cricket for Malden Wanderers, for whom he is recorded as having scored 110* against Woking in 1910.

One of the highlights of 1900 was the second annual athletic meeting of the Malden and Cuddington Jubilee Club, on June 30th, which took place in the 'cricket meadow' that had been kindly lent to the Jubilee Committee by the landlord of the ground, and the tenant of 'New House Farm', **Captain Charles Albert Madge**[2] (b. 1874).

Several of the cricket team either took part in events or acted as stewards on the day. The most interesting result for any of the events saw the first ever mention of young Frederick Blake, in a sporting contest, when he came second in the 150 yards' handicap. For that he won a cricket bat. As the winner of the event won a tool box, it makes one wonder how disappointed Frederick would have been to come second, or whether he had even made an effort to win.

The following year, **1901**, saw only one mention of the Old Malden and Worcester Park team in either the national or local press, when Surbiton United posted the scoresheet for a match that they had played, against them, on June 29th. Although nine of the players lacked initials in the report, it seems as though there were no discernible changes in the team's personnel, but it was impossible to ascertain which Butcher or Skinner played.

Surbiton United had batted first that day at Old Malden and scored 80. Butcher and Skinner took three wickets apiece, whilst Fairminer chipped in with a couple of tail-enders and Burrows bowled the last man. For O.M.&W.P. there were six ducks: Cooper 0, Dare 11, Burrows 17, A. Farmer 3, Fairminer 11, Skinner 0, Banks 0, Butcher 0, F. Farmer 0, Healey 0, Gaskin 0*; Extras 6, Total 48.

Much more information about the Club, in 1901, however, appeared in the 'Malden Magpie' which was basically a non-religious and non-political magazine which appeared on a monthly basis at a penny a copy. The magazine contained plenty of adverts and all the local news from Old and New Malden. All the monthly editions for 1901 are bound up in one slim edition in the Records' Office, in the Guildhall, Kingston, but sadly no further editions appear to exist.

Although most of the cricket news concerned the activities of the larger Malden Wanderers Cricket Club, a small amount of information appeared about, what it referred to as the Malden and Worcester Park C.C., or M. & W. P. C. C., rather than 'Old Malden and Worcester Park'.

The June 1st edition listed the May results and the forthcoming fixtures for June, plus an exceedingly intriguing piece of information about the state of the team.

"The club has commenced fairly well notwithstanding the fact that Captain Blake has been unable to play owing to an injury to his shoulder. G. Burrows' batting and G. Cooper's bowling have been perhaps the most noteworthy features up to the present. The results of matches went as follows:-

May 4th - M. & W. P. C. C. 41 (for 5 wickets), Stamford Green 31

May 11th - M. & W. P. C. C. 32, Wimbledon Spencer 78

May 18th - M. & W. P. C. C. 67, St. Andrews 42

May 25th - M. & W. P. C. C. 81, Wimbledon Spencer 78 (for 8)"

Sadly these results are rather lacking in detail, but it looks as though the Malden side managed two victories, one defeat and a narrow draw in May. Although there's no indication as to where the matches were played it is probably safe to presume that three of them were played at home. The June fixtures showed them playing at home against Mutual, North Brixton, the Earl of Shaftesbury and Surbiton United, whilst the only away fixture was against Sutton Guild. In July there were only three matches listed: at home to 'Rose' and North Brixton, and away, to Stamford Green.

The 'Sporting Life' of June 21st, **1902**, printed the following extremely short and mystifying advertisement on behalf of Malden and Worcester Park C.C.

CRICKET CHALLENGE.

Malden and Worcester Park C.C. (medium) have open June 26 and 27 (at home).—Gaskin, Worcester Park, Surrey.

It was surprising to see that Richard Gaskin still appeared to be the Fixture Secretary and that he felt no need to put his address. As June 26th was a Thursday and the 27th a Friday, had the team started playing mid-week fixtures on a regular basis, or was it a Cricket Week? As the club seemed to have completely ceased providing the 'Comet' with any information, it must remain a mystery.

Only Surbiton United thought it fit to submit a scorecard that year, and had an easy victory over the M.&W.P. team on August 23rd, at Surbiton. Chasing a total of 85, the Park players managed only 22 runs.

The team that day was: H. Hillman 0, J. Blake 3, G. Simmonds 3, E. Spendlove 1, H. Fairminer 0, A. Duck 4, F. Fisher† 0, R. Skinner 1, J. Butcher 3, R. Gaskin 2*, A. Hillman 3, Extras 2. Total 22. R. Skinner took 4 wkts J. Blake 2 wkts, G. Simmons 2 wkts, H. Fairminer 1 wkt , A. Duck 1 wkt.

Out of the five newcomers in this team, it is only possible to identify, with any degree of certainty, two of those players. **Robert Leopold Skinner** (b. 1881), who was listed on the 1901 census as being a member of the Cape Mounted Police, was one of the six sons of William G. Skinner, the wealthy tailor of Portland Place, whilst **John Butcher** (b. 1884), lived with his parents in Idmiston Square, and worked with horses on a farm. John was also a founder member of the W.P.F.C.

The only other mention of the club in 1902, occurred in an article which appeared in the 'Surrey Advertiser' in late September under the heading 'Interesting Cricket':-

"The first match, of what is suggested should be an annual fixture, between the Malden and Worcester Park C.C. and eleven tradesmen of Cheam and District, was played on Wednesday on the ground of the first named at Old Malden, resulting in an easy win for the club. The following were the scores:- M.&W.P.: G. Burrows 8, E. Spendlove 13, F. Fisher 8, C. Dare 43, A. Duck 5, J. Blake 6, H. Skinner 27, R. Gaskin 15, J. Butcher 0, C. Smith 1, F. Blake 4*, Extras 22; Total 155. Eleven Tradesmen: W. Potter 5, J. Dawes 2, F. Smith 3, S. Neil 0, C. Banks 8, H. Fairminer 0, G. Wilson 3, S. Jonas 2*, C. Pratt 1, J. Styles 0, Ned Maynard 0; Extras 2, Total 26.*

In the evening a well attended smoker was held at Mr. Maynard's, 'The Huntsman's Hall', when a capital programme was contributed to by members of the opposing teams and visitors, under the presidency of Mr. J. Styles."

For the Malden & W.P. team, Harold Skinner took seven wickets and E. Spendlove took two, whilst batting at number eleven for the home team was fourteen year old, **Frederick Blake** (b. 1887), who was starting out on an impressive cricketing career in Worcester Park. This match was one of the rare occasions when he was recorded as playing with his brother, John, who was seventeen years older than Fred.

It is interesting to note that two or three of the Tradesmen were actually members of the M.&W.P. Club, and that this match was played on a Wednesday, which, of course, was the day that the shops closed early locally. It makes one wonder whether they were considering turning out a regular midweek side. Twenty years later, Worcester Park C.C. ran a thriving Wednesday side that played over 20 matches per season, and was virtually a separate entity to the Saturday team.

Apart from a fixture which was listed in the 'Comet' on May 6th, **1905**, which stated that Malden Wanderers were due to play Worcester Park, at Worcester Park, there was no further mention of the Malden and Worcester Park Cricket Club, in the press, for over three years, until several of the Surrey newspapers ran the sad story of John Blake's death in January, **1906**. (In the appendix to this chapter, there is an account of his funeral, which was printed in the 'Surrey Mirror', which showed the love and respect with which 'Jack' Blake was regarded not only by his family but by all levels of society and other clubs).

It had been over a decade since those glorious days in the mid-nineties, when Arthur Hann, the schoolmaster, had been the Secretary, and the forthcoming fixtures for the club were listed every week, and match reports appeared quite frequently in the 'Comet'. In the twentieth century, however, it seemed as though no one was prepared to take on the responsibility of contacting the press, and any mention of the team depended upon opposition scribes.

1906 was fractionally better than the preceding three years, as two of the opponents furnished the 'Sporting Life' with short summaries of their matches, minus most of the initials for the M.&W.P.C.C. players. It is interesting to note, however, that both reports list the matches as being played at Worcester Park rather than at Malden. On the 12th of May, they played Athenaeum (late Shepherd's Bush Athletic) at Worcester Park. The Athenaeum declared at 112 for four, with both Buck and Hillman taking two wickets apiece.

In response the home team managed 46 for four wickets. The team that day was:- Drew 5, Burrows 0 (run out), Coates 0, Fairminer 13, Blake 21*, Buck 4*, Extras 3. Hillman, Richards, Graham, Duck and Dearman did not bat.

Four of that team, Burrows, Fairminer, Hillman and Duck, had been in the side for several years whilst two of the others, Drew and Dearman, had played First XI football for W.P.F.C. and had also played cricket for both Cuddington and Cheam Common. The top scorer in the team that day was obviously young Fred Blake, in perhaps the first match after his brother's death.

The second match result in the 'Sporting Life' on June 26th was even briefer: *"Malden and Worcester Park v Atlas - At Worcester Park, the visitors were easily disposed of for 48, owing to the good bowling of Coates and Buck. The home team replied with 115 for nine wickets. F.W. Drew went in first, and carried his bat for 68."*

Frank William Drew (b. 1872), a tailor's cutter who lived at 'Woodlands', Worcester Park, with his family, must have been quite well known to the Atlas team, as he was accorded the honour of being given initials in the report.

1907 saw a slight improvement in the amount and quality of the information provided about the Malden and Worcester Park club as two scorecards of conflicting accuracy were printed in the press. In the first one in the 'Sporting Life', which is reproduced below, the Clapham Park scribe has quite accurately provided one initial letter for all the M.&W.P. players apart from **Charles Noel Gordon Dearman** (b.1867), In the second scorecard, which appeared in the 'Surrey Comet' on July 10th, the scribe of the St. Luke's team, whilst probably listing all the surnames correctly, had allotted the initials in an obviously random fashion. C. B. Fry, for example, probably did not bat at number six for the Worcester Park team, and score a duck. The print quality of that scorecard was extremely poor and is difficult to read.

```
MALDEN AND WORCESTER PARK v. CLAPHAM
PARK.—At Worcester Park, on June 8.
                 Malden and Worcester Park.
Dearman b Dawson ......    2   A Duck  c  Collins  b
H Coates b Cuthbertson     9     Cuthbertson ..............    0
H Firminier b Dawson       0   T Dyer b Cuthbertson...    5
E Richards b Dawson ...   11   W Dyer c Driver b Daw-
A Hillman c Morgan b             son ...........................    0
  Dawson ..................    5   B Strand not out .........    1
T Dalton b Dawson ...      6     Extras ......................    3
A Buck c Spendlove b                                          ——
  Cuthbertson ...........    0        Total ................   42
                 Clapham Park.
C E Horsey b Buck ......   15   W Triggs c Dearman b
A E K Dawson b Buck...      1     T Dyer ...................    6
T H Morgan run out ...     27   W I Large b Buck .......    0
E J Trollope b Buck ...     0   W Driver not out .........   19
E E Spendlove c Dalton          T H Collins run out ......    2
  b Buck ..................    9     Extras ....................   10
W H Horsey b Buck ......    0                                 ——
R A Cuthbertson b T                   Total ................   89
  Dyer ......................    0
```

Although the above scorecard is not at all impressive, especially as far as the batting was concerned, at least it was possible to ascertain that the social composition of the team was changing. It was moving more away from the labouring class towards a more white collar base. The opening batsman, Dearman, for example, had, after all, been educated at a minor private school in Sussex and was the cashier at an engineering firm in 1911.

Of the other players, **Arthur Charles Buck** (b 1876), in the 1911 census was listed as being a civil servant who worked in the Library at the H. M. Patent Office and lived with his wife, Florence, five daughters and a son, in Lincoln Road, which is very close to the current W.P.A.C. Arthur appeared to be the club's main strike bowler in the mid-noughties, along with the Dyer brothers, and in early August made it into the 'London Daily News' honours' list by taking 8 wickets for 15 runs against St. Mark's, Clapham.

Thomas Dalton (b. 1889) was the only son of a draper, who had lived initially in Longfellow Road, but by 1911, had moved to the more desirable Moreton Road. Thomas had played cricket for Cheam Common and was a member of the 1908-09 Championship winning W.P.F.C. team. Sadly, Thomas died fighting for his country in the First World War.

Edgar E, Richards (b. 1875), the top scorer in the team was a skilled craftsman, who was recorded in the 1911 census as being a metal embellisher, who lived at 38, Idmiston Road with his wife, Lilein, four daughters and three sons.

Of the other new players, the last three batsmen in the side were all the sons of gardeners who lived in Longfellow Road. The brothers **Thomas Dyer** (b. 1883) and **William Dyer** (b. 1887) had both been brought up in Longfellow Road and spent most of their lives there. By 1911, Thomas had married Lydia Tompkin and was living with their young daughter at 84, Longfellow Road and was listed as being a gardener, whilst William was still living with his parents and was a Railway Clerk. A short distance away lived another gardener **Bertie Strand** (b. 1875), who played at least 13 innings for Cheam Common the following year, and came third in the batting averages, with an average of 10.4 and also came second in the bowling averages with 45 wickets at 6 runs apiece. Perhaps he became disenchanted with his role as the number 11 batsman for M.&W.P., as by the following year he had moved a to Cheam Common C.C.

The team fared even worse in the match against St. Luke's at Worcester Park, on July 9th, as no-one managed to score double figures. The team that day (with fictious initials omitted) was:- Dearman 0, Coates 5, F. Dyer 6, Buck 9, Richards 4, Fry 0, Dalton 0, Ashenden 1, Duck 4*, W. Dyer 0, Banks 0, Extras 3; Total 32.

In response St. Luke's scored 58 with Buck and Coates picking up three wickets apiece, although they might have taken more wickets as the scorecard was rather incomplete. Two of the batsmen were recorded as being stumped by Dearman with no bowler mentioned, whilst another was simply recorded as being 'hit wicket'.

The Malden and Worcester Park team avoided the realm of historical obscurity in **1908** thanks to the Kingston Brewery scribe submitting two scorecards to the 'Comet', which despite lacking several initials, showed that many of the old guard were still playing and that there had been two or three interesting additions to their ranks, such as that redoubtable sportsman, Dr. William Chearnley Smith.

The 'Watts' in that team might have been **Albert John Watts** (b. 1888), a coal porter, who in 1911 was living with his parents and brother at 82, Longfellow Road, about three houses along from the home of one of the leading players of M.&W.P., Thomas Dyer. The 'Holland', in the team was yet another resident of Longfellow Road. It was either **John Holland** (b. 1869) a chemist at Brocks' Fireworks factory, or one of his two sons **John William Holland** (b. 1890) or his brother **Frederick Charles Holland** (b. 1894). Also living in their house was their sister, Florence, who married Frederick Blake. John junior

Kingston Brewery v. Malden and Worcester Park.

Played at Malden on Saturday, and won by the home club by 40 runs. Score :—

MALDEN.		BREWERY.	
Dr. Smith b Hempster	8	C. J. Brown b Watts	21
F. Blake b Hempster	13	Montague b Dyer	0
Fairminer b Hempster	4	Hempster c Smith b Dyer	0
Buck b Brown	11	J. Bicknill b Buck	26
Watts c Northcote b Tibble	20	Tibble b Buck	5
Hillman b Tibble	21	Cockle c Fairminer b Watts	1
Banks lbw b Tibble	13	Austin c Banks b Dyer	2
W. Dyer c & b Hempster	3	Northcote b Bucks	0
Richards lbw b Hempster	5	Rumble b Dyer	5
Holland run out	4	Francis b Dyer	1
Dendy not out	4	Eldridge not out	4
Extras	5	Extras	5
Total	**111**	**Total**	**71**

became a clerk for a gas company, whilst Frederick followed in his father's footsteps and became a chemist. Both of them, however, were very important figures in the development of Worcester Park Athletic Club. John junior tended to be an opening batsman/wicket keeper, whilst his brother was a very useful bowler.

The highlight of the second match against the Brewery, on August 15th, which was again played at Worcester Park, was probably the half century scored by Arthur Buck, who had been promoted to number three, whilst one of the original members of the team, Arthur Duck, had been relegated to number nine but chipped in with a useful 25 not out. The team that day was:- Dearman 2, Hillman 9, Buck 52, T. Dyer 0, Holland 0, Richards 2, Banks 11, W. Dyer 2, Duck 25*, Bristow 10*, Gregory dnb, Extras 17: Total 130 for 8. The Brewery managed to reach 70 for four, before stumps were drawn, Buck picking up another three wickets and W. Dyer one wicket.

To a large extent the Malden & Worcester Park C.C. seemed to be the poor relative of Cheam Common C.C. in the eyes of the 'Surrey Comet'. A good example of the paper's treatment of the two clubs can be seen in two consecutive articles in the 'Worcester Park' column of the paper on March 13th, **1909**. An account of a Cheam Common C.C. Concert was allotted 41 lines, with seven committee members being mentioned, whilst a whist drive which had been organised by the M.&W.P.C.C. was given three lines with no names. *"The whist drive held recently at the Café Royal was promoted by the Malden and Worcester Park C.C."*

The only other mention of the M.&W.P.C.C. team that year in the 'Comet' occurred in an early season match against Surbiton Hill W.M.C. on May 8th, 1909, which was played at Malden. The team that day was:- F. Blake 17, T. Dyer 0, G. Healey 2, J. Holland 0, W. Dyer 2, T. Dalton 2, A. Hillman 23, E. Richards 0, C. Banks 6, A. Bristowe 0, W. Oaks 0*: Extras 6, Total 64.

In response Surbiton scored 98 runs for 7 wickets before time was called. William Dyer took three wickets, Thomas Dyer two wickets and G. Healey two wickets.

A couple of rather puzzling matches appeared in the 'Wimbledon Borough News' for a team called St. Saviour's Choir and Guild. On June 5th, 1909, it was reported that they had played away to a team called 'Worcester Park'. Although the church side were all out for 22, and 85 in the second innings, the home side only made 14 and 21 for six. The following month they played a team called 'Old Malden', away again, and in response to their 27 runs, Old Malden only made 7 runs in the first innings and 23 for 2 in the second innings. As the team, which was listed for the first match, only contained three recognisable names, Stevens, York and Peters, the matches might possibly have been second eleven games, or possibly church matches that had nothing whatsoever to do with M.&W.P.C.C. The team for the first match was: Stevens 1 (5 wkts), Lambert 0 (5 wkts), Peters 4, York 0, Wicks (capt.) 0, Saville 1, Balls 2, Harwood 1, Parker 2, Diddle 1, Hoskin 2. Total 14.

Another match occurred in the 'Wimbledon Borough News' on August 14th, 1909, however, which was definitely against the M.&W.P. team although it claimed the team was 'Worcester Park': *"Atlas v Worcester Park - These old opponents met at Worcester Park on Saturday, and the result was a win for Atlas. Atlas batted first on a batsman's wicket, but with one exception failed to withstand the bowling of the brothers Dyer - the exception being Savage, who batted well for a useful 24. The innings realised 54. The home team, however, failed to reach even this moderate total, and were dismissed for 41. F. Johnson bowling in irresistible style and capturing 8 wickets for 14 runs."*

No mode of dismissal was given on the scoresheet for each player, just the batsman's name and score. The team that day was:- J. Stevens 4, E. Richards 0, W. Dyer 4, T. Dalton 5, F. Blake 7, T. Dyer 0, J. Holland 2, C. Banks 8*, F. Dyer 1, E. Styles 0, A. Reeve 1, Extras 9, Total 41.

Of the new players to appear in 1909, **Frederick James Dyer** (b.1889) was the younger brother of Thomas and William Dyer. In 1911 he was still living with his parents at 2, Benson Cottages, Longfellow Road, and, like his father, he was a gardener; **John Stevens** (b. 1892) was a house painter who worked for his father, and lived at 3, Royal Cottages, Longfellow Road; **George Edmund Healey** (b. 1889) was a clerk in a Brewery and lived with his father at 6,Wycliffe Terrace, Washington Road. The most influential player, however, was **Ernest Arthur Styles** (b.1884), who, with Frederick Blake, virtually ran the very successful W.P.F.C. Ernest, and his older brother Albert, were both railway clerks who lived with their parents, Joseph and Emily, in Alscott Terrace, Washington Road. Ernest did not appear to be a regular cricketer as he usually batted at number ten or eleven, but obviously turned out for the team when required.

It is interesting to note that, as the Edwardian era moved towards its end, publicity for the Malden & Worcester Park team suddenly increased. More of their matches were reported in the newspapers in the Wimbledon and Croydon areas, which probably meant that they were playing more matches against teams from those two areas. As the football team played in the Wimbledon and District League, and, as many of the players played for the football team, it is highly likely that they had picked up several new fixtures from those areas.

1910 was an important year in the life of Frederick Blake as, on March 19th, he lost the person who had been the greatest influence upon his life, his father, Andrew Blake, who had been involved in a tragic road accident, close to Idmiston Road. Six weeks later, however, Frederick led W.P.F.C. to promotion, by winning the Kingston and District League Division II Championship.

It is highly likely that Fred Blake was also the captain of the cricket team as he was a very good batsman, a reasonable bowler and had the sort of indomitable spirit to inspire others, as was exemplified by the first match in the following table. Despite being injured whilst opening the batting, he came back to take four wickets when Wimbledon Town batted.

Old Malden & Worcester Park - Results 1910					
Date	Opponents	Venue	Result	Score	Individual Performances
May 21	Wimbledon Town II's	Home	Won	147 - 6 v 37	T. Dyer 66, E. Richards 34, A. Hillman 12. F. Blake 9* retired injured W. Dyer 4 wkts, F. Blake 4 wkts, T. Dyer 2 wkts
June 4	Derelicts	Home	N.A.	N.A.	A. Buck 7 wkts, W. Dyer 2 wkts, T. Dyer 1 wkt.
June 11	Mintern	Home	Won	120 -7 v 57	A. Buck 42, F. Blake 34, G. Benson 23* A. Buck 6 wkts, W. Dyer 2 wkts, J. Watts 1 wkt.
June 18	Atlas	Away	Draw	133 v 61 - 7	F. Blake 72*, G. Benson 20. T. Dyer 3 wkts, W. Dyer 3 wkts, F. Blake 1 wkt.
July 16	Mr. Merriman's XI	Home	Won	85 v 84	J. Holland 21, F. Blake 12. A. Buck 6 wkts, F. Holland 1 wkt. Three run out.
July 30	Wimbledon Town II's	Away	Won	147 v 40	F. Blake 83, T. Dalton 18, G. Benson 14. A. Buck 5 wkts, F. Holland 3 wkts, F. Blake 2wkts.
Aug 6	St. Luke's Institute	Home	Won	83 v 62	T. Dyer 14, F. Blake 12, G. Benson 10, F. Blake 5 wkts, F. Holland 3 wkts.
Aug 13	Derelicts	Home	Lost	57 v 62	F. Blake 13, G. Benson 12. F. Blake 5 wkts, F. Holland 3 wkts
Sept 10	South Croydon	Home	Draw	65 - 6 v 54 - 6	Dr. C. Smith 32, C. Dare 17* . A. Buck 5 wkts. "The light was very bad at the finish. The outfield was bad."

Five or six of that team in 1910 really provided the backbone for the Worcester Park Cricket Team of the 1920s, which had Dr. Chearnley Smith as the President of the section, Fred Blake as the captain, John Holland as the vice captain, whilst Fred Holland was the main strike bowler.

Of the two new players to appear on the scene in these matches the only one about whom it was possible to ascertain any information, was **Philip Burchell (b. 1878)** who lived at 2, Ashton Villas, Green Lane, and worked in the City as a Clerk at Liverpool & Martin's Bank. As the Chairman of the Welfare Committee, after the War, it was mainly due to the effort of Philip that the Athletic Club came to be formed, and although his main interest lay in the Tennis section, he did become the Hon. Treasurer of the main club for several years.

The **1911** season continued in a similar fashion with Fred Blake being at the centre of the action in all of the matches which were reported in the press. From the half dozen matches which gained some sort of mention, the season seemed highly successful as five matches were won and one was drawn. All the matches were at home.

Whilst most of the scorecards were found in the 'West Croydon Guardian', the 'Comet' did deign to write the following report on the match against Hyde Farm, which emphasises the importance of Blake to the team:

"Malden and Worcester Park met Hyde Farm at Malden last Saturday, the result being an easy victory for the home side. The visitors batted first and made a good start, 30 runs being registered with only one wicket down but they were all out for 46, F. Blake taking 6 wickets for 17 runs. Malden lost two wickets for one run but Blake and G. Benson carried the score to 87 before the former was caught at the wicket for a splendid innings of 58, which included seven fours and only six singles. G. Benson, although much slower than his partner, played perfect cricket and was not out at the finish with 35 to his credit, the Malden score being 100 for 5."

One notable absentee from the team in 1911 was William Dyer who had deserted the ranks of M.&W.P.C.C. to play for Cheam Common. The end of season statistics, for that club, showed that he topped the bowling averages with 65 wickets at 6.89 apiece, and that he had batted 16 times for an average of 7.81. His younger brother, Frederick, came third in the bowling averages for Cheam Common with 25 wickets. Both William and Frederick were still living with their parents in Longfellow Road, whilst Thomas, who remained true to the Malden and Worcester Park team, was a married man. (As an interesting aside the top batsman for C.C.C.C., in 1911, was another ex-M.&W.P. player, Frank W. Drew, whilst at number four was another of their former players, Gordon Dearman).

At least seven or eight new players appeared on the scene in 1911. An element of doubt over the number is cast by the fact that an 'R. Gaskin' appeared as a tail ender in several of the games. Was this the 'Richard Gaskin' who had been the team's secretary in the 1890s, or was it his son, **Richard Gaskin** (b. 1888), a Gas Meter Maker, who had taken over the mantle of Football captain from Fred Blake in 1910, and who lived with his parents in Old Malden? His brother, **Leonard Gaskin** (b. 1895), was another Gas Meter Maker, who made his debut in 1912.

Of the seven others, who were definitely new players, most of them were white collar workers who lived in the vicinity of Cheam Common Road, and three of them, at least, had connections to the football team, where they played with Blake, Styles, Dalton, Gaskin and J. Watts.

Old Malden & Worcester Park - Results 1911					
Date	Opponents	Venue	Result	Scores	Individual Performances
May 13	Holborn	Home	Won	118 -6 v 52	F. Blake 29, E. Richards 25, T. Dyer 17* F. Holland 4 for 19, T. Dyer 4 for 17.
May 20	Mintern	Home	Won	91 v 22	T. Moscrop 24, E. Richards 24, F. Holland 10*. A. Buck 5 for 7. F. Dyer 5 for 23.
May 27	South Croydon	Home	Won	119 -6 v 46	T. Moscrop 32, F. Blake 24, T. Dyer 23, S. Scott 12*, J. Holland 12. T. Dyer 7 wkts, F. Holland 3 wkts.
July 8	Hyde Farm	Home	Won	100 - 5 v 46	F. Blake 58, G. Benson 35. F. Blake 6 wkts, F. Holland 4 wkts.
July 15	Mr. Merri-man's XI	Home	Won	127 -7 v 104	J. Holland 42*, F. Blake 24, F. Holland 13*, G. Healey 12. F. Blake 3 wkts, T. Dyer 3 wkts A. Buck 2 wkts.
July 22	South Croydon	Home	Draw	66 v 42	F. Blake 12, T. Dyer 10, J. Doel 8*. A. Buck 7 wkts, T. Dyer 2 wkts.

The pick of the crop, **Thomas William Moscrop** (b. 1876), however, did not appear to have any connection to the footballers. Thomas had been born in Kingston and, by 1911, following careers as a butcher and a carpenter, had become an agent for the Prudential Assurance Company, and lived with his wife, Jane, and three children, at 1. St. Margaret's Villas, Longfellow Road.

Another Longfellow Road resident was **Joseph Alfred Philbrick** (b. 1886), a shorthand typist, who lived with his widowed mother and sister at 1, Pennington Cottages, from where they ran a laundry service. Further along the road, at number thirteen, lived **Edward Charles Toomey** (b. 1886), a commercial clerk, who lived with his brother's family, whilst **Fred Holmes** (b. 1883), a copying clerk from York, lived with his wife Louise at 1, Alscot Terrace, Washington Road.

Bertram Ernest Daynes (b. 1882) was a Draper's Assistant, who had lived for much of his childhood with his grandfather, Rueben, at 'Fullbrooks Lodge', and had been a member of the W.P.F.C. 1909-10 league winning squad. Another member of that team had been **James Doel** (b. 1891), who as a child had lived with his family in Longfellow Road. In 1911, however, he was a gardener, who lived with a widow and her family at 'Thorn Cottage', near the 'North End Tavern'. James had also played Football for the league winning First XI in 1909, and eventually married the widow in 1917, shortly before becoming one of the few local victims of the War.

Another member of W.P.F.C. was **Sidney Scott** (b.1887), a chauffeur, who lived with his parents, three brothers and three sisters at Worcester Park Farm. His brother, Albert, another chauffeur, had been the better footballer and had been the vice captain of the First XI and had also represented the League alongside Fred Blake.

It is a little ironic that as the Malden & Worcester Park C.C. drew towards the end of its cricketing life, the 'Comet' decided to bestow a little more publicity upon the club in **1912**. Although none of the upcoming fixtures were listed, it did print one scorecard for the first match of the season and wrote short match reports on five of the following matches, and, at the end of the season, gave a short account of the A.G.M. and for the first time featured the club statistics. A scorecard for the South Croydon game was also reported in two of the Croydon papers.

Old Malden & Worcester Park - Results 1912					
Date	Opponents	Venue	Result	Scores	Individual Performances
May 11	Tillings	Home	Won	130 v 54	T. Dyer 48, F. Blake 24, A. Buck 22. F. Blake 3 wkts, T. Dyer 3 wkts, A. Buck 2 wkts.
May 18	Kennington Tories	Home	Won	72 v 60	M.&W.P. lost first 6 wkts for 15. No additional information.
June 1	Upton C.C.	Home	Won	177-7 v 40	F. Blake 65, J. Holland 51*, T. Dyer 17, E. Richards 15.
June 15	Hyde Farm	Home	Lost	51 v 82	First defeat of the season. Beaten by 'good googly bowling.' G. Benson and J. Holland added 31 for the fifth wicket.
June 22	Cowley	Home	Won	137-4 v 55	C. Dare 39*. T. Dyer, J. Bridgewater & F. Blake hit hard and often. Innings lasted 80 minutes. T. Dyer took a hat-trick.
June 29	South Croydon	Home	Draw	54 v 38-6	G. Benson 14, F. Holland 10. T. Dyer 2 wkts, F. Blake 2 wkts, S. Scott 2 wkts.
July 6	Mr. Merriman's XI	Home	Won	118 v 72	J. Holland 35, C. Dare 32, T. Dyer 29. F. Blake 4 for 11.

Although the match report for the game against Kennington Conservative Club gave no further information than that which is in the above table, some of the other reports make quite interesting reading, and provide some very interesting snippets of information. For the opening match of the season against Tilling's, the reporter wrote: *"A. Buck and F. Blake batted well, retrieving a poor start. Dyer hit very vigorously while compiling his 48, and on several occasions he dropped the ball well over the boundary."* In the match against Cowley, the last six opponents failed to score, whilst John Holland's 35 against Mr. Merriman's XI was described as being 'rather lucky', The top scorer for Mr. Merriman's side was a former Malden and Worcester Park player, H. E. S. Skinner, who was, by 1912, one of the leading Malden Wanderer's batsmen.

On November 2nd, 1912, the 'Comet' printed the following extremely informative account of the club's A.G.M., which reinforced the supposition that Fred Blake had probably been the captain of the team for several years. *"The Malden and Worcester Park C.C. held their annual general meeting at the Plough Inn on Friday in last week. The club's twenty-first season has been very successful, Mr. F. Blake again heading the batting list, whilst Mr. A. Buck is at the top of the bowling averages, positions which they have held for some years. Mr. F. Blake was re-elected captain for next season, with Mr. T. Dyer as vice captain and Mr. J. Holland as Hon. Secretary. The executive wish to inform supporters of the club and secretaries of other clubs, that the Malden and Worcester Park C.C. has no connection whatever with a new club which has taken the title of Worcester Park C.C. The averages of the Malden and Worcester Park C.C. appear in another column on this page."*

Whilst the list of players in the batting averages, on the opposite page, is obviously not complete as there is no mention, for example, of J. Fergusson who scored three runs against Tillings, or S. Scott who batted against South Croydon, at least the person who submitted the averages made sure that the good Doctor Smith was mentioned. The batting averages, however, do reveal another very interesting character, **John William Stevenson Bridgewater** (b. 1892), who, in 1911, lived in a large 13 roomed house called 'Mount Tavey' in Cleveland Road, Worcester Park. At that stage he worked for his father who was a wholesale grocer. Two years later, however, he began a career in acting, and by 1930 he appeared in his first film under the name of Kenneth Kove. His film career, in which he often played 'upper class monocled twits' (imdb), lasted for 35 years and also included appearances in many iconic British comedy series such as 'Hancock's Half Hour' and 'Citizen James' and ended with 'Dr. Terror's House of Horrors'.

The bowling averages, again on the opposite page, were probably less complete as only four bowlers were listed.

The account of the A.G.M. in the 'Comet' had made a rather cryptic mention of another club appertaining to be 'Worcester Park Cricket Club'. Absolutely no

Malden and Worcester Park 1912

Played 17, Won 11, Lost 4, Drawn 2

Runs scored 1,692 for 155, average 10.92. Against: 1,162 for 183, average 6.36

	Inns	N.O.	Most	Total	Aver
F. Blake	15	1	79	256	18.29
J. Holland	15	2	51*	190	15.31
T. Dyer	16	1	48	227	15.13
G. Benson	11	1	36	117	11.79
A. Buck	11	2	32	104	11.55
J. Stevens	15	0	38	159	10.60
F. Holland	14	0	33	100	7.14
J. Bridgewater	11	1	21	61	6.10
E. Richards	16	1	18	83	5.47
J. Philbrick	8	4	8	18	4.50
R. Gaskin	6	1	9	20	4.00
B. Daynes	6	3	8*	11	3.66
E. Styles	6	1	7	13	2.60
L. Gaskin	6	2	6*	8	2
C. Dare	5	2	39*	89	19.65
Dr. Smith	1	0	14	14	14
E. Pilcher	4	0	12	38	9.50

Malden and Worcester Park 1912 Bowling Averages

	Overs	Mdns	Runs	Wkts	Aver
A. Buck	120.2	45	219	42	5.21
F. Blake	88.3	19	177	33	5.36
F. Holland	60.5	8	150	21	7.14
T. Dyer	143	24	351	46	7.63

information about any of the matches played by that club had appeared in any of the newspapers of the time, although the 'Comet' of October 19^{th,} 1912, had reported an account of its A.G.M. under the heading 'WORCESTER PARK C.C.':-

"The annual meeting of the Worcester Park Cricket Club was held at the Drill Inn on Saturday evening, when Mr. G. Haynes presided over a large attendance. The

following officers were elected:- President, Mr. H. Keswick M.P.; Vice-President, Doctor Watson; Captain, A. Head; Vice-Captain, Mr. W. Wellerman; Hon. Secretary, Mr. W. Stent; Hon Treasurer, Mr. G. Haynes; Committee: Messrs. J. Miller, A. Donaldson and S. Pearce, with the officers as ex-officio members.

It was announced that a fixture board had been presented to the club by Mr. Head, and that gentleman was thanked for his kindness. Votes of thanks having been passed to Mr. G. Haynes and Mr. Stent for the interest they had taken in the club's welfare, the remainder of the evening was enjoyably passed with music."

It must have been worrying for the M.&W.P. team who were occasionally referred to as 'Worcester Park' and played at 'Worcester Park', that another team might possibly steal their fixtures or tarnish their reputation. Apart from Henry Keswick, however, the Member of Parliament for Epsom, who was also the President of Cheam Common C.C. and Worcester Park F.C., and the rather roguish **Dr. Percival Humble Watson**[3] (b. 1852), the rest of the company at 'The Drill' appeared to be rather a mystery initially.

At first I wondered whether the team might possibly be a team of gentlemen based around the Tennis Club, but then I discovered that five of those mentioned had been the core of the Cheam Common Second XI that season. As W. Stent had played 13 matches for the Second XI, G. Haynes 11 matches, J Miller 12 matches, A. Head 11 matches and W. Wellerman 7 matches, plus some of them had turned out occasionally for the First team, it seemed highly likely that the Worcester Park C.C. team was a mid-week team, which played on Wednesday afternoons.

William Stent (b 1881) would definitely have been available to play midweek as he was a baker and pastry cook who ran a small business with his wife and brother at 5, Percival Parade, Cheam Common. Of the others, **Arthur Head** (b. 1875) was the manager of a Coach and Motor Builders who lived at 'Caithness', Washington Road: **Arthur Donaldson** (b. 1873) was an assurance clerk who lived with his wife and daughter at 'Jeffort', Hampton Road: **John William Miller** (b. 1880) was a rag sorter who lived at 'Launceston', Lindsay Road, with his wife, four sons and a daughter; **George Haynes** (b.1867) was an auctioneer's clerk who lived in Wimbledon with his wife, daughter and servant.

By 1912, however, Malden and Worcester Park C.C. did appear to be slipping into decline as more and more members seemed to be gravitating towards Cheam Common C.C. Although Charlie Dare had played five matches for M.&W.P. in 1912, he had played on eleven occasions for C.C.C.C. and by the following season was on their General Committee, whilst Doctor Chearnley Smith was one of the Cheam Common Vice-Presidents. An initial-less 'Blake' also appeared in the end of season statistics as he had played at least once for the First XI.

The **1913** season started off in promising fashion for the Malden and Worcester Park Cricket Club when the 'Comet' of March 29th, gave an extremely full report on the club's second annual concert which was held in the Lansdowne Hall. Amongst the numerous acts was Frederick Blake who, as part of the *"humorous element in the programme"*, *"maintained his reputation as a local favourite"*. Whether he sang or told jokes the paper did not disclose, but over the next forty years, or so, he was usually to be found at the centre of any social event.

"The arrangements for the concert were carried out by a committee of the Cricket Club, with Mr. J. W. Holland as Hon. Secretary."

The concert was almost the sum total of publicity received by the club in 1913, although the 'Comet' of August 9th reported that M. Wheeler of Surbiton United had scored 109 versus 'Worcester Park'. Whether this match was against Malden and Worcester Park C.C., or the newly formed Worcester Park C.C. is a mystery. It does, however, look, as though the Malden and Worcester Park C.C. were really struggling in comparison to their larger neighbour, C.C.C.C., who reported in the March A.G.M. that they had acquired eleven new playing members. Perhaps M.&W.P. did not have a full fixture list, or were unable to raise a team, but one of their main players, Thomas Dyer, appeared with his two brothers, playing for Cheam Common II's versus Wandsworth Wesleyan on June 7th, although rather strangely, no mention was made of him or the ten runs that he scored that day in the end of season statistics. What did make another appearance in the Cheam Common statistics for 1913, was the initial-less 'Blake', who both bowled and batted at least once for the First XI.

In **1914**, Cheam Common reported an additional seven new playing members, one of whom was John Stevens, an ex-M.&W.P. player, who went on to win the batting award for that curtailed season. Whether the Malden & Worcester Park team managed to survive to the end of the season is a mystery. The last recorded match that M.&W.P.C.C. played occurred on May 30th, and was briefly mentioned in 'The People' the following day: *"Malden and Worcester Park 66, Devas Institute 56."*

In one of the final matches of the season that was played before War broke out, between Cheam Common and Banstead Asylum on August 22nd. It appeared as though the penultimate nail had been driven into the Old Malden and Worcester Park coffin as it was Fred Blake who took the plaudits for the Commoners for his 43 runs, out of a total of 97, and for his six wickets as they dismissed Banstead for 82. The final nail was obviously the suspension of all cricket because of the War.

There did not appear to be any attempt to revive the club in 1919, and at least three of the M.&W.P. players were elected to the Cheam Common committee in the autumn of 1920. *"Mr. J. Holland, the late Secretary of the Old Malden and Worcester*

Park C.C., which has now ceased to exist, was appointed as successor. Mr. O. C. Foden was elected Captain, with Mr. F. Holland as the Vice-Captain, and the following were appointed the committee:- Messrs. G. Welsh, F. Blake, E. Shrubb, C. Hughes and H. Field."

Malden and Worcester Park - Appendix

[1]**John Blake** was born at 'Baker's Cottage', Cheam Common on the 8th of September, 1870, the fourth out of the twelve children who were born to Andrew and Harriet Blake, although only nine of the children survived to adulthood. Andrew had travelled, with three of his brothers, from Bacton, in Suffolk, in about 1860, to seek work in Cheam. He had started off as a carter in 1861, and followed this with a variety of occupations, which included cowman, pig breeder, shop owner, farmer and builder. Andrew was also a great supporter of both cricket and football in the Worcester Park area, and eventually became the landlord of the grounds for both Cheam Common Cricket Club and W.P.F.C. He must have been particularly proud of the success that two of his sons, John and Frederick, achieved in the sporting arena.

Much of the strength that John showed as a sportsman must have come from working on the farm from a young age. As the second eldest surviving son, a lot of the responsibility for running the farm must have fallen upon his shoulders, which helped to develop a sense of independence and confidence in his own ability, linked to an absence of fear, which led him to be a natural leader of men. His first appearance in the press occurred not in a sporting context but in the report of a court case in which he had tracked a couple of armed poachers across snow covered fields, in the winter of 1885, before helping his father capture one of the men. His answers, when questioned as a witness in court, seemed remarkably clear and confident for a fifteen year old.

As a teenager, John acquired a reputation locally as a fighter. Whether he belonged to a club and followed the rules of the Marquis of Queensberry, of 1857, or whether it was bare knuckle fighting is not known. It seems rather strange nowadays, however, that the preferred method of organising a fight in the 1880s was not via an agent and a promoter, but was initiated through a challenge in the press.

On December 17th, 1887, the following challenge occurred in the 'Sporting Life':-
"R. Stanborough, of Wimbledon, is willing to box J. Blake, of Worcester Park, the best of six rounds for a trophy. A reply through the 'Sporting Life' will receive prompt

attention." Probably slightly more strange was the following challenge from Walter Smith, a nineteen year old gardener, of Longfellow Road, which occurred in the 'Sporting Life' on March 4th, 1889:- *"W. Smith, of Worcester Park, hearing of the boxing abilities of T. Soden, of New Malden, and J. Blake, of Worcester Park will box either of them the best of six rounds. An answer will oblige."*

What makes the challenge of Walter Smith more strange is the fact that John and Walter must have known each other quite well as they were both members of the Queen's Park Harriers. In a team event, that they won by four points, against Chiswick Harriers, in 1890, Walter came fourth and John tenth.

The pair also regularly competed in shorter Athletic events which were promoted by the Amateur Athletic Association and it seems that on the odd occasion they must have bent the rules by accepting payments for their performances, as both of them had to appeal for requalification to the A.A.A. in January, 1893. On February 1st, the 'Sporting Life' reported that their request had been granted *"on forfeiting small prize money"*.

John was still competing in athletic events until the turn of the century. One of his proudest moments must have been when he competed in the first Old Malden Jubilee Sports Day in 1899, which was open to anyone living within a mile of Worcester Park Station. Although the quality of the other five competitors was probably not as strong as those he had run against in his heyday, he won the quarter mile scratch race and was presented with a *'Handsome silver cup by Sir Thomas T. Bucknill, the President of the Club'*. The following year he must have decided to give the others a chance and became a steward for the Sports Day.

John's main sporting love, however, was cricket. He started his cricketing career with Cheam Common in 1889 and played for them until 1891, when he was third in the bowling statistics with 21 wickets. He did not, however, figure in the batting averages which might have been the reason that he joined the newly formed O.M.&W.P.C.C. in 1892. During his short thirteen year career with Old Malden and Worcester Park, he was recorded as opening the bowling and taking more than five wickets on numerous occasions. From 1898, until his premature death in January 1906, he was also the captain of the Old Malden side.

How John died is not recorded in the press, but the effect that it had on all members of the local community is evident from the following tribute to his life which appeared in the 'Surrey Mirror' on January 23rd, 1906:

"Death of Mr. John Blake - Great sympathy and regret have been expressed by all classes in the district with the family of Mr. John Blake, whose untimely death occurred last week. 'Jack' Blake, as he was more widely and familiarly known, was

the eldest son of Mr. Andrew Blake, of Cheam Common, and was partner with his father in the business of farmer, hay and corn merchant and contractor for many years in Worcester Park. The deceased, who was only thirty-five years of age, was well known as an ardent follower of the national summer game, and for the past thirteen years was a popular member of the Old Malden Cricket Club, of which he was captain for eight seasons.

The funeral, which took place on Tuesday last at St. Philip's Church, Cheamside, was largely attended by sympathising friends, among those present in addition to the family, being Mr. Charles Smith, Dr. Chearnley Smith, and Messrs. R. Gaskin, A. Duck, P. F. Woods, C. Perkins, C. Powell, J. Holloway, H. Edwards, A. Hyde, and representatives of the Mutual Cricket Club, while many handsome wreaths were contributed from the above-mentioned clubs and numerous sorrowing relatives and friends."

[2]**Charles Albert Madge** was born on 26th August, 1874, the youngest son of Dr. Henry Madge Madge (another person who chose to repeat his surname), a highly qualified physician of 4, Upper Wimpole Street, London, and Mary, the daughter of David Broun of 'Broxbourne Lodge', Edinburgh. He had attended Westminster School as a boarder between January 1887 and July 1891 and, according to the school records, he was quite a talented musician as well as being an above average athlete, coming second in the Under 14s, 300 yard race.

The 1891 census shows that Charles was a visitor at St. Leonards, Clewer, near Windsor, the home of Sir Theodore Henry Brinckman, 2nd Baronet. The only other person in the house, apart from the twelve servants, was the Baron's son, and Charles's future business partner, Claud William Ernest Brinckman (b. 1873). Their mutual love of horse flesh led to their acquisition of the lease of 'New House Farm' and 'Manor Farm' in Old Malden in about 1895. Over the next five or six years, both Brinckman and Madge figured on several occasions in the press for their winning entries at county shows, both with horses and poultry.

Charles was probably the more dominant, hands-on partner, as Claud married Mary Malthus in 1895 and settled down to live in Fetcham Grove, whilst Charles moved his recently widowed mother, Margaret, and most of his family in to 'New House Farm'. There he quickly became a prominent member of Worcester Park Society.

By 1897 he had become a representative of the Old Malden ward on the Urban District Council, and shortly thereafter, the Guardian of Old Malden. He was also one of the two Secretaries, along with Percy Walters, involved in the construction of the Malden and Cuddington Jubilee Club and Institute, which opened in 1898. Along with his future father-in-law, Henry Hylton Foster of 'Tolworth Hall', he provided a bagatelle table and a billiards table for the Club. (The Worcester Park Beagles provided the Institute with fifty chairs). Charles also allowed the Institute to use the Old Malden Cricket ground for their annual Athletic Events from 1899-1901.

Charles Madge also served with distinction in the Second Boer War with the 6th Battalion of the Royal Warwickshire Militia, and rose to the rank of Captain by 1901. He played a prominent role in Lord Robert's advance on Pretoria and was twice mentioned in dispatches, receiving both the Queen's medal and the King's medal for his service.

He returned to Worcester Park Station on Monday evening, June 3rd, at 6.59 p.m., a hero, after sixteen months away serving his country. According to the 'Advertiser', *"long before that hour the thoroughfare from the station to the farm was thronged with people."* The horses were withdrawn from his carriage so that employees of the estate could pull him, and his family, home along the bunting lined lanes, accompanied by tumultuous cheering and patriotic airs, played by the Worcester Park and Cuddington Band. He was formally welcomed home by members of the District Council, sitting and standing on the local fire brigade's engine.

Sadly, shortly after his triumphal return home, Charles had to resign from all his local positions, as the lease of the farm ended in late 1901, and he had to return to South Africa to help with the repatriation of the Boers. The 'Surrey Times' advertised the sale thus: *"October 2nd at New House and Manor Farms, Worcester Park and Old Malden, Surrey - The whole of the valuable farming stock and produce, including 70 high class shorthorns and pure bred Jersey cows, and 30 grand Shire Horses, Colts and Hackneys: also Stacks of old and new Hay and Straw, by direction of Messrs. Brinckman and Madge, owing to expiration of tenancy."*

Charles spent much of his life after 1902 in South Africa where he worked initially for the Colonial Office, repatriating the Boers. In 1904 he joined the executive of the Transvaal Consolidated Land and Exploration Company and various industrial schemes in South Africa. He became the President of the Transvaal Land Owners Association, Chairman of the South African Anti-Malarial Association and helped to organise the Transvaal Tobacco Growers Association.

Charles did, however, return home in 1910 to marry Barbara Hylton Foster of 'Tolworth Hall' in 1910. Their son, Charles Henry Madge, who was born in Johannesburg, became a famous English poet and sociologist.

Captain Charles Madge resigned his commission in 1905 but continued to work for the South African Army as a member of the Headquarters' Staff of the Union Defence Force in that country. General Smuts, the Second South African Prime Minister praised his work as the Director of the Information Bureau at the Defence

Headquarters thus: *"Colonel Madge has done exceedingly good work......the constant exercise of no small organising ability and sound judgement.......speaks volumes for the good work Madge has done."*

Lieutenant-Colonel Charles Madge transferred to fight with the South African Imperial Forces on the Western Front in World War 1, and died on 10th May, 1916, aged 41, when he was killed by a 'minenwerfer' (a short range mortar), while being escorted around the trenches at the Hohenzollern Redoubt by Colonel Rowley, who miraculously escaped injury. His tombstone at the Bethune Town Cemetery records that he was a member of the South African Defence Force as well as being a member of the Royal Warwickshire Regiment. His death has also been recorded on the South African Roll of Honour.

[3]**Dr. Percival Humble Watson** (b. 1852) was the son of Jane and Robert Watson, a wealthy grocer in Newcastle-upon-Tyne, who at the time of the 1871 census, employed five men and four boys. Jane had a cook, a maid and a nurse to help with bringing up six children ranging in age from one to eighteen. Percival, the eldest child, was listed as being a Medical Student, who studied at the Newcastle School of Medicine and London University. Upon him qualifying as a surgeon his proud father placed the following announcement in the Newcastle Journal:

> Mr P. H. Watson, son of Mr Robt. Watson, of this town, having passed the final examination, held at Lincolns Inn, on the 14th, 15th, and 18th instant, has been admitted a member of the Royal College of Surgeons.

After finally qualifying as a surgeon and physician, Percival returned to Newcastle and married Julia Harvey in 1876, and nine months later they had their only child, Una, which again made the local press. ('Sunderland Daily Echo' 21st July, 1877)

> **BIRTHS.**
> WATSON.—At 12, North Bridge-street, Monkwearmouth, on the 20th inst., the wife of Percival H. Watson, surgeon, of a daughter.

The family continued to live in two or three different homes over the next thirty years or so, in and around the Newcastle and Sunderland area. Their home in Monkwearmouth was obviously too small for a successful doctor, as it only had a drawing room, a dining room, breakfast room, kitchen, nursery and three bedrooms, plus a coach house and stables in a large yard. It was put up for auction in July 1882 and they moved to a larger property in Jesmond, where they had enough space to accommodate a cook and a housemaid.

Percy joined the Freemasons in 1882 and became a prominent member of the 509 Tees Royal Arch Chapter in Stockton. Life must have appeared idyllic to an outsider, but in 1904 the wheels fell off, when it was revealed in the press that Percy had been involved with a fellow doctor's wife.

Dr. John Stanley Manford of Newcastle was granted a decree nisi, on July 14th, 1904, *"on the ground of the adultery of his wife, Charlotte Manford, with Dr. Percival Humble Watson, also of Newcastle."* The Manfords had married in 1898 but it had been an unhappy union. As Percy had been Charlotte's doctor from before the marriage, he continued to attend to her on a very regular basis. After receiving an anonymous letter in 1903, Dr. Manford questioned Percy as to his relationship with his wife. Percy remained silent and received a thrashing.

The following year Percy was struck off the register of the College of Surgeons for five years for 'professional misconduct'. He was re-admitted to the official lists again in 1909, when he presented the College of Surgeons with a petition which had been signed by fifteen fellow doctors from Newcastle.

The court case must have dealt the death blow to his marriage, for, although they remained married, they appeared to have lived separate lives. By the time of the 1911 census, Percy had moved to Worcester Park where he lived at 'Windsor House' with one of his younger brothers, Thomas, who was the branch manager of an insurance company. They lived quite modestly with only one servant, a forty four year old widow to act as the cook and housekeeper. His wife and daughter, however, were living off their 'own means' in a boarding house in Torquay.

In 1913, to assuage his financial problems, Percy decided to sign up as a ship's doctor on a round trip to Bombay. He joined the Anchor liner 'Olympia' in Glasgow and sailed from there to Birkenhead, where he was discovered to have died in his cabin from pneumonia. All he managed to leave, to his brother, was £46-10s.-8d. Julia and Una, however, remained living off their 'private means' for the rest of their lives. Julia died in Hove in 1938, and her daughter died in Brighton in 1964.

Worcester Park Football Club 1900 -1914

For over forty years I had presumed that Worcester Park Football Club was merely one of the many sections of the Athletic Club, which had been founded in 1921. It was not until I met fellow researcher, Robin Fisher, who played football for Worcester Park in the 1960s, that I realised that the supposed child was actually one of the parents, and that the Football Club dated back to 1900.

Robin pointed out that there is a shield in the trophy cabinet at Worcester Park which was presented to the club by the Surrey Football Association to commemorate the foundation of the club in 1900, whilst at the Surrey F. A. offices at the Meadowbank Football ground in Dorking there is a 'Centenary Club' display board, on which, along with other clubs are the words, "Worcester Park founded 1900".

It was thanks to the foresight and enthusiasm of the football club's committee members, along with those of Cheam Common Cricket Club, that a thriving new sports club emerged at Skinner's Field after the trauma suffered by local sport as a result of the First World War.

Whereas the formation of Cheam Common Cricket in 1872 was largely due to the joint efforts of Francis Pennington, the landlord of the 'Old Drill' pub, and to the Rector of St. Philip's Church, the Reverend R. Bigg-Wither, who both wanted to provide the young men of the area with a suitable form of recreation in the summer months, it has proven impossible to obtain the names of the founders of the football club from the Surrey F.A. Much of the credit for the formation of W.P.F.C., however, at least from 1904 when he provided them with a ground, can be traced to the door of a local builder and farmer, Andrew Blake, who wished to provide organised football primarily for his sons, and for members of his extended family.

Andrew Blake was a prominent member of the local community, having arrived in Cheam in about 1872, from Bacton, a small village in Suffolk, with his brothers, David, Abel and George. Andrew had at least a dozen children with his wife Harriet, although not all survived. His youngest son, Frederick, went on to become perhaps the most famous and important of all the W.P.A.C. members, captaining both the football and cricket sections of the club for several years, besides working indefatigably, raising money, to make sure that the club was a success.

The 1891 census showed that Andrew lived at the Coke Shop, Malden Road, which was a couple of houses along from the 'Huntsman's Hall' (now 'The Brook'). He lived there with Harriet, his wife and eight children, and was listed as being a pig and cattle breeder. By the late 1890s, however, he is recorded as farming at Malden Green Farm and he seems to have branched out more towards mixed agriculture. Andrew eventually abandoned farming in September 1900 to concentrate more upon his building projects. An advertisement in 'The Sunday Mirror' showed that he had 8 horses, 19 cows, 75 sheep and 4 stacks of hay for sale at that time.

Towards the end of the century, on November 13th, 1899, Andrew had acquired from Mary Antrobus, the widow of Hugh Lindsay Antrobus, quite a sizeable area of land close to St. Philip's Church, where he built several cottages. The initials 'AB 1901' can still be seen carved into the brickwork of the top terrace block in what is now Lindsay Road.

Andrew had also obtained permission from Cuddington Parish Council to build a road through his property to allow access to the cemetery behind the church. This road became the aforementioned Lindsay Road, which was named after the church's benefactor, who had died on March 18th, 1899.

At the turn of the century, Andrew Blake also acquired from the Antrobus Estate, an area of land further down what is now Lindsay Road, which was called, at that time, Cheam Common Meadows. This was Lot 4 of the Antrobus Estate, an area of 19 acres, 2 rods and 38 poles, for which Andrew paid the princely sum of £1,600.

I had presumed that this was where Ernie Styles had scored the first ever goal for the fledgling club in 1900, until I discovered that, for the first four seasons of their existence, Worcester Park F. C. were hiring 'a meadow', for footballing purposes, from Mrs. Frances Pennington, the landlady of 'The Drill' from 1886 - 1903. This was extremely likely to have been the same meadow, next to the pub, which had been hired to Cheam Common C.C., by her husband, Francis Pennington, in 1872.

In many ways, it might have been more apt to have called Lindsay Road, Blake Road, as many of the properties became inhabited by Blakes or by people who had married into the family over the course of about 20 years. This road was to play an important role in the story of the foundation of W.P.A.C., as it was a hotbed of founder members of the club, many of whom had family ties to Andrew Blake. In fact in the early years of the century Frederick Blake, Andrew's youngest son, and Ernest Arthur Styles were known as "The Lindsay Road Boys."

By 1911 there were 14 houses in the road, three of them being occupied by members of the Blake family, whilst in a fourth lived Andrew's daughter, Ethel, who had married Charlie Dare, who played for Cheam Common C.C. and used to tend their wicket on a Saturday morning. His brother Albert (Bert), who lived nearby in Cheam Common Road, took up the ground-keeping mantle by becoming the groundsman at W.P.A.C. for 30 years from 1929 to 1959. By the time that the Athletic Club was formed in 1921, therefore, five important co-founders of the club were living in the road - Frederick Blake, Charlie Dare, Edwin Shrubb, Arthur Verrall and Ernie Styles.

Not a lot of information exists in the local press, that is, the 'Surrey Comet' and the 'Advertiser' about the players who represented W.P.F.C. during the early years. The esoteric fact that fifteen year old Ernie Styles had scored the club's first goal in 1900, came as the result of a newspaper interview that he, and Fred Blake, gave to the 'Surrey Comet' on March 8th, 1922. In that article Styles was praised for his selfless devotion to the club, having apparently been, according to the 'Comet', the Hon. Secretary of the club for the whole of its existence.

This so-called fact, however, does not quite tally with information obtained by Robin Fisher, from the Surrey F.A., who claimed that the club's Secretary in 1900-01 was actually George E. Turner of 'Birch Villa', Cheam Common, whilst from 1902-06 the job was taken over by **Arthur Ernest Hillman** (b. 1880), a carpenter, of 'Budleigh Cottage', Worcester Park. According to the Surrey F.A., Ernie Styles was the club Secretary in two spells; from 1906 to 1915, and from 1924 to 1947.

A particularly interesting snippet of information that Robin had obtained from the Surrey F.A. about W.P.F.C. is that for the first three seasons of the club's existence from 1900 until 1903, the club colours had been orange and green. This changed to the current blue and white at the end of that season. These remained the basic colours of their kit for the next 116 years. Sometimes the shirts were blue and white stripes and on other occasions they were hoops. Occasionally, according to the Surrey F.A., the club varied this theme by playing in either blue shirts and white shorts or vice versa, whilst for the 1976-77 season they even tried a yellow and blue combination.

The story of Worcester Park Football Club in the early years of the last century is really quite remarkable, for within the course of a few years, a group of relatively young players with the support of a few adults, playing for the first four years in a meadow besides 'The Drill', and then in a muddy field down Lindsay Road, had formed a highly respectable football club, which, by 1914, was one of the leading clubs in the top flight of the Kingston & District League, whilst players such as Fred Blake went on to represent both the League and County in the final season before war broke out.

Just when I had resigned myself to the fact that I would never know the names of the players who represented the club in that first season, Robin Fisher presented me with a mound of information that he had garnered from the 'Wimbledon Herald' and the 'Wimbledon Borough News' which he had discovered at the Morden Heritage Centre.

The first ever recorded match report in the 'Herald' was supposedly for the Reserve team, who played at home against West Ewell on Saturday 23rd February, 1901. I write 'supposedly', as some of the advertisements in the press lead one to presume that the reserve eleven had an average age of about 14. Another reason to doubt that it was a reserve eleven was the fact that at least six of the team were regulars in the First eleven the following year.

"Playing at home, after an interesting game the Reserves won by three goals to one. Both sides showed good form considering the state of the weather and the winners were unlucky in not increasing the score and were undoubtedly the better side.
Worcester Park Reserve team: F. W. Drew, H. R. Turner, W. Hopkins, E. Styles, F. Paye, C. Drew, A. Styles, R. Oxenham, J. Hopkins, A. Hillman, E. Portnall."

The only other match report for that season again appeared to be a Reserve team game which appeared in the 'Herald' on Saturday 13th April, 1901 versus 'Devonians': *"The game was played in miserable weather, and after a one sided exhibition the Parkites ran out easy winners by ten goals to two.*

Worcester Park team: F. W. Drew, W. Hopkins, H. Woods, E. D. Hurles, G. Hawkins, F. Paye, A. Styles, E. Styles, J. Hopkins, E. Foreman, H. Millward.

Goal Scorers: J. Hopkins (7), H. Millward, A. Styles, E. D. Hurles."

Further information about that first season can be found in the initial report for the **1901-1902** season, which was printed in the 'Wimbledon Herald' on the 28th September, 1901: *"Worcester Park, having finished very satisfactorily last year, started its second season by playing Mackenzie Wanderers, a London Junior Cup team, and ran out winners by 3-2.*

A good list of fixtures has been arranged, including Ewell, Ashtead, Leatherhead, Surbiton Rangers, Belmont, Sutton United, Beddington Corner, Old Tenisonians, Old Tiffinians, Wimbledon St. Andrew's, Old Quintinians, London Devonians, Carshalton St. Andrew's, Kingston Albion, and Barnes.

Most of these clubs will play home and away matches, and besides a first team, a fairly strong second eleven will take the field. For that several matches have been arranged, including home and away matches with Westmead Wanderers, Kenilworth, West Ewell, St. Michael's Athletic, Epsom East Street, St. Barnabas Old Boys, Wimbledon Y.M.C.A., and Church Institute (Wimbledon). The club has entered for the Surrey Junior Cup, and has been drawn to play against Wallington Athletic on October 12th, at Wallington.

A good team is available this season, and both defence and attack can be relied upon. The most prominent of last year's team have re-joined, including F. W. Drew, a master between the uprights, W. Hopkins, a most reliable back, and Hugh Woods. A very formidable half line will be selected from F. Cutler, G. E. Turner, R. Turner, G. Hawkins, E. D. Hurles and F. Paye. The front rank will include G. Dearman at centre, on the right J. Hopkins (capt.) and L. Sarll, supported on the left wing by A. Hillman and H. Millward. The latter, who played some wonderfully good games last season, is at present a doubtful starter, owing to an injury to his leg. No doubt he will again take up his old position, which should complete a very dangerous forward line.

The fixture list, as will be seen, is stronger than last year, but the executive, backed up by the support of the local members, will, no doubt, be satisfied with the result of the ensuing season."

Several advertisements also appeared in the 'South London Press' in 1901 which tended to emphasise the youthful nature of the club: *'Wanted, Worcester Football Club, (average age 14, weak second eleven), DATES after November 23rd: S.E. district preferred. Address Charles Salkeld, 40, Stanworth Street, Bermondsey S.E. (Nov 2nd, 1901).'* The advertisements were evidently for Worcester Park F.C.

In another advertisement the average age appeared to have dropped to 13, whilst in an advertisement of December 28th, recipients were asked to contact the Secretary, care of Charles Salkeld and were told that the team preferred to play at home (probably because of their youthfulness).

These adverts, stressing the apparent youthfulness of the Reserves, do not quite tally with the teams listed for the two matches that took place against West Ewell and Devonians in the spring of that year. Of the sixteen players who played in those two games I found fifteen of them listed locally in the 1901 census. Fourteen of these were in full time occupation: Frank Drew - age 28, William Hopkins - age 18, Hugh Woods - age 22, George Hawkins - age 25, Edward Hurles - age 19, Henry R. Turner - age 18, Albert Styles - age 19, Edwin Portnall - age 28, Ernie Styles - age 16, Frederick Paye - age 20, Edward Foreman - age 30, Joseph Hopkins - age 22, Harold Frith Millward - age 24, and Arthur Hillman - age 21. Only Reuben Miller Oxenham - age 14, appeared to tally with the average age mentioned in the advertisements.

Immediately below the Salkeld adverts in the 'South London Press' appeared the following intriguing advert: *'Worcester Cricket Club (14 weak) All dates next season. Apply Charles William Salkeld, 40, Stanworth St., Bermondsey, S.E.'*

It appears as though the members of the club intended to use the 'Drill' meadow all year round, although there is no record of them playing cricket there in the early years of the twentieth century. It was a different state of affairs, however, when they eventually moved to the Lindsay Road field in 1904, as cricket is recorded as being played there up until the early 1920s. This is mentioned by David Rymill in his book 'Worcester Park & Cuddington: A Walk Through the Centuries' where he notes that even after the formation of W.P.A.C. *"The Lindsay Road field continued to be used for both football and cricket by the boys in the area."*

I had presumed that the person who submitted the advertisements in the 'South London Press', Charles William Salkeld, was an adult, but I was way short of the mark, as Charles Salkeld, who was born in Bermondsey in 1888, was the thirteen year old son of a Leather Dresser. It was impressive that a youngster should have had the confidence and initiative to place adverts in the paper, although I could find no connection between Salkeld and the club, apart from the fact that several of the more prominent members of the committee were involved in the fur trade. At that time he would not even have been able to play for the club as he did not live in Worcester Park.

The Club Representatives, George E. Turner and Edward D. Hurles, who attended the Surrey County Football Association meeting at Anderton's Hotel, Fleet Street, before the start of the 1901-02 season, were still in their teens as they were both born in 1882. Despite the fact that the club was newly formed, they were ambitious; they had already entered the Surrey Junior Cup, where they were drawn in Group F, away to Wallington Athletic. It is interesting to note that there were a handful of notable clubs in their group: Beddington Corner, Banstead, Ashtead, Carshalton Park, Wallington, Sutton United, and Mitcham and Ewell.

In 1901 the club and players were young and enthusiastic, and as such they did not always abide by the rules, as is evidenced by the following snippet from the 'Sporting Life' of the 24th October, 1901: *"At an emergency meeting held by the Surrey County Football Association, on Monday evening last, at the York Hotel, Waterloo, the Wallington Athletic and Worcester Park Clubs were ordered to replay their Junior Cup, as the first game was not in charge of an official referee."*

Despite this hic-cup at the start of their second season the club seemed to thrive as can be seen by the following extremely positive article which appeared in the 'Wimbledon Herald' on the 27th September, **1902**, at the start of their third season:

"Worcester Park starts this season with very bright prospects. A good ground, popular officers, including an energetic secretary, happy financial position, and plenty of good sporting members, should at all times make a club a success. A special feature of the Worcester Park club is that all members are entirely local, and therefore, as each man is playing for his own village, enthusiasm of the proper sort is well maintained.

With only one or two exceptions, almost all last year's members will again be available. The membership has been considerably increased. Several new members come with good reputations, especially the brothers W. and A. Patrick, who hail from Pelham, Wimbledon, and they are confidently expected to materially strengthen the team, or, at least, to fill up the gap caused by the partial retirement of J. Hopkins, who, after having 'skippered' the club for two seasons, has, much to the members' regret, felt obliged to resign, owing to an unfortunate strain received last season. It is the hope of all to see him again in the field. The members have undoubtedly found a good successor as Captain in J. Peters, who at all times is a sterling good player, and will, by his energetic example, do his level best to lead his men to victory.

Owing to the late Hon. Sec. (G .E. Turner) having gone abroad, the members had to look round for the right man to fill this important post, and they are to be heartily congratulated upon having prevailed upon Mr. Arthur Hillman, 'Budleigh Cottage',

Worcester Park, to accept the responsible position. Judging by the splendid fixture card he has arranged for the two teams, besides the business-like manner he has started upon his many varied duties, it is confidently anticipated he will do thoroughly all that is required of him.

F. W. Drew will again guard the uprights, and, if required, a splendid reserve will be found in W. Vaughan. G. Dearman and W. Hopkins were last season a tower of strength at the back, and often saved the side from disaster. No doubt is entertained of their being in form. A selection from E. Styles (an indefatigable worker), J. Peters (always 'on the go' and in the right place), H. R. Turner (a much improved player), F. Paye, G. Hawkins, Hugh Woods, and others will give a strong half-back line; while the front rank will be ably filled by the brothers Patrick, A. Hillman, A. Styles, and Leslie Sarll, whose terrific shooting and splendid sprinting powers have not in the least degenerated, and should H. Millward be able to turn out, he will always be considered an acquisition.

The club has again entered for the Surrey Junior Cup, and the fixtures comprise the following:- Ewell II, London Devonians, Leatherhead, Old Tenisonians, Old Quintinians, Belmont, Old Tiffinians, Sutton United, London Swiss, Borough Polytechnic Reserves, Surbiton Rangers, Mackenzie Wanderers, Epsom, Hook, Wimbledon Old Centrals, Malden, and Carshalton Park, with most of whom two fixtures are arranged, the last five being met for the first time. With twenty-eight fixtures arranged for the seconds - captained by Mr. T. Watts - no member can conscientiously complain of the bill of fare provided."

This article must have been written by an enthusiastic member of the committee in an attempt perhaps to encourage more people either to join the club as a playing member or to be a supporter. Whoever wrote the article knew the details of all the fixtures and the strength of the individual members of the team. One or two of the claims, however, such as the condition of the ground, are perhaps a little exaggerated, as was the fact that all the players were 'entirely local'. In the 1901 census Arthur Patrick (b. 1881) and his brother, William (b. 1883), both lived with their family at 167, Merton Road, Wimbledon.

The only match report to appear in the 'Wimbledon Herald', for the **1902-03** season, took place on May 2nd, 1903, for the season's finale against Mackenzie Wanderers.

"The Park had rather a difficulty in getting a good side together for their last match, and knowing the strength of the visitors did not anticipate increasing their goal average, they did not, however, expect such a gruelling as 6-2. The visitors from the start showed that they meant business, their combination was good to see, and ere many minutes elapsed they were in the Park territory, and cleverly evaded the home

backs. Drew had no chance with goal number one. The dose was repeated soon after, when the home team made a determined attack, which resulted in success for the Park, Hillman rushing up and netting the ball. A struggle then took place, the home team trying hard to get level, Rydes, Hopkins, and Hillman, ably fed by Perry, working excellent, but the visitors' backs were as determined, and beat them back. The home defence was again called upon, and a long low shot was badly muffled by the home custodian which put the Wanderers three up, and soon after the teams crossed over.

In the second half the Parkites played very pluckily, but could only gain one more point, splendidly obtained by Will Hopkins. Sarll was incapacitated and could not run, which handicapped a weak team, who were quite outclassed, and had to be on the defence most of the time. It, however, was a very pleasant game quite void of rough play. The home team left the field feeling they had done their best against a much stronger crew. Woods and Turner at back made splendid efforts. Will Hopkins, and E. Styles, were quite at their best, and Rydes missed his right winger. It was generally agreed the best men were Perry and Hillman, indeed the latter played about his best game this season. Worcester Park: F. Drew, Woods, Turner; E. Styles, Perry, York; Sarll, Rydes, W. Hopkins, Hillman, A. Styles."

The anonymous Worcester Park scribe had his work cut out that week as the 'Herald', apart from publishing the account of the Mackenzie game, also published an extremely full account of the 1902-03 season, which is reproduced here in its entirety as it not only waxes lyrical about the footballing prowess of such a small hamlet but also records the progress and development of individual players. Incorporated in the article is an account of their 10-1 defeat by their mighty neighbour, Sutton United, in the Second Round of the Surrey Junior Cup (they had a bye the first round). The gulf between the two sides in 1902 probably was not as wide as it is nowadays. Sutton United had only been formed two years before W.P.F.C., in 1898, through the amalgamation of two local sides, Sutton Guild Rovers and Sutton Association F.C. (formerly St. Barnabus F.C.)

'Wimbledon Herald' 2nd May 1903: *"The season which was finished on Saturday has, notwithstanding various ups and downs, been very successful. A pleasing feature of the club is, that it is composed of village members only, the sources of talent therefore are restricted, but each man is playing for his own hamlet, and for a small club to hold their own so successfully, in fact have a good margin of wins and goals against neighbouring towns with much larger populations to draw upon, speaks volumes for the love of the game evidently possessed by the members. It may here* be noticed the remarkable rate the place is growing; at the pace it is going it bids fair to be very soon become a second Sutton.

The members are again indebted to Mrs. Pennington for kindly placing a meadow at their disposal.

A very entertaining fixture list was arranged for two elevens by Mr. Hillman, the very energetic secretary, and also about twelve Wednesday matches - of the latter I have not the exact record, but honours were about even. By the first eleven 25 matches were played, 12 won, 9 lost and 4 drawn, goals for being 66 with 43 against, while the seconds show a record of 16 games, won 6, lost 8, drawn 2, goals 88 for, 52 against, so that though the wins were slightly against them the goals were not.

Dealing again with the first team the worst licking was in the S.J.C. tie v Sutton United, but here they were surely the victims of misfortune - no doubt the Suttonians were better by three goals to one, but 10-1 was accidental (Remember in 1902 no substitutes were allowed). The Parkites at half-time led 1-0, then Will Hopkins, their most reliable back, was badly fouled and carried off the field unconscious, causing a stoppage of fifteen minutes. Then Drew in goal was badly lamed, and Sutton piled on nine goals. The Park did not mind being snuffed out of the cup so early (second round), but it unfortunately robbed them of several men for some weeks, causing the team to draw upon their second string, but this did not prove a misfortune, inasmuch as several of the juniors proved themselves worthy of their elevation, especially Rydes and Vaughan.

The team had to avenge the defeat on some unfortunates, as 10-1 against looked bad on a card - so Garton Rovers were the victims, and were soundly trounced to the tune of 16-1. A remarkable feature of the games is that no less than eleven times have the defence kept their scoresheet clean, so that leaving out the Sutton match the 33 goals against were scored in thirteen matches. Another feature was that of the four drawn games, two were with Epsom, the first resulting in 1-1, and the second 0-0.

As to the individual play, the loss of the brothers Patrick and J. Peters was a serious matter to the club, but the members do not buckle under for setbacks of this kind. For injuries received W. Hopkins, J. Hopkins and F. Drew were missed for a time, and welcomed back recently. Will Hopkins especially; he is an ideal back in two senses. Dearman for the last few weeks has also been missing, but the club cannot afford to lose him, as with the two named at back, there seems to be an air of safety, and an entire understanding with poor goalie behind. At times the displays they have given during the season have been grand.

One of the most improved players of the season has been Hugh Woods. Taken from half he fell back, and proved a worthy substitute; his kicking powers are well known, in fact 'Hug(h)e' R. Turner too, has proved very useful at back, and if at times erratic, is always a hard worker. But perhaps the hardest out and out worker has been 'Joey Styles', the same week after week, always persevering and full of go.

Of the forwards, of course, first and foremost comes Leslie Sarll. The flying right winger. He has been a tower of strength to the team. His shooting powers are terrific, and his centres grand, and it has been fine tuition for Rydes, who was given a chance early in the season, and played ever since, improving week after week. Great things are expected of him. Hillman, perhaps, has not generally been so well in form this season as last, but he has always been a genuine trier and worker, and with Rydes has done most of the finishing touches to the centres.

About the best acquisition to the team has been Tom Perry at half-back. His play has been splendid all through; never losing his head, he has fed his forwards splendidly, and often stopped an ugly rush. F. Drew, in goal, has been quite up to his usual standard, but recently, owing to business pressure, has had to stand out. The club, however, has been fortunate in obtaining W. Vaughan to ably fill the gap. He has the advantage of youth and height, and is very safe, besides being a good kick.

The Second eleven, perhaps, have lately been a little disheartened by the inroads made upon their team, but they have a sufficient sportsmanlike spirit to know that a good first team is the main thing. Space prevents detailing the second's doings more fully, but special mention must be made of J. Butcher, Nickelson, J. York, Amos, and T. Watts {Captain), who show great promise. It is a pity that M. Mayo, Harry and Edgar Woods are not available on Saturdays."

The **1903-04** season was heralded by the press with the customary optimism. Whilst the scribe regretted the fact that one or two players had moved on to pastures new he felt that this gave a chance for others to step up to the mark. The change in the club colours from green and orange was noted as was the fact that the ground that had been loaned to them by Mrs. Pennington had been worked upon by the committee and was in good condition. 'Wimbledon Herald' October 26th, 1903: *"If this club has not found a lot of new talent, the enthusiasm of the old members appears not a whit abated. I have to hand a splendid fixture card, for which the energetic secretary is to be congratulated. The fixture list totals over thirty matches, the majority of which* *are on the home ground, so that supporters who have the interest of their village club at heart, will have plenty of opportunity of encouraging them.*

The engagements are with Mackenzie Wanderers, Old Tenisonians, Epsom, Borough Polytechnic Reserves, London Germans, Leatherhead II, Maldenians, Ashtead, Sutton Pyro., New Malden, Euneva, Old Quintinians, Ewell, West Ewell, Steinway Athletic, Cottenham Park, Dulwich St. Peters, and Malden Trinity, the last four being met for the first time. It was decided not to enter for the Surrey Junior Cup.

Among the newcomers Mr. Tom Perry was elected Captain, and it is confidently anticipated his selection will not be regretted, he having proved himself to be a thorough good sportsman. The members are still content to let the quill driving remain in the hands of Mr. Arthur Hillman, knowing that a harder worker could not be found, and with a good energetic committee it only remains for the members to buck up. Of the latter, several new players are welcomed, and at least one has a reputation - Mr. Studley, who played for some years for West Norwood - and it is hoped he will greatly assist. Most of the old faces will come up smiling, a good forward line being selected from:- Leslie Sarll, Hillman, A. Styles, Rydes, J. Hopkins, Studley and Fisher, leaving Perry, E. Styles, York, Hawkins, and Butcher to pick from for halves. Four formidable backs are to be found in G. Dearman, H. Woods, W. Hopkins, and R. Turner, while if F. Drew is not always available in goal, W. Vaughan is always willing to fill the gap. The most prominent members are here mentioned, but even then a good many remain to take part in over a dozen good second eleven fixtures arranged for them.

So it would seem to be a discontented man to cater for if he is not satisfied with the menu provided. The club has possibly lost one or two good players for various reasons; their loss is to be regretted, but even this will give an opportunity to some one else, and if the club cannot win all their matches, they always appear to do the next best thing - play their best for victory. The same ground, owing to the repeated kindness of Mrs. Pennington, has been placed at the club's use, and has been got into good order by the committee. Among other noticeable improvements it will be seen that the club's old colours are discarded for prominent dark blue and white stripes."

The ground apparently was not quite as good as the scribe made out, however, as it was slated in the 'Surrey Mirror' less than three weeks later when the First XI played against Leatherhead 2nd XI, who probably submitted the report to the paper;

"The above teams met at Worcester Park on Saturday last, the game ending in victory for the homesters by four goals to nil. The ground was very muddy and

slippery, and was not really fit for football playing, and the visitors failing to exert themselves had three goals scored against them before the half-time. Worcester Park added another goal in the second half, and thus won by four goals to love."

The main item of interest in the preview for the **1904-05** season, was the fact that the club had acquired a new ground. Whether it was the state of the old ground which prompted this move, or whether it was the fact that the landlady of 'The Drill' had retired in 1903. Frances Pennington was by then 71 and had been involved with the pub for almost 50 years, as the landlady or as the landlord's wife. Perhaps the new landlord of 'The Drill', Henry Mortimer Newton, had other plans for the meadow.

The players, however, moved to a much larger ground in Lindsay Road, thanks to the generosity of Andrew Blake. Although it was only five minutes (brisk) walk from the station, it had apparently quite a slope, a point which was mentioned in an account of a Reserve XI match versus Leatherhead, in the 'Surrey Mirror', on December 21st, 1906: *"Leatherhead won the toss and kicked up the slope in the first half."* Sadly the new ground also became extremely waterlogged in winter.

Another benefit of the move to Lindsay Road, was the club's acquisition of Blake's extremely talented son, Frederick, who was to remain associated with the footballers for over fifty years, as footballer, captain and then manager. He made his first appearance in a 1-0 victory over Old Maldenians on October 31st, 1903, aged just 16.

The preview of the forthcoming 1904-05 season, in the 'Wimbledon Herald' of September 24th, 1904, also stated that there were 10 new playing members and that the club was not going to enter any cups or leagues that season. Although most of the fixtures were the same as the previous year the article was interesting as the Second XI fixtures were included and there was some change to the personnel of the First XI: Percy Lloyd and Fred Blake, who were to become stalwarts of the First eleven, were mentioned for the first time, in this article.

"Worcester Park is looking forward to a good season. All last season's players are available, and with about 10 additional playing members the Selection Committee should have very little difficulty in obtaining two elevens. The committee has been fortunate in securing a new ground, which is within five minutes' walk of the station.

The following is the list of matches arranged for the first team:- Borough Polytechnic Reserves, Tenisonians Reserves, Epsom, Old Quintinians, St. Mark's, Sutton Pyro, Ashtead, Leatherhead II, Cottenham Park, Maldenians, and Malden Trinity, all of which were met last season. The clubs to be met for the first time are Gloucester House, Clapham United, Lavender Hill, Eastern United, East Ham, Waddon United, R.H.A. (Woolwich), Raveley, and St. Stephen's. All but Waddon United and St. Stephen's will be met twice. The clubs played last year and missing from the list this year are the London Germans {now defunct), London Devonians, Malden, West Ewell, and Fulham Excelsior. The second eleven have almost a full list with the following clubs:- Park Albion, Epsom II, Stewart's-Lane United, Lavender Hill II, Wimbledon Y.M.C.A., Cottenham Park II, Manor Park, London Rovers, Clapham United II, Malden Trinity II, Burnhill, East Ham Clarence, and St. Stephen's II, all but the latter being met twice. The list is stronger than last year.

Of the first team Ryde and J. Hopkins will both be missing from the forward line, whilst Sarll, outside right, will only be able to assist occasionally. The defence will be chosen from W. Hopkins, Drew (goal), Turner, Fisher, Woods (backs), W. T. Perry, capt., and the brothers Styles, Macey (halves), with Dearman, Walton, Blake, Hillman, Lloyd, and Sarll as forwards. This team should hold its own.

The second team will be strengthened by several new members and Dalton, Heather, Hopkins, and W. Macey have all shown good form at practise. As the club is still kept purely to local membership there is plenty of enthusiasm in the team. The committee has again decided not to enter any cups or leagues. The season commences today versus Gloucester House."

The move to a new ground and the influx of ten new members, plus the emergence of Percy Lloyd and Fred Blake as quality players, certainly seemed to pay dividends for the club, as can be inferred from the following article in the summary of the 1904-05 season which can be found in the 'Wimbledon Herald' of May 6th, 1905:

"Worcester Park: The season which has finished on Saturday was the most successful since the formation of the club. With a larger ground both teams have played more games than in any previous season. The list of members had also increased year by year, and has reached a total of almost 60, 36 of this number being playing members, and all members being entirely local, the interest shown by the supporters is very pleasing. A good fixture list was arranged for both teams with better opponents than either XI had ever before met. By the 1st XI 28 games were played, 16 won, 9 lost, and 3 drawn, the goals for being 73 and 38 against, whilst the 2nd XI show a record of played 23 games, won 7, lost 13, drawn 3, goals for 43, and 54 against. This does not perhaps read well, yet at least five of their opponents might have challenged the Firsts; the rest of the games were fairly even.

Dealing again with the 1st XI it should be stated that about five of the losses were very close and hard fought games, and on nine occasions the splendid defence managed to keep the score sheet clean. Unfortunately Walton and Sarll, two of the best goal-getters and right-wingers, were only able to turn out on very few occasions, and no doubt had they been more regularly in the team the number of wins and goals would have been much higher. Blake in the centre proved himself a splendid shot, and his clever dribbling was a treat to watch. Lloyd and Hillman have greatly improved on the left wing, the former especially. He is very fast, and his centres right across goal have been very noticeable. It is chiefly through his play that so many goals have been scored. As to the halves the same three did duty as in the previous season, the brother Styles and Perry, the skipper, and it is to be hoped that they may be seen together for several seasons to come.

The next line have improved since last season, with Hopkins and Woods and two new men in Verrall and Patrick, who have both come from good neighbouring clubs, and have greatly strengthened the team. Drew, in goal, has played in nearly every game, and has shown that there is plenty of go in him. Some of his saves during the season have won great applause from the spectators.

The Reserves have greatly improved altogether. Clarke, Dalton, the brothers Springetts, and Scott, new members, all assisted the 1st team in time of need. Watts, Cleary, Macey, and Boltuolt played regularly for the Reserves.

The 1st team won against Boro' Polytechnic, Old Tenisonians II, Old Quintinians, St. Mark's, Sutton Pyro (twice), Leatherhead II, Cottenham Park, Grasshoppers, Sumnor (twice), Lavender Hill, Raveley, Fulham Athenian. Lost to East Hill, Gloucester House, Epsom, Lavender Hill, Old Quintinians, St. Mark's, East Ham, Waddon United, and St. Stephen's, and drew with Ashtead (twice) and L'head II.

The Reserves' best wins were Lavender Hill Reserves, Clapham United Reserves, and Wimbledon Y.M.C.A.

The duties of Hon. Sec. for the past three seasons have been carried on by A. E. Hillman, of 'Budleigh Cottage', Worcester Park."

I think one of the most noticeable features of the First XI was the fact that the nucleus of the team had played together for four or five years. If one looks at the sides which turned out in October, 1904, there is a strong feeling of consistency:

October 8th: W.P.F.C. (4) v Old Tenisonians Reserves (1)
F. W. Drew, G. Dearman, A. Styles, W. T. Perry (2) (Captain), J. Macey, P. Lloyd, W. Heather (1), A. Hillman, F. Blake (1), T. Dalton
October 15th: Grasshoppers (1) v W.P.F.C. (3)
F. W. Drew, G. Dearman, Hopkins, E. Styles, W. T. Perry, A. Styles, P. Lloyd, W. Heather, F. Blake (1), A. Hillman (1), L. Sarll (1)
October 22nd: W.P.F.C. (4) v Old Quintinians (2)
Scorers Walton 2, E. Styles 1, W. Heather 1.

October 29th: W.P.F.C. (4) v St. Mark's Kennington (0)

F. W. Drew, Hopkins, Turner, A. Verrall, W. T. Perry, A. Styles, Dalton, F. Blake (2), Hillman (1), W. Heather (1), P. Lloyd

Over the summer of 1905 the football club decided to again forgo the joys and tribulations of league football for the following season, although they decided to enter the Surrey Junior Cup, and renewed most of the fixtures from the preceding four or five seasons. Their Captain from the previous two seasons, W. T. Perry, decided to resign because of work commitments and was replaced by Arthur Verrall. The preview for the **1905-06** season, in the 'Wimbledon Herald', also noted that the club would be using two pitches at the Lindsay Road ground. The article of 23rd September, 1905, merely confirms, ex-President of W.P.A.C. (1993), Cyril Southerby's assertion that there were two football pitches down Lindsay Road:

"Worcester Park will commence the season next Saturday with a home fixture with St. Stephen's, a club which beat them in the last game last season. A full list of games has been arranged for both the first and reserve teams. Of last season's clubs, Gloucester House, Waddon United, Epsom, Old Quintinians, Borough Polytechnic Reserves, St. Mark's, East Hill A, and Leatherhead II, are to be met again this season, whilst the clubs to be met for the first time are Elmhurst, Church Institute, Barnes Reserves, Brixton Burnley, Burwood Athletic, Wimbledon St. Andrew's A, Hillyer's, and Malden Wednesday.

The club has taken the same ground as last season with two pitches, and most of the games will be played at home. Nearly all last season's players have promised to turn out, and it is expected that several of the reserves who showed good form at the latter end of last season will come into the team. W. T. Perry, who was forced to resign the captaincy on account of business, has promised to turn out as often as possible. F. W. Drew will again be seen between the sticks, whilst E. Springett will act in that position for the reserves. A. Verrall, who proved himself such a tower of strength last season at back, will captain the team, and will partner W. Hopkins at back.

The brothers Styles, with W. T. Perry, will form the half-back line, and of the forwards, Messrs. Walton, Blake, Lloyd, Sarll, and Hillman, with the pick of the reserves, should do as well as last season. The first eleven's card is of about the same strength as usual, but the reserves, who have several new members, have a rather stronger list."

On Monday evening, September 10th, 1905, at 7.30pm, the club Secretary, Arthur Hillman, and the club Captain, Arthur Verrall, were recorded in having attended the

28th Annual General meeting of the Surrey Football Association. The 'Surrey Mirror' noted that only clubs who had paid their annual subscription for the ensuing season were sent tickets. At the end of the evening the draw was made for the First Round of the Surrey Junior Cup, W.P.F.C. being drawn away to Kingston St. Luke's, a match which they were to lose 6-1.

There was a definite change of policy following the 1905-06 season, which seemed to coincide with Ernie Styles assuming the mantle of Secretary. Most of the friendly fixtures were discarded as the first XI were admitted into Division 2 of the Kingston and District League for the **1906-07** season. Despite being hindered by a rather restrictive selection policy and a rather sub-standard pitch, they were 'runners up' in **1907-08**: whilst in **1908-09**, they became the Division 2 'Champions'

Kingston & District League 1907-08

2ND DIVISION.

Surbiton Hill W.M.C.	14	12	1	1	54	9	25
Worcester Park	14	10	2	2	32	18	22
Molesey St. Paul's	14	8	5	1	38	19	17
Gigg's Hill	14	6	6	2	31	26	14
Weston Green	14	7	7	0	29	26	14
Cottenham Park	14	2	8	4	18	35	10
Oxshott	14	4	8	2	19	37	10
Hook	14	1	13	0	10	61	2

The state of the ground, however, was a permanent problem which endured year after year, as can be seen by the following extract from the 'Surrey Comet' of December 14th, 1907: *"Worcester Park F.C. will to-day play their fixtures with Summerstown II in the third round of the Surrey Junior Cup Competition. The match was postponed from November 30th on account of the ground being unfit. The kick-off is at 2.30, on the Worcester Park F.C. ground."*

Much of the club's success was due to the fact that it was well organised. It had a strong, focussed General Committee, a Selection Committee, an organised Secretary and their own referees. All these, in their turn, were supported by an array of some of the most important and powerful people in the district, who assumed the roles of President and Vice-Presidents.

The first hint of this successful structure occurred in an account, in the 'Comet' of May 9th, **1908**, of the club's eighth annual dinner, which disclosed the names of a few more of the important characters involved with the club, and revealed that twenty-one year old Fred Blake, who had only joined the club in 1904 had already risen to the position of First XI Captain and seemed to be held in very high regard. From the abundance of complimentary toasts we can glean that Ernie Styles was the Treasurer, Fred Blake was the First XI Captain, Thomas Dalton was the Vice Captain, Joseph Hopkins and Ernest Bartlett (b. 1882) were the referees, and Henry Bartlett was the Chairman for the evening. This Henry Bartlett was either the father or brother of Ernest, as both were called 'Henry'.

"The members of the Worcester Park Football Club held their eighth annual dinner at the Café Royal, Worcester Park, on Saturday. The function proved a great success, there being a large turn-out of members. An excellent repast having been partaken of, the remainder of the evening was occupied with song and sentiment. The chair was occupied by Mr. W. Smith, one of the Vice-Presidents. Mr. E. Styles proposed the toast of 'The President and Vice-Presidents', to which the chairman responded. The toast of the 'Honorary Secretary and Treasurer' was entrusted to Mr. Taylor and Mr. E. A. Styles responded. Mr. A. Hillman, when submitting the toast of the 'Captain', eulogistically referred to the work Mr. Blake had done, and the latter gentleman responded. Other toasts were 'The Vice-Captain', proposed by Mr. W. Lee, and responded to by Mr. Dalton; 'The Referees', proposed by Mr. F. Blake and replied to by Messrs. J. Hopkins and E. Bartlett; and 'The Committee' which was proposed by the Chairman, Mr. H. Bartlett making reply. Music interspersed the toasts, those contributing to the programme being Messrs. L. Patrick, F. Blake, P. Boultoult, H. Boyd, F. Marsh, B. Scales and W. Smith. The duties of the accompanists were ably carried out by Mrs. McGowan and Mrs. Shackleton. A vote of thanks to the Chairman and the singing of the National Anthem concluded a very pleasant time."

The tone of the article was very bullish and self-congratulatory, and there was every indication that the club was going from strength to strength, as can be seen by the fact that at the beginning of the following season they did concede a goal until they were beaten by 4 goals to 1 in a friendly game by Ashtead on October 17th. That was quite impressive for a team which apparently derived its players solely from Worcester Park.

The Annual General Meeting for the **1909-10** season was again held at the Café Royal, with Mr. J. Stenning in the chair, on Thursday evening 20th May, 1909. No mention was made in the 'Comet' of the team's success that season, but *"the statement of accounts showed that the club was in a successful position and that a balance of £4 5s. would be carried forward."* The main topic of conversation at the meeting, was a proposal by Mr. Diddle, which was seconded by Mr. Scott, that the membership of the club should be thrown open to neighbouring districts. This was followed by the election of officers, the President and Vice-Presidents being re-elected en bloc. These officials, and the playing officials can be found in the accompanying membership card on the opposite page.

Two days later, on Saturday 22nd May, the ninth annual dinner of W.P.F.C., was held at the Café Royal with the club's President, Mr. C. W. Smith, in the chair. On this occasion, however, *"there was not a large attendance"*. Obviously two meetings within the space of three days proved too much for the Worcester Park faithful. It is interesting to note that the A.G.M. and Dinner had been incorporated the previous year, and appeared to have been much more successful.

Following their A.G.M. in May, the club decided to extend their catchment area for the 1909 -1910 season. On September 8th, 1909, the 'Comet' reported: *'This season the Worcester Park Football Club will embark upon a programme framed on more ambitious lines, and the membership is now open to residents in Ewell, Raynes Park, New Malden and Cheam, instead of being restricted to Worcester Park as heretofore. A practice match took place last Saturday, and the opening fixture is a home one against Surbiton Hill Working Men's Club, next Saturday. Mr. E. A. Styles is the Hon. Secretary and Treasurer.'*

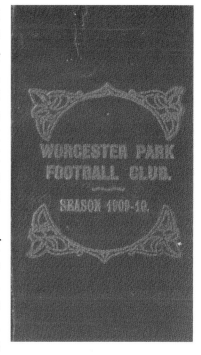

In 2018, I discovered on an online auction site, a small membership card/fixture card for the 1909-1910 season, which had belonged to **Richard Gaskin** Junior (b. 1888) of 9, Idmiston Road, Worcester Park, Malden. Richard was a gas meter maker, as was his 15 year old brother, **Leonard**, whilst his father, Richard senior, was a Tin Plate Worker. Little did I realise that, when I acquired the card, Richard jnr was the First XI goalkeeper and a future Club Captain, and that both he and his brother were also members of Old Malden and Worcester Park C.C.

The card had a dark blue hard cover with the name of the club impressed in gold leaf and measured 2 inches by 4 inches (see photo above). It opened up to reveal all the First and Second XI fixtures for the 1909 -1910 season, and Richard had kindly entered all the results. Sadly the pencil that he used was not as sharp or as clear as one might have hoped. Despite this, I have enclosed an enlarged copy of the rather impressive result sheet on the following page.

It appears obvious from studying the fixture card that there must have been more than one pitch at Lindsay Road as both the First and Second XI's were down to play at home on the same date at least eight times during the season. The Second XI played 19 league matches in the Wimbledon & District League, whilst the First XI played 12 matches in that league and 12 matches in the Kingston & District League (Division II), of which they won 10, drew 2 and lost none. They scored 33 goals and conceded only 3, whilst accumulating 22 points.

The inner two pages of the membership card are also really quite impressive as the names of the committee and the great and good of society, who supported them, were

Member's Name _R. ...._ (handwritten)

1st XI.

Date.	Opponents.	Ground.	Result. For. Agst.
Sept. 11	Surbiton W. M. Club	Home	
18	†Molesey	Molesey	
25	†East Surrey Regt.	Home	
Oct. 2	†Hampton English O.B	Bushey Park	
9	*New Wandsworth Ath	Home	
16	1st rd. Surrey Jun. Cup		
23	†Weston Green	Thames Ditton	
30	*Devas Institute	Home	
Nov. 6	Forest Hill	Home	
13	†Cottenham Park	Raynes Park	
20	*St. Michael's Ch. Inst.	Southfields	
27	†Kingston B.	Kingston	
Dec. 4	*Weston Green	Home	
11	*Devas Institute	Raynes Park	
18	*Oakleigh	Home	
27	*Crusaders	Home	
Jan. 1	*St. Michael's Ch. Inst.	Home	
8	†East Surrey Regt.	Kingston	
15	*Celtic Rovers	Home	
22	†Kingston B.	Home	
29	*New Wandsworth Ath	Earlsfield	
Feb. 5	*Oakleigh	Wimbledon	
12	*Forest Hill	Home	
19	†Hampton English O.B	Home	
26	†Cottenham Park	Raynes Park	
Mar. 5	*Crusaders	Home	
12	†Molesey	Home	
19	*Celtic Rovers	Raynes Park	
26	St. Kilda	Home	
April 2	Surbiton W. M. Club	Surbiton	
9	Wandsworth Wesleyan	Home	
16	West London Old Boys	Home	
23			
30			

†Kingston & District League. *Wimbledon & District League.

2nd XI.

Date.	Opponents.	Ground.	Result. For. Agst.
Sept. 11			
18	Bevill	Home	
25	*Ravenswood II.	Home	
Oct. 2	*Loretto	Home	
9	*Southfields E. School	Southfields	
16			
23	*Battersea Celtic	Home	
30	*Sth. Wimbledon Wes.	Wimbledon	
Nov. 6	Fulham Primitive	Home	
13	*Battersea Celtic	Earlsfield	
20	Oakleigh Athletic	Home	
27	*Universe	Home	
Dec. 4	*Crusaders II.	Raynes Park	
11	*Sth. Wimbledon Wes.	Home	
18	*Y.M.C.A. II.	Wimbledon	
27			
Jan. 1	*Raynes Park	Raynes Park	
8	*Universe	Earlsfield	
15	Moreton	Home	
22	*Colliers Wood II.	Home	
29	*Raynes Park	Home	
Feb. 5	*Y.M.C.A. II.	Home	
12	Oakleigh Athletic	Home	
19	*Southfields E. School	Home	
26	*Colliers Wood II.	Merton	
Mar. 5	*Crusaders II.	Home	
12	*Rayleigh	Home	
19	*Ravenswood II.	Southfields	
26			
28			
April 2	*Rayleigh	Home	
9	*Streatham Grove	Home	
15	Fulham Primitive	Home	
23			
30			

*Wimbledon & District League.

J. W. Heath, "The" Athletic Printer, 102, Merton High Street, Wimbledon.

172

players and ex-committee members, William T. Perry, Arthur Verrall and Edward Hurles, who were all in their late twenties or early thirties, and more mature pillars of the community such as Andrew Blake and Dr. William Chearnley Smith.

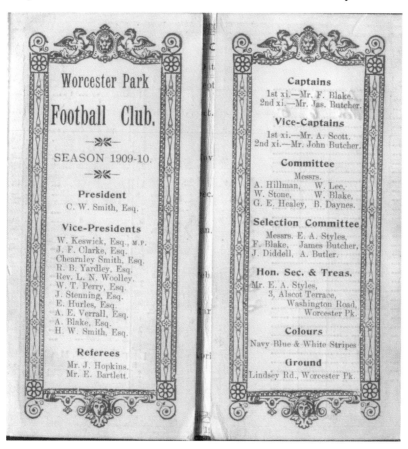

Worcester Park Football Club.

SEASON 1909-10.

President
C. W. Smith, Esq.

Vice-Presidents
W. Keswick, Esq., M.P.
J. F. Clarke, Esq.
Chearnley Smith, Esq.
R. B. Yardley, Esq.
Rev. L. N. Woolley.
W. T. Perry, Esq.
J. Stenning, Esq.
E. Hurles, Esq.
A. E. Verrall, Esq.
A. Blake, Esq.
H. W. Smith, Esq.

Referees
Mr. J. Hopkins.
Mr. E. Bartlett.

Captains
1st xi.—Mr. F. Blake.
2nd xi.—Mr. Jas. Butcher.

Vice-Captains
1st xi.—Mr. A. Scott.
2nd xi.—Mr. John Butcher.

Committee
Messrs.
A. Hillman,   W. Lee,
W. Stone,   W. Blake,
G. E. Healey,   B. Daynes.

Selection Committee
Messrs. E. A. Styles,
F. Blake,   James Butcher,
J. Diddell,   A. Butler.

Hon. Sec. & Treas.
Mr. E. A. Styles,
3, Alscot Terrace,
Washington Road,
Worcester Pk.

Colours
Navy Blue & White Stripes

Ground
Lindsey Rd., Worcester Pk.

The President of the Club was **Charles William Smith** (b. 1834), a 75 year old widower, who lived at 'Malvern Lodge', Worcester Park, a 17 room house which he shared with a cook and four servants. He had been retired for over 20 years by this time, after making a fortune as a fur merchant. Charles had been a great benefactor of St. Mary's Church (see David Rymill) and was the sort of patron that an up-and-coming football club might need.

Of a similar age was **William Keswick** M.P. (b. 1834), a Scott who had been born into a wealthy shipping family, and had spent much of his life working for the family company in Hong Kong and Japan. In 1899 he had won a bye-election and became the Conservative M.P. for Epsom, a seat that he held until his death in 1912. Keswick was about the only Vice-President who did not live locally as he lived at Eastwood Park, Great Bookham. The local M.P. probably was not a regular on the touchline at Lindsay Road on a wet November afternoon. Having his name in the fixture card, however, added a certain gravitas and prestige to the club.

Of the other Vice-Presidents: **Leonard Napier Woolley** (b. 1870) was the Vicar of St. Philip's Church; **James Stenning** (b. 1854) was a furrier's assistant who lived at 'Sydney Villas', Washington Road; **Robert Blake Yardley** (b.1859), of the Yardley Lavender soap family, was a retired barrister, a County Councillor and a local Councillor who resided at 'The Birches' in the London Road, Cheam; **John F. Clarke** (b. 1847) was a chartered accountant living at St. Andrews, Cuddington; **William Thomas Perry** (b. 1877) was an insurance manager who lived at 'Fairlight' Kingsmead Avenue, Worcester Park; finally **Henry Walter Smith** (b. 1846) was a law clerk who owned the Café Royal in Cheam Common Road, a Tea Room and Restaurant which was run by his wife, Hazell Elizabeth Smith.

The two referees named on that page were, as might be expected, slightly younger: **Ernest Bartlett** (b. 1882) was a carpenter who lived at 8, Cheamside, whilst **Joseph W. Hopkins** (b. 1879) was a potter who lived in the Malden Road, Cheam.

Of the Committee members apart from Fred Blake, Ernie Styles and Arthur Hillman, the only ones that there appeared to be any information on, in the 1911 census, were **John Diddell** (b.1872), an 'outworker' who resided with his family at 1, Daisy Cottages, Longfellow Road; **Albert Scott** (b. 1883) a butcher, living with his parents at Worcester Park Farm; **John Butcher** (b.1883 in Thakeham, Sussex), a gardener, who lived with his wife and daughter at 68, Idmiston Road, Malden, and his brother **James Butcher** (b 1890 in Thakeham), a Post Office worker, who still lived at his parent's home at 78, Idmiston Road. This was the very same road where **Richard Gaskin**, who became the First XI Captain in 1910, was also living.

The celebrations which followed the First XI becoming Division II Champions in the Spring of 1910 were sadly marred by the death of Edward VII on May 6th. The club's annual dinner, which was due to be held the following day, was an extremely muted affair, as was recorded in the 'Comet' the following week: *"The annual dinner of the Worcester Park F.C. was held at the Café Royal on Saturday evening, about thirty members being present. Mr. J. Stenning was in the chair. Owing to the death of his Majesty the King the proceedings were of a quiet nature, no toasts being submitted and no music indulged in. The only item in the programme after dinner was the presentation to members of medals won in the Kingston and District Football League competitions, the following being the recipients:- Messrs F. Blake (Captain), A. Scott (Vice-Captain), E. Styles, T. Dalton, J. Butcher, R. Gaskin, F. Marsh, J. Watts, T. Stevens, J. Diddell, G. Hawkins, G. Hilton, B. Daynes and J. Doel.*

The main points of interest to be gleaned from the A.G.M. which occurred on the following Wednesday was that it was just as difficult to get money from certain members in 1910 as it is over a hundred years later; and that Fred Blake stood down as Captain in favour of Richard Gaskin. Although Fred had growing commitments as he had married Florence Maud Holland in 1908, and had had a son, John Vivian, on May 16th, 1909, what probably led him to relinquish the post of Captain was the death of his father, Andrew Blake, on March 19th, in a tragic road accident.

In the inquest which was held at the 'Drill Inn' on Wednesday evening March 23rd, 1910, the coroner, Mr F. J. Nightingale, heard that at about 2.15p.m. on the previous Saturday afternoon, a Mr. Ralph Gregory was driving a covered van of provisions towards Worcester Park at a speed of approximately 3 to 4 miles per hour when a light spring cart driven by Andrew Blake travelling at about 6 to 7 miles per hour, collided with him at the corner of Idmiston Road. One of the witnesses claimed that it looked as though Andrew had lost control of the horse as it seemed to be going rather fast. The cart overturned and Andrew lay mortally injured on the kerb about twenty yards away. Dr. Chearnley Smith visited Andrew at 6p.m that evening, two other doctors having already attended to him, but found that he was comatose. He died later on that evening.

In his will, Andrew asked his trustees, Harriet, his wife, and William, his son, to sell his property and to divide the proceeds between his children; William, Edwin, Minnie, the wife of Reginald Shaw, Alfred, Herbert, Ethel, the wife of Charles Dare, Harriet, the wife of Percy Boitoult and Frederick Blake. By a strange coincidence Andrew's younger brother, George, with whom he had run Malden Green Farm, was thrown out of a cart in 1919, an accident which was supposed to have led to his death two years later.

Perhaps Fred Blake felt a sense of guilt over his father's death, despite the fact that the Coroner had returned a verdict of 'Accidental Death', which had been caused by cerebral concussion and heart failure. As the accident occurred at 2.15pm on a Saturday afternoon, it makes one wonder whether Andrew Blake was actually speeding to a match so that he could watch his son play.

Fred probably still had great influence over the running of the First XI, however, as he was still on the selection committee, whilst his brother-in-law, John Holland (b. 1890), had been installed as the team's Vice-Captain at the annual general meeting.

Mr. J. Stenning presided over the A.G.M of the football club which was held at the Café Royal, on Wednesday evening May 11th, 1910. The 'Comet' that week reported that: *"Mr. E. Styles (Hon. Secretary) presented the financial statement, which showed that the club possessed a balance in hand of £2 10s. 3½d. It was mentioned that a number of subscriptions were still outstanding and that when those were got in they would bring the total balance up to £6 15s. 3½d. The report stated that the club had been very successful in matches during the season, and only 19 goals were scored against 87 made by the club.*

The election of officers was then proceeded with. Mr. C. W. Smith was re-elected President, and with the exception of the late Mr. A. Blake, all the Vice-Presidents were re-elected. The following officers were elected:- Mr. R. Gaskin and Mr. B. Daynes, Captains first and second elevens respectively; Mr. J. Holland, Vice-Captain, first eleven; Mr. E. Styles, Hon Secretary; Messrs. Stone, Hillman, W. Blake, H. Bartlett, J. Butcher and T. Dalton were appointed the committee; and the selection committee comprised Messrs. E. Styles, J. Diddell, B. Daynes, F. Blake and A. Butler. Votes of thanks to the Chairman, Captain and Secretary were heartily accorded."

For the **1910-11** season the First XI played in the South Suburban League Division 1, alongside teams such as Carshalton Athletic, Sutton United, Redhill, Summerstown, City of Westminster, Beddington Corner, Mavis and Kingston, whilst the Reserve team languished near the foot of Division III of the Wimbledon & District League.

Wimbledon & District League - Division III - 1910-1911 Season							
Clubs	P	W	D	L	F	A	Pts
Bevill	18	17	1	0	86	14	35
Morgan Recreation Res	18	14	2	2	46	15	30
New Wandsworth Res	18	9	2	7	39	27	20
Crusaders III	15	9	0	6	35	25	18
Southfields Evening School	18	8	2	8	28	22	18
Y.M.C.A. Res	15	6	0	9	24	35	12
St. Andrews Athletic	18	4	3	11	18	45	11
Worcester Park Res	18	5	1	12	14	57	11
Corporation Res	15	3	3	9	14	46	9
Broomwood Wesleyans Res	15	3	1	11	13	26	7

For the **1911-12** season the teams remained in their respective divisions; the First XI finishing the season as 'Runners - up' in Division 1 of the South Suburban League.

For the two pre-war seasons both the First Eleven and the Reserves reverted to the Kingston and District League. Whilst the Reserves languished in Section 3B of Division III, the First XI were admitted to Division I, finishing 2nd in 1912-13, and 3rd in 1913-14. The team might have been even more successful but for the fact that they had to play many of their matches without Fred Blake who was picked to play several representative games for both the League and the County. He was awarded a Surrey Junior Badge on the 17th September, 1913 and a full county cap on May 9th, 1914. Albert Scott also played representative games for the League that season.

It is interesting to note that according to the Surrey F.A., the registered ground for the club for 1912-14 was Lindsay Road, whilst the changing room was the Café Royal. It was extremely useful having a Vice-President like Henry W. Smith, who owned a restaurant, and would let the club use it both for meetings and for changing purposes.

Not all the games, however, that the club played were without incident, as an article in the 'Surrey Advertiser' of 14th February, 1914, indicates: *"At the meeting of the Surrey County Football Association on Wednesday evening, C. Peacock, of Molesey and St. Paul's United was reported for deliberately kicking an opponent in a Kingston & District League match v Worcester Park. The Council decided to suspend the player until further orders."*

Four months later, however, a more serious conflict broke out, which virtually suspended all competitive football for over four years, and signalled the end of league football at Lindsay Road. On September 16th, the Advertiser sadly reported:
"The Emergency Committee of the Kingston League and Teck Charity Cup Committee, which met on Saturday, at the Angel Hotel, Thames Ditton, reported that it was a source of considerable satisfaction for the committee to learn that at a time when they were needed for the service of the King, practically whole teams had joined the colours, whilst the ranks of others had, and would probably still further, become severely depleted. While not omitting consideration of the claims of those unable to serve in the ranks, the committee felt that competition football should be suspended for the present season, and it requested the Hon. Secretary to call a meeting on Tuesday, September 15th, to confirm and adopt this decision. The committee, however, trusted that all clubs would retain membership of their County association. The report was signed on behalf of the committee by Mr. J. A. Peel (Chairman) and Mr. E. Wyatt (Hon. Secretary)."

Worcester Park Football Club, like most clubs in the country, ceased all footballing activities in 1914, for over four years, as many of their players heeded the call to arms, some never to return. For those who did return, there was only to be one more season, 1919-20, playing football for W.P.F.C., before the club was disbanded and absorbed into W.P.A.C.

****

Appendix Potted Biographies of W.P.F.C. players starting with those who appeared in the teams from the 1900-01 season. The 1901 census proved most useful.

Frank W. Drew was born on February 8th in Holloway, London. In 1901 he was a tailor's cutter living at 2, The Woodlands, Cheam Common, with his wife Clara, a widow, and two step children. By 1939 he had become a master tailor. He played for the club until at least the 1905-06 season and was also a stalwart of Cheam Common C.C. The 'Herald' referred to him as *"playing up to the usual standard"* and *"there's still plenty of go in him."* He became a Vice-President of W.P.A.C.

George E. Turner was born in 1882 in Mile End Old Town, London. He was a bank clerk who became the club's first Secretary at the age of 18. In 1901, he was living with his uncle, Henry, and cousin, H.R.J. Turner, at 'Birch Villa', Malden Road, Worcester Park. He left the club and emigrated in 1902.

Henry Roland James Turner was born in 1883 in Camberwell. He was the son of Henry Turner, a retired butcher, and was still living at 'Birch Villa' in 1911. He was a copyist in the Patent Office, and played for the club for at least the first four or five seasons.

William George Hopkins was born at Hemel Hempstead, Hertfordshire, in 1883. In 1901 he was living with his father, James, a potter, his mother, Mary, three brothers and two sisters, at 'Oakendene', Malden Road, Cheam. He married Florence Pickett in 1907 and moved to 2, Poplar Cottages, Cheam Common. The 'Wimbledon Herald' said he was *"a tower of strength at the back."*

Joseph William Hopkins was the elder brother of William and was also born in Hemel Hempstead in 1879. In 1901 he worked, in Cheam with his father, James, as a potter. He was the First Eleven Captain for the first two seasons of the fledgling club's existence. In that first season he was credited with scoring 7 goals in a 10-2 victory over Devonians. After his playing career was curtailed through injury, he became one of the club's referees. Sadly he was killed in 1917 whilst serving with the 9th Battalion of the East Surrey Regiment.

Edwin Portnall was born in 1872 in the small Wiltshire village of Chicklade. In 1891 he was serving in the 3rd Battalion, the Wiltshire Regiment. By 1901, however, he was working as a labourer in Cheam and lodged in the same house as the Hopkins' family. By 1911 he had returned to Long Woodford in Wiltshire, where he married the following year.

Ernest Arthur Styles was born on 5th May, 1884, to his parents, John Joseph and Mary, who lived at 2, Blake Cottages, Longfellow Road, Cheam. Ernest lived there with his parents, elder brother, Albert, and sister, Bertha. In 1901 they moved to 3, Alscot Terrace, Washington Road. At the age of 16 he was credited with scoring the first goal by a Worcester Park player. In his time as a member of the club he was the Secretary on two separate occasions, for a total of 32 years.

In 1945 the Surrey County Football Association presented him with a gold medal for his thirty years continuous service as Chairman, Hon. Sec. and Treasurer. He seemed to have an inexhaustible supply of energy, both as a player and as an administrator. He was described as *"A most valued member of the club as never had."*

Albert Charles Styles was born in 1881 in Cheam. In 1901, both he and Ernest were still living at home and were both railway clerks. By 1911, however, he had married Florence Evelyn Hurles, the sister of a fellow W.P.F.C. player, Edward Dudley Hurles, and they lived, with their son Clifford at 'Fernlea', Donnington Road.

Edward Dudley Hurles was born in Lewisham in 1882. By 1891, Edward was living in Washington Road, Worcester Park, with his parents and four sisters. Ten years later the family were to be found living at 'Rosebank' in Cuddington, and by this time he was a clerk at the Railway Clearing House. Although he married Catherine Hastings and moved to live in Acton in 1908, he still remained a Vice-President of the club. The 'Wimbledon Herald' notes that along with G. E. Turner, H. R. Turner, G. Hawkins and F. Paye, he *"played in a formidable half back line."*

Hugh Arthur Woods was born in 1879 in Fen Stanton in Huntingdonshire. By 1901, Hugh was an electrician, living in an eight roomed house, above the shop, in Park Terrace with his father, Francis, his mother, Leah, and seven siblings, three of whom were involved in the butcher's trade. In 1910 he married Elizabeth Cordelia Ledger at St. Philip's Church. By 1911, the pair had become the landlord and landlady of the Queen Victoria pub, North Cheam, and remained there until 1924. Elizabeth's parents had been landlords of the pub from 1887.

The 'Wimbledon Herald' commented that he was *"A most prominent and reliable back, one of the most improved players of the season, well known for his strong kicking power, a noted goal scorer."*

Edgar Arnold Woods, the younger brother of Hugh, was born in Fen Stanton, in 1882. By 1911, of the eight members of the family who were still living at 1, Park Terrace, four of them, including Edgar, worked in the family owned butcher's shop, whilst the youngest worked as a fishmonger's assistant. On the 19th of April, 1916, in another example of how close knit the W.P.F.C. community was, Edgar married Margaret Scott, the sister of Albert Scott, in Kingston. By 1939, when he and Margaret and their two sons lived in Cuddington Avenue, he had graduated to managing his own butcher's shop.

Hugh appeared in team lists as early as the first season. Edgar, however, was not acknowledged in the press until the end of the third season when the 'Herald' wrote: *"It is a pity that M. Mayo, Harry and Edgar Woods are not available on Saturdays."* On several occasions, however, progress reports in the press merely mentioned the player's surname: ergo 'Woods' could have been Hugh or Edgar.

Frederick Edward Paye was born in 1880, in Cheam, the youngest son of William Paye, a labourer. The family, which included Caroline, his mother, and four siblings, lived, in 1891, at 4, Pottery Cottages in the Malden Road, Cheam. By 1901, William was working for the waterboard and the family moved to Reservoir Cottages in Banstead. Frederick, however, had a job as a brick burner, probably at the brickworks in Cheam. In 1902 he married Alice Cole (b. 1875), and by 1911 they were living with their four young children at 5, St. John's Cottages, Cheam Common Road.

Edward Foreman was one of the oldest members of the team in 1901, having been born in Wistow, Huntingdonshire in 1870. By 1901 he was a carpenter living in Bushey Road, Sutton, with his wife, Ada Margaret, whom he had married three years earlier at St. Saviour's Church, Chelsea, whilst he was a resident of Cheam parish, which must be why he qualified to play for W.P..F.C. By 1911 he lived with his wife, four sons and a daughter at 'Wistow', Cheam Road, Sutton.

Reuben Miller Oxenham was a true local lad. He was the youngest player listed in the team sheets for the 1900-01 season, having been born in Cheam on 16th February, 1886, and was baptized three years later at St. Philip's Church. Reuben's father, Alfred, was a printer and the family, which included two brothers and a sister, lived at 12, Poplar Place, Malden Road, Cheam. When he entered the R.A.F. in 1916, his occupation was listed as being a photographer. He was discharged in 1917, suffering from a gunshot wound to his left hand. Following the war, in 1922, he married Annie Hudson, a secondary school teacher. The 1939 register shows that he was a plumber and decorator, and that he and his wife were living at 186, Cheam Common Road, where they remained for over thirty years.

Arthur Ernest Hillman, who was born in 1880, was one of nine children living at 'Knowle Cottage', Longfellow Road with his father, Herbert, a carpenter, and mother, Susan. Although Hillman was still living at 'Knowle Cottage' at the time of the 1901 census, by the time that he became the secretary of W.P.F.C. in 1902, he had moved into a two room first floor flat in 'Budleigh Cottage', Longfellow Road, which he rented from his mother for 4s 6d per week. Apart from being a regular first eleven footballer and an excellent secretary he also served on the club's committee in 1909-10, and was still supporting the club thirty years later when he lived at 6, Beverley Gardens. The 'Wimbledon Herald' stated in the club column, *"How well the club valued his service, the enormous heavy work load he undertook."*

George Hawkins was born in Reading in 1875 and in 1901 he was a building labourer who lived with his widowed mother, two brothers and two sisters at Garth Cottage in Morden. For the first decade of the twentieth century he was a vital member of the Park first eleven. By 1911 George was a labourer on a golf course and the family had moved to 4, Burdett's Cottages in Cheam. George had risen to the rank of foreman green keeper by the time of the 1939 register. Back in 1901, however, he was recorded by the 'Herald' as being part of a *'formidable line'* along with G. E. Turner, R. Turner, F. Paye and F. Cutler.

Harold Frith Milward, who was born in Malden in 1876, was the son of a rather important figure in the community, Thomas Frith Millward, who among his various roles had been an assistant tipstaff to the court, a collector of rates and taxes, postmaster for the district, agent for the management of Thomas Weeding's estates and the vestry clerk for both Cuddington and Malden parishes. His sons, Harold Frith and Thomas William, became Milward Bros (dropping an 'l'), estate agents. The brothers also acted as coal merchants, stationers and had a drapery department.

Charles Noel Gordon Dearman who was born in 1866 in St Pancras, London, was usually referred to in match reports as Gordon. Dearman was older than most of the other players in the team and also came from a more privileged background. Further information on him can be found in the chapter on Cheam Common C.C. for whom he was one of the star performers. He must have been quite fit as he was still playing football, for the first eleven, in 1905-06, when he would have been nearly forty. The 'Herald' referred to him as being *'a tower of strength at the back'*.

Leslie Sarll was an auctioneer's clerk who was born in Hounslow in 1881, the son of George, a tailor. By 1901, he was living with his mother, Priscilla, a widow, his elder brother, Sidney, and his sister, Edith, at 5, Mycliffe Terrace, Cheam Village. The flying right winger seems to have been an extremely important component in the club's success in the first three seasons, and the reports bemoan the fact that he was unable to play quite as often in the 1904-05 season. He was, *"A tower of strength to the team with his shooting powers which are terrific and his centres grand."* Leslie married Jessie Chardin in 1912, but unfortunately he died young in 1923, six years after his brother died whilst serving as a lance corporal in the Royal Engineers.

Arthur Verrall was a shoemaker's son who was born in Reigate in 1880. The last record of him in Reigate was in a school attendance record from 1892. His next appearance occurred when he married Alice Bumpstead at St. Stephen's Church, Wandsworth on October 10th, 1903. The following year he made his debut for W.P.F.C., and by the 1905-06 season he was the First XI Captain. The 1911 census showed him living with his wife, Alice, daughter Audrey and son Clifford, at 'Dunedin' Lindsay Road, two houses away from Fred Blake. Arthur was listed as being a domestic chauffeur in 1911, an occupation which led to him being used as a driver in the Army Service Corps in the First World War. His military record shows that he was short and stocky for although he was only 5ft 7¼ inches tall he weighed over ten stone.

Arthur Ernest Patrick was an insurance clerk who was born in Wandsworth in October 1880. He and his brother joined the club at the start of the 1902-03 season. At that time they were living with their mother at 167, Merton Road, South Wimbledon. They only stayed at the club for about a season. Arthur did return on

December 2nd, 1907, to marry Gertrude Anne Walsh at St. Philip's Church, Cheam Common. By 1911 Arthur, Gertrude and their son had left the area and were living in Essex.

William Alexander Patrick, the younger brother of Arthur, born on 18th November, 1883, was the only member of his family to be born in New York. In 1901 he was listed as a clerk. Ten years later he was lodging at 46, Melbourne Road, Merton Park, and was an insurance clerk. The joys of being a clerk must have drained away, as by the time of the 1939 register he was driving a newspaper delivery van.

Louis Douglas Patrick was the youngest of the Patrick brothers, who was born in 1890. He joined the club at the same time as Arthur Verrall, for the 1904-05 season. He stayed at the club until at least 1908. By 1911, however, he was a draper's clerk, living with his parents in Prittlewell, Essex.

Bertram Ernest Daynes was born, the son of a sixteen year old baker's porter, in East Dereham, Norfolk, on 29th May, 1882. As the father was very young it looks as though he was raised by his grandparents. By 1891, the family were living at 'Fullbrook Lodge', Malden. Ten years later his grandfather was a gardener and Bertram was a draper's assistant. In 1907 he married a local girl, Gertrude E. Reeve at St. John's Church, Malden and by 1911, Bertram, who was by then a salesman, was the Captain of W.P.F.C. Second XI, and the family were living at 64, Idmiston Road with their 2 year old son.

Frederick Arthur Rides, whose name was usually misspelt as 'Rydes' in the press, was born the son of a gardener on January 2nd, 1887. In 1891, he was living with his parents, and sister Gertrude, at 'Providence Cottage', Longfellow Road. As a fifteen year old, in 1902, he was already making a name for himself as a footballer at Worcester Park. In March, 1907, however, he left the area when he enlisted in the Royal Marine Light Infantry, Chatham Division, where he stayed until at least 1911.

William Robert Vaughan, who was considered a more than useful understudy in goal for Frank Drew in 1902, was an extremely interesting character. He had been born in Le Marchant Barracks, Southbroom, Wiltshire, in 1883, the eldest child of William and Sarah. His father, at that time, was a Sergeant in the Wiltshire Regiment. By 1901 he was living with his parents, four brothers and two sisters in Washington Road, Worcester Park. Both he and his father were listed as being clerks for the Waifs and Strays Society, an organisation which had been set up in 1881, by the Church of England, to help destitute children. In 1882 the Society had 2 homes and 34 children in its care, but by 1902 this figure had risen to 90 homes and 3,071 children. The office's headquarters in 1900 were at the Medical Examination Hall in Savoy Street, but moved to the Old Town Hall in Kennington in 1907. The Society also ran an emigration scheme whereby children were sent to receiving care homes in Canada.

In 1904, W. R. Vaughan married Dorothy Evaline Rides, the sister of Frederick A. Rides, and by 1911, William and Gertrude were living with their 1 year old daughter Eileen at 'Ashley Villas', Coombe Gardens, New Malden. By the 1920s the family had moved to 16, Whiteladies Road, where William continued working for the Waifs and Strays. The Canadian Passenger Lists showed that he made several trips to Quebec and Toronto in order to inspect the local Waif and Stray homes.

In 1932, following the resignation of Dr. Westcott as Secretary of the Association, his place was taken by the then Assistant Secretary, William Robert Vaughan, *"who had originally join the Society as an office boy."* In 1949, William, *"much to his chagrin",* had reached the retirement age of 65, and was forced to retire. The changes which he had forced through for the Society left it in a very strong position, however. After leaving the Society he became the General Secretary of the Fairbridge Society, an organisation devoted to the emigration of children.

Mark Thomas Watts, who was born on the 17th October, 1881, tended to be known to his fellow team-mates as Thomas. He was the son of Thomas, a labourer, and Emma, and lived with them for the first 30 years of his life in various dwellings in Longfellow Road. During the 1902-03 and 1903-04 seasons, he was the Captain of the Park Reserve XI. He eventually left home when he married Florence Eliza Sycamore on the 12th of August, 1912. By this time he had graduated from being a labourer to a gardener. Thomas and Florence had moved to Lower Court Road in Epsom by 1932.

William Francis Macey was born in Kingswood on the 12th November, 1878, the son of Thomas B. Macey, a Blacksmith and Farrier from Somerset, and Rosina, his wife. The family lived in Ewell in 1891 and moved to Longfellow Road by the time of the next census. William doesn't appear on that census but surfaces as a W.P.F.C. player in the 1904-05 season. He does, however, appear on the 1911 census as being married to Jessie and lived in Donnington Road, Cuddington. He was listed as following in his father's footsteps, in that he was also a blacksmith and farrier.

Even less is known about **Joseph Macey** who was born in 1882 and appeared on the 1901 census as living with his parents at 'Hope Villa', Longfellow Road. He too, like his brother and father, was also a blacksmith and farrier. Both Joseph and William seemed to exist in that rather indeterminate area between the first eleven and the Reserves.

Frederick Blake was born in Cheam on the 24th October, 1887, to Andrew Blake, a farmer, and Harriett, his wife. Fred was the youngest of twelve children and looks to have been rather an after-thought as he was six years younger than his nearest sibling. At the time of his birth the family were living at the Coke Shop in the Malden Road, Cheam Common. By 1901, the family had moved to 'Ingomar', in Cuddington, where they lived in a house next to Edward D. Hurles, one of the founding members of W.P.F.C. At this time Andrew was still being listed in the census as a farmer. Shortly after this, however, the family moved into one of the new houses that Andrew had built in Lindsay Road.

Frederick was an extremely skilful footballer who made his debut, in the press, in a 1-0 victory over Old Maldonians on October 31st, 1903, and by the age of 19 had risen to become the Captain of the First XI for the 1907-08 season. This was a position he was to hold on several occasions over the next 20 years, along with the captaincy of the cricket team. His most successful season was 1913-14 when he was selected to play for the League and County on several occasions.

By 1911, Fred was an engineer, who was still living in Lindsay Road, with his wife and young son, John Vivian (b. 1909), in a five roomed house called 'Bacton'. He had married Florence Maud Holland in 1908, a nineteen year old girl from Longfellow Road, the sister of John William and Frederick Charles Holland, with whom Fred had played both Football for W.P.F.C. and Cricket for Old Malden and Worcester Park.

Frederick and Florence were still living in Lindsay Road until at least 1930, but by 1936 they had taken up residence at 86, Oaks Avenue, Cuddington, with their second son, Robert (b. 1915). By this time Frederick did not seem to be playing football but was still the Captain of Worcester Park C.C. First XI and a Vice-President of the club. He was also a very successful engineer and businessman, having a garage locally and another in London. In the 1950s it is rumoured that Diana Dors, the famous model and actress, lived above his London garage. When he died on the 14th November, 1961, at St. George's Hospital, Westminster, he left an estate of £8,000. By 1964, according to Robin Fisher, a memorial gate to him had been erected at the entrance to the club.

William Thomas Perry was one of the most interesting characters to grace the Lindsay Road pitch. He had been born on the 24th May, 1877, in Leytonstone, Essex, the son of Elizabeth and John, a policeman. By 1881 the family were living in Paddington, before moving to Lambeth where they remained until 1901, by which time William was an Insurance Clerk. The family must have moved to Worcester Park shortly thereafter as William was playing at half back for W.P.F.C. in the 1902-03 season. The 'Herald' rated him as being *'the best acquisition to the team'* that year, and the following season the club appointed him captain of the First XI, a post which he held for two seasons before he had to hand over the mantle because of work commitments. He carried on playing, when possible and was listed as being a Vice President of the club, in the 1909-10 membership card.

From 1905, when he became a Freemason and was accepted into the United Grand Lodge of England, his career really took off. The Freemason Register showed that he was living at that time in Hampton Road, Worcester Park. By 1911 the family, which included his younger brother, Frank Owen, had moved the short distance to

'Fairlight', Kingsmead Avenue, Cuddington, and by this time William had graduated into being an Insurance Branch Manager.

Football seemed to take second place to his career, however, as there was no further record of him being a W.P.F.C. member. In fact there is no further trace of him at all, until he appeared on a ship's manifest in November, 1917, emigrating to the USA. He lived in the States for several months before settling in Canada for a short while, where he still worked in Insurance. He was obviously a high flyer in the Insurance world as he seemed to spend the next 20 years travelling, First Class, between England, Canada, the States and South Africa. Often his address was given as such prestigious places as the Ontario Club in Toronto, or the R.A.C. club in Pall Mall. Although he married a Lilian Mary Perry, in about 1925, who lived at 'The Grange', St. George's Road, Bickley, Kent, she rarely accompanied him on his trips. He was still travelling solo across the Atlantic in 1956 at the age of 79.

Thomas Dalton was born in Bermondsey in 1889, the son of Mary Ann Hunter and Thomas George Dalton, a carpenter. By 1901 he was another of the Park players living in Longfellow Road. He first appeared as playing for the First XI in 1904, at the age of 15, and was one of the medal winners when the team were the Kingston and District League Division II Champions in the 1909-1910 season.

On 14th May, 1910, he was elected on to the club's committee along with five others, and on Wednesday 18th September, 1912, along with Ernie Styles, he attended the League's 35th A.G.M. At the start of the war his parents and brother emigrated to New York State, whilst Thomas remained to fight the Hun. (Further information about him is in the chapter on WWI).

John William Holland, who was born in Clapham in 1890, and his brother, **Frederick Charles Holland,** who was born in Worcester Park in 1894, were yet again part of the W.P.F.C. clan who lived in Longfellow Road in 1901. John was to prove to be one of the most important architects behind the formation of W.P.A.C. in 1921. (More information about him and his brother can be found in the chapters about the First World War and Cheam Common C.C.)

Not a lot is known about their footballing careers, although John must have been relatively competent as he was appointed Vice-Captain of the First XI at their A.G.M. in 1910. Both John and Frederick played in the first ever recorded football match played at Skinner's Field in 1920, and Frederick was elected to the football committee that year, along with Fred Blake and Ernie Styles.

On August 7th, 1918, Frederick, who was a lance corporal in the 23rd London Regiment of the Royal Fusiliers, married Ethel Rose Hillman (b. 1902), the sister of Arthur Hillman. Frederick was living at this time at 111, Longfellow Road, and his bride-to-be was at 131, Longfellow Road. This was yet another example of the close knit community in which many of the players lived, and the way the players were often bonded together through marriage.

On September 10th, 1919, John married Marjorie Montgomery Shiells of 4, Percival Parade, Worcester Park, at St. Philip's Church. The Best Man was his brother-in-law, Frederick Blake, who had married his sister, Florence Maud Holland.

****

The following certificate was awarded to the Football Club in 2000 by the Football Association, to record their centenary. It is on the wall in the clubhouse next to the shield.

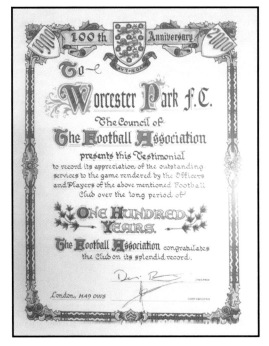

The shield below was presented to the club by the Surrey F.A. in 2000.

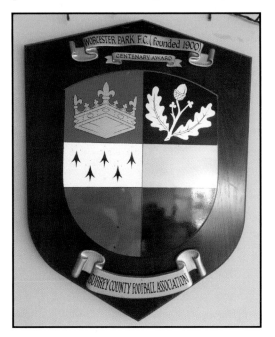

W. G. Grace and the Worcester Park Beagles

When I began to research this book I must admit that I had never heard of the Worcester Park Beagles, nor had I any idea that the most famous cricketer in the history of the game, Dr. William Gilbert Grace, had ever visited Worcester Park.

Beagles were, in the late nineteenth century, primarily hounds that were used for hunting hares and foxes, and the huntsmen would follow them on foot. W. G. Grace had been an ardent huntsman in his native Gloucestershire and had followed the Clifton Foot Beagles for many years, as he found that following the hounds was an excellent means of exercise during the winter months. The local newspapers record him as being a regular follower of the Worcester Park Beagles for at least a decade from the turn of the twentieth century, and he was even on the Beagles' committee in 1907. The fact that he scored the first hundred for any Worcester Park team, albeit for the Worcester Park Beagles, was one of his feats that invariably gets overlooked in the annals of cricketing history.

I did not realise at first that there was any connection at all between the Worcester Park Beagles and the formation of Worcester Park Athletic Club, until I discovered, however, that the two organisations had been neighbours at one point in their respective histories: the kennels had been literally a stone's throw from our present pavilion. I also found that some of the people associated with the formation of the club were also employed by the 'Beagles', and that the 'Beagles' had several fine cricketers in their midst, including the greatest cricketer of the Golden Age of Cricket.

As one wanders down Green Lane from Central Road there is a shallow stream on the left that usually flows extremely slowly in a straight line between the road and the boundary of the sports ground. This is Beverley Brook, which according to David Rymill, was originally called 'Beverey' or 'beaver rithe' ('rithe' indicating a streamlet). The stream is usually only three or four inches deep during the summer but in periods of excessive rainfall can reach depths of over three or four feet, causing flood damage to the clubhouse and the adjoining properties in Green Lane. Severe summer storms can cause flash floods and I have even witnessed beer barrels floating out into the centre of the square, and barefooted players carrying their wives, girlfriends and children over the flooded bridge to safety. It was this danger from flooding which led the Environmental Agency to build flood defences around the clubhouse in 2014.

When one reaches the new bridge by the entrance to the clubhouse the stream turns sharply away from the road before rejoining it about a hundred yards further on by Back Green, the area of land which is now a wetland conservation area. This 'island' of land between the stream and road is now occupied by six semi-detached houses and 'Brook View Lodge' retirement home. Over two hundred years ago, however, on the area of land closest to the present pavilion stood a cottage which was called, at various times, either 'Tattle Arbour' (or Harbour), 'Harbour Cottage' or 'Cold Harbour', whilst where 'Brook View Lodge' stands was the red brick kennel block of the Worcester Park Beagles.

This island of land is something of an administrative anomaly. On the Enclosure Map of 1806 and the Tithe Map of 1840 it was the only parcel of land on the north side of Green Lane that was in the Parish of Cheam. The remainder of the land on the north side of the road, along with Skinner's Field (the home of W.P.A.C.) and Back Green, lay in the Parish of Malden. In those days Beverley Brook was the parish boundary. The 1930s O.S. maps, however, show the Municipal & Urban District Boundary which separated Kingston and Sutton as running through the centre of the W.P.C.C. cricket square. Nowadays the ward boundary follows the railway.

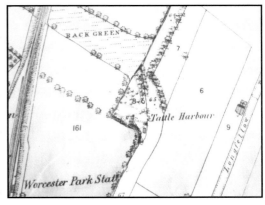

'Tattle Cottage' was shown as being on the island of land in 1806 and belonged to a James Carpenter. He still owned the property in 1840, although the Occupier was one William Clark, and the Tithe Map of that year informs us that it was called 'Tattle Harbour' and that in area it was just over half an acre in size and consisted of a cottage and orchard. The census of 1841 shows Sam Clark, an agricultural labourer, and his family living there. (O.S. maps reproduced with the permission of the National Library of Scotland.)

The above map shows the cottage on the 1868 OS map. In the midst of the orchard there was a well which is easier to see on the 1897 OS map (to the left). Note the lack

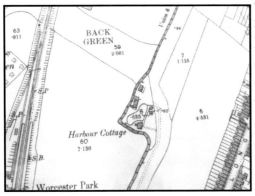

of houses in Longfellow Road in 1868. The railway had only been there for nine years. By 1897, however, the area was becoming quite built up. The 1897 map shows that the orchard had disappeared and that in its place were two red bricked kennels.

By the 1880s the cottage, which apparently had six rooms, had passed into the hands of William and Martha Saitch and their eight children, several of whom feature in the early years of the Worcester Park Athletic Club story. In 1881 William Saitch, was listed as being a carman or carrier. He probably carried goods to and from the nearby station. By 1891 he was listed as being a greengrocer whilst his sons, John and William F., bore the brunt of the carrying business. By 1901, William was described as being a general labourer, whilst by 1911, aged 75, he was a roadman.

The kennels in the grounds of 'Tattle Harbour Cottage' were built in 1885 by **Colonel George Pilkington Blake**[1] (b. 1835) who was the Master of the Surrey Union Foxhounds from 1884 to 1886. In 1884 he was reported as having moved his hounds from Fetcham to his home at 'New House Farm', but because of sewage problems had to move them to Green Lane. The 'Illustrated Sporting and Dramatic News' in January, 1900, said that, *"The kennels, situated a few hundred yards away from Worcester Park Station, are built substantially of red brick, and are roomy and dry, though the approach is bad."*

When George retired in 1886, a new Master was elected and the hounds were moved. There was, therefore, a void in the local hunting scene which needed filling. This void was exacerbated by the fact that another local Hunt Master, with the same surname, 'Squire' **Charles Blake**[2] (b. 1817) who had been the Master of the Morden Harriers from 1863, resigned at the 'Spring Hotel', Ewell, in 1886, whereupon that Hunt appears to have folded.

In the summer of 1886 a dozen hounds, a draft from the Eton Beagles, and a hunting horn were purchased by the W. P. Beagles. Another twelve 15½" studbook beagles were also acquired in the autumn before the first general meeting of the Hunt supporters on October 11th. Despite boundary disputes with other packs, the Worcester Park Beagles quickly became one of the most prestigious packs in the country, whilst a shortage of hares was met by importing several from the Elvedon Estate, the home of Prince Duleep Singh in Suffolk.

In December, 1900, the 'Illustrated Sporting and Dramatic News' ran a long article about the Worcester Park Beagles, which described them as being: *"Among the most well known packs of beagles in the United Kingdom. The Worcester Park is one which holds a high position …. They are very level and compact, showing plenty of quality, exceptionally fast and true, hunting always well together ….Altogether the Worcester Park Beagles are an ideal pack and the sport they show is first rate and could not be beaten anywhere."*

The 'Illustrated Sporting and Dramatic News' also featured several photographs of the Hunt in action. The posed picture above shows some of the main participants in the Hunt meeting at 'New House Farm', Old Malden, in 1900.

In 1901 William Saitch charged the Hunt a ground rent of three guineas a year for the kennels. William, or perhaps his son William F., crops up several times in the Hunt's records as doing a variety of odd jobs around the place. His eldest son, John (b. 1862), ran a carrying business from the cottage and also did a variety of jobs for the hunt, such as ferrying the hounds to and from meets, procuring horse meat and biscuits, and supplying coal. William's youngest son, Arthur (b. 1881), also worked in the kennels and had started as a kennel lad in 1889 at 6 shillings per week. At that time he seems to have been the only person employed by the Hunt. Towards the end of the century, however, Arthur had graduated to become a kennel huntsman at 18 shillings per week, whilst a boy was occasionally employed at 2 shillings a week. Arthur died in 1902. aged 21. Another of the Saitch boys, Charles (b.1876), also crops up on several occasions in the Hunt's accounts and on the 1901 census was listed as being a Beagle kennelman.

By the time Worcester Park Athletic Club was formed and Skinner's Field came in to use in 1921, the kennels had become exceedingly disease ridden. The kennel books from 1905 onwards reveal increasing numbers of deaths amongst the brood bitches and their whelps. By 1921 the situation was intolerable as Mr Jamieson, the Master, revealed at their A.G.M., when he reported that nearly all the early puppies had died.

By the mid-1920s hunting was also becoming extremely difficult in the East Surrey region as the area became more built-up. The final hunt from Worcester Park was held in 1921 although the kennels continued to be in use for another five or six years. In 1923 the Beagles merged with the Buckland pack, which met near Dorking, to form the Worcester Park and Buckland Beagles. As early as 1905 the Hunt had decided that it was necessary to find new kennels but it was not until February 1927 that new kennels were built at 'Well Cottage', Mugswell, Chipstead and the pack eventually moved.

For the first five years of W.P.A.C.'s existence, therefore, the baying of the Beagles must have been a constant feature of sport at Skinner's Field. Perhaps it was the ghostly echo of their howling down the years that caused their descendants to be unjustifiably banned by W.P.A.C. in about 2012, or was it just rabid cynophobia.

One renowned dog lover, however, was the greatest cricketer of the age, **Dr. W. G. Grace**, who, as a child, used to play cricket in the family's orchard at 'The Chestnuts', at Downsend, in Gloucestershire, with his sisters fielding and the three family dogs, Don, Ponto and Noble barking their encouragement.

W.G. was born on July 18th 1848, in Gloucestershire, and began playing first class cricket in 1865, a career which lasted for 44 years

until 1908, during which time he scored 54,896 runs and took 2,836 wickets. By 1898, at the age of 50, however, he must have felt that he was reaching the end of his playing career, and so accepted a post in London, tasked with setting up the London County Cricket team, for the Crystal Palace Company. It must have been quite a blow for Gloucestershire Cricket Club and the people of Gloucester to lose such a renowned superstar. When questioned by a reporter from the 'Cardiff Times' in October 1898, he gave an assurance to his interviewer that he would be able to play in most if not all of his old county's matches, adding, with that peculiar smile of his, *"That is if they think me good enough."*

Any desire that he might have had to continue playing for his old county did not tally with the ideas of his new bosses who managed the Crystal Palace Company. The company that owned the pleasure grounds at Sydenham had been looking for a major attraction to draw in large crowds during the summer months. W. G. Grace was to be that attraction. His contract only allowed him to play for teams outside the Crystal Palace organisation by permission of the directors of the company. They did apparently allow him to play his final Test Match for England in 1899.

W. G. Grace was the star attraction of the London County team and it was hoped that he might be able to save the company, which had struggled financially for several years. It was, however, only a short term fix, as the company was eventually declared bankrupt in 1909.

There was already a cricket ground in the gardens at Crystal Palace, along with a football ground, which had been the venue for the Cup Final from 1895 (until 1914), and a cycle track. W.G. quickly drew up plans to improve the main pitch and to develop two more pitches on the site. He also designed a new pavilion, and was both the manager and secretary of the newly formed London County Cricket Club.

Grace also arranged an impressive list of first class fixtures and attracted a host of decent players, such as Billy Murdoch, to agree to play for the club. A tremendous amount of work must have been involved setting up this new venture virtually from scratch, as anyone who has ever tried to arrange fixtures would know. The degree of his success can be seen by the following extract from the 'London Daily News' of the 5th of April, 1901: *"Mr. W. G. Grace has secured a programme of 13 first-class matches for the London County Club the list of fixtures comprising out and away fixtures with Surrey, Warwickshire, Derbyshire, Cambridge University and the M.C.C. and one match with the South Africans. Apart from the first-class fixtures, 75 matches have been arranged."*

For a while W. G. seemed to have been the answer to the prayers of the owners of the company as his team attracted crowds of thousands to watch the cricket at Crystal Palace, as can be seen by the photograph on the following page, which shows the

Grand Old Man batting on the London County C.C. ground in about 1902. The crowd around the boundary appears to be about four or five deep. (courtesy of John Fox)

The Grace family left Gloucestershire in December 1898 and he was already fully engaged in his work by the following month as can be seen by this short snippet from the 'Cambridge Daily News' of January 23rd, 1899:

"Dr. W. G. Grace is now settled in his new home near the Crystal Palace with his wife and daughter. He is already immersed in work connected with forthcoming athletic shows at the Palace. It is hardly likely that he will have much time for county play this season."

Apart from sacrificing playing cricket for the county he loved, he had also to forgo hunting with the Clifton Beagles. At a farewell meal given in his honour by that body in December, 1898, he claimed that some of the most pleasant times he had spent in that neighbourhood had been with the beagles and when he was younger with the foxhounds.

It did not take him long to be attracted by the prestigious Worcester Park Beagles who tended to meet most Saturdays and Wednesdays during the winter months. It would have been a relatively straight forward journey by train from Crystal Palace to Worcester Park. He could possibly have been recommended to visit them by G. H. Longman, a whipper-in with the hunt, with whom he had occasionally played cricket during the 1880s. On January 14th, 1899, 'The Surrey Mirror' records that:-

" On Wednesday the Worcester Park Beagles visited Headley at the invitation of Mr. Walter Cunliffe, of the 'Highlands', who entertained the company to a sumptuous luncheon. The company which was very large, included Dr. W. G. Grace (the renowned cricketer) and his two sons. Hares were plentiful and several good runs were made."

The Doctor's acceptance by the Beagles was probably a formality but that was not the case for ordinary mortals, as the following passage from an extremely informative book, edited by James Stracey, entitled 'The History of the Worcester Park and Buckland Beagles' suggests. The book was published in 1986, by the Surrey and North Sussex Beagles, to mark the centenary of the pack.

"The Worcester Park was a Hunt Club, and had the reputation of being a rather exclusive affair and one to which it was an honour to belong. Every aspirant to membership was scrutinised with care, proposed, seconded and then balloted for - 'one black ball in three to exclude'."

Although many of the members were farmers, as they often owned the land over which the hunt passed, the remainder tended to be members of the upper echelons of society, and W.G. self-evidently passed muster.

In the early years of the twentieth century, William Gilbert Grace must have been a regular visitor to the 'Huntsman's Hall' at the end of Green Lane, now 'The Brook', where the huntsmen used to meet. The illustration below is from an advertisement for the Inn which gives a rather idealistic picture of what the pub looked like on a hunt day. Although there are a couple of horses in the picture only the Master of the Hunt tended to ride on horseback, although George Henry Longhurst, the whipper-in, was allowed to ride a pony for several years following an attack of Typhoid in 1907.

(Illustration courtesy of John Fox)

It is rather awe-inspiring to think that such a great cricketer as W. G. Grace probably walked to and fro across the W.P.C.C. cricket field, on many an occasion whilst exercising the hounds. (I often wonder if he ever considered its potential as a cricket ground). He certainly appears to have known the area intimately, as is shown by this newspaper article from the 'Dundee Evening Telegraph' of the 26th January 1900:

"Dr. W. G. Grace is keeping himself fit till the cricket season opens by trotting after the Worcester Park Beagles, The wily doctor, it is said, knows the short cuts, and generally gets in at the death."

The presence of the 'Doctor' at the various meetings was probably more noteworthy in the local newspapers than the activity of the hounds. The 'Dorking and Leatherhead Advertiser' of the 24th January, 1903, wrote,

"The Worcester Park Beagles had a meet at Ashtead on Wednesday, and a capital day's sport was provided over Mr. Walter Cunliffe's estate. Dr. W. G. Grace was present at the meet, and followed the beagles."

From James Stracey's book I also discovered that the Doctor not only followed the hounds but was also a prominent member of the committee. On March 8th, 1907, he proposed at a committee meeting that an offer from the Surbiton pack to re-define their boundaries should be accepted. The motion was defeated - his reputation as the greatest cricketer of his age obviously failed to sway the meeting.

Apart from being involved with the running of the Hunt, W. G. was also a useful member on the social side. From the rather limited newspaper articles available it is apparent that he organised an annual cricket match for the members of the Beagles with the London County Cricket Club over at Crystal Palace. I was fortunate enough to find accounts, which varied in detail, of all nine of the matches played between the Worcester Park Beagles and L.C.C.C. for the years 1900 to 1908. With the help of the good 'Doctor' and numerous 'ringers' the Beagles won four of these matches and drew the other five.

It is interesting to note that despite the fact that the 'Doctor' had left his beloved Gloucestershire behind, their local newspapers were still interested in his activities, even when he played for the Beagles. Many of the sports articles of the day were obviously syndicated, as the same articles could be found literally, word for word, in Dundee, Cardiff or Leeds. The Gloucester papers, however, often offered facts which were absent from the other papers, which makes one wonder whether the 'Grand Old Man' was still in constant touch with them.

The first match between the Worcester Park Beagles and the London County team took place on Saturday the 19th May, **1900**, at Crystal Palace. The newspaper reports of this first game are a little sketchy and lack the detail of the later contests. The 'Sporting Life' did record the score for the match, but the on-line photo copy was that poor that one could only ascertain that Worcester Park had scored 207 runs. Fortunately 'Lloyd's Weekly Newspaper' of Sunday 20th May, 1900, was more legible, and it was possible to establish that the match had been drawn: *"Worcester Park Beagles, 207; London County Council (?) 187 for nine."*

As a record of the first match between the Beagles and the London County Cricket Club (not 'Council'), it left a lot to be desired, especially as none of the participants was named. It is highly likely that the Beagles might have featured some prominent cricketers, who were associated with the Hunt, such as the 'whipper-in', **George Henry Longman**[3] (b. 1852), or his son, **Henry Kerr Longman**[4] (b. 1870), their friend and local schoolmaster, **Arthur Sidney Tabor**[5] (b. 1851) **Colonel John Henry Bridges**[6] (b. 1852), **Robert Henderson**[7] (b. 1865) and **Thomas Paine Hilder**[8] (b. 1867). (More about these characters in the Appendix to this chapter).

It was purely by accident that whilst surveying a list of centurions for 1900, in the 'Sporting Life' of January 9th, 1901, I came across the following information: *"WALKER L.- May 19th, London County v Worcester Park Beagles - lbw Stewart - 106"* **Livingston Walker**[9] (b. 1879) had only made his debut for the L.C.C.C. the previous week against Worcestershire and obviously impressed the great man in this non-first class match.

A more interesting fact regarding the first ever fixture between the Worcester Park Beagles and London County was gleaned from the 'Gloucester Citizen' of Monday, 21st May, regarding a match, the previous Saturday, which failed to mention the name of either team; *"In attempting to stop a hard return, when bowling in a match on Saturday, Dr. W. G. Grace severely damaged his left hand. He, however, went in to bat with one hand, but only made six runs."*

The injury to his hand must have been quite severe as, on Monday May 21st and Tuesday May 22nd, although the Doctor was on the L.C.C.C. team sheet to play against Oxford University that day, alongside L. Walker, various newspaper reports of that game commented upon the fact that the Doctor was absent.

Another interesting fact about that first Worcester Park Beagles' match was that W.G. was obviously playing for London County C.C. Perhaps this was a result of the rather restrictive contract that he had signed with the Crystal Palace Company, and which tied him firmly to the company. For most of the later encounters, however, he appears to have ignored the contract and played for the Beagles.

In **1901** W. G. was particularly successful, and became the first ever recorded player for any Worcester Park team to score a century. Although his 'ton' was noted in several papers, such as 'The Gloucester Citizen' and 'The Gloucestershire Echo', the only newspaper to feature the scorecard was 'The Sportsman' of Monday May 27th. Sadly the online image is too faded to reproduce, but most of it is legible:

"Quite a fashionable gathering witnessed this match at the Crystal Palace ground on Saturday. M. Bisset, the South African, Dr. W. G. Grace and C. B. Grace were assisting the visitors, while B. C. Cooley and F. Prince, two of the South African Cricketers played for London County who were dismissed for 164. C. B. Grace secured four wickets for 2?? runs and Bell six for 47. The visitors soon passed their opponents' total, W. G. playing a fine innings of one hundred and fourteen, in which were twenty 4's. Cooley was credited with all five wickets that fell at a cost of ?? Runs. The Beagles won by 189 runs, with five wickets in hand. Score:

London County *- J. M. Campbell 41, B. C. Cooley 0, C. S. Gordon-Smith 19, Rev. K. Clarke 0, C. Prince 5, H. C. Stapleton 5, R. C. Darke 13, A. H. Madava 3, C. Raywood 12, W. L. Roper 1, C. Wade 3*, Extras 6. Total 164.*

Worcester Park Beagles *- M. Bisset 48, T. P. Hilder 14, N. M. Reid 9, W. G. Grace 114, C. B. Grace 63*, F. P. Francis 29, H. Willis 45*, Extras 25, Total 353 for 5 wkts.*

Did Not Bat: R. C. Stapylton, Capt. Willoughby, A. W. Gordon, and R. T. P. Anson."

A more prosaic account of the occasion was recorded in the 'South London Press': *"The week-end London County club matches are always of an interesting nature as the G. O. M. generally whips up a good side. Last Saturday the Doctor was opposing his club and assisting the Worcester Park Beagles, together with his younger son, C. B. The father scored 114, while his son obtained 68 not out. It was a pretty sight to see father and son batting together at the wicket, knocking the London County bowling about to all parts of the field. The juvenile Grace has much of his parent's skill, and should develop his powers with more experience. He is a much better cricketer than his elder brother, W. G., jun., who never did take seriously to the game, much to the Doctor's regret."*

Apart from the 'Grand Old Man's' century the main point of interest in the match was the inclusion of three of the 1901 unofficial South African touring team, that visited England, whilst the Boer War was still being waged. The tour was much more arduous than current tours as it lasted over three months, and they played a total of 25 matches. As the tour was unofficial no test matches were played.

The second match of the tour had been the previous week, when they beat the London County side by 61 runs. This must have been when Grace took the opportunity to persuade, **Bertram Clifford Cooley**, **Charles Frederick Henry Prince** and **Murray Bissett**, to forego their rest day. Of these three, Murray Bissett was the most famous and played in three test matches. He had already captained the national side, in his first two matches against England in 1898-1899, at the age of 22. Later in his career he was knighted and became the Governor General of Southern Rhodesia.

The **1902** match between the two teams warranted a much more detailed account in the 'Sporting Life' of May 26th, and illustrates what a popular social event the game must have become locally. *"Members of the Beagles were very much in evidence at the Crystal Palace on Saturday on the occasion of this annual match, and the Doctor, who again supported the Beagles, presided over the luncheon at which about 200 were present, the fair sex being prominent. The scoring on both sides was not heavy, Dr. Grace (37) for the Beagles and E. H. Lulham (31) for the County being the chief contributors. For the County, P. G. Gale took six wickets for 53 runs, and Kenward three for 37; while Dr. Grace dismissed five of the County for 34, and Bell four for 39, Beagles winning by 48 runs. Scores:-*

WORCESTER PARK BEAGLES.

R. Chetwynd Stapylton b Kenward	0	C. B. Grace c Hayward b Gale	19
F. G. Colman c Benton b Gale	19	P. P. Francis b Bell	0
B. M. Bell c Gale b Campbell	16	T. A. Straker b Kenward	5
C. G. Boosey l b w, b Gale	16	Dr. W. G. Grace c Kendle b Kenward	37
Captain Willoughby c Norman b Gale	0	H. Willis, jun. b Gale	1
T. P. Hilder c Norman b Gale	7	B. Wallach not out	3
		Byes, &c.	6
		Total	**129**

In the second innings R. C. Stapylton scored not out 13, F. G. Colman run out 2, C. G. Boosey not out 27, C. B. Grace c Newman b Haywood 9, H. Willis, jun. b Newman 22; bye, 1.—Total (three wickets), 74.

LONDON COUNTY.

N. F. Norman run out	0	A. P. Todd b W. G. Grace	1
P. G. Gale c and b Bell	3	E. M. Lulham l b w, b W. G. Grace	31
C. E. C. Kendle b Bell	6	F. Benton not out	3
A. Worsley absent	-	Kenward c Hilder b W. G. Grace	7
A. P. Newman c and b Bell	0	Byes, &c.	8
J. Bell c Hilder b W. G. Grace	12		
C. Haywood c Colman b Bell	5		
Admiral C. Campbell b W. G. Grace	6	**Total**	**81**

Umpires: Dickenson and Galpin.

One can imagine the well-heeled followers of the hunt, and their good ladies, descending en-masse on the marquees at Crystal Palace for the day's entertainment, whilst to cater for 200 at lunch was quite impressive. For some of these encounters between the L.C.C.C. and 'The Beagles', the day was often referred to in the press as 'Ladies' Day'.

'The Sporting Life' provided a scorecard that has withstood the ravages of time and is reproduced above. I also discovered a faded photograph, which is reproduced on the following page of some of the players and their supporters sitting in front of the pavilion, with what might be W. G. Grace standing on the right hand side. It is definitely a photograph of one of these matches and appears to be dated 1902.

For the Worcester Park Beagles, the side's opening batsmen were the young pairing of **Frederick D. G. Colman**[10] (b.1881), the mustard magnate, who was probably the wealthiest player in the team, and **Richard G. H. Chetwynd Stapylton** (b. 1880), who was a clerk with a stock broking firm. Richard was a member of perhaps the most important family in the Worcester Park area, as his grandfather, the Canon Rev. William Chetwynd Stapylton, had been the vicar of St John's Church, Old Malden for 44 years from 1850 to 1894. The vicar's curate and lodger, the Rev. G. Lewis, had played in one of the first recorded games in the Worcester Park area, between Malden and Worcester Park in September 1851, which Canon Stapylton had probably instigated. Richard's uncle, Frederick Chetwynd Stapylton had been the joint master of the hunt in 1889, whilst Richard's father, Edward, was a committee member.

Francis Philip Francis (b. 1852), although he failed to score on the day, was a regular participant in these contests. Francis had been born in Upminster, Essex, the son of a wealthy solicitor. His cricketing credentials were quite impressive as he had played cricket for both Worcestershire and Essex, and was on the committee of Kent C.C.C. Francis was yet another stockbroker involved with the Beagles and lived for much of his life at 'Rowan Brae' in Claygate.

Probably the youngest member of the Beagles' side was the third oldest son of W.G., **Charles Butler Grace** (b. 1882), who, like his father, was a keen beagle-follower. C. B. was named after a Tasmanian cricketer, Charles Butler, with whom his father had stayed when touring Australia. C. B. Grace, who was an exponent of lob bowling, only played four first class games for London County.

At the opposite end of the age scale was **Henry Willis jun.**, who was probably the oldest player on the Beagles' side, having been born in 1841. He lived at 'Horton

Lodge' in Epsom, and was a member of the London Stock Exchange. As a cricketer he had failed to impress in the one first class game that he had played for Surrey against Yorkshire in 1868. He did, however, captain the Epsom side for many years, where he must have played with fellow committee members of the Beagles such as George Henry Longman and Colonel Bridges.

A rather enigmatic short account of that 1902 encounter between 'The Beagles' and L.C.C.C. appeared in the 'Westminster Gazette' on Monday May 26th, which demonstrates that Grace appeared to be a law unto himself, and raises a few questions such as 'Why Waring?' and 'Who on earth is Norman Gale?':-

"A cricket mystery has been solved. 'What's become of Waring?' - otherwise 'W. G.' - they were asking at Lord's last week when the "Old 'Un" mysteriously vanished during the progress of the M.C.C. v All Ireland match, and Mr. W. L. Murdoch had to take his place. Today the little mystery is explained. The 'Doctor' had betaken himself to the Crystal Palace to play for that distinguished side the Worcester Park Beagles. And against his own London County team too! Of course he made top score, took numerous wickets, and generally did great execution. Another of the 'Beagles' we notice was 'c Norman b Gale'. Perhaps Mr. Norman Gale will oblige with a 'copy of verses' on the incident."

As an ex-English teacher I feel that it is sadly remiss of me that I failed to realise that Norman Gale was a famous Victorian poet, story teller and publisher, who in 1894 had produced a body of work called 'Cricket Songs'.

The first account of the **1903** match that I found was, predictably, in 'The Gloucester Citizen' of 25th May, 1903: *"For once in a way W. G. Grace played against the London County team at the Crystal Palace on Saturday. During the winter he follows the Worcester Park Beagles to keep himself fit, and it was for a team representing that body of sportsmen that "the Doctor" turned out. Batting first the Beagles hit up 240, to which "W. G." contributed 92 by delightful batting. London County soon lost W. L. Murdoch for a single but L. O. S. Poidevin, the young Australian, and Major F. Fleming hit very hard indeed, and were not separated until both had made centuries. After the wicket had added 223 runs Fleming was run out, and time was soon after called. The game was left drawn, with London County only 5 runs short of victory. Major Fleming made 115, Poidevin 110 not out, and the total was 236 for two wickets."*

A fuller account of the match was found in the 'Sporting Life' of the same date under the title *'Heavy Scoring and a Close Finish'*:-

"There is always a big gathering at this meeting held at the Crystal Palace, and on Saturday there was again a big gathering of friends with ladies predominating. As in

previous matches W. G. Grace followed the Beagles and opposed the County, and together with T. P. Hilder, made a fine stand, the doctor being in great form, and was unfortunate in missing his century by eight runs, his 92 including nine 4's, four 3's, and eight 2's. Hilder's score of 75 comprised a 6, nine 4's, four 3's and eight 2's, the Beagles closing their innings for a big total of 240. With considerably less than three hours to bat, London County went to the wickets. Murdoch was out for a single. Major F. Fleming and L. O. S. Poidevin (the Australian) commenced hitting freely, and fighting against time this pair, amid considerable excitement, worked the total to 224 when Major Fleming was run out for 115, including a 6 and fourteen 4's. With still a few minutes to bat twelve more runs were added, but London County just failed by five runs to win when stumps were drawn after a most exciting finish. Poidevin, who was applauded for his brilliant effort of 110 not out, hit thirteen 4's."

Scores :—
WORCESTER PARK BEAGLES.—F. G. Colman c Gale b Murdoch 10, B. C. Covell c Campbell b Murdoch 5, R. M. Bell b Murdoch 6, T. P. Hilder c sub b Campbell 75, C. C. Macaulay run out 6, W. G. Grace c Colegrave b Campbell 92, H. Willis b Poidevin 0, P. P. Francis b Campbell 25, B. Jayaram b Fleming 6, Captain Willoughby not out 0, L. Covell c Gale b Campbell 0 : byes, &c., 15.—Total, 240.
    LONDON COUNTY.—W. L. Murdoch st Covell b Grace 1, Major F. Fleming run out 115, L. O. S. Poidevin not out 110, J. M. Campbell not out 6.—Total (for two wickets), 236. P. G. Gale, C. J. Posthuma, R. H. Dillon, H. H. Burton, H. Colegrave, T. B. Woodfall, and C. C. Finch did not bat.
    Umpires : Messrs. Dickinson and Galpin.

William Lloyd (Billy) Murdoch (b.1854) in 1903 was virtually at the end of his first class career. Apart from captaining the Australians on four tours of England, he played in the first Ashes' match (1882), scored the first test double century and the first triple century in Australian domestic cricket. He eventually settled in England and played for both London County and Sussex, whom he captained. In 1892 he also toured South Africa with England and played in one Test.

Murdoch's fellow Aussie in the London County side was **Leslie Oswald Sheridan Poidevin** (b. 1876) who had an average of over 57 for New South Wales. He came to England to study medicine and qualified to play for Lancashire in 1904, helping them to win the County Championship that year. The following year he scored 1376 runs for the Red Rose County at an average of 44, and continued to play for them until 1908. In total, however, he only played 149 first class matches but succeeded in scoring 14 centuries and 31 fifties. He was also a very good tennis player who represented Australia in the Davis Cup in 1906.

Recently copies of an interesting journal entitled 'Cricket', have appeared online. It was founded in 1882 and appeared every Thursday. On June 25th, 1903, that newspaper wrote that Poidevin *"is a batsman of the very highest class. Next year he will be qualified for one of the Metropolitan counties, and if he is able to appear regularly for the side should do much to restore it to the high position it formerly occupied in the cricketing world. During the past few weeks he has exceeded the hundred on three occasions for London County, making 110* v Worcester Park Beagles, 116 v Dublin University, and 172 * v Lancashire."*

Prior to the advent of the 'Cricket' paper online, the only mention of the **1904** match was a brief one-liner in the 'London Daily News' of June 6th, 1904, which blandly stated that:- *"Worcester Park Beagles 230, London County 189."*

It was an annoying quirk of the 'London Daily News' that they always listed the winning side first, rather than the home team. Any thought that the match had been played at Worcester Park, however, was dispelled by the following brief article in the 'Cricket' newspaper on Thursday, June 9th, which tended to focus primarily upon the 'Grand Old Man', rather than the match: *"For the Worcester Park Beagles, Dr. Grace on Saturday scored 65 against the London County C.C. at the Crystal Palace, took two wickets and stumped no fewer than four men, all off the bowling of R. M. Bell. This is not by any means the first time that the Doctor has kept wicket. The most notable occasion on which he acted as wicket-keeper was in the match at the Oval between Australia and England in 1884, when the present colonial secretary, (Right Honourable Alfred Lyttelton) giving up the gloves to W. G., went on to bowl and took four wickets with lobs. The Doctor caught Midwinter off him."*

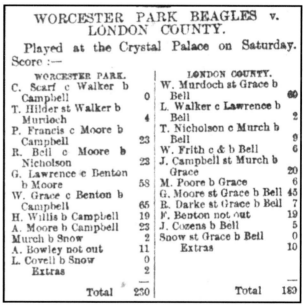

WORCESTER PARK BEAGLES v. LONDON COUNTY.
Played at the Crystal Palace on Saturday.
Score :—

WORCESTER PARK.		LONDON COUNTY.	
C. Scarf c Walker b Campbell	0	W. Murdoch st Grace b Bell	80
T. Hilder st Walker b Murdoch	4	L. Walker c Lawrence b Bell	2
P. Francis c Moore b Campbell	23	T. Nicholson c Murch b Bell	9
R. Bell c Moore b Nicholson	23	W. Frith c & b Bell	6
G. Lawrence c Benton b Moore	58	J. Campbell st Murch b Grace	20
W. Grace c Benton b Campbell	65	M. Poore b Grace	6
		G. Moore st Grace b Bell	45
H. Willis b Campbell	19	R. Darke st Grace b Bell	7
A. Moore b Campbell	23	F. Benton not out	19
Murch b Snow	2	J. Cozens b Bell	5
A. Bowley not out	11	Snow st Grace b Bell	0
L. Covell b Snow	0	Extras	10
Extras	2		
Total	230	Total	189

As London County C.C. were unable to meet the requirements of the M.C.C. as to the number of home fixtures they could provide in 1905, they lost their first-class status and much of their kudos. In many respects Crystal Palace was not an ideal venue for a cricket ground and by 1904 L.C.C.C. was already struggling to attract top class players. W. G. Grace was no longer the player that he had been, whilst others such as

Murdoch and Poidevin had either retired or moved on to pastures new. More importantly the number of paying spectators was beginning to flag.

The 'Pall Mall Gazette' mourned the passing of first-class cricket at Crystal Palace in quite an interesting article of the 22nd April, 1905, entitled 'Unfair Criticism', in which it blames in equal measure the inaccessibility of the ground and competition with The Oval and Lord's as reasons for the club's demise, rather than the standard of cricket that the London County Club provided.

"Regret is very general at the absence this season from more or less regular participation in first-class cricket of the London County Cricket Club. Without much doubt this venture - if it may so be termed - has, says 'C. B. Fry's Magazine,' not met with anything like the success it deserved. That it has not done so is very materially due to what appears at first sight to be a trivial cause, but which in these go-ahead days of haste and hurry in all things, has undoubtedly acted as a deterrent factor. Reference is made to the train service, and to the generally prevailing opinion of inaccessibility associated with the Crystal Palace. To the individual not really keen on going to Sydenham the mere mention of the Palace in preference to the Oval or to Lord's was treated with contumely. As a fact, very seldom have first-class fixtures at these three grounds been allowed to clash, though at times, of course, it was quite unavoidable. Then, again, the absence of a competitive element about the L.C.C.C. first-class matches also very probably affected the attendances. The public of today must have 'blood.' The charge laid against the L.C.C.C. elevens that they were not first class was, on the general run of the five years during which the club held a first-class certificate unfounded. Now and then non-first-class cricketers appeared in its elevens in first-class fixtures, but the same may be truthfully said every year about almost any county eleven. Besides, London County Cricket Club, through the championship, did more in a way of encouraging talent in this way than it was possible for any other club to do, and one may be quite sure W. G. Grace would not give a place in any of his elevens for a first-class match to anybody who had not got some first-class cricket somewhere in his composition. In some quarters the criticism in this direction was anything but fair."

The **1905** L.C.C.C. versus the Worcester Park Beagles match was probably quite a sombre affair as W.G.'s eldest son, a hunt follower, W. G. Grace junior (b 1874) had died on the Isle of Wight on March 2nd. He had been quite a promising cricketer, having obtained his cricket 'blue' at Cambridge, and had played first-class cricket for both Gloucestershire and London County.

From the brief one-liner in the 'London Daily News' of 5th June,: *"London County, 237, Worcester Park Beagles, 183",* one might be forgiven for thinking that the

L.C.C.C. had won the 1905 encounter. Fortunately 'The Sportsman' printed the full scorecard, which indicated that 'The Beagles' still had three wickets to fall at the close of play. It is strange to note that the score was almost identical to that in 1904.

```
       LONDON COUNTY v. WORCESTER PARK
                    BEAGLES
         Played at the Crystal Palace on Saturday.  Score:
                         LONDON COUNTY.
  B. Kenward, c Scarf, b      F. Benton, b Colman .... 10
    Colman.. ............ 12   P. A. Layman, c Grace,
  A. Marshall, c Francis.b       b Bell ................. 21
    Snow .................. 1   T. Cassells, c Francis, b
  P.G.Gale, lbw, b Colman  5     Grace................... 27
  F. R. Waterer, c Bell, b     R. H. Darke, not out..... 7
    Grace................. 26   Batty, b Grace........... 0
  O. H. Moor, c and b Bell 53   Extras................... 3
  L. C. Smith, c Murch, b                               --
    Colman.. ............         Total.............237
            WORCESTER PARK BEAGLES.
  C. Scarf, c Gale, b         W. G. Grace, c and b
    Marshall .............. 0   Kenward ................ 36
  Murch, b Waterer........ 91  P. P. Francis, b Gale ... 22
  H. C. Laurence,c Smith,     H. Wills, not out........ 0
    b Marshall............. 5   Extra .................. 1
  T. P. Hilder, c Batty, b                              --
    Cassels ............... 6   Total (7 wkts)...185
  E. M. Bell, b Marshall.. 22
    G. Colman, L. Covell, and Snow did not bat.
```

The opening batsman for the 'Beagles', who scored 91 runs and was merely called 'Murch', was an old team-mate of the Doctor, **William Henry Murch** (b. 1862). He had been born in Bristol and played cricket for Gloucestershire between 1889 and 1903, when he left the West Country to play for the London County C.C. The following year he played against the 'Beagles' but was not quite as successful.

His opening partner, who failed to score for the second year running, was **Charles Scarf** (b. 1867) an agent for a wool merchant. Charles had been born in Birmingham, but by 1901 was living in Thames Ditton and played cricket for Surbiton.

The **1906** match, which had returned to being played in May again, received a more comprehensive coverage in both the 'Sporting Life' and 'The Sportsman', which reported the match thus: *"It was Ladies' Day with the London County C.C. on Saturday, on the occasion of this annual fixture and the presence of a number of ladies in the pavilion, as well as in the ground, and the attendance of a band, imparted an infrequent scene of gaiety. The game resulted in a fairly even draw, the conspicuous features being the batting of Wells, of London County C.C., who in eighty-eight hit a five and nine 4's, and the bowling of Dr. W. G. Grace and Covell for the visitors. The veteran secured five wickets for 36, and Covell three for 23. Score:"*

```
                    London County.
Admiral  Sir  C. Camp-       S. E. Walmsley c Bouch
  bell b Bell           3       b Grace ................. 6
L S Wells b Grace ....  88   Murch c Covell b Grace  6
J E McPherson c Covell       F S Gothard c Scarf b
  b Bell ............... 16      Grace .................. 0
J H Todd c Marshall b        H L Parry c Bond b
  Covell ............... 18      Grace .................. 0
P R Waterer b Covell ... 1   P G Gate not out ....... 0
F  Benton  c  Willis  b         Extras ................. 1
  Covell ............... 0                          ——
                                     Total .........139
                Worcester Park Beagles.
F P Francis c Waterer        R M Bell c Penfold b
  b Wells .............. 15      Wells .................. 1
C Scarf b Waterer ...... 18  L  Covell  st  Todd  b
Lawrence   c   Gale   b          Wells ................. 15
  Waterer .............. 17  A Marshall not out .... 24
E R Bouch c Murch b          Penfold not out ........ 6
  Waterer ............... 8      Extras ................. 5
H P Holder c Penfold b                              ——
  Waterer ............... 7       Total (8 wkts)...129
H  Willis  st  Todd  b
  Waterer ............. 13
W. G. Grace did not bat.
```

Batting at number nine for the 'Beagles' was the imposing figure of the 6' 3" tall, Australian all-rounder **Alan Marshall**[11](b. 1883), whilst **Edwin R. Bouch** (b. 1866) was yet another quite wealthy local stockbroker, who hailed from Bromley. **Richard M. Bell** (b.1874), who played in several of these fixtures came from a quite well-to-do family in the Brighton Road, Sutton. He had spent some time in Australia, and in the 1901 census he was listed as being an Australian merchant's clerk. He was a reasonable bowler and had played for both London County and the Gentlemen of Surrey (according to the 1910 Wisden). Sadly the 1939 register showed that he ended his days in the Long Grove Mental Hospital at Horton.

By 1906, however, the press were becoming conscious of the lack of first-class cricket being played by W.G. Grace, who was by then 58 years old. Although his performances upon the cricket field were beginning to wane, he was still a very competitive and competent sportsman in other fields, as is stressed by the following article in the 'Derby Daily Telegraph' of the 28th May, 1906.

"With little call yet made upon him in this season's cricket, the veteran, W. G. Grace, is keeping his eye in with golf and bowls. Golf and beagling are his chief winter sports, and in golf he may often be found playing with Mr. Gilbert Jessop, perhaps inwardly confessing that a little knowledge is a dangerous thing, since it is apt to lead the unpractised player into many traps undreamt of in the cricket field. In bowls this season the doctor enjoys an unbeaten record. He is the skipper of the London County Bowls Club, and led them to victory last week against a strong side of the Banbury Club. He is as noted for his rink generalship as he is in the beagling field for the power of his voice and his ability to be somewhere on the track, if not in at the kill."

The **1907** match, which was rain affected, was reported in the 'Sporting Life' of June 3rd:

The good 'Doctor' appears to have been playing for both teams. Not only did he open the batting for L.C.C.C., but then caught their number five batsman out. He was perhaps of the opinion that the crowd had come expressly to watch him play. Sadly the game was abandoned before he could bat for a second time.

It is surprising the number of interesting characters that W. G. managed to persuade to play for the Beagles. **Leonidas De Toledo Macondas de Montezuma**[12] (b. 1869) was the son of a wealthy Brazilian Naval Lieutenant, whilst **Cyril Theodore Anstruther Wilkinson** was born in Durham in 1885, the son of a cricketing vicar, A. J. A. Wilkinson, who played 19 first class matches. In the 1911 census Cyril was listed as being a civil servant, 3rd class clerk. He was, however, quite a sportsman and played cricket for Surrey from 1909. He captained them to victory in the Championship in 1914 and in the two post war years. He retired from first class cricket in 1920 but continued to play club cricket into his sixties. In his final game in 1953 for Sidmouth, at the age of 67 he scored a fifty and took all ten wickets.

Cyril T. A. Wilkinson also played Hockey 4 times for England, once as the captain, and also won a Gold Medal at the Antwerp Olympic Games in 1920. Following this success he became an international hockey umpire and vice-president of the Hockey Association. In 1954 he was awarded a C.B.E. for his service to the sport.

The final game in the series between the Worcester Park Beagles and the L.C.C.C. occurred in **1908**, the year that the London County team eventually folded. The match again merited a mention in the 'Gloucestershire Echo' of the 25th May: *"W. G. Grace turned out for the Worcester Park Beagles against the London County on Saturday. The Doctor's side won easily, and he himself took six wickets for 34 runs and scored ten runs."*

```
                    Worcester Park Beagles.
C B Grace b Wells...........  34   K Keeler c G Gillespie b
C Scarf c Benton b Wells ...  30     Wells ........................  5
R M Bell c G Gillespie b           G H Lawrence lbw b J
  Keliher ...................  11     Gillespie ..................... 15
A Brandt b J Gillespie......  48   H Halketh-Crickett not out   1
L Covell c Campbell b Wells   6    T P Hilder b Wells...........  5
W G Grace c sub b J                   Extras .................... 12
  Gillespie .................  10
L Newitt c Keliher b Wells    3       Total ...............180
        1st Inns.        London County.        2nd Inns.
G S Gillespie c H Crickett b
  W G Grace ................  13   b C B Grace .................  0
Ian M Campbell c and b Bell..  10   st H Crickett b C B Grace. 39
L S Wells not out .........  23   c Covell b C B Grace.........  5
F R Waterer b W G Grace.....  6    c Brandt b C B Grace ......  5
J D Gillespie c Brandt b W G
  Grace ....................  0    c Covell b Keeler .........  23
E P Kay b Bell .............  4    not out ....................  9
J C Keliher b W G Grace ....  0    not out ....................  7
P W Taylor b Bell ..........  0
S E Walmesley c Covell b W G
  Grace .....................  1
W L Parry b W G Grace.......  0
F Benton b Bell ............  14   c H Crickett b Bell.........  9
  Extra ....................  1       Extras ..................  2
     Total ...........  72            Total (6 wkts) ... 99
```

A much more comprehensive account of the game, however, appeared in the 'Sporting Life' of the same date: *"At the Crystal Palace on Saturday the Beagles, who were assisted by Dr. W. G. Grace and C. B. Grace, defeated London County by 108 runs. For the Beagles W. G. Grace took six wickets for 38 runs, and R. M. Bell four for 33, while L. S. Wells (six for 79) and J. D. Gillespie (three for 58) were the pick of the losing bowlers. C. B Grace secured four for 46 on London County again going in."*

It is strange to note that amongst all the gentry of the Beagles, their wicket keeper, the aptly named **Halkett Crickett**, was a working class youngster, who had been born in Ewell in 1890. The 1891 census showed him and his mother, Minnie, as being visitors in the home of Charles Grafham, a painter and decorator in Ewell. Ten years later, however, his mother had disappeared and Halkett had been adopted by Charles Grafham and his wife. He was still living with the family in 1911 when his occupation was listed as being a general porter. He served throughout the First World War, becoming a captain in the Royal Army Medical Corps, whilst between 1924 and 1939 he was a surgeon in the Merchant Navy.

****

Worcester Park Beagles Appendix

[1]**George Pilkington Blake** (b. 1835) was an extremely colourful character who lived in Worcester Park in the 1880s. He had been born at 'Thurston House', near Bury St. Edmonds, Suffolk, the only son of James Bunbury Blake, and grandson of Sir James Blake, 5th bart. Despite hailing from Suffolk there does not appear to have been any relationship to Andrew Blake and his brothers, who also came from the same county.

His mother was Catherine Pilkington, one of the daughters and heiresses of Sir Thomas Pilkington 7th bart., who had been a wealthy mill and landowner from 'Chevet Hall', near Wakefield, in Yorkshire. She brought a fortune of over £40,000 to the marriage, whilst James was only worth between £3,000 and £5,000. Her eldest sister, Louisa, had married the heir to the Blake title, Sir Charles Henry Blake.

Following his education at Rugby School, George opted for a military career, and at the age of seventeen and a half, he bought a commission as an Ensign in the 74th Highlanders. The following year, on the 24th August 1853, he arrived in India, where he served for almost five years until May 29th 1858. Whilst in India he was promoted to the rank of Lieutenant and transferred to the 84th Regiment, and thence to the 100th Foot, with whom he served with distinction in the Indian Mutiny. Following the death of his Captain, during General Havelock's relief of Lucknow in 1857, George led the advance guard into the beleaguered city. There he spent nine weeks defending the besieged town until the Mutiny was eventually suppressed. For this feat of bravery he was promoted from Lieutenant to Captain and received the Indian Mutiny Medal with two clasps. One of these clasps was awarded for the Capture of Lucknow and the other for its Defence.

Following his return to England as a war hero, he retired from the military in 1860 and married Adeline King, the third daughter of Sir James King King, Esq., M.P. for Herefordshire. The wedding ceremony, which was performed by the Bishop of Hereford, at St. George's, Hanover Square, was recorded by the 'Hereford Times', under the heading 'Marriage in High Life'. They were certainly celebrities who, over the following twenty years, were regularly listed as attending all the leading society events from balls and banquets to the races.

The couple moved to 'Sparrow's Nest' near Thurston that year, with its regulation six servants, including a groom. There they began to raise a family. George, however, still seemed to yearn for army life, and in June, 1862, he joined the 2nd Battalion of the Suffolk Rifle Volunteers, on a part time basis, with the rank of Captain. By the late 1860s he had moved from the Rifle Volunteers to the Suffolk Yeoman Cavalry where he was promoted to the rank of Lieutenant Colonel in 1876, and eventually to the honorary rank of Colonel in June 1882. According to the 'London Gazette' he resigned his commission in January 1887, but was *permitted to retain his rank and to continue to wear the uniform of the regiment on his retirement.*

Apart from his role as a father to his growing family of a son and three daughters, his duties with the Suffolk Yeomanry, and the work involved in being a Justice of the Peace for the County of Suffolk, George became an avid huntsman in the 1860s. With the help of some friends and relatives, he started a pack of staghounds, and hunted the countryside around Ipswich for five or six years. After relinquishing these hounds he hunted regularly with the Essex and Suffolk Fox Hounds.

George appears to have been a rather ruthless and flamboyant character who was not averse to the sort of publicity that a more reserved man would have shunned. This was particularly true in some of the legal cases in which he found himself embroiled, often with members of his own family. In 1874 following the death of his father, James Bunbury Blake, George managed to persuade his mother to move out of 'Thurston House', into a small cottage, so that he and his family could live there. He also tricked her into signing a document which in essence gave him access to her fortune. When he sacked a faithful gardener, however, who had been with the family for over 25 years and also cut down some trees, the relationship with his mother finally broke down, and she eventually took him to the High Court at Westminster in 1879, and again in 1880.

Col. George Pilkington BLAKE
(1835-1915)

These cases made all the national papers and the local 'Bury and Norwich Post' of February 11th 1879, devoted over 20,000 words to the court proceedings. It was a case of infinite intrigue worthy of an Agatha Christie Mystery, most of which hinged around the missing will of James Bunbury Blake, which strangely disappeared shortly before his death. George's 80 year old uncle, Admiral Patrick John Blake, voiced his opinion, and also put it into writing, that the will had been destroyed by his nephew. This, in its turn, led to another court case in June of that year when the Admiral was accused of both libel and slander.

Following his eviction from 'Thurston House', George and his family moved initially to Kensington, before relocating to 'New House Farm' in Worcester Park, although his role as a Lieutenant Colonel in the Suffolk Yeomanry Cavalry meant that he still returned to his home county on a regular basis for parades and social occasions, such as the point-to-points for which the Hussars were famous, and which were events where George could enter some of his prize horses, such as 'Ironmaster'.

The Colonel, who, according to 'The Stage' of May 30th, 1884, was *interested in theatrical matters'*, appeared to be also a theatrical agent and erstwhile producer, with a penchant for actresses, as was revealed in another couple of legal cases which made the papers whilst he was living at 'New House Farm'. In May 1884 he was sued for breach of contract by a famous Music Hall singer, dancer and actress, Miss Fanny Leslie (b.1850). At one stage he proposed to build a new theatre, run by the actress Emily Duncan, where Fanny could perform. When he failed to find a suitable venue for her act, however, his two word telegram to her, "Engagement Off" was deemed unsatisfactory by the court and he was fined £250 plus costs.

In June, 1885, he ordered a padlock bracelet for Miss Florence Clifford, who was then acting at the Comedy Theatre. He presented the bracelet to her in front of witnesses, but, because it was not the right size, it had to be returned to the jewellers. Florence, subsequently collected the bracelet from the jewellers, who were then taken to court by the Colonel on the grounds that they had returned it without his permission. He lost the case and had to pay costs, although the case did make for some interesting headlines in the press - 'Colonel Blake and the Actress' ('Evening Star') and 'An Actress and her Admirer' ('Western Morning News').

Despite all the adverse publicity that he had received, Colonel Blake was invited to take the mastership of the Surrey Union Fox-hounds, at a meeting held at 'The Swan' in Leatherhead, in April 1884. He accepted the offer, and at once set about building suitable kennels and stabling at 'New House Farm'. This, in turn, led to conflict with the local council because of the increase in sewage which emanated from the farm, thereby leading to his eventual decision to build new kennels in Green Lane in 1885.

'The Sporting Gazette' hailed Colonel Blake's election to the Mastership of the Hunt, as he was *"a fine horseman and a good sportsman, and he was willing to take the country on the terms of hunting it at least two days a week (Tuesday and Saturday), and be prepared to give up his whole time to the interests of the hunt."*

George resigned from the Hunt at the end of 1886, possibly because of a disagreement over the amount that had to be paid in members' subscriptions. He wanted the members to pay £1,500 per annum, rather than the £1,250 that they were already paying. Hunting was definitely a rich man's sport as an inflation calculator reveals that £1,500 in 1886 would equate to over £196,000 in 2020.

Following their relatively brief foray into Surrey, the Blakes returned to Thurston, where George continued to sit on the Bench, and appeared at local regimental events and steeple chases. Sadly his wife, Adeline, died in 1890, after a lingering illness, and George eventually married a wealthy widow, Adela Mary Lavinia Duffield, nee Theobald, in 1893, and they made a new life for themselves in Kent, where George continued to hunt until he was 78 years old. He died in 1915 and left £10,965 0s 3d.

[2]**Charles Blake,** who was unrelated to his namesake George Pilkington Blake, was born, the son of a wealthy farmer in 1817, at Idmiston, in Wiltshire. In 1834, at the age of seventeen, he was articled, as a solicitor's clerk, to Charles Bridges, of Winchester and London. Much of his five years' apprenticeship seems to have been

spent in Bridges' offices in Finsbury Square, London and, in November, 1839, he was admitted as an Attorney-at-Law to Her Majesty's Court of the Queen's Bench.

Charles married his first wife, Mary Ann Elstob, the daughter of Dryden Elstob, a shipbuilder from Peckham, in 1842. Mary was twenty years older than Charles, who was living in Norwood at the time of the wedding. Apart from being a solicitor in the city, Charles was also involved in several new property developments being undertaken in the Norwood area, where it is interesting to note that another Idmiston Road exists, the precursor to the road and square of that name in Old Malden, in an area that Charles also helped to develop.

Although the 1851 census shows that Charles and Mary Ann were living in Bermondsey, by the time of the 1861 census they had moved to 'Blue House Farm', near the junction of West Barnes Lane and what is now Blakes Lane, which was named after Charles. By 1865, according to David Rymill, Charles had taken a 99 year lease from Merton College, on Motspur Farm on condition that he built at least 10 large houses upon the 170 acres of land.

In 1883, Mary Ann died, and the following year Charles married Elizabeth Rosalie Gush who was 22 years his junior. In 1893 the couple moved to 'The Laurels' in Motspur Park, which at a later date became 'The Rookery'. This, at a much later date, became the clubhouse of the London University Sports ground, where Sidney Wooderson broke the world mile record in 1937. In the 1980s this ground was hired by Worcester Park Cricket Club, for their Third XI fixtures, and now, of course, the site is the training ground for Fulham Football Club.

Charles Blake appeared to be a newcomer to the Morden Hunt when he took over the Mastership of the pack of *'Real old English Harriers, blue mottled and lemon pied'* (Stracey) in the spring of 1863. According to James Stracey, Mr. Blake was an extremely secretive Master who took great pains in covering his tracks and never advertised meetings, basically eschewing all publicity.

Charles did, however, acquire the reputation of being an eccentric, possibly because he continued to wear an old fashioned top hat as the Master of the Hunt rather the more modern flat cap. He was, however, extremely popular amongst the locals who always referred to him as 'Squire Blake' and, when not hunting, Charles used to be ferried up to his office at 4, Serjeants' Court, Temple, in a dog cart, driven by his huntsman, Billy Poole. When he retired as the Master of the Hunt in 1886, after twenty three years in the job, he gave his prize dogs to the local farmers, which also increased his popularity.

Although Charles was a solicitor, who was supposed to work within the confines of the legal system, his practice in the City did occasionally fall foul of the law. In 1852, for example, his clerk was charged with forgery and embezzlement, whilst in December, 1879, a solicitor called Charles Blake was sentenced to six months' hard labour for fraud, despite there being a recommendation of mercy from the Jury. On a more local level he also found himself at odds, on several occasions, in the 1880s and 1890s, with the Malden and Coombe Urban District Council, for allowing sewage to flow into a ditch at South Lane, near 'New House Farm'. He, in his turn, tried to blame the owner of that property, Thomas Weeding Weeding.

[3]**George Henry Longman** (b. Aug 3rd, 1852) was probably the most famous cricketer associated with the Worcester Park Beagles, apart from W. G. Grace himself. G. H. Longman was undoubtedly one of the most well known amateurs in England during the second half of the nineteenth century, despite only playing 68 First Class games. He was a dashing, hard-hitting batsman, part time wicket-keeper and leader of men. It is interesting to speculate how famous he might have been had he devoted more of his time and energy to cricket rather than to hunting and the family business. Despite only hitting eleven half centuries and having a highest score of 98, some of his innings and his fielding feats were the stuff of legend. James Stracey, when he edited his book in the 1980s, dreamt of an idyllic time, *'When W. G. Grace and G. H. Longman played cricket for the hunt and when hares were hunted in country now urbanised.'*

Longman had been born at Farnborough Hill in Hampshire, the son of Thomas Longman, one of two brothers who owned the Longman publishing company, which later became Longmans, Green & Co. of Paternoster Row. He certainly had a privileged upbringing, as by time of the 1871 census the family were living in Eaton Square. It must have been an 'Upstairs, Downstairs' sort of life with a butler, under footman, lady's maid etc., whilst on one side lived Lady Scott and on the other the Earl of Erne.

As a youngster he must have been quite talented at cricket before he went to Eton, as he played for the College First XI for four years and captained them in 1871. He was also President of the Eton Society and Master of the Eton Beagles.

The first real indication of his potential as an outstanding cricketer probably occurred in the prestigious Eton versus Harrow game that was held at Lords in July 1871. The match, which was the forty-seventh in the series, was attended by about 20,000 spectators over the two days, including the Crown Princess of Germany.

The following account from the 'Illustrated London News' of July 21st takes up the story: *"Eton won the toss, and sent the Hon. F. G. Brace and A. S. Tabor to the wicket. Nothing particular occurred till the two men were out for 29, and G. H. Longman (the Eton captain) and A. W. Ridley got together. These two made a wonderful stand; indeed, in spite of constant changes in the bowling it seemed impossible to separate them, especially when the former was missed after scoring 20. They made 126 runs before their partnership was dissolved by a fine ball that took Longman's bails."*

Longman made 68 runs out of the partnership whilst A.W. Ridley notched up 117 out of a total of 308, which enabled the Eton lads to triumph convincingly by an innings and 77 runs.

The following year Longman went to Trinity College, where, apart from taking on the roll of Master of the Trinity Foot Beagles he gained a blue at cricket for Cambridge and featured in what was undoubtedly the most emphatic win against Oxford in the 38 years' history of the competition to that date. Before a crowd of 12,000 at Lords, Longman and his fellow old Etonian, A. S. Tabor (50), put on 104 runs for the first wicket.

The impact that two freshmen had made in setting a record opening partnership in the Varsity match amazed many of the onlookers, In writing about it, over 50 years later in the 1929 'Wisden', in an article entitled 'My Years at Cambridge', Longman said an ardent Oxonian was sitting in the pavilion and up to him came another with the eager question, *'Well how is it going?' 'Going! There are two little freshmen in, and they've got the hundred up without a wicket.'* In a way, this feat was the highlight of both Longman's and Tabor's careers and just about eclipsed anything else they ever achieved. Even in the early years of the Twentieth Century, mention of their names would cause genuine cricket lovers to return to that glorious day at Lords in 1872 when two precocious freshmen had had the audacity to notch up a century opening partnership.

Longman was eventually out for 80 in an innings that was not in his usual aggressive style. It was reported in the 'Morning Post' of June 25th, 1872, as follows:
'Longman was run out for an admirable contribution of 80, his obstinate defence and steady play having done much to "breaking the heart" of the Oxford bowlers. He had been at the wickets for three hours and 20 minutes, was missed when he was 38, and his chief hits were seven 4's, a 3, and seven 2's. He was loudly cheered.'

Being run out was rather an habitual way of being dismissed for Mr. Longman, as his first two innings for Eton at Lords had also ended in that fashion. He also carried on that tradition for Hampshire as, in one of his first matches for that county against Kent, in 1876, he was again run out.

W. Yardley, who had scored the only century in the history of the 'Varsity Cricket Match in 1870, added another 130, as the Light Blues amassed 388 runs, which enabled them to win by an innings and 166 runs. Before the game the Dark Blues had been the 2-to-1 favourites but they were outclassed by the quality of the Cambridge batting and their keenness in the field. It is curious to note that A. W. Ridley, who had scored a ton for Eton the previous year was batting for Oxford, down at number eight in the first innings, and was undefeated on 18* at number nine in the second innings.

The 1872 win was the only victory that G. H. Longman experienced against Oxford, as they lost the next three with him captaining the losing side in both 1874 and 1875. The Light Blues should, however, have, won the 1875 match but for a brave call by the Oxford captain, A. W. Ridley, (who went on to play for Sutton C.C.) in an incident which was recalled in the 'Yorkshire Evening Post' of August 29th, 1916, following Ridley's death: *"Mr. Ridley was the Oxford captain in the 'Varsity match of 1875. Cambridge needed 7 runs to win with two wickets in hand, when, to everyone's astonishment, Ridley went on to bowl lobs. There must have been still greater surprise when he ended the match with three balls, giving Oxford the win by 6 runs. He bowled W. S. Patterson and A. F. Smith, so it is recorded, each with a low straight ball on the leg-stump, neither delivery turning an inch. In his "Chats on the Cricket Field", Mr. W. A. Bettesworth elicited from Mr. G. H. Longman, of the Light Blues — prominent later in Hampshire County cricket — that when the last man went in, he offered him sal volatile to steady his nerves. He refused, scored a duck, lost the match, and then said afterwards that he really wished he had accepted the nerve steadier."*

In total G. H. Longman played 27 matches for the University in four years, scoring 1,019 runs at an average of 22.15. He scored four half centuries, with the 80 that he had scored in his first Varsity game being his highest score. On the fielding side he managed 11 catches and one stumping.

There were certain similarities between G. H. Longman's University and County careers, as he also played 27 matches for Hampshire, over a ten year period from 1875 until they lost their first class status in 1885. He also scored four half centuries for them, his highest knock being 78 against Surrey in 1884. Although his batting average of 17.46 for Hampshire was not overly impressive, he did take 20 catches and made 3 stumpings.

In addition to these matches Longman played four times for the M.C.C., once for the Gentlemen of England in which he scored 98 against Cambridge University, once for the Gentlemen of the South, once for the South of England and seven times for the Gentlemen versus the Players. He also played with W. G. Grace for the Gentlemen in 1876 and scored 70 on a difficult pitch out of a total of 153. Altogether, therefore, he played 68 first class matches in fifteen years, and, whilst there were no hundreds, he played several crucial and match winning innings.

It was whilst playing for the Gentlemen versus the Players at Prince's ground in early July 1876 that he really demonstrated his athletic ability in the field when he dismissed the last man, Allan Hill, off the bowling of W. G. Grace to end the match. The following is Wisden's description of that catch:- *"The innings was ended at long-*

field-on by 'the catch of the season' made by Mr. Longman, who was then fielding at deep long off, close up to the people in front of the new road in course of formation. With body bent back over some of the visitors, and right arm extended still farther over, he caught and held the ball with that right hand in such grand style that a roar of admiring cheers rang out, and all who witnessed it agreed it was the finest catch they had seen that season. It was hard lines for Hill to suffer defeat from so fine a drive but his consolation must be he suffered from a catch in a thousand."

After his first class career ended, George Henry Longman did, however, continue playing for Epsom for several seasons until about 1894 and possibly participated in one of the Beagles' matches in the early years of the last century. He also joined the Surrey Committee in 1894, and remained a Committee member until his death 44 years later in 1938. He became the President of Surrey County Cricket Club from 1926 until 1929 and from then onwards was the Hon. Treasurer from 1929 until 1939.

He was also an extremely keen golfer, winning several monthly medals at Epsom G.C. around the turn of the century and played in celebrity golf tournaments into his 80's. He even played the day before he died, in his sleep, at the age of 86.

Longman joined the Worcester Park Beagles in 1890 and was a very useful acquisition for the Hunt, as he had already been the Master of the Eton Beagles and the Trinity College Foot Beagles, besides having his own pack at his father's house at Farnborough Hill. He was an extremely keen huntsman, and on weekdays would arrive early at the kennels from his home at 'West Hill House', Epsom, *'while it was still dark so as to hunt from dawn until he had to catch the train to London for business'.*

Unlike the majority of Beagle followers who hunted on foot, G. H. Longman rode a pony as he had been severely incapacitated sometime during the mid-1890s by an attack of typhoid. From 1900 until 1904 he also became the Master of the Surrey Union Foxhounds whilst retaining his links with the Worcester Park Beagles.

[4]**Henry Kerr Longman** was born on March 8th, 1881, the son of G. H. Longman. Like his father, Henry played cricket for both Eton and Cambridge. He showed quite a lot of promise and, in 1899, for Eton, he shared in an opening stand of 167 at Lords, against Harrow, with F. O. (Francis Octavius) Grenfell who won a V.C. in August 1914, and was killed on August 24th 1915. Both scored 81 runs in the second innings of a drawn game.

Henry went up to Trinity College, Cambridge, and initially it seemed as though he would surpass his father's feats there. He must, however, have suffered greatly by being constantly compared to his father, as is shown in the following article from the 'Dundee Evening Post' of 27th April 1901:- *"H. K. Longman, the Eton captain, has* made a capital start at Cambridge, scoring over a hundred in the Trinity College Freshmen's match on Monday and Tuesday. He will be following exactly in the footsteps of his father, Mr. G. H. Longman, if he should be so fortunate as to get his Blue as a Freshman. Cricketers whose memories go back to 1872 will not need to be reminded that G. H. Longman made 80 the first time he played against Oxford at Lords, he and A. S. Tabor sending up the hundred for the first wicket - a feat never before performed in the University match. Mr. G. H. Longman is a member of the Surrey committee, and the young batsman now at Cambridge is qualified for the county."

Another article in the 'Dundee Evening Post' later that week, under the title 'A Week's Cricket in England' again praised Longman junior, whilst reminding their readers of his father:- "The first 'century' of the new century has been scored at Cambridge by a Freshman, Mr. H. K. Longman. He is the son of Mr. G. H. Longman, a famous Etonian and Cambridge bat in the early seventies, who is now a partner in the great firm of publishers whose name he bears. Mr. H. K. Longman, who was the captain of Eton last year, played two lovely scores of forty-four and eighty-one against Harrow in 1899. Last season he was abnormally consistent, averaging forty-five, whilst his largest innings was only sixty-nine. His form at Winchester was brilliant. Personally he is a splendid specimen of a healthy young Englishman, clever at work, good at games, and with a delightful boyish carelessness which made him wear his I Zingari sash the wrong side out the first time he put it on. He is qualified for Surrey, but, it is said, he might help Hampshire if he chose."

After scoring a sparkling hundred against Yorkshire at Fenners in May, 1901, at the age of twenty, it looked as though he would be an exceptional player. The following is an account of that innings in the 'Lancashire Daily Post' of Saturday, May 25th, 1901. They mistakenly call him G. H. Longman:

"G. H. Longman, who on Thursday scored 150 out of 335 for Cambridge against Yorkshire, is still merely a boy. He opened the Varsity's innings in company with Harper at twelve o'clock, and was not dismissed until half-past five. It is only his second match in first class cricket. He made his hundred in three hours and twenty minutes, the exact proportion of his figures to the full score being at that point 101 out of 227. Longman, without any special brilliance of style, keeps a good straight bat, and gets most of his runs in front of the wicket, though he has a fairly good square cut, and keeps the ball well down. His batting far outshone anything seen on the Light Blues' side. "

This innings was a false dawn, however, as Henry only played 32 First Class matches in a rather lacklustre career that spanned 20 years. Most of those matches were played in either 1901 for Cambridge or in the three years after the First World War for Middlesex. He did play three or four games for Surrey before the War, and overall he averaged 20.50 runs per innings, scoring four half centuries and one hundred. When not playing for Cambridge in 1901, he opened the batting for Epsom on several occasions.

Henry's career was probably disrupted by the fact that he became a career soldier, taking a Commission in the Gordon Highlanders in 1902, after just one year at Cambridge. The following year he played six games in Scotland for Aberdeenshire. From 1904 onwards he was to be found playing several non–first class games in the South of England and the odd Surrey game. He still retained his penchant for batting, however, as can be seen by the fact that whilst playing for the Aldershot Army Corps in July 1908, (according to the 'Army and Navy Gazette') he scored 126 in the first innings and 113 in the second. He retired from the army in January 1909, and spent a couple of years playing cricket in Yorkshire before the Great War.

He did return to the Army in 1914 and served in the First World War as a Major in the Gordon Highlanders winning a D.S.O. and an M.C., and eventually rose to the rank of Lieutenant-Colonel.

[5]**Arthur Sidney Tabor** (b. 1852) was one of the most prominent members of society in the Parish of Cheam, having a lifelong connection to the prestigious private prep school, Cheam School. Arthur was a pupil at the school where his father, Robert Stammers Tabor, was the Headmaster from 1856 until 1890. After university he returned to teach at Cheam School, and upon his father retiring in 1890, Arthur took up the baton and became the Headmaster from 1891 until 1920. For sixty-four years, father and son, ruled the school.

When Arthur went to Eton he played for the First Eleven at cricket for three years from 1869. He was always considered a promising opening batsman at school but, apart for one innings, failed to deliver. His main claim to fame is what he achieved at Cambridge, particularly in the Varsity matches. In 1872 with Longman he scored 50 out of an opening partnership of 104 in one hour and three quarters, in 1873 he scored 3 and 45, and in 1874 he scored 52 on a difficult pitch, the highest score of the match. Later that year he played his only game for the Gentlemen versus the Players alongside W. G. Grace.

Whilst at University he played a few games for Middlesex and, in 1878, he also turned out once for Surrey. Overall his first class career was rather disappointing as he only played in about 28 games and averaged a paltry 14.20 with the bat with a top score of 59. He scored no hundreds and had only a handful of fifties.

From 1875 he was a classics teacher at Cheam School, which obviously limited his opportunity to play cricket. He did, however, turn out quite often for the M.C.C., the

Free Foresters and the Eton Ramblers, and in July 1887 he scored 70 for the M.C.C. versus Rugby School. It is quite surprising to note that he often ended up opening the batting in several of these matches with his old school and university friend, G. H. Longman - probably in the hope that they would repeat their deeds of 1872.

Tabor is also recorded as guesting in many high society social games such as a match, in August 1886, when he played for Mr. V. W. R. Van de Weyer's Eleven versus the Hon. K. P. Bouverie's Eleven at Windsor, against Prince Christian Victor. In 1889 he was also mentioned as playing for Colombo in Ceylon against a touring side led by G. F. Vernon.

Arthur S. Tabor also had quite an excellent reputation locally as a cricketer and, in August 1881, he helped Cheam win the Surrey Challenge Cup by beating the holders, Farnham, at the Oval. By 1886, however, he seemed to have switched his allegiance to Sutton, where he joined up with his old Eton colleague, A. W. Ridley, as playing members of the club's Committee.

Most of his Social Cricket and Club Cricket, however, ceased when he became the Headmaster of Cheam School in 1891. Apparently he was exceedingly hardworking and only allowed himself a break from his work on Tuesday afternoons for a round of golf, although he did occasionally organize a team of his old Cambridge friends to visit Cheam in order to play against the staff of his school.

Cricket was the main sport played at Cheam School in the sixty-four year reign of Arthur Tabor and his father. Numerous of the boys went on to play for Cambridge but only one, Bere, played for Oxford. Between 1864 and 1895 there were only seven years in which there was no Cheam boy in the Cambridge side, and in one year there were four. During that time Cambridge was captained by a Cheam boy on seven occasions. H. K. Longman was the last in the line of Cheam boys to play for Cambridge.

Amongst the old boys several made the grade at cricket. One of the most famous was the Hon. Ivo Bligh (b.1859) who led the tour to Australia in 1882/83 and succeeded in regaining the Ashes which had been lost the preceding season. On that tour to Australia were two fellow Cheam Boys, George and Charles Studd. Bligh also became President of the M.C.C. in 1900/1.

The Studds of Cheam School was one of the most famous cricketing families of all time, all six playing for Eton, five for counties, four for Cambridge and two for England. The three eldest, George, Charles and Kynaston, captained Cambridge in successive years and all played in the famous victory of Cambridge over the Australians, who included Spofforth and Giffen, by six wickets in 1882. They were that famous that 'Punch' referred to them as 'a set of studs'.

Although several other boys went on to play first class cricket, I feel that special mention must be made in the appendix of **Robert Montagu Poore**[13].

The cricketing facilities at Cheam School were extremely good, although precisely where they were is difficult to ascertain. Some clue, however, can be gained perhaps from this paragraph from Edward Peel's book on Cheam School:

"The cricket field, with the pavilion and the row of ancient elms on one side and the railway line on the other, was a fine setting for the game. There were four separate pitches, the best of which was said to have no superior in Surrey."

A. S. Tabor was a firm disciplinarian and took this approach both in the classroom and on the sports field. On a games' afternoon he could often be found, sitting on a chair, at the centre of the four pitches bellowing instructions through a megaphone to the players on all four pitches. He not only wanted the best for his own pupils but wanted to improve the playing conditions for all youngsters. To this end, in 1892, he chaired *'a meeting of masters of English preparatory schools, convened for the purpose of discussing the best means of promoting the cricket education of boys under the age of fifteen.'* Their main recommendation was to introduce a slightly smaller, lighter ball for youngsters.

Even after he had ceased to play cricket, Arthur Tabor took an active role in supporting the game, and served for at least twelve years, until his death in 1925, with his old partner, George Henry Longman, on the Committee of Surrey C.C.C.

[6]**Colonel John Henry Bridges** was the son of a vicar, who was born on March 26th, 1852, in Horsham. According to the 1910 copy of 'Wisden', Bridges played both for Winchester College and Surrey. He studied law at Oriel College, Oxford, in the early seventies, and proved himself to be quite an accomplished all-round athlete. In the College's Sports Day in 1871 he won the High Jump, the Long Jump, the Hurdles and throwing the Cricket Ball, besides coming second in the 100 yard dash. He failed, however, to gain a 'blue' for cricket.

After finishing University he entered the Inner Temple in 1876, which was the year that he also played two first class matches for Surrey against Cambridge University. These two matches marked the end of his first class career but he carried on playing for several local teams, including Epsom and Beddington Village, for several years. On the scoresheet of one of the Beddington matches on 18th August, 1888, he was listed as opening with another of the Hunt's committee, one Robert Henderson. Although Bridges lacked Henderson's skill with the bat, he was still an outstanding batsman at club level and is recorded as scoring 137* out of 231, for Beddington Village on the 12th August, 1876, against Croydon Early Closing

Bridges was also an extremely good archer and competed at the Summer Olympics in London in 1908, where he came fifth in the double York round event with 687 points. He also competed in the Continental style event.

Stracey's book on the Worcester Park Beagles also showed that the Colonel was a frequent huntsman in the early years of the twentieth century. He was, after all, an extremely wealthy man who had plenty of time to hunt. He lived locally, in 1901, at Ewell Court with his young son and two daughters and employed eleven servants. His only occupation at that time appeared to be that of a Justice of the Peace. In 1939, at the age of 87, he became the Master of the Surrey Hunt.

[7]**Robert Henderson** (b.1865 in Wales) had played 148 matches for Surrey between 1883 and 1896. Following a brilliant debut season as an eighteen year old for Surrey in 1883, in which he scored over 500 runs and took 35 wickets, his career was interrupted by illness for three years. He was relatively successful upon his return and scored over 500 first-class runs again in 1889, which led to him being named as one of Wisden's nine players of the year in their 1890 Almanack. In 1892 he was even selected to play for the Players against the Gentlemen at Lords.

Robert eventually retired from cricket at the age of 31 to become a commercial clerk, and lived in a relatively modest fashion at 13, Bridge Road, Wallington, for the rest of his life. Unlike most of the remainder of the Hunt he only employed one servant. Henderson continued to play occasionally for Beddington for several seasons, hunted, and was elected the Hon. Sec. of the Beagles in 1909.

[8]**Thomas Paine Hilder** (b. 1866) was born at 'The Lindens', Penge, the only son of the five children of a wealthy stock broker, Thomas Paine Hilder senior and his wife, Emma. They were looked after by a cook, a parlour maid, two house maids, a kitchen maid and a nurse.

Young Thomas was educated at Eastbourne College where he proved to be a good sportsman. In the College Sports Day in 1883 he came first in the quarter mile, second in the 120 yard hurdles and second in the Open Mile. He also frequently opened the batting for the College in the early 1880s. Later in the decade he began a lifelong connection with the Bickley Park side and was recorded as chipping in with 134 runs for them, out of 443, versus Guys Hospital on June 9th, 1888. Later that year he also top scored with 61 runs, for an M.C.C. team versus Brightling Park.

By 1891, T. P. Hilder was listed in the census as being a stock dealer and worked with his father, who was on the Committee of Kent C.C.C., at the London Stock Exchange. Cricket was the younger Thomas's main love in the Summer whilst in the Winter he was the Captain of the West Kent Football team, for whom he is recorded as playing at half back in 1892.

Thomas was also a prominent member of the Worcester Park Beagles and was recorded as being on their committee in 1905. In his early days with the Hunt, according to Stracey's book, T. P. *'is described as having been almost as fast on his legs as the hare.'*

Thomas married Katie Madeline Pillans in 1905 and they moved into 'Cadlands', a twelve room house, in Chislehurst. As they had no children they settled for just a cook and a maid to look after them.

[9]**Livingston Walker,** who was named after the famous explorer, was born in 1879, into a Methodist family in Urmstone, Manchester, the youngest of five sons of a wealthy Lancashire merchant, John Maddock Walker. The following year John moved his family to Anerley Road, Penge, Croydon, in 1880, where he be apparently became a very popular member of society, and continued to work as a merchant for Reynolds, Walker and Son, and later became a Justice of the Peace.

Livingstone attended The Leys School, near Cambridge, which had been founded by the Wesleyan Methodist Church for the sons of laymen in 1875. It was there, according to the 'Norwood News' that he *"acquired the thorough knowledge, skill, and love of the game. He subsequently became a Surrey 'colt' and afterwards played in Surrey's 2nd XI."*

The young Livingston came to the attention of W. G. Grace, in 1900, whilst opening the batting for Anerley. He was invited to play a few games for London County that season and was eventually selected to play two matches for Surrey.

The following year was Walker's most successful season in his short career, as he played fifteen matches for Surrey and a further nine for London County, scoring more than a thousand runs at an average of over 31. His only two hundreds occurred in that year and he had a top score of 222 against the M.C.C., in a match that saw him take part in a third wicket partnership of 281 with the Great Man. Following that match, W.G. had the ball mounted and had it presented to the young player.

In 1903, because of a lack of a more suitable or experienced amateur, Livingston Walker became the Surrey Captain. The 'Norwood News' commented on June 27th that, *"It is a remarkable fact that, when appointed, Mr. L. Walker was only 23 years of age, reaching his 24th birthday last Saturday. It is believed such a young captain for a first class county is unique…..It may be added that Mr. L. Walker is another striking example of muscular Christianity. Notwithstanding his captaincy, he retains his post of secretary to the Wesleyan Sunday School at Annerley, and is devoted to the duties."*

His tenure as the county captain was not particularly successful as the side only finished eleventh out of fifteen teams. This virtually signalled the end of a short and interesting first class career, which lasted from 1900 to 1904 and included 94 first class matches.

By 1906 Livingstone was a merchant, living in Shanghai, where he continued to play cricket for the Shanghai C.C., which was a popular destination for touring teams and the armed forces. He eventually became the club's captain, as is mentioned by Pelham Warner in his marvellous book 'Imperial Cricket' (1912):-

"Shanghai, blessed with natural advantages, also has the fortune to include amongst its club team several first class players, two of the best known being

Capt. E. J. M. Barrett, late of the Malay States guides, now in the Shanghai police, who has done yeoman service for Hampshire on more than one occasion, and L. Walker, the present Shanghai captain, who has skippered Surrey. The Shanghai ground is a magnificent one, the same size as the Oval; the wicket is good, and so is the light, and here, owing to the climatic differences, it is a summer game."

The outbreak of War, in 1914, found Livingstone back in England, where he became a Lieutenant in the Sussex Yeomanry. Three years later he married Joyce Mewburn, the daughter of a J.P. from Kent, in what appears to have been quite a lavish wedding. The following year they had their only child, Richard, and in 1919, Livingstone went to work yet again in Shanghai, accompanied by his family. They finally returned to England in 1923, and settled in the village of Hildenborough in Kent.

[10]**Frederick D. G. Colman** (b.1881), lived at 'Nork House', Banstead, with his widowed mother, a younger brother, a niece, a nephew and eighteen servants. His occupation was listed as a Mustard Manufacturer. His father, Frederick, who had died in January, 1900 had been the Chairman of J. & J. Colman Limited of Norwich that produced one of the most iconic of British products - Colman's Mustard.

On Wednesday evening, 25th March, 1903, Frederick attended a ball which had been thrown in his honour at Nork Park. The event, which was organised by his mother, was attended by numerous Lords, Knights of the Realm and Ladies. *"The young squire is very popular among all classes, his genial disposition having secured for him a host of friends and well wishers."* ('Surrey Advertiser'). Among the multitude of presents which were showered upon him, pride of place went to the present that he received from his mother, a handsome hunter, which had secured premier honours at the previous year's county show in Guildford.

Despite his youth, Frederick was already the Captain of the highly successful Nork cricket team in 1902, and had been elected to the Beagles' committee in 1901 and became the Master of the Surrey Union Foxhounds from 1904 to 1910. Eventually Lieutenant Colonel Frederick Gordon Dalziel Colman OBE became the Master of the Belvoir Hunt in 1930.

W.G. Grace not only knew Frederick Colman as a fellow huntsman and cricketer, but he starred in what is undoubtedly one of the most iconic advertisements of the twentieth century, for Colman's Mustard.

[11]**Alan Marshall** was probably the most interesting player in the Beagles' team in 1906. The 6' 3" tall, batting all-rounder was born in 1883 in Queensland, Australia, where he played club cricket for Paddington, in Sydney. He only played eleven games for Queensland, who were not in the Sheffield Shield in those days, before he arrived in England in 1905. He then proceeded to score 2,752 runs, at an average of 56.16, and took 118 wickets at an average of 16.41 (ESPNcrickinfo) that year, for the London County C.C. The following year he was apparently even more successful for the club, and scored over 3,578 runs at an average of 76.16, and took 167 wickets at 14,10 apiece.

By 1907 Marshall had qualified by residency to play for Surrey and scored over a thousand runs for them that season at an average of over 25. Following his feat of scoring 1931 runs for them the following year at an average of over 40, he was named as the Wisden Player of the year in 1909. He returned to Australia in 1910 having played 119 first class matches in England, and having notched up over 5,000 runs at an average of almost 28. He also picked up 119 wickets at 22.84 apiece.

Sadly for the world of cricket he became yet another cricketing casualty of the First World War. Having enlisted in the Australian Army in 1914 he was sent to Gallipoli where he caught enteric fever, and eventually died on the 23rd July, 1915, at the Imtarfa Military Hospital on the Island of Malta.

[12]**Leonidas De Toledo Marcondes de Montezuma** was born in Crowborough on the 16th April, 1869, the sixth of nine children. Although both his parents were born in England, his father, who at one stage had been a Captain in the Brazilian Navy, was the son of Viscount Jequitinhonha, Councillor of State and Senator of the Empire of Brazil.

By the time of the 1881 census, although his family was living in South Norwood, Leonidas was a boarder at the Royal Naval College at Greenwich. There isn't much indication that he pursued a naval career, however, as much of his teenage years appeared to be spent either playing cricket or taking part in bicycle races for the Norwood Safety B.C. throughout the southern counties.

As a teenager Leonidas appeared to be primarily a bowler, who played for a variety of teams in the Croydon area including South Norwood College, Norwood, Selhurst, Carshalton, Spencer, Beddington, Epsom and the Thespians. Rarely a week passed without him being mentioned in the Norwood press, mainly for his bowling feats. One of his first appearances in the 'Sporting Life', however, occurred in July, 1885, when he played in a Royal Naval School match, Past versus Present. For the Past team he opened the batting and top scored with 46 runs and also took a couple of wickets. In the 1890s he played on several occasions for the Kensington Club.

By 1891, Montezuma was playing for Surrey Second XI with the likes of Charles Burgess Fry and Tom Richardson, at grounds such as Trent Bridge. Although he played several Second XI games his performances probably were not impressive enough to warrant a First XI spot. In 1898, however, he made his debut playing for Sussex, for whom he qualified by birth, against Essex at the County Ground in Leyton. In total he played eight First Class games that season with a top score of 80*. That was almost the end of his First Class career, although he played one final game in 1904 for London County.

Leonidas tried a variety of careers, mostly without success, and at one stage, in about 1895, he was committed to the Bethlem Hospital at Beckenham, with what is now suspected to be bipolar disorder. This was a disease that seemed to trouble him most of his life until his death in the City of London Mental Hospital at Stone in Kent in 1937.

[13] **Robert Montagu Poore** was born in Dublin in 1867, the son of a Retired Army Major and an Irish mother. He was educated initially at 'Edgeborough', a boarding school in Guildford, before moving to Cheam School.

Poore showed no real love for the game of cricket until he was serving in the army in India as a Major and began playing for the Europeans. He basically learnt how to play from books. He was sent to South Africa and in 1895/6, after some debate as to whom he should play for, he found himself playing in three Test matches for the South Africans against Lord Hawke's English side. In 1899 he scored 1551 runs for Hampshire at an average of 91.23, scored seven centuries in a two month period, with a top score of 304, and was made one of the Wisden Cricketers of that year. He was a typical English colonial officer with a solar topee being his headwear of choice in hot weather. Legend has it that when a young colleague asked him how to tackle Harold Larwood, he boomed, "Charge him, sah. Fix yer bayonets and charge him."

The 6 feet 4inches tall Poore was an impressive athlete. He was the lawn tennis champion of West India and Matabeleland, a first class polo player and an expert swordsman. During one fortnight in 1899, he won the man-at arms event in the Royal Tournament, he played in the winning inter-regimental polo team, and scored three consecutive tons for Hampshire.

"Together joined in cricket's manly toil."—*Byron.*

Cheam **Common** Cricket Club

Probably one of the oldest organised cricket clubs in the Worcester Park area, for which we have records, was the Cheam Common Cricket Club which, to a large extent, can be considered as the true pre-cursor of Worcester Park Cricket Club. It was their brave decision to disband in 1919, and to re-form as the Worcester Park Athletic Club, which led to the formation of the current club shortly after the Great War, in 1921.

Back in the 1870s Cheam Common stretched roughly from the outskirts of Cheam Village to Worcester Park Station. It was still mainly an area of rolling fields that supported a thriving pastoral economy. One only has to look at the early censuses to see that the majority of men of employable age were either farmers or agricultural labourers, with a smattering of brickwork labourers. Never having seen any sheep in the area, I was surprised to learn that three or four of the residents listed their occupations as shepherds. The arrival of the railway station in 1859 had led to the gradual development of blocks of houses in the Longfellow Road area for railway workers and early commuters.

The effect of this expansion locally is perhaps best summed up by this short passage from 'The Croydon Advertiser', of June 12th, 1873 - entitled 'The New Church at Cheam Common': *"Thursday was the day fixed for laying the foundation stone of the new church of St. Philip, Cheam Common. This outlying hamlet of Cheam which now numbers about 120 houses, and a population of 700, has sprung up on the extreme border of the parish, close to Worcester Park Station, and it has long been evident that forming, as it does, a separate and increasing village, it was fully entitled to, and urgently needed, a church of its own. For five years past a curate has been resident in the district and services have been held on the Sunday, first in a cottage, and afterwards in the temporary Infant School-room, but as building still went on, and population thickened, it was determined to make an effort to supply the want of a permanent home for the worship of God. An excellent site was liberally presented by Mr. H. Lindsay Antrobus ....."*

Two of the prime movers behind the formation of the club in **1872** were a parson and a publican, who came from totally different backgrounds. The local vicar, at that time, was the **Reverend Reginald Fitz-Hugh Bigg-Wither** who was born in 1842 at 'Tangier House', Wootton St. Lawrence, Hampshire, the son of a local landowner and Justice of the Peace, the Reverend Lovelace Bigg-Wither. Reginald was educated at home by a governess until he was about eight and then was sent to a small private prep. school, with two of his brothers, in South Vale, Croydon. He finished off his education at Pembroke College, Oxford, and was recorded in 'Bell's Life in London and Sporting Chronicle' of June 7th, 1863, as opening the batting for Pembroke

College versus New College. In the three or four innings which made the press, he never scored more than 3 runs - he was evidently keen but not particularly talented.

The publican, who came from one of the oldest families in the area, was **Francis Pennington** who was born in Cheam in 1826, the son of another Francis Pennington, who was the landlord of 'The Drill Inn' or 'The Old Drill' from 1839 until 1847. Strangely in the 1861 census, it was known as 'The Jolly Farmer', but reverted by 1871 to 'The Drill'. The Penningtons retained the licence until 1903. From 2010 'The Drill' has been renamed the 'H. G. Wells', although the Worcester Park C.C. Old Farts, who used to meet there, still referred to it as 'The Drill'.

There is very little of note on the cricketing front for the Penningtons, although Francis Pennington the elder was reported in 'Bell's Life', on February 2nd 1840, as taking part in a bird shooting match for two sovereigns at 'The Plough', Malden, against J. Allen, a local gamekeeper. Francis had to shoot at six pigeons whilst the gamekeeper shot at six sparrows. The gamekeeper won.

Field Sports seemed to be the order of the day for the Pennington family. Joseph Pennington who, in 1840, owned 16 acres of land on Cheam Common in the vicinity of what is now Washington Road, took part in another interesting shooting match at 'The Drill Inn' in January 1841, as was recorded in 'Bell's Life': *"The friends of the trigger met on Thursday last at 'The Drill Inn', to witness a long-depending match between Mr. Joseph Pennington and Mr. E. Bowry, for £15 a side, at twenty-one yards, thirteen birds each; the shooting was very good, and Mr. Pennington was the winner by a bird. Several other matches were shot by the same party and their friends, after which the company retired to 'The Drill Inn', and partook of a fine haunch of venison, which, with the wines, was greatly approved of."*

Francis Pennington, apart from being a publican, a farmer and a landowner, also seemed to be a follower of the sport of kings, and gained a mention on two or three occasions in the racing pages of 'Bell's Life'. He might possibly have kept race horses in the stables and meadow adjoining the pub.

The Landlord did, however, have four sons, Francis, Eustace, Sidney and Edward, who could form the nucleus of a cricket team, which, in its turn, would provide the pub with an additional source of revenue. 'The Drill', therefore, became the first headquarters of Cheam Common C.C., and, throughout the Club's 49 year history, there was a noticeable link between the club, the church and a pub.

One of Francis's sons, **Eustace** (b. 1858), was also an enthusiastic musician, and at the age of fourteen, prior to the building of St. Philip's Church, played the harmonium for the services that were held in the local Church Hall. After the church was built young Eustace was the first organist, a position that he held for several years until the arrival of the Rev. F. Goldsmith (later Bishop Goldsmith) to the parish in 1881. Eustace lived all his life in Cheam and was eventually buried at St. Philip's in 1934.

As the population of Cheam Common grew, the young dynamic vicar, the Reverend Reginald Bigg-Wither, must have become conscious of the growing number of young men locally who needed spiritual and physical guidance. What better means of channelling their energy than by forming a cricket club. It was to this end that he organised a meeting of like minded members of the church in July 1872.

In the 'Cheam and Cuddington Parish Magazine' (C.&C.P.M.) of August 1872, there was the following article: *"At a meeting held at the Parsonage, Cheam Common, on Saturday July 14th (present Reverend R. Bigg-Wither, Messrs. James Cuff, James Taylor, Francis Pennington, George Coombers, Charles Powell and Henry Bryant - Mr. J. Cuff in the chair) it was decided that a cricket club be started for the working men of Cheam Common. The Reverend R. Bigg-Wither was able to announce that due to the kindness of Mr. Pennington, a suitable field for playing on could be found, and that owing to the kindness of neighbouring gentlemen he should be able to start the club with a box of bats, balls and stumps etc."*

Of the seven gentlemen listed at this inaugural meeting five of them lived in the short stretch of Cheam Lane between 'The Drill' and the 'North End Tavern'. In the 1871 census, **Francis Pennington** (45) was listed as being a licensed victualler, whilst **James Cuff** (41) was a beerhouse keeper and builder, **Charles Powell** (27) was a bricklayer, **Henry Bryant** (40) was a labourer, whilst **James Taylor** (34) was a carpenter. Other members of this club found in this small area of Cheam Lane were **William Joscelyne** (27) a carpenter, **Thomas Connor** (25) a painter and grainer and **William Blackett** (42) a bricklayer. These men and their children, therefore, formed the backbone of Cheam Common Cricket Club for the next twenty or thirty years. Whilst many cricket clubs at that time catered for the privileged in society, Cheam Common C.C. was, at this time, definitely a working man's club.

"A Committee was thereupon formed, with Mr. Pennington engaging to act as Secretary and Treasurer. A set of rules were drawn up of which the following are of most importance. The annual subscription to be 8 shillings, payable as convenient by quarterly or weekly instalments, but all sums due from members to be fully paid up at each quarter. No swearing or bad language to be used on pain of expulsion from the club. Anyone who wishes to join should give his name to Mr. Pennington, in order that he may be billeted for in committee."

The first cricket pitch for Cheam Common C.C., therefore, was probably the field behind 'The Drill', which in 1840 measured 2 acres, 1 rod and 4 poles in size; the barn behind the pub probably also acted as the changing room. The field was quite adequate in size but, having been a meadow, it was probably not conducive to good cricket. In fact the state of the pitch caused concern from the start of the club and probably became more so as the team progressed and the players developed their ability.

There is, however, a record in 'Bell's Life and Sporting Chronicle' of Sept. 7th, 1845, of the field behind 'The Drill' being used for a cricket match over a quarter of a century before Cheam Common C.C. was formed. What is really amazing about that match, however, is that the first Chairman of Cheam Common C.C., James Cuff, had played, as a 14 year old lad, alongside his brother, William, a bricklayer.

"MATCH AT CHEAM. - A match was played at the Drill Inn Ground, Cheam, on Tuesday last, between eleven players chosen by Mr Madgwick, and eleven chosen by Mr. Taylor. Score: Mr. Taylor's side 28 and 37 - total 65; R. Tribe obtained 16 and 0, H. Taylor 1 and 3, A. Brookes 1 and 0, J. Harris 3 and 6, R. Harris 0 and 0, T. Clark 1 and 1, D. Harris 0 and 0, W. Cuff 1 and 5, J. Cook 1 and 1, J. Cuff 0 and 2, F. Boury 0 and 9; byes 4 and 10.

Mr Madgwick's side 50 and 16 - total 66 (with ten wickets to go down); Varnes obtained 15 and 8, Rayner 0 and 5, Stamford 13, Harrison 0, Simmonds 0, Rowley 0, Wood 1, Stevens 1, Madgwick 10, Shepherd 0, Hill 0; byes 10 and 3."

That the formation of the club was a success was evident in the next mention of it in the 'Cheam and Cuddington Parish Magazine' of October, 1872:- *"The Cheam Common Cricket Club is in a flourishing state, and although it was not started until the middle of July, it numbers on its books 40 subscribing members.*

On August 26th a match was played in Mr. Pennington's field between the Married and the Single, which in being a sort of inauguration of the new Club attracted no small interest. The Bachelors going in first obtained 78 runs, notwithstanding the excellent bowling of Messrs. Bryant, Connor and J. Taylor. The Married were disposed of by the destructive underhand of Mr. Millward for 34.

In the second innings the Bachelors added 78 to the score, thus leaving their opponents 132 to make up. It was late, however, in the day, and they only succeeded in scoring 28 with the fall of 8 wickets.

Notwithstanding the showery state of the weather it was altogether a most pleasant day and we hope that next year the funds of the Club will allow for a small outlay on the ground, which sadly needs improvement. This Club is heartily recommended to all friends."

It is interesting to note that the inaugural game was a low scoring double innings match which set the pattern for many years to come. The low scoring was probably due to the state of the wicket rather than to the devastating quality of the underarm bowling. It is also fascinating to note that many of the games continued after the match was won or lost, presumably so that those who had not batted could have a go, or perhaps it was to fill in time until the pub opened. Matches often continued in this fashion up until the 1950s.

As it was a relatively late start to the first season, only a small amount of cricket appeared to have been played but the 'Croydon Advertiser and East Surrey Reporter' did manage to provide a very faded scoresheet for a match, played between the fledgling club and the more mature Cheam Village side, on the 14th of September 1872. As this was the first recorded match by the club, I have reproduced it below.

"CRICKET - Cheam Common CC v Cheam CC - This match was played at Cheam Common on the 14th September. It will be seen that only eight on each side turned up at the pitching of the wickets, and the Commoners were slightly beaten."

Cheam Common

	First Innings		Second Innings		
F. Pennington	Not Out	7	b	J. Earl	0
Ed Pennington	b J. Norrington	0	b	J. Earl	3
S. Pennington	Run Out	2	b	J. Norrington	2
E. Pennington	Run Out	5	Ct J. Earl b	J. Norrington	4
H. Blackett	c Barnes b J. Earl	0	Run Out		1
R. Smith	b J. Norrington	0	b	J. Norrington	0
W. Green	b J. Norrington	0	b	J. Earl	0
A. Coomber	ct E. Brown b J. Norrington	0	Not Out		2
Extras		7			1
		21			13

Cheam

	First Innings		Second Innings		
J. Earl	b S. Pennington	7	ct F. Pennington	b E. Pennington	1
H. Bassett	ct Ed Pennington	5	b F. Pennington		2
G. Barnes	b S. Pennington	0	Run out		1
F. Constable	b E. Pennington	0	b F. Pennington		0
R. Bassett	ct Ed Pennington	1	ct Ed Pennington	b F. Pennington	0
E. Brown	b S. Pennington	0	b E. Pennington		1
J. Norrington	ct E. Pennington b S. Pennington	2	Not out		20
E. Norrington	Not Out	0	b E. Pennington		8
Extras		3			7
		18			40

This was not a very auspicious start for the Commoners, although they did 'win' the first innings. Apart from being three players short, the team was extremely young and inexperienced, featuring the four young Pennington boys, Francis (17), Edward (11), Sidney (12) and Eustace (14); plus additional youngsters such as Henry Blackett (11) and Richard Smith (12). There is no trace of the other two players on the 1871 census, although A. Coomber was probably the son of George Coomber who was on the club's committee.

The Cheam Village Club, which had a longer history, was also struggling for players in the mid-1870s, but they were far too good for the new boys in the second innings, and again carried on batting even after they had won.

Not a lot of work appeared to have been done before the start of the following season as was apparent from the following article in the Parish Magazine of May **1873**: *"re Cheam Common Cricket Club - The Reverend R. F. Bigg-Wither appeals on behalf of this club, which was opened so successfully last year. The only thing now needed to establish the club on a firm basis is the improvement of the ground, the use of which has been kindly given by Mr. Pennington. It is the only field in the neighbourhood at all adapted for the purpose, and it is estimated that an outlay of from £15 to £20 would meet all requirements; and if this sum could be collected during the summer it would encourage the members, and the work of laying down chalk, drains, fencing etc. might be begun immediately on the close of the season. The fact of the ground lying very low and having been laid out in lands, of which the subsoil is strong clay, make this absolutely necessary."*

Despite the poor condition of the ground, Cheam Common managed half a dozen fixtures that season, the results of which were listed in the November Parish Magazine: *"The first season of this young club has been most successful. Adjoined is a list of Matches played and the scores of the first innings. The Reverend R. Bigg-Wither in reference to his appeal for funds to improve the Cricket Ground heartily commends this Club to the support of all friends."* (C & C Parish Magazine)

CCCC	91	'Star & Garter' CC, Battersea	49
CCCC	171	North Cheam School	30
CCCC	47	'Star & Garter CC (return)	64
CCCC	157	Worcester Park CC	41
CCCC	77	New Malden CC	16
CCCC	63	New Malden (return)	58

There was no indication of the dates of the first four matches on this list, the start times, the venues for the away matches, or the names of the individual players. The Worcester Park C.C. team appeared to have been an occasional team based around the St. John the Baptist church in Old Malden. This was probably the seed, which, eighteen years later, developed into the Old Malden and Worcester Park side. If that match had been played away, it would probably have been played in the grounds of one of the large houses between Malden and Nonsuch Park.

The final two matches against New Malden, however, did make the local press and show the change which had occurred in the team's personnel. The first of these matches was reported in the 'Surrey Comet' on September 6th, 1873, under the title 'Cheam C.C. v New Malden Village'. The scorecard, however, rectified this error and called the team 'Cheam Common': *"Last Saturday a match was played on Cheam*

Common between the above clubs, the result being a disastrous defeat for New Malden, whose eleven were disposed of for the small total of 16 in their first innings; and as they only scored 41 at the second attempt, Cheam scored a single innings victory with 18 runs to spare. Beardshaw (15) and Hoather (10), as the score shows, were the only players on the losing side who made anything like a stand against the bowling of the Cheam men, but it is rather singular to notice the fatality which befell New Malden in the first innings, not one of the ten wickets being bowled. (two Hit Wicket and three were Run Out). H. Bryant and Thorns were the chief scorers for Cheam 'wides' coming next in numerical order towards piling up the 77 runs."

The Cheam Common team was: J. Taylor (4), C. Powell (3), J. Simmonds (8), Thorns (7), Bryant (19), Connor (9), W. Powell (1), B. Thorns (11), T. Powell (2), Joscelyne (0), Pennington (0), Extras (13). Connor took 5 wickets in the first innings, whilst Taylor took 6 in the second innings.

The second match which was played at New Malden was reported in the 'Surrey Comet' of September 20th, 1873 under the title 'Cheam Common C.C. v New Malden C.C.' *"Played at New Malden, on Saturday, and after a very exciting contest ended in favour of the visitors by five runs. Powell, Connor, and J. Capp (15) batted well for their respective sides. W. Thorns trundled the ball in a very effective style, taking five out of the six wickets that were bowled."* (He actually took 6 wickets).

CHEAM COMM	
C. Powell c Tilley b Fryer	16
J. Taylor b T. Phillips	0
W. Thorns c Heather b Woola- cott	5
T. Conner b J. Capp	15
B. Thorns c F. Capp b Fryer	4
H. Bryant b J. Capp	4
J. Symons b J. Capp	1
E. Pennington not out	2
W. Powell b Fryer	0
T. Powell b Fryer	0
R. Johnson ht wkt b Fryer	0
B 13, w 2	15
	—
	62

One game that was not deemed worthy of mention in the Parish Magazine was one which occurred on the 4th of October, 1873, between Cheam Common and Cheam Juniors. The team was almost completely different from that which had played against New Malden and might possibly have been a Colts' game. It did, however, merit a write-up in the 'Croydon Advertiser and East Surrey Reporter' the following week.

The Cheam side was J. Norrington (16), J. Ockenden (0), G. Barnes (4), J. Earl (11), G. With (1), H. Hammond (3), J. Bryant (19*), A. Day (0), F. Norrington (0), A. Barnes (0), R. Bassett (0). Extras 16: Total 70.

For Cheam Common Eustace Pennington took 7 wickets and Francis Pennington 3.

"CRICKET - A match was played at Cheam Common, on Saturday, October 4th, between Cheam Common C.C., and the Cheam Junior C.C. The following is the score:"

(Sadly the scorecard was too faded to reproduce, but is in the following table).

Cheam Common					
First Innings			**Second Innings**		
E. Pennington	ct J. Norrington b J. Earl	0	Thrown out by	J. Bryant	10
Ed. Pennington	ct J. Norrington b Hammond	0	b	H. Hammond	0
F. Pennington	b H. Hammond	9	b	H. Hammond	2
W. Green	ct Barnes b Hammond	2	ct Bryant	J. Earl	1
A. Bryant	b J. Earl	1	Not out		5
G. Cuff	run out	2			
F. Coomber	b J. Earl	4			
W. Goodey	st Barnes b Hammond	2			
H. Blackett	b J. Earl	1			
R. Smith	Not out	0			
(Substitute)	b Hammond	1			
Extras		5	Extras		8
		27			26

Although the Cheam C.C. side appeared to have won this encounter so convincingly, in 1873, the fortunes of the two clubs appeared to go in separate directions for a few years. The Parish Magazine for June **1874** said that as the Cheam C.C. club were unable to find a suitable ground, *"it is desirable that the club remain in abeyance for this season;"* but although the Cheam Common men had a pitch which was far from satisfactory, however, they had, *"a more prosperous story to tell."*

The Reverend Reginald Fitz-Hugh Bigg-Wither was, by 1874, the President of the Club, Mr. James Taylor was the Captain, Mr. Pennington was the Treasurer and Mr. Charles Powell was the Secretary. This Committee met on the first Monday in April 1874 to audit the accounts and to discuss the fixtures, which had already been arranged with Worcester Park, Battersea and New Malden.

Despite the first match against Worcester Park being lost, the team again defeated New Malden, whilst the game on the 11th July against *"an eleven of 'The South Western' from Nine Elms"* was interrupted by thundery showers, *"which told against high scoring"*. They did, however, win that game by 58 runs to 48 runs, and also beat Worcester Park in the return match by 100 runs versus 52 runs.

The Parish Magazine of November 1874 stated that Cheam Common C.C. had had *"an altogether satisfactory season winning 5 out of 8 matches."* That might not seem like a lot of games in a season but it should be remembered that they only played on Saturdays as playing upon the Sabbath was frowned upon. Just thirty years prior to the inauguration of the club there had been numerous reports of young men being fined for playing cricket on a Sunday, especially if it was during the time of church services.

Under the title *'Cricket-Playing on Sundays After Divine Service'*, 'Bell's Life in London and Sporting Chronicle' of August 20th, 1843, published the following article:

"On Tuesday Lord J. Manners, after noticing the case of six lads at Hurley, in Berkshire, who were fined 15 shillings each for playing cricket on a Sunday, asked the Attorney-General whether it was illegal for the working classes or others, who had only one day in the week for recreation, to play cricket or other hand games after divine service on Sunday, and if so, whether it was legal for the rich to drive out in their carriages on that day. The Attorney-General said his noble lord had not stated whether in the case he had mentioned the lads were playing in their own parish, for if they were within their parish undoubtedly they were not liable to any punishment, but there was a statute by which they were liable to fine if they played on Sundays out of their parish."

The Cheam Parish Magazine of November, 1874, also listed the following results: on August 15th Cheam Common had played Nine Elms at home and won by 12 runs; on August 29th they lost a close match against New Malden 120 to 124; and finally on August 31st they had defeated the Battersea Club in the return match scoring 68 runs in the first innings, plus 63 for 6 wickets in the second innings against Battersea's 30 all out in the first innings. The match against the Battersea Club was the first recorded incidence of Cheam Common playing on a Bank Holiday. To turn out two teams that weekend was impressive and showed the growing popularity and strength of the still rather inexperienced club.

The only match report which appeared in the 'Surrey Comet' in 1874 occurred on September 5th, for a narrow defeat by New Malden. As 244 runs were scored that afternoon it suggests that the New Malden pitch was far superior to the Cheam Common one, and, as the New Malden victory was achieved *"amid some excitement"* it also suggests that there was probably a reasonable crowd there to watch the game *"This match was played at New Malden last Saturday, and amid some excitement ended in favour of Malden by four runs only. For the winners J. Capp made 64 without giving a chance, while W. Thorns played a fine innings of 42 for the losers. Woollacott's underhand bowling seemed rather puzzling; he obtained just half the wickets."*

The Cheam Common team that day was: *Millward (1); Thorns (42); Conner (11); C. Powell (13); Bryant (12); Frances (9); T. S. Powell (4); Taylor (1); J. Powell (8); F. Pennington (0*) - Extras 18 - Total 120.*

William Thorns (b. 1846) was a butcher who worked for his father in the High Street, Cheam, whilst **Charles Powell** (b. 1844) and his brother **Thomas S. Powell** (b. 1853) were both bricklayers who lived with Charles' young family in the Pottery Cottages, Cheam Lane. Both brothers had been born in Bristol, the sons of a milkman, and settled in Cheam some time after the 1861 census. J. Powell might possibly have been their brother, John (b. 1851), who was also born in Bristol.

By **1875** the young Reverend Reginald Bigg-Wither had wandered off to pastures new and with him went nearly all the publicity which the Cheam Common team received in the Cheam and Cuddington Parish Magazine. A couple of years later, apart from being a curate, Bigg-Withers was also to be found managing the Reigate Youths' Institute, which gave the young men of that area the rare opportunity to further their education. He was, according to the local paper, *"indefatigable in his exertions for its success."* It was quite a blow for Cheam Common C.C., however, to lose him, as, without his drive and enthusiasm in providing a cricket club for the young men of the area, Cheam Common might not have come into being, and indirectly Worcester Park Athletic Club.

Apart from providing the local youngsters in Cheam Common with a successful cricket team, the Rev. Bigg-Withers had overseen, in 1873, the construction of the new church of St. Philip at the top of Cheam Common Hill. Two years later, however, the church had a new vicar, the Rev. T. G. Browne, who did not seem to have Bigg-Withers' enthusiasm for cricket. As a result the Parish Magazine tended to focus more upon the activities of St. Dunstan's Church, in Cheam, and on the plight of the local village side, Cheam Village C.C.

In comparison to the Cheam Village side, the Reverend Bigg-Wither had, however, left behind him a team built upon a strong foundation, It was a team which was steadily improving and expanding and had acquired quite a good reputation locally. The final mention of the team in the Parish Magazine was in June **1875**, when it merely stated that they had been defeated by Worcester Park on May 15th, *"after a pleasant game on a beautiful day",* and a return match had been fixed up for June 19th on the Cheam Common ground.

As the decade progressed, therefore, all mention of Cheam Common C.C. in the Parish Magazine was replaced by an increasing number of articles on Education and the Temperance Society. The fact that the Headquarters of Cheam Common C.C., at that time, was a public house, 'The Drill', could have been another reason for the paucity of publicity they received, as pubs were hardly renowned for their sobriety.

Basically, after 1875, the only information on Cheam Common C.C. occurred in occasional snippets garnered from either the national or the local papers. Fortunately there are enough records of their games to be found, either online or on microfiche, to ascertain the club's progress and to spot within the ranks of the players, the families and individuals who helped with the eventual foundation of W.P.A.C.

By **1878**, the club had started to play regularly on public holidays. Two interesting Bank Holiday Monday games were reported in the 'South London Press' in 1878, which were both played at Cheam Common, against a team called 'Atlas'. In the first game, on June 10th, the Commoners only managed 23 runs in the first innings and 33 in the second innings, thereby losing by an innings and 15 runs. A month later, however, on July 8th, thanks to the strategic use of 'ringers', the result was reversed. *"These clubs played the return match on Monday on the ground of the former (Worcester Park, Cheam), which, after a one sided game all through, resulted in an easy victory for the Cheam by an innings and 30 runs. The Cheam mustered a good team from their own and the Sutton Club with Colts, which accounts for so easy a victory."*

The 'Croydon & East Surrey Reporter', of June 21st **1879**, provided a short account and scoresheet for another meeting between Cheam Common C.C. and Cheam Village C.C., which revealed that several of the players, who had played in 1872, were still playing for both clubs. It is interesting to note that the Killick brothers, a pair of painters and decorators from Ewell, William (b. 1852) and Alfred (b. 1858), who both played regularly for their home village, ended up on this occasion, playing for opposing teams.

Probably the most interesting character in the Cheam Common side was another cricket-loving, wicket-keeping cleric, the

CHEAM v. CHEAM COMMON.—This match was played on Cheam Common on Saturday last, and resulted, after an exciting and sharp fight for time, in a victory for the visitors by 3 wickets. Score :—

Cheam Common.

W. Aldridge, b Keates	14
F. Aldridge, run out	4
Rev. H. Lucas, b Keates	13
W. Killick, ht wkt, b Brown	0
C. Powell, b Stevens	9
T. Connor, lbw, b Stevens	15
A. Gibson, c and b Stevens	0
W. Abbot, b Stevens	3
S. Pennington, lbw, b Keates	0
T. Venus, run out	2
E. Pennington, not out	2
Extras	13
	75

Cheam.

J. Ockenden, jun., c Powell, b Connor	15
W. Bryant, c and b S. Pennington	31
H. Keates, st Lucas, b Gibson	1
W. Ockenden, b Connor	8
C. Norrington, jun., b Venus	4
C. Stevens, c Powell, b Venus	3
A. Ratcliff, run out	6
E. Brown, jun., not out	0
Extras	8
	76

A. Killick, A. Day, C. Farncombe did not bat.

24 year old, **Rev. Herbert Hamilton Lucas** (b. 1854) from the small parish of Filby in Norfolk, who, for a short time, was a curate at St. Dunstan's Church in Cheam.

H. H. Lucas had started his cricketing career at Uppingham School, before playing for Caister in his home county of Norfolk. He had also attended Trinity College, Cambridge, at the same time as the local Cheam cricketing star, A. S. Tabor, although there is no record that he played cricket there. He was ordained into the clergy in March, 1878, and joined the Rev. C. H. Rice at St. Dunstan's, Cheam, the following month. Lucas left the Parish in early July to become the Rector of Preston in Rutland, and on Tuesday, July 8th, shortly after his move, he top scored with 27, whilst opening the batting for his new parish versus Manton. Later that year he returned to Filby where he followed in his father's footsteps by becoming the Rector of All Saints.

It is also interesting to note that the Rev. H. H. Lucas had opened the batting for Cheam versus Ewell in their first match of the season, in 1879, as was reported in the 'Croydon Advertiser' of May 24th. In that game, young Sidney Pennington of 'The

Drill Inn' had opened the bowling for Cheam, whilst W. Killick and A. Killick, who were to play in the Cheam versus Cheam Common match, the following month, had both been playing for Ewell. There was obviously great friendship between the local teams, as they were able to call upon each other if short of players, although finding replacement players must have been very difficult before the telephone era.

In a way it is lucky that so many newspaper accounts exist from the early days of the club, in the 1870s, as there is a dearth of information for the next decade. **1880** started in promising fashion with two short match reports appearing in the press in the first six weeks of the season. The first one was reported in the 'South London Press' on Saturday May 22nd: *"Cheam Common v Atlas - On Whit Monday these clubs played on the ground of the Cheam at Worcester Park, Cheam, and after an enjoyable day's cricket ended in a victory for the Atlas by eight wickets. The Cheam, in their first innings, scored 23, and their opponents 44. In their second innings the Cheam fared much better, scoring 67, owing to Lockwood's 30 not out. The Atlas then went in again, having 47 runs to win, which they obtained for the loss of two wickets."*

The fact that the reporter on three occasions referred to the home team as 'the Cheam', makes one wonder whether the match was actually a Cheam Common fixture, or whether it was a mistake in the press. Another reason for believing that there might have been a mistake was the fact that the team's top scorer, the Yorkshire professional cricketer, Lockwood, was a regular Cheam player. But there again, as it was a Bank Holiday game, C.C.C.C. might have drafted in a few 'ringers'.

The second account occurred in the 'Surrey Comet' of June 12th, for a match versus new opponents: *"Wimbledon Spencer v Cheam Common - Played at Cheam on Saturday, and left drawn for want of time. Scores: Wimbledon 99, and Cheam Common 34 for 4."*

The only indication that the club still existed over the next few years, however, was the fact that Sidney Pennington was recorded as representing the club in several hundred yard handicap events. In October, 1883, Sidney took part in the North London Harriers 100 yard Open at Tufnell Park and came third in his heat. In September of the following year he won a 120 yard open handicap at Stamford Bridge with a 12 yard handicap. He also came second in a race at Romford that month whilst representing Cheam Common C.C.

The next mention of the cricket club, in the 'Croydon Advertiser', occurred for a match played on April 27th, **1889**. It was a low scoring, incomplete match played at Cheam Common, against Sutton Star. The match started at 3.00 p.m., which is a far cry from the 11.00 a.m. or 12.00 noon starts for some of today's matches. When I began playing in the early 1970s, 2.30 p.m. starts were still quite common.

The Sutton Star side were skittled out that day for 59 runs, thanks mainly to the bowling of T. Pierce, who took seven wickets, and G. Blake who chipped in with three tail-enders. In response the Commoners managed 22 for four before play was curtailed. The Cheam Common side that day was G. Cooper (3), W. Hook (4), G. Dearman (3), T. Pierce (7), C. Powell (3*), J. Cuff (1*), F. Stuttaford, G. Blake, W. Hammond, H. York and P. Peters did not bat.

The J. Cuff in this team was probably **Joseph Cuff** (29), a bricklayer, who lodged with another Cheam Common player, Tom Connor, rather than James Cuff who was 58 by this time. **James Cuff** was the first of four landlords of the 'North End Tavern' who were heavily involved with Cheam Common Cricket Club throughout its history. The other three were Charles Powell (1875-1891), Arthur Morris Watts (1891-1913) and Harold Watts (1914-1937).

```
         Cheam Common.
C. Powell, b Ockenden  ..    0
G. Cooper, c & b Sillence    0
C. Dearman, not out    ..    9
J. Blake, b Ockenden   ..    0
J. Cuff, c Rice, b Ockenden  0
W. Hammond, b Ockenden       0
E. Pennington, c Smith,
     b Sillence   ..    ..   1
S. Pennington, c Hale, b
     Sillence          ..    0
C. Everest, not out    ..    0

     Extras    ..    ..  5
        Total         —  15
   H. York and P. Peters did
not bat.
```

Two further games appeared in 'The Comet' that season. The first one occurred on May 18th, 1889, against old rivals Cheam. The Cheam side batted first that day and managed to amass 128 runs on the notorious Cheam Common wicket. In response the home side struggled and by the end of play were 15 for 7, a total which included six 'ducks'.

Due to the close proximity of the clubs, matches between Cheam Common and Cheam Village appear to have been regular newsworthy social occasions, which probably accounts for the frequency with which these matches appeared in the press, and in this chapter.

Despite the rivalry engendered by these games, there seemed to be an off-field camaraderie between the two clubs, as there are several occasions when Cheam players turned out for Cheam Common and vice-versa. Charles Powell, for example, despite being a founder member of Cheam Common Club, and a regular in the team for over thirty years, turned out for Cheam on numerous occasions in the mid 1880s. As the landlord of the 'North End Tavern' he was probably a popular addition to the team, whilst, in his turn he might have gained a few more customers..

The third match to be reported in 'The Comet', in 1889, was another poor batting performance by the home side, on June 30th, against Surbiton Hill, but at least one of the players managed to score double figures. The team that day was:- W. Hook 16, G. Cooper 0, Eus. Pennington 7, Ed. Pennington 1, J. Cuff 0, C. Powell 4, W. Hammond 2, J. Styles 0, J. Connor 0, C. Ross 2*, W. Aldridge 0. Extras 5, Total 37. In response Surbiton Hill scored 43 all out with J. Cuff and Eustace Pennington taking five wickets apiece.

It is interesting to note from these three matches that, besides Charles Powell, three of the Pennington brothers were still playing for the club, in 1889, 17 years after the club's formation. It also appeared that Cheam Common was no longer exclusively a working man's club. The match on April 27th, was the first one that recorded the presence of **Charles Noel Gordon Dearman**, aged 24, who, along with his brother, **Henry W. Dearman** (16) made their first appearances for the club that season.

The Dearmans lived at 'St. Katherines', a rather impressive house on the London Road, North Cheam, along with their parents, another brother, three spinster sisters and a servant. Their father had been a civil servant but, by the time of the 1891 census, was recorded as 'living on his own means'. Charles had apparently learnt his cricket when he attended a private school, 'St Saviour's', in Ardingly. He was obviously of a different class from the rest of his team mates both socially and ability-wise and easily topped the team batting averages two years later.

Another fascinating feature of those three matches from 1889 was the appearance of two members of the Blake dynasty. **George Blake** (b. 1844) who played against 'Sutton Star', had arrived, looking for work, in Worcester Park, in the mid-1870s, from Bacton, a small village in Suffolk, with his three brothers Andrew, David and Abel. Against Cheam, one of Andrew's sons, **John Blake** (b. 1871), made his first recorded appearance for the club although he was to spend most of his cricketing career from the early 1890s, playing for local rivals Old Malden and Worcester Park, a team that he captained for eight seasons.

Another noteworthy match which was played on September 20th, **1890**, at Cheam Common, revealed how fragile the home side batting could be on a damp wicket. St. Mary-the-Less declared their innings closed with the score at 59 for eight, Joseph Cuff having taken 5 wickets. The home side, in response, managed to lose six wickets for 16 runs before the match was abandoned because of rain, with only Police Constable Hammond scoring: - *"Hook 0, Cooper 0, Dearman 0, T. Pennington 0, E. Pennington 0, F. Pennington 0, Hammond 14*, Fairman 0*, extras 2, Total (for six wickets), 16."*

The fourth Pennington brother, Francis, turned out on that occasion, whilst T. Pennington was actually his brother, Edward, who was apparently known as 'Ted'.

By **1891**, however, there had been quite a change in the overall composition of Cheam Common C.C., when they amalgamated with another local club, Cuddington C.C., a team which also dated back to the early 1870s. From 1891, therefore, the two teams became known as Cheam Common and Cuddington CC, but the alliance never seemed to be a happy marriage and, by 1898, they had divorced.

One benefit of the merger seemed to have been an increase in media publicity. This might have been due to the fact that one of the Cuddington players, F. H. L. Shipton was listed in the 1891 census as being a journalist. As such he must have had connections at the 'Comet' and 'Advertiser', for, after a decade of virtual silence, interesting scoresheets began to appear in the press, containing a handful of new names, such as the Head family who lived in Cuddington and R. Legge.

At least thirteen matches were mentioned in the press in 1891, a summary of which has been included in the Appendix. It is interesting to note that most of the matches played by Cheam Common tended to be played at home and were usually extremely low scoring affairs, which probably suggests that they might still have been playing in the meadow behind 'The Drill'. It must have been a popular venue, however, as some of the teams chose to play there twice in the season, rather than playing the more traditional home and away format. The lack of runs, however, often left plenty of time for a second innings (not included in the table).

Although the majority of the reports, which occurred in the 'Croydon Advertiser', were extremely short and basically just provided the scores of the leading batsmen for each team, on the odd occasion additional information appeared in a summary of the previous week's outstanding performances.

This was certainly the case for the match against Broomwood when the 'Advertiser' reported that: *"J. Cuff had the following excellent bowling analysis, namely:- 8 overs, 2 balls, 3 maidens, 14 runs and six wickets. In the course of his operations he performed the 'hat trick'."* Only one Broomwood batsman, E. Williams (10) crept into double figures. It is impossible to tell what type of bowler Joseph Cuff was, but in one match **Thomas Skilton** (b.1858), a labourer from Longfellow Road, managed to obtain a stumping off his bowling.

On another occasion, in the match against Mr. C. Woods XI, who were shot out for 22 runs, F. L. Head *"had the following bowling analysis - nine overs and three balls, five maidens, seven runs and seven wickets, performing the 'hat-trick'."*

Francis Lane Head (b. 1872) was one of the new class of player from a more refined, social background. In 1891, he was still living at 'Arundel House', in Cuddington, with his widowed mother, Caroline, a lady of 'private means', who had had seven sons, and no daughters, and had become a widow by 1871. Francis, who was listed as a scholar was the youngest of four brothers, all of whom had received a good education, and were still living at home: Arthur (b. 1862) was a doctor; Ernest E. Head (b.1869) was a medical student; and Frederick D. Head (b. 1967) was a law student. Francis headed the bowling averages in 1891, whilst Ernest and Frederick had both shown that they could bat.

Even better than the scoresheets, at the end of the season, October 31st, 1891, the 'Croydon Advertiser' published the players' statistics (See the Appendix)

A win ratio of 70% was quite impressive when one considers that only two of the batsmen succeeded in averaging over 10 runs per innings for the season and not a single fifty was recorded. Whilst the pitches were often a nightmare for the batsmen, for the bowlers, however, they were paradise as can be seen by the bowling statistics.

At some point in the first 30 years of the club's existence, Cheam Common Cricket Club moved from the meadow behind the 'Drill Inn' to a field alongside Cheam Common Road, between Lindsay Road and Ruskin Drive, on the site of the modern Christ Church & St. Philip's Church.

As the 1891 statistics suggest that the team were apparently playing upon an extremely poor wicket, it could have meant that they were still playing at 'The Drill', where, as we know from the Parish magazines of the 1870s, the players were not very happy with the condition of the field. But would they continue playing upon a poor pitch for almost 20 years? Perhaps, however, the new field was no better or the square still needed time to bed in.

Francis Pennington, their original patron at 'The Drill' had died in 1886, and the pub passed in to the hands of his widow, Frances. Perhaps it was the death of Francis that led Cheam Common C.C. to move their headquarters from 'The Drill' to the 'North End Tavern' and to the field opposite the pub.

One snippet in the press which tends to support the theory that they had already moved to the ground opposite the 'North End Tavern' by the early 1890s, was found in a 'South London Press' report of another low scoring two innings' game played against Wasp C.C. on Bank Holiday Monday, 7th August, **1893** - *"This match was played near Worcester Park on Monday, the Wasp adding another victory to their list. Blake and Austin bowled splendidly for the losers."*

When the match report mentioned 'Worcester Park' it was obviously referring to the station. As the 'North End Tavern' is much closer to the station than 'The Drill'; therefore, it seems to suggest that, by 1893, it was more than likely that they were playing at the ground near Lindsay Road.

Another reason for thinking that they might have moved to the site opposite the 'North End Tavern' before 1891, was the fact that all the landlords of that particular inn had held positions of responsibility within the club. James Cuff and Charles Powell had both captained the team, and, although Arthur Watts seemed to be lacking in cricketing ability, almost as soon as he became the Landlord of the pub in 1891, he became the Treasurer of the club. The fact that the newspapers of the day often referred to the 'North End Tavern' as the club's 'headquarters' also supports the idea that they had moved to the ground near St. Philip's Church.

Although the Wasp team on August Bank Holiday Monday 1893, only managed to score 57 and 50 that day, C.C.&C., in response, could only managed 28 and 23 runs in each of their innings, and not one of their players managed to reach double figures. Austin, however, did pick up nine wickets that afternoon and John Blake eight. The team that day was Eades, Cooper, Dearman, Powell, Austin, Blake, Pennington, York, Cuff, Dare and Styles - no initials as it was a Wasp report.

For some time, I was of the opinion that the field opposite the 'North End Tavern' had belonged to Andrew Blake, until I found a Conveyance map of 1905 in the Woking Record Office, which showed that it had belonged to the Reverend Edward William Northey, a local landowner who lived in Epsom. The club might possibly have rented the ground from the Rev. Northey, before he sold it in 1905 to Francis Pennington junior. Northey also rented out to Andrew Blake a narrow strip of land between the houses that Andrew had built in Lindsay Road and the Cricket Field. The Conveyance plan also showed a 'Proposed New Road', Ruskin Drive, to the south of the cricket ground, and beyond that another couple of narrow strips belonging to Francis Pennington.

The **Francis Pennington** (b. 1855) who bought the ground, was a local builders' merchant and the eldest son of the Francis Pennington, who had been instrumental in forming the club in 1872. Francis (jnr) had played in the very first recorded game for the club, and was carrying on his father's good work by providing the club with a permanent ground upon which to play. The 1901 census showed that he was still living at 'The Drill' public house with his brother, Edward, and his mother Frances, the Landlady. When his mother retired in 1903, after over 42 years working at 'The Drill', she moved with her two sons to a cottage in Cheam Common Road called 'The Lagoon'.

At some stage, after 1905, the ground had passed into the hands of the Blake family, as an article in the 'Comet', in November 1915, said that Mr. W. Blake, who had inherited the ground in 1910, kindly lent the Cheam Common Cricket Ground for a local Army recruitment rally. On that occasion *"A considerable crowd marched through the streets of Worcester Park behind the Raynes Park Band, until they reached the cricket field, where they listened to several short speeches."*

By today's standards the cricket field in Cheam Common Road would have appeared to have been a very tiny ground, as the Conveyance plan showed that it was only 200 feet wide. Of course, the playing area might possibly have extended over some of the Blake land or over the site of the proposed new road, Ruskin Drive, as that was not built until after the First World War.

Although the ground might not have been conducive to high scoring, it is obvious, however, from Cheam Common's results in 1891 that they were quite a successful club and, as such, by the mid 1890s they were attracting much stronger opponents. In the 'Sporting Life' of July 22nd, **1895** it listed, as an upcoming game at Cheam, a match of Cheam Common and Cuddington versus Surrey Club and Ground. To my surprise I managed to find the match report despite it being listed as a Cheam match rather than a Cheam Common match.

"Surrey Club and Ground v Eighteen of Cheam and Cuddington

The above match was played at Cheam on Monday last, and after an exciting game the home side won by 1 run. Of course the wicket after the heavy rain was all in favour of the bowlers, small scores being the result. The Surrey Club were first to bat, and out of an innings of 107, three batsmen were responsible for 70 of the runs scored off the bat, Henderson playing in fine form, being not out 39. Against this total the local side made 108, winning as above stated, by 1 run. Bentley played well for the winners. Lisle Nice and Austin bowled well, the former taking seven wickets at a cost of 23, and the latter 4 for 21 runs." 'The Sporting Life' July 24th, 1895.

For Surrey the team was: Watts (5), Higgins (20), Ayres (1), G. P. R. Windlaw (3), H. C. Pretty (9), Corden (0), W. T. Grayburn (2), Henderson (39*), Baker (11), Plaistow (1), Nice (9).

Several of the Cheam Common & Cuddington side had not appeared in previous match reports, and had probably been drafted in from other local teams to strengthen the side. Neil and Surridge, for example, were Cheam players. The team that day was: E. Gilbert (18), F. L. Head (1), C. Bentley (27), H. C. Preece (10), F. D. Head (6), S. Neil (0), P. Coote (10), A. Toppin (3), F. Bale (6), W. Markham (0), J. Thoms (3), E. Surridge (0), F. T. Eades (2), H. Austin (5), F. Weadon (0), F. Potter (2*), F. H. Shipton (0), F. Pennington (0).

What was particularly surprising about this scoresheet was that 17 men were out. Did the last man stand? Unfortunately we shall never know!

As a result of their defeat at the hands of 18 men of Cheam Common, the Surrey Club and Ground returned the following season intent on revenge with a much stronger side.

The 'Sporting Life' of the 17th August, 1896, had advertised a match at Cheam of Eleven of Cheam Common versus Surrey Club and Ground, just below a list of the county matches. Below that, it then listed fifteen players.

ELEVEN OF CHEAM COMMON AND CUDDINGTON C.C. v. SURREY CLUB AND GROUND.

The following is the team to represent Cheam Common and Cuddington at Cheam to-day (Monday) :—H. E. Preece, C. Bentley, H. Austin, F. Eades, F. Hale, H. Martin, E. Clarke, J. Baker, C. Humphrey, F. Potter, G. Dearman, J. Dare, J. Thorns, F. Shipton, and A. N. Other.

All day games, in the 1890s, seemed to have been very popular with the residents of Worcester Park, especially on Bank Holidays, as there was probably a lack of alternative amusement available locally. The crowd must have been greatly impressed by the performance of some of the County players, who showed that top class batsmen could prosper even on the Cheam Common wicket.

What was surprising, however, was the fact that the match report actually made it into the following day's 'Sporting Life' under the title *'Twelve of Surrey Club and Ground v Sixteen of Cheam Common and Cuddington CC'*. It must have been a bit of a logistical nightmare turning out a team on the day, however, for although fifteen players had been listed as being in the team on Monday morning, only about ten of those actually made up the final sixteen that day.

The match report was really quite detailed for what was, after all, a minor match, and included a more complete scorecard than usual, which has been reproduced below.

```
SIXTEEN OF CHEAM COMMON AND CUDDINGTON.
F. Eades b Lees              6 | H. Austin l b w, b Lees      1
P. H. Dagg c Pearce l Keene 3 | T. Frisk c Parton b Keene    5
R. Clarke b Keene           6 | G. Thorns b Keene            1
C. Humphreys b Keene        0 | F. Shipton b Lees            4
J. Jenner c Braund b Lees   0 | G. Burrows not out           2
A. Betteriss b Lees         1 | A. J. Mercer c Wilson b Lees 0
J. Hale b Lees              1 |      Byes, &c.               6
P. Potter b Keene           3 |                             ──
G. Dearman b Lees          0 |      Total              39
J. Dare b Lees              0 |

                    SURREY CLUB.
Ayres c Hale b Dagg        37 | Lees c Hale b Clarke          2
Braund l b w, b Austin      2 | W. T. Graburn c Jenner b
R. G. Parton b Austin       0 |   Clarke                    14
Henderson b Clarke         75 | Earle c Burrows b Shipton    10
W. G. Cobb b Hale          14 | Keene not out                2
C. E. Wilson b Austin      17 |      Byes, &c.              28
Pearce b Clarke            15 |                             ──
E. W. Corbett b Clarke      0 |      Total              216

                  BOWLING ANALYSIS.
                CHEAM.—FIRST INNINGS.
            O.   M.   R.  W.              O.   M.   R.  W.
Lees       16    8   13   9 | Keene     16    4   20
                SURREY CLUB.—FIRST INNINGS.
Shipton    13.2  2   40   1 | Isey       9    3   12   1
Austin     23    5   46   3 | Hale      12    3   40   1
Clarke     23    9   51   5 |
```

The Surrey players managed to score 216 runs from 85.2 overs, which does seem remarkably slow scoring until one factors in the fact that an over in the 1890s was probably only five balls, although if they were still playing by pre-1889 rules, an over would have only been four balls in length.

"Henderson scores 75: This annual fixture was played yesterday (Monday) before a numerous attendance on Cheam Common. The locals, having won the toss batted first, but the bowling of Lees and Keene proved very deadly, the first named taking nine wickets for 13 runs, and the latter six for 21, the innings closing for the small total of 39, not one of the batsmen being capable of obtaining double figures. On the visitors going in runs came very freely, the last wicket falling for 236, of which Henderson contributed 75 in faultless style, not giving a single chance during the innings, the Club and Ground thus winning by 177 runs."

It is important to remember that Surrey C. C. had won the County Championship in 1894 and 1895, and as such were the County Champions. It is not surprising, therefore, to see that there was a reasonable crowd there to watch the Surrey side which included several up and coming players, and one or two players like **Robert Henderson** (see page 219) who was in the twilight of his career. Blighted by ill-health, Henderson could still post a good score on the rather tricky C.C.&C. wicket. Cheam Common and Cuddington, in their turn, had strengthened their side by adding George Burrows, the young Worcester Park and Old Malden opening batsman, to their ranks. It was, however, a shame that he batted number 15 and was unable to show his true potential.

The home side had been destroyed by a nineteen year old quickie from Yorkshire, **Walter Scott Lees,** who was born on Christmas Day, 1876, and went on to have a long and varied career with Surrey from 1896 to 1911. In all he played 364 First Class matches, and he also took 26 wickets in five Test match appearances. His opening partner **John Keene** (b. 1873), a left arm medium pace bowler, only managed three matches for Surrey out of a total of 27 first class matches.

Of the other Surrey players, **William Turbett Graburn** (b. 1865), a Yorkshireman, was another player whose career was in decline as he had already played his last game (of two) for the Surrey First XI, whilst **George White Ayres** (b. 1871) played 25 matches for Surrey as a batsman between 1892 and 1899 (without scoring a fifty) before moving to Essex for a season in 1899.

Probably the star of the future, for that team, however, was **Leonard Braund** (b 1875), who only played 26 first class matches for Surrey, before resurrecting his career with Somerset in 1901, when he scored over a thousand runs and took over 100 wickets in that season. Despite Braund having to qualify for Somerset by residency, and despite the First World War interrupting his career, between 1896 until 1920 he scored over 17,000 first class runs which included 25 centuries, and he also took over 1,100 wickets. Braund also played 23 times for England, for whom he averaged over 25, and scored three hundreds.

The departure of the Cuddington players in about 1897-98 led to a falling off in publicity for the Cheam Common side for the next decade or so, although the Cuddington team, which had taken many of their star players, continued to make the sports pages. Any mention of Cheam Common, however, tended to be as a result of their opponents submitting press reports of their matches. These match reports were not always very flattering towards the Commoners. Cheam Common, for example, merited a mention in the awards' section of the 'London Daily News', of the 7th of June **1905**. Apparently the previous Saturday, *"G. F. Barham, who, bowling for Travers C.C. against Cheam Common, captured six wickets (five clean bowled) for no runs, he bowling 7 overs."*

A similar article, which dwelt upon the frailty of the Cheam Common batting featured in the 'South London Press' of May 29th 1908, under the heading 'Cheam Common v Cowley': *"Playing at Cheam Common, on Saturday, for the Cowley C.C., A. Wormleighton took 6 wickets for 5 runs. G. Simpson was top scorer with 29.*

Scores: Cowley, 80; Cheam Common, 33. This is the twelfth season of the Cowley C.C., and with a playing membership of twenty-six, they look like advancing well into their teens."

Despite the virtual anonymity of the club in the Edwardian era, Cheam Common apparently continued to thrive and appeared to have been able to turn out a relatively capable Second XI. A couple of matches which were not reported in the 'Surrey Comet' have recently appeared online in the 'Croydon Guardian' from 1905 and 1907. These matches were obviously submitted by their opponents, Beulah II's, and included both a full match report and the relevant scorecard. Whilst the results are irrelevant, the scorecards in particular introduce a handful of new characters to the story, some of whom went on to play a more prominent role in the Cheam Common side and eventually figured in the creation of Worcester Park Athletic Club.

The first match, which was probably a Second XI affair, was recorded at length in the 'Croydon Guardian' of July 22nd, **1905**. It seemed to be one of those strange Victorian/Edwardian games where the opponents carried on batting long after the game was won, presumably until the local hostelry was open.

"Beulah visited Cheam Common C.C. at Worcester-park, and after an exceedingly pleasant game defeated them by two wickets and 40 runs. Cheam Common took first knock but made a bad start, Fox being bowled with the first ball of the match, and four wickets fell for 11 runs. With the exception of Dalton (15) the home team's batmen failed to make anything like a

BEULAH v. CHEAM COMMON.—Played at Worcester-park on Saturday. Score: —

CHEAM COMMON.

J. Fox, b Manchee	0
C. Jarvis, b C. Clegg	2
J. Cleary, b Manchee	3
E. Thompson, b Manchee	7
T. Goldsmith, c H. Clegg, b Manchee	5
A. Fox, b Manchee	0
T. Dalton, c H., b C. Clegg	15
H. York, b Manchee	0
H. Small, not out	4
E. Springett, c sub, b C. Clegg	6
W. Oakes, b Manchee	2
Extras	3
	—
Total	47

BEULAH.

S. Manchee, not out	22
C. Tagg, c Fox, b Goldsmith	8
C. Clegg, c Thompson, b Fox	14
H. Clegg, b Fox	8
G. S. Hurren, c Dalton, b Jarvis	11
H. E. Player, st, b Jarvis	1
E. Amos, b York	0
S. Colling, b York	7
E. G. Champion, b York	2
F. H. Player, not out	0
Extras	14
	—
Total (for 8 wickets)	87

The rest did not bat.

stand against the bowling of Manchee and C. Clegg. The innings closed at 47...."

As Beulah had started the innings two men short and quickly lost Manchee with a damaged finger, the Cheam Common captain graciously allowed the Beulah scorer to bat. The wicket appears to have been a little lively, as apart from Manchee's injury, the other opener was caught off his hand and H. Clegg had to retire injured at one stage. *"....in order to play out time, the total was taken to 87 for 8 wickets. Manchee, on resuming his innings, although his finger was still very bad, increased his score to 22 not out.... York, Fox and Jarvis were the most successful of the home bowlers."*

At least six of the Cheam Common players lived locally and the team seemed to have had slightly more manual workers than the First XI. **James Cleary** (b.1872 in Ireland) might possibly have been the captain as he had previously had First team experience. He was listed in 1901 as being a jobbing gardener who lived opposite the ground at 3, North End Place, within a stone's throw of the 'North End Tavern'.

Joseph Fox (b. 1871) and his brother **Albert Fox** (b. 1878) had both been born in Reading but by 1905 were living in Cheam Common Road. Joseph was a wire worker whilst Albert was a cellarman. **Henry York** (b.1864) was a carpenter from Longfellow Road, whilst **Ernest Thompson** (b. 1882) was a jewellery salesman, who lived in Washington Road. **Thomas Dalton** (b. 1889), the top scorer, was the youngest player in the team and lived with his parents in Longfellow Road. This was his only recorded cricket appearance for Cheam Common, although he became a regular for Old Malden & Worcester Park C. C. and became one of the star players for the newly formed W.P.F.C.

Beulah II's proved too strong for the Cheam Common side again in August **1907**, and according to the 'Croydon Chronicle and East Surrey Advertiser', *"administered the order of 'the knock' to the men of Cheam"*. The home side had been skittled out for a lowly 40 on that occasion, of which Sawyer contributed 18 runs. In return Beulah managed 64 runs, although James Cleary did take seven wickets.

The Cheam Common side that day was: Springett (2), Williams (4), Patrick (0), Sawyer (18), Norton (0), Boitoult (1), Perkins (5), Cleary (2), Crowther (3), Buckle (0*) and Armitage (0).

Apart from Thomas Dalton, at least four of the other players, in those two matches against Beulah, appear to have been members of W.P.F.C.:- James Cleary had been an occasional First XI player, **Louis Patrick** (b. 1890) was the youngest of three brothers who had played football for Worcester Park, **E. Springett** was a goalkeeper, whilst **Percy Boithoult** (b. 1886) was a Second XI player. Percy was a commercial clerk from Cockfosters who in 1903, at the age of seventeen, married Harriet (Queenie) Blake, and thus, along with Walter Charlie Dare and the Holland brothers became another member of Frederick Blake's extended family.

Although no initials were given it is highly likely that the match against Beulah was the first recorded instance of the appearance at the club of a **Charles William Crowther** (b. 1884), a school teacher from Wimbledon, **Frederick George Williams** (b. 1875 in Dorset), who lived at 'Springfield', Cheam Common in 1911, and **Alfred Armitage** (b. 1867). The last two mentioned men moved into the area in the early years of the century. Williams was still living in Brixton, until at least 1904, where he worked as a civil servant; whilst in 1901 Armitage was a Church of England clergyman in West Ham. He appears to have given up the cloth with his move to Worcester Park, becoming a company director and Justice of the Peace. Both Williams and Armitage were to become important figures, fifteen years later, in the formation of Worcester Park Athletic Club. Frederick Williams became the Chairman of the Club and Alfred Armitage the first President.

The **1908** season began in promising fashion, publicity-wise, when the 'Surrey Comet' indicated, in late February, that the club had made important improvements to the ground: *"The members of this club are already eagerly awaiting the opening of the season. Further improvements to the ground have been carried out during the winter, which should greatly improve the facilities for practice."*

This short report heralded an unprecedented avalanche of information, in the 'Comet', which started three weeks later with a relatively full account of the Spring A.G.M. of the club. This was the first time in thirty-four years that the captain, secretary, treasurer and committee had been named.

"The general meeting of the Cheam Common Cricket Club was held at the 'North End Tavern', Cheam-side, on Saturday evening, Mr. Crowther presiding. At the outset the Chairman referred to the success of the series of smoking concerts promoted during the past season, by means of which a sum of £7 had been raised for the improvement of the club ground. On the motion of Mr. A. J. Rolfe, seconded by Mr. G. Perkins, the thanks of the club were unanimously accorded to the entertainment committee.

The Secretary pro. tem., Mr. F. G. Williams, read a letter from Mr. C. Jones, the secretary, resigning the office on account of continued ill-health, and the resignation was accepted with regret. Mr. H. Buckle, 'The Retreat', was then selected for the vacancy. Mr. A. M. Watts was re-elected Treasurer, the other officers appointed being:- Captain, Mr. G. W. Perkins; Vice-Captain, Mr. F. G. Williams. A vote of thanks was passed to the latter gentleman for his valuable services as Hon. Secretary during the past few months. Mr. Keswick, M.P., was again elected President, and the Vice-Presidents are: Major E. F. Coates, M.P., Dr. Chearnley Smith, Mr. C. W. Smith and Mr. R. B. Yardley. The committee comprises Messrs. J. Cleary, A. J. Donaldson, F. Rickard, H. T. Gilbert, J. E. Sawyer, W. S. Norton, C. Crowther, B. Strand and P. Peters; and the selection committee is the Captain, Vice-Captain and Mr. Cleary.

The first match is announced for May 2nd, and the whole of the fixtures for the coming season have already been arranged."

Although no report of the match on May 2nd exists, the 'Comet' did feature eleven scorecards for Cheam Common C.C. in 1908. Suddenly from having very little information, there is too much to include herein. These scorecards, therefore, have been summarised and included in the appendix. They do, however, reveal that the team played most of their matches at home, which suggests that Cheam Common, which was still a very rural village, must have been an attractive place to play.

As an added bonus the 'Comet' also provided the team statistics at the end of the year (again in the Appendix), which seem to indicate that 1908 had been an extremely average season, with eight victories and nine defeats for the First XI. Frank Drew was the outstanding batsman whilst Henry Thomas Gilbert was the leading wicket-taker. The overall impression to be had from the statistics, however, is that it was more preferable to have been a bowler rather than a batsman in 1908, and that more work probably needed to be done on the ground.

*This group of moustachioed players was the Cheam Common side of **1908**. (Courtesy of John Fox)*

The new cordial relationship between the 'Surrey Comet' and Cheam Common C.C. continued to flourish in **1909**, and began with an account of a highly successful fund-raising concert which the Club had organised at St. Philip's School on Wednesday evening March 10th:- *"under the able management of Mr. H. Buckle (Hon. Secretary of the club) who was assisted by a committee comprising Messrs. G. Perkins, H. Gilbert, W. S. Norton, F. G. Williams, F. Rickard, and J. E. Sawyer."*

This was followed a month later with a short account of the Club's Spring A.G.M., which, although missing information on the state of the ground, the financial state of the club and the number of members, it further emphasised the fact that the running of the club had by 1909 moved even further into the hands of the middle class.

"At the recent general meeting, held at the North End Tavern, Worcester Park, the chief business was the election of officers. After two years of hard and highly appreciated work as Captain, Mr. G. W. Perkins resigned this position, and he is succeeded by Mr. F. G. Williams. The other appointments were:- Vice-captain, Mr. J. E. Sawyer; Hon. Secretary, Mr. H. Buckle; Hon. Treasurer, Mr. A. M. Watts; Committee, Messrs. F. Rickard, C. Crowther, P. Peters, A. Donaldson, W. S. Norton, H. T. Gilbert, G. W. Perkins, H. Field, E. Armitage and J. Cleary: Selection Committee, Messrs. F. G. Williams, J. E. Sawyer and J. Cleary."

Amongst the new characters who were mentioned as being either involved with the concert or on the Club's Committee: **Henry Thomas Gilbert** (b. 1872) was a stockbroker's clerk who lived in the Malden Road; **John Edward Sawyer** (b. 1876) was a civil servant who lived in Washington Road; **George Perkins** (b. 1877), who had been the First XI captain in 1908, was a tailor who lived in Washington Road; and **William S. Norton** (b. 1865) was a clerk who lived in Hampton Road.

The 'E. Armitage' mentioned as being on the Committee, seems not to have had any connection to Alfred Armitage. Instead he was probably **Ernest George Joseph Armitage** (b. 1880), the son of a commercial traveller, who had been born in Camberley. Ernest was a commercial clerk in a silk warehouse who married Minnie Peirson in 1904, before moving to Chestnut Road, Raynes Park in 1906, where they brought up their three children.

Henry Buckle (b.1874), the Hon Secretary of the club, was another commercial traveller, who lived at No.1, The Retreat, next door to Edwin Ashley, one of the leading C.CC.C. batsmen. Another committee member of the club, and occasional player, who was also present at the concert was **Frederick Rickard** (b. 1865) who lived in Cheam Road, Worcester Park, with his wife and son in 1911. He worked in the warehouse of an auction house.

The 1909 season was evidently not a brilliant one for Cheam Common C.C. as only two of the batsmen averaged double figures, W. W. Champness with 12.5, and F. G. Williams with 11, which included the top score of the season, a less than impressive 36 runs (again the averages and results can be found in the Appendix). Part of the reason for the club's poor performance, apparently, was the weather as there was above average rainfall in June, July and September, which obviously did not help the bowlers as the leading wicket taker, H. Gilbert, only managed 44 victims.

The annual dinner and A.G.M. of the cricket club was held in **1909** at the 'North End Hotel' on Wednesday November 10th. The pub had obviously been upgraded from a 'Tavern' to a 'Hotel', in the extremely full report which occurred in the 'Comet' that

Saturday, under the heading, 'Members of the Cheam Common Club Meet at the Festal Board'. Mr. A. Hamilton, one of the vice-presidents, was in the chair, and was ably assisted by the club captain, Mr. F. G. Williams, whilst, "A recherche dinner had been provided by the host and hostess, Mr. and Mrs. Watts."

Following the loyal toast and Mr. Crowther's rendition of 'Hearts of Oak', "'Cheam Common Cricket Club' was submitted by the Chairman in a short but complimentary speech, the name of Mr. F. G. Williams, the captain, being coupled with the toast. The Chairman deplored that the season, with regard to play, had been bad owing to the excessive rains, but in spite of that he understood the club had won 7 matches and drawn 2. He hoped the coming season would be more prosperous.

Mr. Williams, in responding, said that although they had not been as successful as they should have liked, yet they were very good losers, and were sportsmen. Financially they were in a very good position, and he wished to take that opportunity of thanking the tradesmen and others of the district for their support in the past.

Mr. F. W. Drew gave the toast of 'The Officers and Committee' coupling with it the name of Mr. H. Buckle, the secretary. In Mr. Buckle, he said, they had a gentleman whose heart and soul was in the welfare of the club, and this function was the only opportunity they had of thanking him for all he did. A good secretary, he said made a good club, and Mr. Buckle, by his work, had ensured the latter by his abilities. The toast was received with loud applause. Mr. Buckle thanked them for the way they had received the toast, and said he hoped to have even more members next year.

During the proceedings the Chairman presented a bat to Mr. W. W. Champness, that player having obtained the highest batting average during the season; and for the honour of having secured the highest number of wickets, Mr. G. W. Perkins was the recipient of a pair of gloves." (He had the best bowling average).

Further toasts and musical recitals were made by Messrs. Crowther, Donaldson, Bowskill, F. W. Drew, W. W. Champness, G. W. Perkins, Mr. Sutherly (on piano) and a local builder of Alma Parade, George William Young (b. 1874).

Although the weather in **1910** was mainly dull and cool the performances of the Cheam Common First XI showed a notable improvement over the previous year, as they won eleven out of the eighteen matches played, sixteen of which are summarised in the Appendix, thanks to the 'Surrey Comet' and the 'Wimbledon Borough News'. George Perkins led the way in the first game by scoring 50 runs, before nobly retiring. Nowadays a batsman might possibly consider retiring once he reached a century, but to actually score a fifty upon some of the wickets that they played on, seemed to be a remarkable feat. In the home match against Tadworth,

W. W. Champness's 23 runs were highlighted by the 'Comet' as they had been scored on what they described as *'a difficult wicket'*.

The full scorecard for the August Bank Holiday game versus Grosvenor, which was a double innings match, was also reproduced. Sadly, however, only one match appeared for the Second XI, when they beat Grayshott, at Cheam Common, on June 18th by 44 runs, the score being 64 v 20. *"P. Peters 26* played a good innings for Cheam."*

Amongst the additional information that appeared in the 'Comet' was the following interesting snippet of information, which concerned the acquisition of a promising new player who turned out for the club in the final match of the season:
"J. Atkinson the well known Mitcham bowler, who is now resident in Worcester Park, played for the winners and took 5 wickets for 9 runs."

The end of season A.G.M., which was held at the 'North End Tavern', revealed that the averages of both the leading batsman and bowler showed a significant improvement upon the previous year's performances. On this occasion the 'Comet' provided a rather blurred version of the statistics. Frank Drew won the batting prize for his 240 runs from 10 innings, whilst Harold Watts took 75 wickets at under five runs per wicket: Leonard S. Hudson won a *"pair of carvers"*, which were presented to him by Mr. Jim Prior, for the best all round performance throughout the season.

Before the festivities for the evening began, Henry Buckle was presented with a silver cigarette case, by Mr. Williams, the First XI Captain, as a sign of the appreciation of his fellow cricketers for all the work that he had undertaken, on their behalf, for the previous three years. He was replaced as the Hon. Secretary by **Henry Plaw** (b. 1862), a police pensioner, who lived in Donnington Road in 1911, six houses along from the former captain, George William Perkins.

The festivities that followed the A.G.M. included several musical items and a performance by one of the cricketers who rarely appeared in the 'notable performances' column. His talents obviously lay elsewhere: *"Mr. Cyril McKechnie, a member of the club, mystified all with his clever card tricks and sleight of hand."*

1911 was a turning point for C.C.C.C. in many ways, as it was the most successful season ever for the First XI. They also turned out a regular second team and tried their hand at mid-week cricket. (See the list of fixtures in the Appendix although one might need a magnifying glass as the font is extremely small). The Club also appeared to have an extremely conscientious press officer as most of the scorecards appeared in the press, often with a short account of the highlights of the matches. All accounts of Cuddington C.C, however, seemed to have vanished, and several of those mentioned as playing for Cuddington, a few years earlier, had returned to the C.C.C.C. fold.

The 'Surrey Comet' of the 28th October of that year, gave not only a thorough review of the club's progress for the season, but also produced a comprehensive statistical breakdown of the individual players' batting and bowling for 1911. (Again in the Appendix).

"The season of 1911 is the most successful the club has ever experienced. The first eleven have played 24 matches, winning 16, drawing 4 and losing 4.The fixture list has been a strong one, and the results prove that the Cheam Common eleven must now rank as a really good side.

Frank Drew, for the third time in five years, again heads the batting averages, and to him and W. W. Champness, the club owes a great deal for the fine starts they have often given the side.

Most of the other regular members of the side have batted well at different times, someone generally getting runs when these were needed. The bowling, which has been mainly in the hands of W. Dyer and Watts, has been very strong. W. Dyer finishes at the head of the bowling averages, and wins the prize annually presented by Mr. W. J. Mills. Both Watts and W. Dyer have excellent figures, considering the strength of their opponents.

The fielding of the team is one of its strong points, the importance of this being always emphasised by the captain, Mr. F. G. Williams, not only by theory but also by example. The second eleven has been run this season, and, although only winning two matches out of twelve, it has scored the very useful double purpose of unearthing some likely players for the first eleven in the time to come, and also of enabling more of the members to indulge in match practice. W. Stent has done very useful all-round work, and has earned the prize that was set aside for this eleven. Two Wednesday matches were also played by the club."

When compared to the 1891 statistics, the 1911 statistics show that the wickets that they played on must have been immeasurably better. As a result, the batting averages had improved considerably whilst the bowling averages had predictably worsened. At last batsmen were reaching the half century mark although there was still no sign of the elusive ton for a Cheam Common player.

The bowling attack of **William Dyer** (b. 1887), a resident of Longfellow Road, and **Harold Watts** (b. 1893) must have been rather special, as on more than one occasion they bowled a side out unchanged. Dyer, the older of the two, in particular, seems to have been rather potent. In a match against the West Streatham Institute on August19[th] that year, according to the 'Surrey Comet': *"W. Dyer began to bowl in startling fashion, getting three of the visitors' wickets in the first over, and in all he took eight wickets for 15 runs. Cheam won by 55 runs, the Streatham players being dismissed for 36."*

Harold Edmund Watts was an extremely important figure in the W.P.A.C. story. He seems to have been brought up for most of his young life by his uncle, Arthur Watts, the landlord of the 'North End Tavern' and Hon. Treasurer of Cheam Common C.C. His father, Ernest, a wood engraver, had been living at the 'North End Tavern' in 1891 but there is no record of him after the birth of his son in 1893.

Living opposite the ground obviously gave young Harold ample opportunity to practise as a youngster; that, and his tall, lean frame, helped him develop into an excellent quick bowler and hard hitting batsman. Harold was the first recorded player from Worcester Park to take 10 wickets in a match, albeit in the second innings of a game, and he also hit one of the first ever recorded hundreds. In 1925, he followed in his uncle's footsteps and became the landlord of the 'North End Tavern' where he hosted many social events on behalf of the new Athletic Club which lacked a large pavilion in the early years. Even today Harold Watts is remembered by the cricket section, as the Harold Watts' Trophy is still awarded annually to the person, not necessarily a cricketer, who has contributed the most towards the success of the club.

The potency of the Dyer/Watts attack is shown in an account of the match against their old rivals Cheam Village in the 'Comet' of July 1st, 1911:

"In Cheam Park on Saturday, there was a match possessing much interest, the opposing teams being Cheam Common and Cheam Village. Against the bowling of Dyer and Watts the Village team only made 34 runs, six of the team only adding two to the total. Watts also proved to be in good form with the bat, his 32 being a notable contribution in a total of 89." Watts took six wickets and Dyer three.

Probably one of the most interesting matches in 1911 occurred, on September 23rd, against a scratch side cobbled together by an ex-player of the club, **John Elson** (b. 1868). The previous week's paper had mentioned that, *"some years ago Elson was a player for Cheam Common C.C., but for some considerable time past he has been coach at Westminster College."* It is interesting to think that the poor pitches of Cheam Common might have helped in the development of someone who had decided to take up cricket as a career, although it is difficult to work out when precisely he played for the club.

John Elson had been born in Nottinghamshire and, in 1891, was on the ground staff at Trent Bridge, when he was hired to act as the professional for Sidmouth in Devon.

The 'Exeter and Plymouth Gazette', reported on May 18th that Elson, *"has received good recommendations from some of the prominent cricketers of Nottingham. The Hon. Secretary of the Sidmouth Club heard of Elson through Shaw and Shrewsbury, of the same cricketing county. I shall expect after this to find Elson giving a good account of himself this summer. He is about 24 years of age, and is described as a good medium pace bowler."*

Elson married his local sweetheart later on that summer in Sidmouth and appeared to spend most of that decade living in Devon. By 1901, however, he was the Cricket Master at Westminster School and lived with his wife and four children in the Groundsman's House, Vincent Square, Westminster. They were still living there in 1911 but by 1939 he had retired and was living at 156, Washington Road, Worcester Park. In the 1939 register his occupation was listed as, *"professional cricketer/ groundsman retired."*

William Dyer's brother, Frederick, had starred with the ball in the Elson match taking a hat trick against the visitors, but Mr Elson's team's score, of 100 for 8, was twenty runs too much for the home team.

One important character who, surprisingly, failed to figure in the First team averages was **Dr William Chearnley Smith**, who appeared, on July 15th, 1911, opening the batting and top scoring with 15 runs for the Seconds against St Barnabus's. He also chipped in with a couple of wickets that game. Perhaps being a doctor made it difficult for him to commit to playing First team cricket regularly, and he, therefore, contented himself with an occasional game for the Second XI.

William Chearnley Smith was born on June 4th, 1865, in Kentville, Nova Scotia, Canada, before moving on to be educated at the famous Merchiston Castle School in Edinburgh, where he excelled at sport, playing for both the school first fifteen at rugby and the first eleven at cricket, besides being a good golfer. Following school, he studied medicine at Edinburgh University from where he graduated in 1890. In 1891 he married Isabella Scott from Kelso and they had a daughter, Hilda Margaret Alison Smith. At some stage he left Scotland and went to work at St. George's Hospital, Tooting. In 1900-01 he volunteered to serve in the South African War as a Surgeon Captain, in the 8th Battalion, the Imperial Yeomanry.

According to Sir Alexander Houston, a fellow Merchistonian in the 'British Medical Journal', *"Chearnley Smith was a great athlete, and his handsome face and figure and breezy personality made him seem almost like a god to his admiring schoolfellows. Later, Chearnley Smith played 'rugger' for Edinburgh University and, I think, for St. George's and the United Hospitals."* In 1930, Chearnley Smith apparently told Houston that he only had two athletic regrets; one being that he had never been chosen to play for Scotland at rugby, although his friends thought him good enough; and the other was that he had only come second in throwing the cricket ball at school, even though he had thrown it over a hundred yards,

For almost thirty years after the Boer War, Dr. William Chearnley Smith became one of the most prominent figures in Worcester Park, society, and rarely a week passed by in the local paper without it recording him as having attended an accident, a coroner's autopsy, a cricket match or a social function. By 1911 he was recorded in the census as living with his wife, daughter and a couple of servants at 'Elm Lodge', Worcester Park, Malden. Ten years later he was one of the founding fathers of the Athletic Club, and eventually became an extremely popular President of the Club.

Another important member of the Cheam Common side, in 1911, who helped form the Athletic Club a decade later, was W. W. Champness. He is another example of the fact that the social composition of the club had altered considerably over 40 years, away from being predominantly a working man's club, towards being an all inclusive organisation.

William Weldon Champness was born into a strong Methodist family in Louth, Lincolnshire in 1875, and was educated at a Wesleyan School in Somerset where he played cricket for the Independent College. In the 1890s he moved to North East London where he worked in various children's homes and orphanages whilst continuing to play cricket in Hackney as an all-rounder. Upon moving to Cheam, besides joining the local cricket club, he became quite an important figure in the Free Trade Union movement.

The 'Comet' for June 24th, 1911, under the heading 'Political Appointment' informed the reader that *"Mr. W. W. Champness, of Westwood, Worcester Park, has been appointed assistant secretary of the Free Trade Union, in succession to Mr. G. Wallace Carter, who vacates the position at the end of June to take over other political work."* In January 1914 he became the General Secretary of the movement, besides remaining an important figure in the Methodist Movement for the rest of his life. It also seems likely that he might have used his secretarial skills to improve the club's coverage in the local press.

Sadly, despite the team's success on the cricket field, tragedy struck another popular founder member of W.P.A.C. which probably affected them all to some degree. The 'Comet' of July 15th, 1911, informed the reader that Edith, the 31 year old wife of **Edwin Reginald Ashley** (b 1880), a clerk for a stout and ale merchant, had passed away after an operation: *"Much sympathy has been extended to Mr. Ashley, who resides at the Retreat, and is a prominent member of the Cheam Common C.C., in view of the bereavement he has sustained by the somewhat sudden death of his young wife, which occurred at St. Anthony's Hospital, Cheam, after an operation. The funeral took place at St. Philip's yesterday, and amongst the floral tributes was a wreath from the members of the cricket club."*

Despite this setback, 1911 was a good year that, besides seeing the Coronation of George V, was a year made for cricket and good performances, with a severe heatwave and drought lasting from July through to September. In comparison **1912** failed to be a memorable year either for Cheam Common or for the country in general. The cricket season throughout the land suffered from the wettest August on record which culminated in severe flooding particularly in East Anglia.

The statistics posted in the newspaper at the end of that season make quite dismal reading in comparison to 1911. Only four batsmen in the First XI scored over 30 in an innings, the top score being 39* by R. Ashley. Welch topped the averages with 247 at an average of 13.7. Harold Watts was second in the averages with 192 runs at 10.7. Watts, however, dominated the bowling attack, taking 84 wickets at 4.8 apiece. He actually averaged over 5 wickets per game (although some games were two innings' affairs).

In all the First XI managed to play 19 matches in 1912, won 10, lost 7, drew 1 and tied 1. For the Second XI, W. W. Champness played 6 matches and topped both the batting and bowling averages with 11.8 and 5.7. Fewer scoresheets for the First XI made it into the local press that year, which could have been down to the fact that Champness played fewer First XI games.

The account of the opening practice match on April 27th, 1912, and the ensuing evening's celebration, gives a fascinating insight into life in England prior to the First World War. One can imagine the scene in the smoke be-fugged room of the 'North End Tavern' as the members enthusiastically toasted the health of their departing captain, F. G. Williams.

"The Cheam Common C.C. opened their season on Saturday with a match between the first XI and the next fifteen, the former winning by 70 runs - 110 to 40. In the evening a smoking concert was held at headquarters, the North End, at which function opportunity was taken to present to Mr. Fred Williams a Tantalus as a slight recognition of the good and efficient services he had rendered to the club both as a member and as captain. The presentation was made, on behalf of the members, by Mr. G. Perkins, who voiced the regret every member felt at the fact that circumstances would not allow him to continue as their captain. Mr. Williams thanked the members for their kind and tangible expression of appreciation, and assured them that although he was unable to continue as their captain his interest in the club would not diminish and that he would still do his utmost for them in any other way possible. The health of Mr. Williams was enthusiastically drunk, and a most enjoyable evening was passed in harmony. The Tantalus was suitably inscribed."

Even though the match reports for the 1912 season tend to be short and basic, they often present one with a snippet of information which is missing from the scoresheet. A good example of this was the following account, from the 'Comet' of July 20th, of a catch by Reginald Ashley who had so tragically lost his wife the previous year:

"Cheam Common and Mitcham II were opponents last Saturday in a game which was full of exciting features, Cheam Common winning by ten runs with scarcely five

minutes to spare. The wonderful catch with which Foster was dismissed will ever be remembered on the ground, Ashley securing the ball high up with his right hand after running along the boundary for fully twenty-five yards."

The following summer in **1913** was not particularly noteworthy weather-wise but in a way it was very special. It was the last, peaceful summer before the world was thrown into chaos; it was the end of a Victorian/Edwardian way of life. Britain still had an Empire and most of the world was shaded pink.

The way of life of the whole country, however, was about to be irrevocably altered, and yet I feel that they probably sensed it for, as I read the 'Comet' over the years leading towards 1914, I became more and more aware of photographs and articles of a militaristic nature, relating to local regiments either on parade or on military manoeuvres. For the cricketers of Cheam Common, however, 1913 was that last, serene summer of innocence.

The press was again particularly kind to Cheam Common C.C. in 1913 and published in detail their A.G.M.s and statistics for the season. In a way there was too much detail and I briefly toyed with cutting back on the accounts. Every name mentioned, however, is important, as these names are the foundation stones of the present day club. These often lengthy articles merely show that their meetings followed the same format and faced the same problems as our own meetings a century later. It is for this reason that I have included them in full.

The report of the A.G.M. from March, 1913, shows that the club was progressing nicely, both in numbers and financially, whilst the committee was headed by a galaxy of local dignitaries. Under the heading, *"A Large Accession of Members Reported at Annual Meeting"* was the following report: *"The annual general meeting of the Cheam Common C.C was held at the headquarters, the 'North End', on Wednesday evening, when Mr. W. W. Champness presided over a large attendance.*

In his report, the Hon. Secretary, Mr. H. Plaw, stated that for the coming season the list of fixtures had been prepared, and with the exception of June 14th, all the dates were filled, the first match taking place on April 26th. For the second eleven 14 matches had been arranged. Financially the club was in a sound condition, as after meeting all liabilities there was an acceptable balance in hand. Referring to the ground, the secretary stated that during the past winter considerable improvements had been carried out which would increase the area for the preparation of pitches.

The officers were then elected as follows:- President, Mr. H. Keswick, M.P.; Vice-Presidents, Major E. F. Coates, M.P., Dr. Chearnley Smith, Messrs. Charles Smith, W. W. Champness, G. W. Perkins, and F. G. Williams.

Mr. Hudson was unaminously re-elected Captain of the first eleven, and Mr. G. Welsh Vice-Captain. Mr. W. W. Champness was elected Captain of the second eleven. The general committee appointed comprised Messrs. C. Dare, H. Field, G. Percival, J. E. Sawyer and G. Young; and the selection committee Mr. W. Dyer and the captains of the first and second elevens.

Further business conducted was the revision of the rules and the nomination of eleven new members to the club. In this latter connection it was stated that the club now possessed approximately 30 playing members, and this was considered most satisfactory.

Votes of thanks to the retiring officers and the Chairman closed the meeting."

The fact that two M.P.s were officers of the club demonstrates that the club had quite a good reputation locally, and in the cricketing world. **Henry Keswick** was born in 1870 in Shanghai and attended Eton College and Trinity College, Cambridge. He was the Conservative M.P. for Epsom from 1912 to 1918 and was actually the local M.P. as Cheam and Cheam Common at that time were part of the Epsom Rural District.

Major Sir Edward Feetham Coates Bart. (b.1853) was the Unionist M.P. for Lewisham from 1903; he was also a Justice of the Peace, and the Deputy Lieutenant of Surrey. Sir Edward Coates had lived in Cheam Road, Ewell, with his family for over 20 years, as they were listed as living there in the 1881, 1891 and 1901 censuses. It is highly likely that during that time he would have visited the ground on a Saturday afternoon, and he would have known some of the members socially, such as Dr Chearnley Smith.

The final, full, pre-war season was probably the most successful ever as can be judged from the following extremely full account of the end-of-season A.G.M., which was recorded in the 'Surrey Comet' of October 18th, 1913, under the heading, *'Cheam Common C.C.: Successful Season Reviewed': "The annual meeting of the Cheam Common C.C. was held at headquarters, the 'North End Tavern', on Saturday evening, Mr. W. W. Champness presiding over a large attendance of members. Mr. Watts, the Hon. Treasurer, presented the financial statement, which showed that the receipts, including a balance brought forward of £2 8s.10½d. had been £31 11s. 0½d., and the expenditure £29 17s. 11d., leaving a balance in hand of £1 13s. 1½d. The balance sheet having been passed, the Chairman announced that the only officers to be elected at that meeting were the Hon. Secretary and Hon. Treasurer. Messrs Plaw and Watts were thereupon unanimously re-elected and thanked for their past services.*

Mr. L. Hudson, captain of the first eleven, presented his annual report, stating that looking at results in general it was a great pleasure for him to again report a very successful season, ten matches being won, five lost and five drawn. There was no need to apologise for the losses, as they were sustained at the hands of such good clubs as Epsom, Hook and Walton.

History was made on one occasion when the team had a record score of 234 against Grafton. The batting of the eleven had been beyond all expectation, and fine individual performances had marked the play, the most notable being the 78 not out of F. Drew against Banstead. Several fifties had also been registered. Ashley led the batting average with 22.5, and took the batting prize presented by Mr. W. W. Champness. (Applause.)

The bowling had been in trustworthy hands. Harold Watts headed the list with 58 wickets, and won the bowling prize presented by Mr. A. Rides. (Applause.) W. Dyer was next with 56 wickets. Fielding was the weakest spot, and any suggestion whereby it could be remedied would be welcome. He hoped that the good fortune of the eleven would continue. (Applause.)

Facts about the Second XI: Mr. Champness, Captain of the 2nd XI, said it was with considerable satisfaction that he had to report a record season. Of the 20 matches played, 12 had been won, 7 lost and one drawn, as against only one match won last season. (Applause.) At the beginning of the season the team was quite an unknown quantity, but victory in the opening match inspired confidence, and they found that although deprived of the assistance of certain of last season's players they could nevertheless win matches. The best performance of the team was the victory at Earlsfield, against St. Andrew's, a club superior to them in all points of the game, yet they managed to win a sporting match by seven runs. In this match F. Dyer took nine wickets and hit the stumps seven times. (Applause.) Dyer won the bowling prize with the splendid record of 67 wickets for 4.6 runs. (Applause.) The batting prize was won by a new-comer, W. Field, who was an acquisition to the team.

After referring to the fielding and missed catches, Mr. Champness said it must always be remembered that the second eleven ought to be more or less recruits for the first eleven. The good spirit of the game was everything, and he hoped the lesson of 1913 would help them to attain success in every department of the game next year.

The reports having been adopted, and both Captains thanked, a discussion took place as to the means for improvement, and Mr. Shrubb suggested practices under match conditions. The Chairman considered this a very good suggestion, and it should be acted upon. Regarding the upkeep of the ground and pitches, Mr. Foden moved the appointment of a sub-committee, but Mr. Young's amendment that the appointment of a groundsman be considered, was carried.

It was agreed that the annual dinner should be held this year, the committee for this function being Messrs. Hudson, Perkins, Williams and Welsh, with the Secretary and Treasurer, were appointed a concert committee.

The advisability of arranging home matches on Bank Holidays for the second eleven was discussed and approved, and a vote of thanks to the Chairman terminated the meeting."

One notable new comer, who figured quite prominently in the batting averages was **Oliver Cornelius Foden**, who had been born in 1887, the son of a printer in Alvaston in Derbyshire. He spent most of his youth in Derbyshire before qualifying as a elementary school teacher in 1907. In 1911 he was living in Clapham with his young wife, Nellie, before they moved eventually to Oaks Avenue in Worcester Park.

O. C. Foden was a great organiser and leader of men and became the earliest First XI captain of W.P.C.C. The photograph, below, which was kindly provided by David Rymill shows the highly successful 1913 side, with Oliver Foden standing second from the right in the back row.

The Cheam Common Cricket Team 1913 (Courtesy of David Rymill)

1914 began like any other year with the traditional pre-season A.G.M. being held in the 'North End Tavern' at 8 p.m. on Saturday evening, March 28th. This meeting was fully recorded in the 'Surrey Comet' on April 4th under the heading *'Decision to Appoint a Groundsman'*: *"Mr. W. W. Champness presided over a large attendance of members of the Cheam Common Cricket Club at the general meeting, held at the 'North End' on Saturday evening. The Hon. Secretary, Mr. Plaw, announced that the membership was over fifty, and that the finances were in a sound condition, there being a balance in hand of £6 6s. 7½d,. Which included a profit of £4 14s. 6d. from the concert. With the exception of an away match for August Bank Holiday, the fixture lists of both elevenes were complete.*

The Hon. Secretary was heartily thanked for his services.

The election of officers was then proceeded with Col. The Hon. F. L. Colborne and Mr. A. Rides were added to the list of vice-presidents. Mr. Champness was elected Captain, and Mr. G. Welsh Vice-Captain of the first eleven; and Messrs. W. E. Field and A. Styles Captain and Vice-Captain respectively of the second eleven. Mr. F. G. Williams, with the Captains of both elevens, was appointed to the selection committee. The following were elected to form the general committee:- Messrs. G. W. Young, O. C. Foden, E. R. Ashley, E. Shrubb and L. S. Hudson; Messrs. J. Hopkins and J. Styles were selected as official umpires.

The Chairman announced that acting on the suggestion brought forward at the last general meeting, the committee recommended that a groundsman be appointed. If the members agreed with the committee's recommendation, he felt sure they would find the appointment a great advantage to the club. Mr. Dare had been approached with a view to taking over the duties, and had agreed to accept them on certain conditions. The recommendation of the committee was agreed to.

A proposition to allow juniors to become members of the club at half-fee was rejected.

A proposition to raise the subscription to 7s. 6d. did not meet with approval. Eventually it was proposed by Mr. Hudson that the minimum subscription be 5s. and the rule altered accordingly.

This was carried, several members, however, not voting. Seven new members were elected, and a vote of thanks to the Chairman and officers closed the meeting."

Leonard Stranger Hudson was born on March 3rd, 1888, in Bexley, Kent, the youngest of nine children of George Hudson, a joiner. The 1911 census showed that Leonard was a local government civil servant who was living at 'Blantyre', Cheam

Common Road, the seven roomed house of **William James Hopwood**, his wife, Annie, and three young daughters. This was to become one of the most important families in the inter-war history of the Athletic Club, as W. J. Hopwood was to become the General Secretary of the club for at least fifteen years, whilst his wife and daughters were usually in charge of all the catering for the club's social events.

Leonard was the captain of Cheam Common C. C. from 1911 until the start of the war, by which time he had moved to 'White Heather', Donnington Road. Initially he was in a reserved occupation and served in the local army reserves. Eventually, however, he joined the 5th Regiment, the Gordon Highlanders, where he attained the rank of Lance Corporal, before being wounded on July 27th, 1916, whilst serving in the trenches at Bazentin-le-Grand. It was fortunate for him that he was invalided out as many of his fellow soldiers who were wounded that day were later killed in action. His army records show that he was quite a small man as he was only 5ft 3¾ins tall.

Following the war, Leonard returned to Worcester Park and on April 10th, 1920, he married Doris Beatrice Wilson. They lived at 'Goshen', Hampton Road, from where he became a prime instigator for the formation of an Athletic Club for the returning soldiers and for the youth of the area. He was to become not only an invaluable playing member of both the cricket and bowls sections, but also a hard working committee member and Vice-President of the Athletic Club until the mid-1930s.

Most of the club's fixtures in 1914 appeared to be listed in the 'Comet' each week, and on an odd occasion a short match report was included of the previous week's matches. The Second XI continued their previous season's good form by beating Benhilton II's at home on May 2nd. *"Score:- Cheam, 161 for seven, declared; Benhilton, 23 and 56. For the winners the best scorers were P. W. Rampton (41*), C. Dare (33), E. Shrubb 33, J. W. Argles (22) and W. E. Field (19)."*

This brief match summary threw up another couple of interesting white collar workers. **Percy William Rampton** (b. 1888) was the fourth eldest out of 15 children of a merchant who lived in Liverpool Road, Kingston. In 1911, Percy, a surveyor, was still living at home with his parents, ten of his siblings and only one servant, whilst **Joseph William Argyles** (b. 1895), was the son of a vicar, who lived with his widowed mother at The Retreat, Worcester Park. Joseph was a clerk for a company of Indian Army Agents before the War, and became a shipping manager after being invalided out of the Army with a severe wound to his left leg.

On May 16th, the First XI, had a comprehensive victory over Clapham St. John's in Merton Park: *"J. Stevens (49) and O. C. Foden (22) made 71 out of 112. St. John's team had a distinct tail, and their total being 83. Cheam Common won by 29 runs."*

On Wednesday, July 1st, the Club turned out a team against Ashtead and recorded one of their largest scores: *"Playing for Cheam Common against Ashtead on Wednesday week, Welsh batted brilliantly during his compilation of 88 runs. His club declared at 250 for seven, but time did not permit of Ashtead getting further than 123 for four wickets. On Saturday, Cheam Common defeated Hook by 41 runs, 141 to 100."*

By the beginning of August, however, war was breaking out all over Europe and Britain was being dragged into the affray. On August 7th the British Expeditionary Forces arrived in France and people were beginning to question as to whether all sport should be cancelled. Before listing that week's Cricket Fixtures, the 'Comet' on August 8th solemnly noted: *"Since last Saturday a vast change has been wrought. Ordinary conditions have been exchanged for the extra-ordinary, and the rapidity with which the normal life of the country has been supplanted by the abnormal is not the least startling in the development of affairs during the last few days.*

The question is 'Shall England play whilst she is at war', but when the matter is given calm and dispassionate consideration the answer must be in the affirmative, even though our cricket fields are taken over for military operations, as is the case at the Oval at the present time.

So far as is possible let the ordinary life of the country proceed along its well-ordered lines, and as recreation is essential to health now more than ever desirable - there is no reason why cricket and other sports should not continue."

The committee of the M.C.C. met on the evening of Monday the 10th of August, under Lord Hawke, to discuss the remaining county championship matches. After the meeting a statement was issued which said that the county championship competition would continue as would the programme of matches which were still due to be played at Lords.

CRICKET.

THE GAME TO CONTINUE.

Pronouncement by the Marylebone Club.

Despite these brave words that cricket would carry on, it became extremely noticeable in the following weeks, in the 'Comet', that all club cricket and football seemed to have ground to a virtual halt, and remained so until 1918/19.

The final reported Cheam Common game occurred on Saturday August 22nd, although the Club was listed as having fixtures against Epsom Rovers and Wimbledon Police for the following Saturday. Despite living close to the Lindsay Road ground, the most successful player that day, Fred Blake, had played most of his cricket for Old Malden and Worcester Park C.C. This match was his first notable appearance for the Commoners, in what appears to have been their last game of cricket for over four years, *"Cheam Common's 97 was a winning score against Banstead Asylum on Saturday, the Banstead players being all out for 82. Blake's 43 was a capital effort for the winners, and he also took six wickets. Cheam Common's second team also won, 67 to 59, against Croydon St. Mary's."*

The final mention of Cheam Common Cricket Club occurred in the 'Surrey Comet' of November 14th, 1914, when those members not on active service were invited to an informal soiree at their old headquarters. It lacked the detail of previous end of season occasions but at least a few of the members were mentioned, if not the overall success rate for that season.

"Cricket Club Concert - The members of the Cheam Common Cricket Club had a "free and easy" concert at the 'North End Inn', on Saturday, and advantage was taken of the occasion to present the prizes won during the past season as follows;- Batting, first eleven, John Stevens; second eleven, James Doel; bowling, first eleven, J. Atkinson; second eleven, J. Rampton; fielding, H. Field."

Countless clubs disappeared for ever in the autumn of 1914 as many of their members died in battle and their grounds became overgrown and neglected. Cheam Common Cricket Club was lucky, however, as many of its committee members and players survived. These men had the ability and desire to resurrect an even better club in place of the old one - a club which proved to be an integral part of the local community. They were the men behind the creation of Worcester Park Athletic Club.

****

Statistical Appendix for Cheam Common

Cheam Common & Cuddington - Results 1891					
Date	Opponents	Venue	Result	Scores	Individual Performances
May 9	Ettrick	Home	Won	99 v 65	C. Dearman 28, W. Hook 20, H. Fairminer 12
May 16	Cheam	Home	Won	47 - 9 v 45	F. Head 16, P. Peters 10* F. Head 6 wkts. (Cheam only 9 men)
June 13	St. Mary - the-Less	Home	Lost	33 v 66	C. Powell 16
June 20	St. John's Wimbledon	Away	Lost	53 v 85	C. Powell 14
July 18	Nassau S.P.	Home	N/A	N/A	
June 27	St. Mary's Newington	Home	Won	69 - 3 v 47	W. Hook 33, R. Legge 12, C. Dearman 10
July 4	Broomwood	Home	Won	77 v 45	C. Dearman 33, W. Hook 12, F. Head 11 J. Cuff 6 wkts, J. Blake 4 wkts
July 11	Cheam	Away	N/A	N/A	
July 25	St, Mark's Kennington	Home	Draw	100 - 4 v 51 - 5	Eus. Pennington 37, W. Hook 31, R. Legge 16* J. Cuff 3 wkts.
Aug 1	Mr. C. Wood's XI	Home	Won	90 v 22	H. Fairminer 25, E. E. Head 24, C. Dearman 11, J. Cuff 10*. F. L. Head 7 wkts, J. Cuff 3 wkts
Aug 3 B.H.	Norwood Wanderers	Home	Lost	56 v 60-5	R. Legge 25, C. N. G. Dearman 14 T. Skilton 3wkts, W. Hook 1wkt, F. Head 1 wkt
Aug 8	Ettrick	Home	N/A	N/A	
Aug 22	St. Mary's Newington	Home	Won	73 - 6 v 54	R. Legge 21, C. Dearman 20, C. Powell 12 J. Blake 4 wkts, J. Cuff 2 wkts
Aug 29	Epsom Police	Away	N/A	N/A	
Sept 5	St. Mary's- the-Less	Home	Lost	61 v 65-4	C. Dearman 14, Eus. Pennington 14*
Sept 12	Epsom Police	Home	Won	46 v 31	R. Legge 12, A. Ray 10, J. Blake 8* W. Cole 4 wkts, J. Blake 3 wkts
Sept 19	Broomwood	Home	N/A	N/A	
Sept 26	Garton	Home	Won	51-4 v 36	H. Fairminer 26, W. Hook 10 J. Cuff 5 wkts, J. Blake 5 wkts

Cheam Common & Cuddington C.C. Averages 1891					
Matches played 20; won 14; lost 5; drawn 1.					
Name	Inns	N.O.	Most	Runs	Average
C. N. G. Dearman	21	2	42*	268	14.2
R. Legge	14	1	25	132	10.2
E. E. Head	6	0	24	58	9.4
C. Powell	14	4	16	94	9.4
H. Fairminer	17	2	26	129	8.9
Eust. Pennington	11	3	37	67	8.3
W. Hook	21	0	33	161	7.14
J. Cuff	17	3	18	88	6.4
G. Cooper	14	2	25	66	5.6
P. Peters	8	2	10*	30	5
F. L. Head	9	0	16	36	4
Other members:- T. Skilton 3.4; W. Hammond 3.3; E. Pennington 1.3.					

Cheam Common & Cuddington C.C. Bowling Averages 1891					
	Overs	Mdns	Runs	Wkts	Average
F. L. Head	108.3	31	171	37	4.23
J. Cuff	177.2	51	321	67	4.53
J. Blake	58.2	12	112	21	5.7
H. Fairminer	81.3	7	197	23	8.13

By the following season Francis Lane Head, and his brothers Ernest and Frederick, were all turning out for Merton on a regular basis. Francis rarely appeared to bowl for Merton and seemed to concentrate more upon his batting. By 1898 Francis and Frederick had moved on to play for Hampton Wick. John Blake also deserted the Cheam Common ranks in 1892 when he joined the newly formed Malden & Worcester Park C.C.

Cheam Common & Cuddington - Results 1908					
Date	Opponents	Venue	Result	Scores	Individual Performances
May 23	Cowley	Home	Lost	33 v 80	W. Oakes 10 H. Gilbert 5 wkts, G. Healey 4 wkts
May 30	West Streatham Institute	Away	Won	48 v 43	G. Healey 10, G. W. Perkins 10 H. Gilbert 4 wkts, B. Strand 2wkts, G. Healey 2 wkts
June 6	Walton	Home	Lost	34 v 44	H. Gilbert 5 wkts, F. G. Williams 3 wkts
June 13	Grosvenor	Home	Won	65 v 43	H. Gilbert 32, J. Cleary 13 H. Gilbert 5 wkts, G. W. Perkins 2 wkts
June 20	Duchy	Home	Lost	25 v 179-7	F. G. Williams 11 & 2 wkts, B. Strand 2 wkts, H. Gilbert 2 wkts
June 27	Beulah	Home	Lost	27 v 99	H. Gilbert 4 wkts, J. Cleary 3 wkts
July 4	Walton	Away	Draw	53-4 v 142-9	B. Strand 28, F.W. Drew 15* F. G. Williams 4 wkts, F. W. Drew 2 wkts
July 11	Grosvenor	Home	Won	96 v 71	B. Strand 41, H. Gilbert 33 H. Gilbert 5 wkts, B. Strand 3 wkts
Aug 3 B.H.	Fulham Club & Institute	Home	Lost	87 v 128	F. G. Williams 37, D. Norton 20, J. Cleary 9 B. Strand 4 wkts, F. G. Williams 3 wkts
Aug 8	Bovill	Home	Won	126-4 V 29	F. G. Williams 52*, P. Burchell 32*, H. Gilbert 21, Dr. Montgomery 13 B. Strand 7 wkts, H. Gilbert 3 wkts
Aug 15	Kingston Brewery	Home	Draw	130-8 v 70-4	A. C. Buck 52, A. Duck 25*, C. H. Banks 11, A. Bristowe 10. A. C. Buck 3 wkts

'Surrey Comet'
July 4th, 1908.

Cheam Common First XI 1908					
Played 23, Won 9, Lost 8, Drawn 4					
	Inns.	N.O.	Runs	Total	Aver.
F. W. Drew	9	2	259	62*	37.2
F. G. Williams	18	1	239	52*	12.9
B. Strand	13	0	135	41	10.4
P. Burchell	7	1	49	32*	8.2
P. Peters	7	2	36	15	7.2
H. T. Gilbert	17	1	111	33	6.9
J. Cleary	16	4	73	15*	6.0
G. Healey	12	0	66	19	5.5
G. W. Perkins	11	0	44	11	4
J. E. Sawyer	13	1	47	15	3.9
C. Crowther	9	0	32	15	3.5
W. S. Norton	13	1	35	20	2.9
W. Oakes	9	1	21	10	2.6
BOWLING					
	Overs	Mdns.	Runs	Wkts	Aver
H. T. Gilbert	164.1	37	313	57	5.5
B. Strand	126.1	23	273	45	6
P. Burchell	20	3	52	8	6.5
F. G. Williams	92.2	9	287	34	8.4
G. Healey	50.3	9	136	16	8.5
F. W. Drew	32.4	4	74	8	9.2
G. W. Perkins	38.5	2	133	11	12.0
J. Cleary	41	3	145	9	15

'Surrey Comet'
February 27th, 1908.

CHEAM COMMON CRICKET CLUB.—The members of this club are already eagerly awaiting the opening of the season. Further improvements to the ground have been carried out during the winter, which should greatly improve the facilities for practice.

					Cheam Common - Results 1909

Date	Opponents	Venue	Result	Scores	Individual Performances
May 1	Malden Wanderers	Home	Lost	54 v 91-6	F. W. Drew 12, J. Sawyer 9 H. Gilbert 3 wkts
June 5	West Streatham Institute	Home	Won	30 v 26	J. Sawyer 11 L. S. Hudson 4 wkts, H. Perkins 4 wkts
June 19	Wesley O.B's	Home	Lost	82 v 98-6	H. Gilbert 20, J. Cleary 12, A. Lock 11, W. W. Champness 11. L. S. Hudson 2 wkts, J. Cleary 2 wkts
July 3	Beulah II's	Home	Lost	27 v 82	H. Gilbert 3 wkts, Perkins 3 wkts, J. Cleary 2 wkts
July 31	F. W. Drew's XI	Home	Lost	45 v 188-9	J. E. Sawyer 15 L. S. Hudson 4 wkts, H. Gilbert 3 wkts
Aug 7	Wandsworth-Melville	Away	Won	95 v 48	L. S. Hudson 27*, H. Gilbert 17, H. Watts 11, J. E. Sawyer†11 H. Watts 5 wkts, H. Gilbert 3 wkts
Aug 14	Beulah III's	Home	Lost	62 v 98	J. E. Sawyer 17. H. Gilbert 4 wkts, L. S. Hudson 4 wkts, W. W. Champness 2 wkts
Sept 18	Mr. Armitage's XI	Home	Won	N/A	Tea provided by Mrs. Noakes at the Huntsman's Hall. It was followed by a smoking concert.

'Surrey Comet'
August 7th, 1909

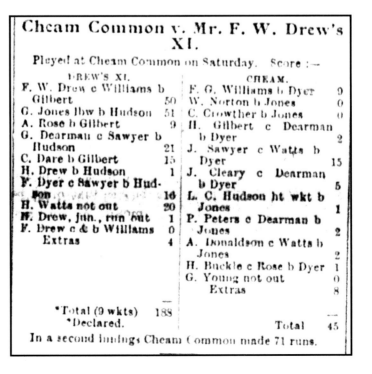

Cheam Common v. Mr. F. W. Drew's XI.

Played at Cheam Common on Saturday. Score :—

DREW'S XI.

F. W. Drew c Williams b Gilbert ... 50
G. Jones lbw b Hudson ... 51
A. Rose b Gilbert ... 9
G. Dearman c Sawyer b Hudson ... 21
C. Dare b Gilbert ... 15
H. Drew b Hudson ... 1
F. Dyer c Sawyer b Hudson ... 16
H. Watts not out ... 20
W. Drew, jun., run out ... 1
F. Drew c & b Williams ... 0
Extras ... 4

*Total (9 wkts) ... 188
*Declared.

CHEAM.

F. G. Williams b Dyer ... 9
W. Norton b Jones ... 0
C. Crowther b Jones ... 0
H. Gilbert c Dearman b Dyer ... 2
J. Sawyer c Watts b Dyer ... 15
J. Cleary c Dearman b Dyer ... 5
L. C. Hudson ht wkt b Jones ... 1
P. Peters c Dearman b Jones ... 2
A. Donaldson c Watts b Jones ... 2
H. Buckle c Rose b Dyer ... 1
G. Young not out ... 0
Extras ... 8

Total ... 45

In a second innings Cheam Common made 71 runs.

268

Cheam Common C.C. First XI 1909					
	Inns	N.O.	Runs	Highest	Aver
W. W. Champness	13	1	150	35	12.5
F. G. Williams	21	0	230	36	11.0
J. Cleary	23	0	191	28	8.3
F. W. Drew	13	0	91	20	7.0
H. Gilbert	21	0	135	26	6.4
J. E. Sawyer	23	1	133	17	6.0
L. S. Hudson	19	1	102	27	5.7
A. Lock	10	1	40	11	4.4
G. Perkins	12	1	46	14	4.2
C. Crowther	10	1	32	8	3.6
W. Norton	18	0	58	10	3.2
P. Peters	14	1	22	5	1.7
Bowling					
	Overs	Mdns.	Runs	Wkts.	Aver.
G. Perkins	76.3	17	162	32	5.0
J. Cleary	46.1	4	110	13	8.5
L. S. Hudson	126.3	13	397	42	9.5
H. Gilbert	206.5	50	450	44	10.2
W. W. Champness	31.1	6	95	9	10.6
F. G. Williams	53.5	7	204	16	12.8
A. Lock	23.4	4	65	5	15

'Croydon Chronicle'
August 21st, 1909

CHEAM COMMON v. BEULAH III.

Played at Worcester Park on Saturday and resulted in a win for Beulah's third string by 36 runs. Cheam Common, 62 (Sawyer 17, extras 12); Beulah III., 98 (L. Oatway 23, W. E. Ollis 19, S. Pearce 14, extras 18). For the winners R. J. Walder captured seven wickets cheaply.

Date	Opponents	Venue	Result	Scores	Individual Performances
May 14	St. Michael's Institute	Home	Lost	90 v 95-8	R. Ashley 26, Dr. Smith 20, H. Plaw 14, L. S. Hudson 13, G. W. Perkins 10 H. Watts 5 wkts, G. W. Perkins 2 wkts
May 16	Cowley	Home	Won	N/A/	Won Bank Holiday game by 2 runs
May 21	Belmont II's	Away	Won	161-8 v 54	G. W. Perkins 50, H. Plaw 35, F. G. Williams 34, H. Watts 18* and 6 wkts. L. S. Hudson 4 wkts
June 4	Grosvenor	Home	Won	126-6 v 22	F. W. Drew 64, F. G. Williams 20, W. W. Champness 13 H. Watts 6 wkts, L. S. Hudson 4 wkts
June 11	Tadworth	Home	Won	61 v 48	W. W. Champness 23 ("Difficult wicket") H. Watts 5 for 13, L. S. Hudson 4 wkts
June 18	Streatham Institute	Away	Lost	29 v 108	H. Watts 4 wkts, F. G. Williams 4 wkts
July 9	Coventry Park (2 men short)	Home	Lost	57 v 77	H. Watts 17, H. Plaw 13, C. Crowther 9 F. G. Williams 4 wkts, H. Watts 3 wkts
July 16	Walton-on Hill	Away	Lost	44 v 66	H. Watts 14 & 4 wkts. G. W. Perkins 3 wkts, H. Plaw 2 wkts
July 23	Clapham Villas	Home	Won	44 v 23	W. W. Champness 16 H. Watts 7 wkts, W. W. Champness 3 wkts
Aug 1 B.H.	Grosvenor	Home	Won	118 & 63-7 v 105 + 62	L. S. Hudson† 37 + 18, F. W. Drew 24 +18* H. Plaw 5 wkts, H. Watts 2 + 5 wkts, F. G. Williams 2 + 0 wkts, J. Cleary 0 + 4 wkts
Aug 13	Tadworth	Away	Won	67 v 61	H. Watts 23, J. E. Sawyer 14* H. Watts 4 wkts, G. Perkins 4 wkts
Aug 20	Beulah II's	Home	Won	109 v 36	L. S. Hudson 41, J. Cleary 17, H. Watts 17 J. Cleary 5 for 6, H. Watts 3 wkts
Aug 27	Grosvenor	Home	Draw	126-5 v 95-8	F. W. Drew 77*, J. Cleary 16, R. Ashley 12 H. Plaw 5 wkts, G. Perkins 2 wkts
Sept 3	Cowley	Home	Won	88 v 58	F. W. Drew 30, J. E. Sawyer† 17, H. Plaw 11 H. Watts 5 wkts, G. W. Perkins 3 wkts
Sept 10	Tadworth	Away	Lost	20 v 61	G. W. Perkins 4 wkts. H. Watts 2 wkts F. G. Williams 2 wkts. R. Ashley 2 wkts
Sept 24	Stamford Green	Home	Won	50 v 28	J. Atkinson 11, H. Plaw 10 J. Atkinson 5 for 9, Dr. W. C. Smith 5 wkts

Cheam Common - Results 1910

Cheam Common C.C. First XI 1910

Played 18, Won 11, Lost 6, Drawn 1.

	Inns	N.O.	Highest	Runs	Aver
F. W. Drew	10	2	77	240	30.00
W. W. Champness	11	0	28	133	12.09
R. Ashley	12	0	43	120	10.00
L. S. Hudson	17	1	41	153	9.56
H. Plaw	18	2	35*	130	8.12
H. Watts	18	1	23	135	7.94
G. W. Perkins	12	1	50	76	6.91
F. G. Williams	16	1	34	89	5.93
J. Cleary	16	2	17	73	5.21
J. E. Sawyer	17	3	17*	64	4.57
P. Peters	11	2	7*	33	3.67
D. Foster	7	1	9*	12	2.00
W. S. Norton	12	2	4	18	1.8
C. Crowther	6	0	9	10	1.66

The following also batted: F. Rickard 1-7-1-4-1, E. Armitage 0-0*, J. Fox 1-4, H. Buckle 0-1-0-1, A. Donaldson 0-2-3*, C. McKechnie 5*-0, A. Lock 6-0, Dr. W. C. Smith 8-20-8, J. Atkinson 11.

Bowling

	Overs	Mdns.	Runs	Wkts	Aver.
H. Watts	195	52	306	75	4.08
J. Cleary	22	2	65	13	5.00
L. S. Hudson	72.2	8	149	25	5.96
G. W. Perkins	58.3	9	142	18	7.88
H. Plaw	45	6	148	16	9.25
F. G. Williams	37.2	2	138	14	9.57
W. W. Champness	38	5	90	8	11.25

The following also bowled: Dr. W. C. Smith 14-1-42-5, R. Ashley 6.1-0-25-3, A. Lock 6-1-27-0, J. Sawyer 6-0-15-0, F. W. Drew 2-0-7-0. J. Atkinson 5 for 9.

Cheam Common - Results 1911					
Date	Opponents	Venue	Result	Scores	Individual Performances
May 6	Walton-Hill	Away	Won	68 v 25	H. Plaw 15, C. Dearman 13, J. Sawyer 10 H. Watts 7 wkts
May 13	Stamford Green	Home	Lost	110 v 121	G. Welch 25, W. W. Champness 18, E. Shrubb 13, C. Dearman 13, H. Watts 10 & 4 wkts, G. Percival 3 wkts, H. Gilbert 2 wkts
May 20	Hook & S'boro	Away	Draw	117-7 v 113-7	W. W. Champness 35, R. Ashley 18, L. S. Hudson† 16, G. Perkins 16. W. Dyer 2 wkts
June 24	Cheam Village	Away	Won	89 v 34	H. Watts 32, F. W. Drew 18 H. Watts 6 wkts, W. Dyer 3 wkts
July 1	Mitcham	Home	Won	130-8 v 98	R. Ashley 28, F. Williams 28*, J. Atkinson 17, F. W. Drew 12, L. S. Hudson 12, W. W. Champness 10 H. Watts 3 wkts, W. Dyer 3 wkts, J. Atkinson 3 wkts
July 8	St. Michael's Institute	Away	Draw	92 - 9 v 114	W. W. Champness 18, H. Watts 16*, F. W. Drew 10 H. Watts 4 wkts, W. Dyer 2 wkts, L. S. Hudson 2 wkts
July 15	Tadworth	Away	Won	158-7 v 41	H. Watts 48, H. Gilbert 35, C. Dearman 35, G. Welsh 15, G. Perkins 14 H. Watts 5 wkts, J. Atkinson 5 wkts
July 22	Belmont	Home	Won	115-9 v 61	F. W. Drew 40, L. S. Hudson 30, F. Williams 22* W. Dyer 11 & 7 for 27, H. Watts 3 wkts.
Aug 5	Manor Asylum	Away	Won	125 v 78	R. Ashley 42, F. Williams 19, F. Drew 12, W. W. Champness 10, C. Dearman 10 W. Dyer 5wkts, H. Watts 3 wkts, F. Dyer 2 wkts
Aug 7 B.H.	Westbourne Park Inst.	Home	won	140 + 70-6 v 89 + 116	W. W. Champness 66, F. Williams 20, E. Shrubb 18 H. Watts 5 wkts, F. Williams 2 wkts C. Dearman 26*, F. W. Drew 18, F. Williams 12* H. Watts 3 wkts, W. Dyer 3 wkts, 3 run out
Aug 12	Walton Hill	Home	Lost	50 v 73	Last man, W. Dyer 11 runs H. Watts 6 wkts, H. Gilbert 2 wkts
Aug 19	W Streatham Institute	Home	Won	91 v 36	E. Shrubb 27, H. Plaw 21*, F. W. Drew 16, W. Dyer 10 runs & 8 for 16 (3 wkts in first over)
Aug 23	Newlands Wednesday	Home	Lost	71 v 101	F. Williams 15, H. Watts 13, L. S. Hudson 11. H. Watts 7 wkts.
Aug 26	Belmont II's	Home	Won	159 v 53	C. Drew 44, L. Hudson 17, H. Watts 14*, F. Williams 10 W. Dyer 6 for 12, F. Williams 4 wkts
Sept 2	Manor Asylum	Away	Lost	70 -115	F. Drew 21, E. Shrubb 12 H. Watts 3 wkts, F. Williams 2 wkts, G. Perkins 2 wkts
Sept 9	Stamford Green	Away	Won	130-9 v 42	F. W. Drew 54, L. S. Hudson 17, H. Watts 14*, F. Williams 10 & 4 wkts. W. Dyer 6 for 12
Sept 16	Hook & S'boro	Home	Won	66 v 43	L. S. Hudson 16, J. Atkinson 13 J. Atkinson 6 for 17, W. Dyer 4 wkts
Sept 23	Mr. J. Elson's XI	Home	Lost	80 v 100 - 8	H. Plaw 14, F. W. Drew 13, C. Dearman 10, R. Ashley 10 J. Atkinson 3 wkts, F. Dyer 3 wkts + 'hat-trick'

Cheam Common C.C. Batting 1911					
	Inns	Not Out	Total Runs	Highest Score	Average
F. W. Drew	19	1	376	82	20.88
W. W. Champness	20	1	339	77	17.84
H. Watts	21	3	254	48	14.13
G. Dearman	21	3	248	33*	13.77
H. Gilbert	9	1	97	35	12.12
L. S. Hudson	17	2	160	30	10.66
F. G. Williams	16	3	133	38*	10.23
R. Ashley	16	0	149	42	9.31
E. Shrubb	17	2	132	22	8.80
H. Plaw	19	3	138	30*	8.62
W. Dyer	16	3	102	19	7.81
G. Welsh	22	2	158	44*	7.80
G. W. Perkins	7	1	46	16*	7.66
J. Atkinson	9	1	49	17	6.12

Also batted:- F. Dyer 9, 1, 24, 9, 3; J. Sawyer 10, 0, 17, 10, 1, 70*; G. Percival 4; P. Peters 1*;
J. Cleary 1*,5,1,0,1; F. Rickard 0*,0; C. Drew; 0,1,1*9,44,2; W. Stent 0,0,7,0,1; H. Field 6;
W. Norton 3; L. Satherley 1,1*; A. Donaldson 0; C. McKecknie 0.

Cheam Common C.C. Bowling 1911					
	Overs	Mdns	Runs	Wkts	Aver
W. Dyer	149.1	20	448	65	6.89
H. Watts	182	28	567	76	7.46
F. Dyer	64	9	197	25	7.88
J. Atkinson	93.3	25	229	28	8.17
F. Williams	27.3	1	119	11	10.81

Also bowled:- H. Gilbert 28.4-6-56-6 ; R. Plaw 28-2-121-9; L. Hudson 7-1-30-2;
R. Shrubb 2-0-13-1; G. Dearman 5-2-14-0; W. W. Champness 2-6-8-0;

G. Percival 13-1-46-4; J. Cleary 5-0-25-2; G. Welch 5-0-40-0; F. Drew 2-0-13-0;

G. Perkins 23.2-2-64-7; L. Satherley 3-0-19-0; R. Ashley 3-1-7-1.

The best batting averages in the 2nd XI were those of W. Stent and H. Field
with an average of 5.

In bowling W. Stent took 26 wickets, H. Gilbert 18 and A. Puttock 13.

Cheam Common - Results 1912					
Date	Opponents	Venue	Result	Scores	Individual Performances
Apr 27	Club Match	Home	Won	110 v 40	N/A First XI v Next Fifteen.
May 4	Walton	Away	Lost		N/A
May 18	Cowley	Home	Won	97 v 24	H. Watts 5 for 6, F. Dyer 5 for 18
May 23	Cheam	Away	Won	72 v 64	N/A
May 25 B. H.	Westbourne Park Inst.	Home	Won	38 v 26 155 v 54	F. Dyer 5 wkts, H. Watts 4 wkts
June 15	Hook & S'bro	Away	Lost	99 v 102	N/A
July 20	Malden Brotherhood	N/A	Won	92 v 48	N/A
Aug 5 B.H.	Grosvenor	Home	Won	48 + 127-3 v 95 + 70-9	H. Watts 18 & 4 wkts, F. Dyer 4 wkts Pearce 30*, H. Watts 27, W. Champness 19, E. Shrubb 7 & 18. H. Watts 5 wkts, L. S. Hudson 4 wkts

'Surrey Comet' August 10th, 1912

In the last innings of the match between Cheam Common and Grosvenor, at Cheam, on Monday, the home side had the very hard task of getting 127 to win with only 55 minutes at their disposal. They set about the Grosvenor bowling in workmanlike fashion, and made the winning hit with the last ball of the match. The last 48 was made in fourteen minutes. The feature of the innings was the superb hitting of Watts and Pearce, who scored 27 and 30 respectively.

'Surrey Comet' May 30th, 1912

CHEAM COMMON v. CHEAM.—On Saturday, at Cheam, the Common C.C. won by eight runs, 72 to 64.—Cheam Common II. lost to Carters' Grasshoppers by nine runs, 54 to 63.

Cheam Common C.C. First XI 1912

Played 19, Won 10, Lost 7, Tied 1, Drawn 1

	Inns	N.O.	Runs	Highest	Aver
Welsh	18	0	247	37	13.7
Watts	18	0	192	28	10.7
Hudson	17	0	180	31	10.6
Williams	10	2	83	17	10.4
Dare	11	0	110	24	10
Champness	10	0	94	28	9.4
Pearce	7	1	55	30*	9.2
Ashley	15	1	126	39*	9
Dearman	12	0	98	24	8.2
Shrubb	15	3	91	18	7.6
Upperton	6	2	25	?	6.3
Percival	7	1	37	?	6.2
F. Dyer	14	3	33	?	3
Plaw	16	4	19	?	1.6

Also Batted: Blake, Cleary, Drew, W. Dyer, Field, Franklin, Gill, Haynes, Head, Miller, Perkins, Peters, Phillips, Satherley, Sawyer, Dr. Smith, Stent, Turner

Bowling

	Overs	Mdns.	Runs	Wkts	Aver.
Watts	190	47	402	84	4.8
Gill	34	6	108	18	6
Plaw	32	5	81	10	8.1
F. Dyer	86	9	278	34	8.2
Percival	30	2	85	10	8.5
Ashley	28	3	101	11	9.2
Williams	17	0	78	6	13
Hudson	29	5	96	6	16

Also Bowled: Haynes, Pearce, Perkins, Satherley and Stent.

Cheam Common C.C. Second XI 1912

	Inns	N.O.	Runs	Highest	Aver
Champness	6	0	71	35	11.8
Pearce	7	0	74	40	10.6
Cleary	9	2	59	16	8.4
Stent	13	0	104	24	8
Lee	12	4	44	9*	5.5
Beardmore	13	1	60	20	5
Haynes	11	0	52	18	4.7
Sawyer	7	0	32	17	4.6
Miller	12	0	49	12	4.1
Field	9	0	28	18	3.1
Head	11	0	22	8	2
Peters	9	1	15	5	1.9
Wellerman	7	0	13	5	1.9

Also batted: Crowther, Dare, Donaldson, F. Dyer, Percival, Phillips, Satherley, Shrubb, Turner, Welsh, Williams

Bowling

	Overs	Mdns.	Runs	Wkts.	Aver.
Champness	13	2	34	6	5.7
Pearce	46	8	120	17	7.1
Stent	125	26	361	50	7.2
Head	50	9	158	17	9.3
Miller	37	4	127	12	10.6
Haynes	24	3	92	8	11.5

Also bowled: Beardmore, Cleary, F. Dyer, Percival, Satherley, Shrubb, Turner, Wellerman, Williams

Cheam Common - Results 1913					
Date	Opponents	Venue	Result	Scores	Individual Performances
June 14	Wandsworth Wesleyan	Home	Won	95 v 38	2nd XI. Barnard 16, Sawyer 15, Shrubb 12 W. Dyer 8 wkts, T. Dyer 2 wkts
Aug 2	St. Barnabus Epsom	Home	Drawn	64 - 4 v 146 - 9	N.A.
Aug 4 B.H.	Grafton	Home	Won	238 v 59 + 79	Gill 39, Welch 36, Champness 28, Evans 26, Ashley 19, Williams 14, Percival 14 Percival 7 for 21, Gill 3 wkts Evans 3 wkts, Gill 3 wkts, Evans 2 wkts
Aug 9	Walton-Hill	Home	Won	115 v 61	H. Watts and W. Dyer bowled well. Percival's excellent catching at slip.
Aug 9	St. Andrew's Earlsfield	Away	Won	86 v 79	2nd XI. Dearman 22, Plaw 16, Champness 11 F. Dyer 9 for 37
Sept 20	Banstead II's	Home	Draw	111 - 4 v 39 -6	F. Drew 78*

'Surrey Comet'
August 9th, 1913

Cheam Common made a club record on Monday by scoring 238 runs against Grafton. The last-named were rather feeble opponents, two innings only producing 138 runs. In Grafton's first innings Percival took seven wickets for 21 runs. On Saturday Cheam's match against Epsom St. Barnabas was drawn, the Epsom team declaring at 146 for nine and getting four Cheam wickets for 64.

'Surrey Comet'
September 27th, 1913

In Cheam Common's last match of the season, against Banstead II., last Saturday, chief honours went to F. Drew, who hit a brilliant 78 not out, out of the total score of 111, for four wickets.

This is the season's highest individual score for the club, and this distinction is a fitting ending to all Drew's fine performances for Ewell this season. Banstead made the poor reply of 39 for six wickets, and Cheam Common had to be content with a draw, very much in their favour.

Both Frank W. Drew and J. Atkinson seemed to have transferred their primary allegiances to Ewell C.C. by 1913. F.W. Drew was still living at 2, The Woodlands in Cheam. The property was owned by one of the original members of C.C.C.C., Eustace Pennington.

Cheam Common First XI 1913					
Played 20, Won 10, Lost 5, Drawn 5					
	Inns.	N. O.	Runs	H. S.	Aver.
E. R. Ashley	11	1	225	50	22.5
L. S. Hudson	17	2	252	37	16.8
G. Welsh	17	0	251	60	14.8
O. C. Foden	15	1	206	50	14.7
F. G. Williams	16	3	147	29*	11.3
J. Doel	8	2	57	22	9.5
W. Dyer	14	2	79	18	8.8
H. Watts	11	1	88	57	8.8
E. Shrubb	15	1	115	32	8.2
F. H. Cornell	14	4	77	20*	7.7
G. Percival	12	0	66	24	5.5
H. Plaw	10	2	17	8	2.1
Also batted - Barnard, Blake, Champness, Dearman, C. Drew, F. Drew, F. Dyer, Evans, Gill, Marsh, Perkins, Peters, Phillips, Satherley and Dr. Smith					

Cheam Common C.C. Bowling Averages 1913					
	Overs	Mdns	Wkts	Runs	Aver
H. Watts	137	25	52	375	7.2
W. Dyer	120	26	49	379	7.7
G. Percival	86	25	28	224	8.0
F. G. Williams	37	6	10	144	14.4
H. Plaw	23	3	6	106	17.7
Also bowled - Ashley, Blake, Champness, Cornell, Doel, F. Dyer, Evans, Foden, Gill, Hudson, Perkins and Satherley.					

'Surrey Comet'
August 16th, 1913

Cheam Common's second team had a very interesting finish with Earlsfield St. Andrew's, the Cheam team winning by seven runs, 86 to 79. Dearman (22), Plaw (16), and Champness (11) were the principal scorers for the winners, and F. Dyer proved to be in wonderful form with the ball, taking nine wickets for 37.

Cheam Common - Results 1914					
Date	Opponents	Venue	Result	Scores	Individual Performances
May 2	Benhilton II's	Home	Won	161 - 7 v 23 + 56	2nd XI. P. W. Rampton 41*, C. Dare 33, E. Shrubb 33, J. W. Argyles 22, W. E. Field 19
May 16	Clapham St. John's	Away	Won	112 v 83	J. Stevens 49, O. C. Foden 22
June 1 B. H.	Cobham	Away	Won	98 v 29 + 50	
June 1 B. H.	Battersea Imperial	Home	Won	122 + 127 v 87 + 73	2nd XI
June 6	Baroda	Home	Lost	66 v 107	Foden 37. Champness 4 wkts
June 6	St. Cuthbert's	Away	Won	111 v 94	2nd XI. Shrubb 48, Styles 27. Shrubb 4 wkts
June 13	Effingham	Away	Won	128 - 7 v 31	Rampton 7 wkts. Williams 3 wkts
June 13	Wimbledon Primitive M's	Home	Lost	57 v 63	2nd XI
July 1	Ashtead	??	Draw	250 - 7 v 123 - 7	Welsh 88
July 4	Hook	??	Won	141 v 100	N/A
Aug 22	Banstead Asylum	Home	Won	97 v 82	F. Blake 43 and 6 wkts
Aug 22	Croydon St. Mary's	Away	Won	67 v 59	2nd XI

'Surrey Comet'
June 6th, 1914

CHEAM COMMON C.C. VICTORIES. — Two matches were played by the Cheam Common C.C. on Whit Monday. The first eleven met Cobham, at Cobham, and made a single innings score of 98, against 29 and 50. Hampton, for the visitors, scored 43 runs and took four wickets in four consecutive balls. Playing at home on Whit Monday against Battersea Imperial, the second eleven scored 122 and 127, against their opponents' 87 and 73.

'Surrey Comet'
August 29th, 1914

Cheam Common's 97 was a winning score against Banstead Asylum on Saturday, the Banstead players being all out for 82. Blake's 43 was a capital effort for the winners, and he also took six wickets. Cheam Common's second team also won, 67 to 59, against Croydon St. Mary's.

World War I and the Formation of W.P.A.C.

It is strange to think that the events which happened on June 28th, 1914, in the Bosnian capital of Sarajevo, when Gavrilo Princip assassinated the Archduke Franz Ferdinand and his wife Sophie, led not only to a World War but also indirectly to the formation of Worcester Park Athletic Club.

Although First Class Football continued during the 1914-1915 season, and Cricket was played throughout the war in certain Northern leagues, such as the Lancashire League, in the Cheam Common and Worcester Park area all organised sport ground to a complete halt in the autumn of 1914, because so many of the players had volunteered for active duty. The final competitive game that was played locally, that I discovered, occurred on October 10th, 1914, when *"Worcester Park F.C. will play Kingston Minerva F.C. on the ground of the first-named, all proceeds to be given to the War Fund."*

In total 34 members of Cheam Common C.C., many of whom were also members of W.P.F.C., were recorded as taking part in the conflict, whilst several others were engaged in activities which supported the war effort, such as the "Athletes' Volunteer Force". This company was formed primarily by members of the Cricket Club who were either too old to enlist or were in reserved occupations, and was run entirely on militaristic lines. The following extract from the 'Surrey Comet' of November 8th, 1914, makes the organisation sound like a slightly younger version of the Home Guard: *"Last week circulars were issued throughout the district with the object of calling the attention of men to the proposal to form a company of Athletes' Volunteer Force, and asking for names to be enrolled. The result was that by Saturday last, 60 names had been handed in.*

Encouraged by this excellent response, a meeting was held at the Café Royal on Wednesday evening when there was a crowded attendance, Mr. O. C. Foden presided. A roll-call of men enlisted having been taken, Mr. F. W. Drew, the Secretary, explained the objects of the movement, and read a letter from the War Office expressing approval of the movement. The conditions of regulating enrolment were outlined, and these showed that men over the age of 18 who were ineligible to join any branch of his Majesty's Forces and who furnished legitimate reasons for not doing so, could become members."

Among the members of the local sporting fraternity, who were listed as serving on the committee of the Volunteer Force were **Robert Blake Yardley**[1] (b. 1858), Messrs. Hudson, Welsh and Perkins, Dr. Chearnley Smith, F. W. Drew and Sergeant **Philip Burchell**[2] (b. 1878). The Captain of the organisation, which had its headquarters at the 'North End Tavern' was the First XI skipper of Cheam Common

C.C., Oliver Foden, whilst Mr. W. R. George was the range officer. The paper noted that whilst many of the rifles had to be borrowed, the men at least had the privilege of practising at the range of the Wimbledon shooting ground every Sunday morning, as the local vicar had given the men a blessing to drill on Sunday mornings before church, and in the afternoon. Sadly for the sportsmen amongst the company, however, although some of the drilling took place in Mr. Scott's barn, the majority of it took place upon the cricket field.

Saturday afternoon April 10th, 1915, was a red letter day for the volunteer force when their own miniature rifle range was unveiled in a field owned by Mr. Randall in Lindsay Road. A hut had been built with a removable wall which allowed five men at a time to shoot from a prone position. The troops, watched by a large crowd, had been marched from Balmoral Road to Lindsay Road under the command of Captain Foden to be presented to Capt. L. P. Pennethorne who performed the opening ceremony.

By early 1915 the local Volunteer group had now become D Company (Worcester Park), part of the 11th Battalion (Mitcham) Surrey V.T.C. On Sunday afternoon, June 13th, a large number of people assembled to witness the 11th Battalion march through the district on a 'recruiting day'. The parade assembled in Green Lane and marched along Longfellow Road to Malden Green. Later in the day, led by the Raynes Park Band, they then proceeded to the cricket ground, which had been kindly lent to the Battalion by Mr. W. Blake, where the crowd listened attentively to a series of short speeches. The cricket field had been festively arrayed with colourful bunting and flags provided by Messrs Brock and the local Institute. 'D' Company was under the command of Captain O. C. Foden, that day, who was ably assisted by the President, R. B. Yardley C.C., Platoon-Commander Fish and Sergeant Burchell.

For those who were young enough to enlist, and who weren't in reserved occupations, membership of the local VTC provided an invaluable training experience, as the Company's Secretary, Frank W. Drew noted in a letter to the local paper dated November 24th, 1915: *"Twenty-five members of our unit have left to join the Forces, and most of them have since expressed their gratitude for having been made practically efficient before they left."*

It was rather surprising that, in a war where so many soldiers died, out of the 34 members of the Cricket Club, there were only two acknowledged fatalities, James Doel and Joseph Hopkins, who were both also members of W.P.F.C. James had won the Second XI batting award at Cheam Common in the 1914 season and had also been a medal winner for the football club in 1910, whilst Joseph had been the first Captain of W.P.F.C. in 1900, and later on became the official umpire for the cricket team and a referee for the football club.

James Doel (b. 1891) had been one of at least seven children of William and Rosina Doel, who lived in a three bedroomed house in Longfellow Road. By 1911, however,

James, a gardener by trade, had moved out of the family home and was residing in a four roomed house, 'Thorn Cottage', Cheam Common Rd. with a widow Minnie E. Bamping (b. 1869) and her five children who ranged in age from 5 to 22.

James enlisted in the 2nd (City of London) Battalion (Royal Fusiliers) in 1915 and quickly rose to the rank of sergeant. In January 1917, despite a twenty years' age gap he married Minnie, and was shipped out to France on January 22nd. He died less than four months later at the Second Battle of Bullecourt, on May 14th, one of over 14,000 British and Australian casualties. Minnie was paid a War Gratuity, in November 1919, of £11 10s., and hopefully received a pension.

Sadly a year before James's death, his family had also suffered the loss of his younger brother, **Robert George Albert Doel** (b. 1896), who had enlisted in the Royal West Surrey Regiment in April, 1915, aged just 19. His military records are rather damaged but paint a poignant picture of a rather frail 5ft 5¼" tall youngster who only weighed 100lbs. Just over a year later on July 3rd, 1916, he went missing, presumed dead.

The military records of **Joseph William Hopkins** (b. 1878), a potter by trade, are much more complete, and, in a way, are even more moving. In 1911, he and his family had lived at 2, Briar Cottages, Cheam Common, near Frank Drew. Despite being over 36 years old at the outbreak of war, he enlisted in the 9th Battalion, the East Surrey Regiment on the 5th of November. At first he was appointed to the Railway Companies Surrey National Reserve, but was eventually sent abroad in June 1916. He was posted to the front on 3rd April, 1917, where he probably took part in the Third Battle of Ypres. In the chaos of war, on August 5th, he was posted as being missing, perhaps captured, and possibly a prisoner of war. His wounded body must have been discovered the following day as he was admitted to hospital on the sixth and was recorded as having died of his wounds three days later on the ninth of August at 12.50 pm (Some of the army records are quite detailed and some are occasionally wrong). Joseph had suffered from shrapnel wounds to his lower right leg and his left hand.

Joseph William Hopkin's body was buried in the 'Wood' or 'Forest' cemetery, Menin, whilst his wife, Annie, who by this time was living at 13, York Terrace, Cheam, had to bring up three young children, Gwendolin (b. 1903), James (b. 1907) and Doris (b. 1912) on a war pension of £1 9s. 10d. per week.

One local casualty of the war who was not mentioned by either the cricket club or the football club, was W.P.F.C. 1st XI forward, and committee member, **Thomas Dalton** (b. 1889). Thomas had been a stalwart of the 1910 medal winning team, and had even been the top scorer in a cricket match for Cheam Common C.C. against Beulah in 1905, while he was still only fifteen years old.

Thomas appears to have been an only child who was born in Bermondsey to a father who was a draper's assistant. By 1901, the family were living at St. Martin's Place, 1, Longfellow Road. The 1911 census showed that the family were socially upwardly mobile, as by that time, they had moved to a seven roomed house, 'Montrose' in Moreton Road. Although he was 22 years old by this time, Thomas, however, was still living at home and had a good job in the Civil Service. Two years later, however, his father died, and the following year Thomas enlisted in $1^{st}/5^{th}$ Battalion of the East Surrey Regiment in Wimbledon.

Thomas's military record is very minimalistic but it appears as though he was a lance corporal in the East Surrey Regiment, which was shipped out to the Near East in October, 1914. He eventually died in Turkey on July 1st, 1916, and his name appears on the Cuddington Cemetery War Memorial. There is no record that his widowed mother, who died in 1919, received a pension..

1919 - On January 18th, 1919, the Peace Conference assembled in Paris and whilst the politicians tried to resolve the many problems still facing Europe, in Worcester Park the returning soldiers began to consider more mundane matters such as the resurrection of their sports' clubs.

Cheam Common C.C. was the first local club to spring into action with a short advertisement on the 22nd of March informing the people of Worcester Park and Cheam that a meeting was going to be held at 7.30 that evening at their headquarters, 'The North End Tavern'. The meeting was reported the following week under the heading *'Cheam Common C.C. to Resume Activities after Interval of Four Years'*:

"There was a large attendance of members of Cheam Common Cricket Club, at a general meeting held at Headquarters, 'The North End Tavern', on Saturday evening. Mr. Williams presided, and referred to the fact that no fewer than 34 members of the club had joined his Majesties' Forces since the outbreak of war, a record of which, he thought, any club might be proud. He moved that the gratitude of the club be conveyed to them, and that the names be placed on permanent record in the minute book. This resolution was seconded by Mr. Perkins and carried unanimously.

Referring to Messrs. J. Doel and J. Hopkins, members who had made the supreme sacrifice in the war, Mr. Foden proposed, and Lieut. Burchell seconded, that their names should be noted in the minutes, and that the club's condolences be sent to their respective families. This was carried by a standing vote.

The election of officers led to Mr. G. Welsh being appointed Captain, Mr. Cornell Vice-Captain, Mr. Watts Treasurer and Mr. Plane Secretary. It was decided to ask Sir Roland Blades, M.P. for the Division, to accept the presidency.

It was stated that, owing to the excessively wet weather recently, it had been impossible to get on to the ground to estimate what the requirements would be to bring the pitch to a fit condition. After four years of disuse it was feared the cost of preparation would be heavy.

The Hon. Secretary announced that he had already received several challenges from old opposing clubs."

The only match which appeared in the press for that season was their victory over Weston Green on Saturday, 17th May, when they *"succeeded in defeating them by 57 runs. Drew was the highest scorer for the winners with 42 not out, and F. Holland took seven wickets for 16, T. Dyer three wickets. Scores:-*
Cheam Common: G. Welsh 2, W. Blaber 7, J. Holland 7, F. Holland 4, F. W. Drew 42, F. Cornell 1, H. Watts 4, W. Whittaker 4, T. Dyer 16, A. Styles 0; extras 10 - Total, 100.   Weston Green - Total, 43."

The match report does not indicate where the match was played although I suspect that it was at Weston Green, as the Cheam Common pitch was in such a poor state that apparently no home matches were played there for at least two years after the war. Judging from the fact that all the Cheam Common players were accorded initials I suspect that the report was written by Frank Drew, who had held secretarial posts in the past. It is a shame that only ten of the Cheam side were listed and that the score did not tally. Perhaps the absent player scored the missing three runs.

Although Frederick Blake was not playing, it looks as though three other ex-members of the now defunct Old Malden & Worcester Park team had been successfully integrated into the side: **Thomas Dyer** (b. 1883), **John Holland** (b. 1891) and **Frederick Holland** (b. 1894). The last two were both brothers-in-law of Fred Blake, and all three of them lived in Longfellow Road

At the end of the season, on Thursday October 2nd an emergency meeting was called: *"Mr. F. Drew presided over a meeting of members of the Cheam Common C.C. on Thursday, called for the purpose of discussing the question of a ground. He explained that owing to the present ground being unused since the outbreak of the war, the condition had become so bad that the cost to make it playable and to drain the ground would be very great. It was decide that every effort should be made to obtain a suitable ground."*

Worcester Park F.C. began their activities slightly later in the year in preparation for the 1919-20 season. They did, however, find their circumstances drastically altered after the five year break. When they returned to playing league football in the autumn of 1919, the 1st XI were no longer a First Division side but had been relegated to playing in the Fourth Division, whilst the Reserve XI were reduced to finding friendly fixtures wherever possible, as can be deduced from this following advertisement in the 'Comet' on the 25th of November, 1919: *"Worcester Park F.C. 2nd XI require home and away matches. Average age 16-17, weak.*
Apply F. S. Collett, Lillie Villa, Worcester Park."

The 2nd XI had, however, with the help of the First XI skipper, Clifford Hughes, played at least one match a couple of months earlier as was recorded in the 'Comet' of September 20th, 1919: *"Worcester Park Junior F.C. - Playing the first match of the season at home on Saturday, Worcester Park Juniors drew with Cremyll House, New Malden, a much heavier and older team. The goal scorers for the home side were C. Pease and C. Dare. It was the fine playing of C. Hughes at back and the goalkeeping of T. Phillips which staved off defeat."*

There was, however, a definite attempt to try to return to a feeling of normality, and to resurrect the pre-war social atmosphere of the club. What better way than a 'Football Club Concert'! *"Under the auspices of the Worcester Park F.C. a successful concert was given at the Institute on Saturday evening (November 1st), the hall being crowded. It opened with the chorus 'Here we are again,' by the Worcester Park Concert Party of eight ladies and gentlemen."*

According to the Surrey F.A., Ernie Styles was no longer the Secretary of W.P.F.C. but had been replaced by **Frederick Sydney Collett**[3] (b. 1901) for the 1919-20 season. It was difficult to find much information about Collett apart from the fact that he did score a goal that season for the club and had also played cricket for Cheam Common. When Collett left the area at the end of the season, he was replaced for the 1920-22 seasons by Arthur Hillman, who resided at 131, Longfellow Road.

The club was also recorded as playing at Kingsmead Avenue instead of at Lindsay Road for the 1919-20 season. It could be that, as with Cheam Common Cricket Club, the ground had fallen into a sorry state after five years lack of use. There again, it might have reverted back to being used for agriculture.

What was surprising, however, was that St. Philip's Church was listed, by the Surrey F.A., as being the club's changing room, rather than the Café Royal. The fact that Ernie Styles was a sideman at the church might have been influential in gaining the club access to the Church, as the club's former generous Vice-President, Henry Smith, who had allowed them to use the Café Royal before the war, had sadly died in 1916, and perhaps his widow, Hazel, no longer felt quite as happy in having a group of muddy footballers changing in her tea room.

It might possibly have been divine influence which led to the First XI finishing runners-up in Division IV, that season, and being promoted to Division II for the 1920-21 season. This promotion also saw them move from Kingsmead Avenue to Skinner's Field, changing just across the road at the Huntsman's Hall.

1920 - Cheam Common C.C. The year began with a very interesting letter written to the editor of the 'Comet', on January 24th, from Leonard Hudson, an ex-Captain of the Cricket Club. Under the heading '*Sport in the District - The Difficulty of Finding a Field* *for Play'*, Hudson bemoaned the fact that the returning soldiers, and the youngsters of the area, completely lacked the facilities whereby they might indulge in *'healthy and manly games'*. Whilst expressing his fears for the future of the cricket club as their ground was unusable, he makes the first recorded reference to the fact that some people in Worcester Park had already begun to discuss the possibility of forming a local sporting Athletic Association.

"To The Editor; Sir, To those who have been during the past few years at grips with the enemy on the Continent, and also to those of whom it was not demanded that they should face the enemy at close quarters, but who nevertheless passed through anxious and nerve-racking times in this country, the return of their pre-war pastimes will be as welcome as a 'woodbine' to a sentry on the fire-step. Eagerly is the youth of our land looking forward to opportunities for developing its manhood on the cricket and football fields.

It requires very little imagination, therefore, to understand the disappointment that must be felt by those who are responsible for keeping sport alive in Worcester Park and who, since the Armistice, have been trying hard in face of many difficulties to launch an Athletic Association, to find that they are brought face to face with the hard fact that they cannot secure a field for the purpose. The authorities of the Cheam Common Cricket Club, which has no mean history in the annals of Surrey cricket, have this project in view of forming such an Association, but the sub-committee appointed for the purpose of scouting around for a ground for even cricket alone has had to admit failure, with the result that their 1920 fixtures will have to be played away from home, the same as last year.

There is considerable apprehension felt that this state of things, if it must continue, will almost certainly lead to the disbanding of this old club with the resultant shock to sport in the district.

I feel convinced that the urgent need of a suitable ground only requires ventilation in every possible way and the chief grievance under which we are labouring will speedily be removed.

It is surely a debt which is owing to our boys who have given us victory that every encouragement should be given to them and to the younger generation in their participation in healthy and manly games. Has it been forgotten already that it was a Surrey Battalion that once went 'over the top' with a football at its toes? - Yours faithfully, L. S. Hudson, Hampton Road, Worcester Park."

The movement towards fulfilling the dreams and ideas promulgated by Leonard Hudson, in January, took a giant step forward a couple of months later on Friday night, March 19th, when Cheam Common C.C. held their Annual General Meeting at the local Institute. It was reported the following week in the 'Comet' under the heading 'Worcester Park Athletic Club': the first time that W.P.A.C. had ever been mentioned in the press, and over eighteen months before the club came into existence.

"Cricketers assembled in full strength at the annual meeting of the Cheam Common C.C., which was held at the Malden and Cuddington Institute on Friday last week, under the chairmanship of Mr. O. C. Foden. The meeting was an enthusiastic one, and showed determination to overcome the one great difficulty which was being experienced with regard to the ground. It was decided that the old ground used prior to the war should be rented this year as a practice ground, whilst efforts will be made to secure a more suitable pitch for next year. The financial statement was presented and disclosed the satisfactory balance in hand of £30.

On the retirement of Mr. H. Plaw from the Secretary-ship, a resolution was passed, amid acclamation, according him the sincerest thanks for having so earnestly, and conscientiously, carried out his manifold duties during many years of service. Mr. J. Holland, the late Secretary of the Old Malden and Worcester Park C.C., which has now ceased to exist, was appointed as successor. Mr. O. C. Foden was elected Captain, with Mr. F. Holland as the Vice-Captain, and the following were appointed the committee:- Messrs. G. Welsh, F. Blake, E. Shrubb, C. Hughes and H. Field.

A full discussion took place with reference to the general question of sport in Worcester Park, and the meeting decided to change the name of Cheam Common C.C. to the Worcester Park Athletic Club. This significant change was regarded as the first stage in the realisation of the ideal that all forms of local sport should be catered for by the Athletic Club, whenever the time was ripe for such a step and whenever the difficulties as to the ground were satisfactorily met."

It is interesting to note that half of the eight committee members mentioned, Fred Blake, Clifford Hughes, John Holland and Fred Holland were also playing members of W.P.F.C. and, as such, it is not surprising that the footballers were also thinking along the same line as the cricketers.

W.P.F.C. Shortly thereafter, on Monday evening, May 10th, **1920**, at a General Meeting of the Worcester Park F.C., which was held in St. Philip's Church Room, the assembled members had decided that pending a meeting of the two committees the club should form the football section of the newly formed Athletic Club. (My thanks to Robin Fisher for discovering this snippet in the 'Comet').

The first mention of the Football Club, in 'The Comet', in 1920, was an account of a Whist Drive and Dance that was held at the Institute on Saturday 15th May, with the Club Captain, Clifford Hughes, acting as the M.C., and with Arthur Verrall's daughter, Audrey, on piano. Prizes for the event were donated by Messrs. W. Bemrose, F. S. Collett and E. Hughes, whilst Mr. Chitty was responsible for the refreshments. Before the close Clifford Hughes made an interesting and informative speech in which he thanked, *"the company for the support accorded that evening, and during the past season, said the club was open to both honorary and playing members, and a meeting was to be held shortly for enrolment. Referring to the successful work of the Hon. Sec. throughout the past season, Mr. Hughes said that he felt sure all present would join in wishing Mr. Collett success in his new venture abroad. This sentiment was endorsed by hearty cheers."*

The A.G.M., which was held prior to the new season, on Friday August 13th, 1920, was a more practical and business like meeting. Over 50 members attended the Girl's School that evening and were presided over by Clifford Hughes, who was also elected First XI Captain for that season. The other elected officers were: E. Richards - Vice-Captain: Arthur Hillman - Hon Secretary and Treasurer; and the Committee was made up of Ernie Styles, Fred Blake, E. Bird and Fred Holland.

"The statement of accounts showed a balance in hand of £5 16s., and this was considered exceptionally satisfactory owing to the heavy expenses which have been met. Twenty-six members, both playing and honorary, were elected, and the selection committee were appointed to take office immediately."

The club probably needed a new influx of blood as they intended to turn out two sides in Division 2 and 4 of the Kingston and District League. In addition to those games they had also applied to enter the 'Teck' Charity Cup, the Surrey Junior Cup, the Surrey Charity Cup, and the Minor Cup competitions.

The club was no longer going to play at Kingsmead Avenue but had managed to hire **Skinner's Field**, in Green Lane, from **Thomas Weeding Weeding**[4] (b. 1847). The Recreation Ground Committee of Cheam Council had already been in negotiations with Weeding earlier that year about purchasing a ten acre plot of land from him in Brinkley Road, for £3 per acre, to provide a Recreation Ground and allotments. As an important County Council Official, Landowner and former sportsman, Weeding seemed more than amenable to provide land for recreational purposes rather than just for housing development.

The meeting ended with a vote of thanks to George Noakes, the landlord of the 'Huntsman's Hall', who had agreed to provide a dressing room for the club. A couple of months prior to this meeting George Noakes had become another casualty of the infamous Cheam Common Hill, an accident blackspot. On May 22nd, the 'Comet' reported: *"As Mr. George Noakes, of the Huntsman's Hall, was riding his cycle down Cheam Common-hill on Wednesday evening the handle-bar became loosened and turned round, causing him to lose control of his machine, and he was thrown to the ground sustaining injuries to his face, hands and arms."*

The first recorded game played at the new venue in Green Lane, was a Surrey Junior Cup game, which kicked off at 2.45p.m. on the 23rd of October, 1920, against Wimbledon St. Barnabus. They won that game 7-1: the team being:- J. Phillips, Roper, J. Holland, Pritchard, Herbert, F. Holland, C. Taylor, F. Blake, Watts and F. Richards.

"Worcester Park, at home in the first round, gave Wimbledon St. Barnabas a severe beating, netting seven times without response. As the score indicates, the home forwards were in fine fettle, and none more so than F. Blake, who helped himself to four goals, C. Taylor (2) and Watts obtaining the other points. If the Park can maintain such form they should account for Cremyll House in the first round of the 'Teck' Cup competition to be played at Worcester Park to-day."

It was the start of another highly successful season which saw the First XI finish as runners-up in Division Two of the Kingston and District League. That was quite impressive for a team that had been placed in Division Four the previous year, a place occupied for the 1920-21 season by the club's Reserve eleven.

The footballers did, however, have to hire another ground that season at Hooper's Farm whilst apparently work was being carried out on the main pitch at Green Lane. This meant that they started off the following season, as members of W.P.A.C. in a rather perilous financial position. It is no longer clear where Hooper's Farm was, but it was probably near 'The Plough' as a small notice appeared in the 'Comet' of January 1st, 1921, advising spectators not to go to the Green Lane ground as it was under water but to go to the field opposite 'The Plough'. If so, this would probably have been on the ground which became the Columbia Gramophone Company Sports ground in 1929, near the current Columbia Avenue.

To cover the additional costs incurred that season of having to hire additional pitches the Football Club organised several fundraising social events in 1921. The first of these events to be mentioned in the 'Comet' was a concert which was held at the Institute on Monday evening, January 3rd. The event, which attracted a large audience, was an evening of song, dance, prestidigitation and sketches. It appeared to have been a great success, thanks in no small measure to the club's multi-talented musical director, Mr. Fred Blake. *"There were many encores during the evening. The accompaniments were capably shared by Miss A. Verral (who also contributed pianoforte selections) and Miss Haynes."*

1921 Cheam Common C.C. The first meeting of the cricketers was reported in the 'Comet' on March 12th 1921, under the heading *'Worcester Park Athletic Club'* although they had not at that point in time, formally amalgamated with the footballers.

"The annual meeting of the Worcester Park A.C. was held at St. Philip's Church-room, on Wednesday, Mr. W. W. Champness presiding. The balance-sheet for 1920 showed a satisfactory credit balance of £8 0s. 10d. Mr. A. Armitage was elected President, and the Vice-Presidents, with the addition of Mr. W. J. Bridger, were re-elected. Mr. O. C. Foden and Mr. F. Blake were appointed Captain and Vice-Captain respectively of the first cricket eleven, but the selection of similar officials for the second eleven was left to the committee. The following will constitute the committee: Messrs. W. Brewer, C. Hughes, W. Field, G. W. Welsh and E. Styles. It was agreed that the selection committee should consist of the Captains of each eleven, the Secretary and Messrs. F. G. Williams and J. Phillips. Messrs. Burchell and Cornell were appointed auditors. The committee was instructed to proceed forthwith with the amalgamation of the different branches of the club."

The Welfare Committee of the United Services Federation. The committee members responsible for the amalgamation of the cricket and football clubs acted with surprising speed and, within a month, both clubs had agreed to amalgamate and to lease Skinner's Field from Mr. Weeding.

There was, however, one small problem for, despite the fact that both the cricket and football clubs had shown a small profit for the previous year, more funding was required if they were to realise their dream. As a result the committee members decided to approach the United Services Fund, which had been set up in 1919, under Lord Byng, to care for the interests of ex-servicemen and their dependents.

On April 7th, 1921, an extremely important meeting was held by the local Welfare Committee of the United Services Federation, which seemed to have the financial clout and the determination to make things happen on the sporting front. To some extent the U.S.F. could be seen as the catalyst which led to the merger of the football and cricket clubs, although the fact that many of the officers of this organisation were also on the committees of both clubs was clearly an advantage.

Two days later, the 'Surrey Comet' reported on probably the most important meeting in the history of Worcester Park Athletic Club, under the heading *'Ex-Fighting Men and Sport'*: *"A meeting of ex-Service men was held in St. Philip's Girls' School, Worcester Park, on Thursday evening for the purpose of confirming the action of the local Welfare Committee of the United Services Federation in negotiating for a field for use as a sports ground. Mr. A. Armitage presided over a gathering of about 50 men, being supported by Mr. P. Burchell, Chairman of the Welfare Committee, and Mr. W. R. Fairhead, Hon. Secretary.*

Mr. Burchell reported that there were 519 ex-Service men in the district. The ground under consideration, and which the committee had been offered on lease, adjoined Worcester Park railway station. The lease was for seven years, at a rental of £35 per annum. The meeting was asked to confirm the action of the committee and to delegate trustees as the proper authority to obtain the money grant from the United Services Federation and to utilise it in the preparation of the ground.

It being decided to accept the lease on the terms stated, four trustees were elected, viz., Messrs. A. Armitage, R. B. Yardley, P. Burchell and G. W. Young. The sports club to be formed will have the title of the Worcester Park Athletic Club, and the ex-Service men in the existing cricket and football clubs expressed their willingness to amalgamate and to form the nucleus of the new sports club. Tennis and bowls sections are to be formed. For the purpose of organising an athletic meeting to be held later in the year, a committee was elected pro tem. as follows:- Messrs. Welch, Hughes, Styles, Powell, Langley, Foden and Young with Mr. Shrubb as Hon. Secretary."

W. P. A. C. (Cricket Section) While the members waited for the legal documents to be drawn up, and the acquisition of the ground, life carried on as normal. Less than a week after the momentous meeting at the Girls' School, the cricket section organised a dance on Wednesday 13th April at the Institute. The event, which was attended by a large crowd, was arranged by Messrs. C. Hughes (M.C.) and G. Welsh, with Audrey Verrall again on the piano.

Only a handful of match reports for the former Cheam Common C.C., under the guise of 'Worcester Park', appeared in the 'Comet' in **1921**, but it was interesting to note that they did appear to play a fair percentage of these games at home. This was in sharp comparison to the previous two years when all matches had to be played away from home. The lack of a suitable home ground was, after all, one of the club's main reasons for deciding to form the Athletic Club. There had even been talk of the club folding because of the lack of a suitable ground.

The first match played at home, since 1914, was a bit of a mismatch against Cheam II's on May 7th. The team, which was now referred to as 'Worcester Park' in the press was made up of several familiar faces: *"L. Hudson 7, E. Shrubb 15, V. Alton 19, F. Blake 11, C. Hughes 23, O. Foden 10, H. Brewer 31, C. Dare 22, J. Holland 2*, E. Welsh and F. Jeffries did not bat. 8 extras, Total 168 for 8 wickets."*

The Cheam side only made 42, the wickets being taken by Brewer (3), Jeffries (3), Alton (2) & Hughes (1).

Cheam must have realised that the new Worcester Park side was not a team to be taken lightly for, on July 23rd they turned out their First XI for their home fixture versus virtually the same Worcester Park side, but the result was still the same. Cheam batting first scored 97 runs, losing wickets to F. Blake (3), T. Phillips (3), C. Hughes (2) and H. Brewer, whilst the Park easily passed that total, notching up 155 runs, thanks mainly to Fred Blake (54). Clifford Hughes (34) and Edwin Shrubb (24).

The match report in the 'Comet' of May 21st showed that the team was really thriving, as they managed to turn out three sides over the Whitsun weekend. What is more impressive is that they even managed to stage an all-day event for the Whit Monday game, something that we can rarely achieve these days. The end of season A.G.M. mentioned a Pavilion which would have been ideal for helping to stage such an event, especially if a lunch and tea had to be provided.

As two of the games were at home that weekend, it shows that a considerable amount of remedial work must have been done on the ground over the winter, although the scores suggest that the pitches were far from ideal. Perhaps the club was not entirely confident of acquiring a new ground and had decided to retain the Cheam Common ground as back-up in case the new ground failed to materialise.

"Worcester Park Athletic Club played two cricket matches on Saturday, and an all-day match on Whit Monday, winning two out of the three. The team which met Epsom Rovers at Horton, on the first day, proved victorious by 103 runs, the scores being Worcester Park 143, Epsom 40. F. Holland, for the visitors, took six wickets for 15 runs. In the match at home against Havelock Athletic B team, Worcester Park lost by 40 runs, 49 to 89. The visitors to Worcester Park on Whit Monday were the Alanstone C.C., who scored 65 in the first innings and 46 in the second. The totals of Worcester Park were 77 and 66 respectively, the home side thus winning by 32 runs."

The only other match reports appeared in the 'Comet' of June 4th, and recorded a rather impressive First XI performance at Ashtead, plus a Second XI score of over a hundred at Cheam Common: *"Worcester Park Athletic Club - The first cricket eleven played an away match against Ashtead A.C. first eleven on Saturday. The visitors were in excellent form, and after taking the score to 207, declared at the fall of the ninth wicket. C. Dare played a fine innings for Worcester Park, making 75 not out. Ashtead's total was 89 for six wickets. Rain interfered somewhat with the innings. - Worcester Park second eleven were at home on Saturday to Bradbank C.C. second XI, and succeeded in vanquishing the visitors by 116 runs, the scores being:*

Worcester Park 139, Bradbank 23. For the home club, T. Phillips and C. Dare jun., scored 40 each."

W.P.A.C. On Saturday 22nd of October 1921, the 'Comet' broke the momentous news for local sportsmen that, on Tuesday 18th October, Cheam Common Cricket Club and Worcester Park Football Club had formally agreed to merge, under the bold headline *'ATHLETIC CLUB FORMED - Primarily for Ex-Servicemen: Sports Field Secured.':* *"A gratifying culmination of the efforts of the Worcester Park Ex-Servicemen's Welfare Committee was reported at a meeting held on Tuesday evening in St. Philip's Girls School, and presided over by Mr. A. Armitage.*

It was stated by Mr. P. Burchell that arrangements had been made, and terms agreed upon, for securing Skinner's Field, adjoining Worcester Park Station, as a recreation ground for an athletic club for the district. Mr. Burchell explained that with the object of forming such a club, which was essentially for the benefit of ex-Servicemen of the district, the Welfare Committee appointed at a meeting held some time ago, had worked hard to make provision for sport of all kinds. A sum of money had been procured from the United Services Fund which would go towards the cost of laying out the ground etc. The committee had now come to terms with Mr. Weeding, the owner of the field, and had secured possession of it for the next eight years. The meeting that night had been called to hear of the project, and to form the athletic club.

The Chairman said it was gratifying to learn of such satisfactory arrangements, which he hoped might become permanent and not for eight years only, so that the present and future generations in the district might always have a sports field. He moved a resolution that the club be formed, and that it be designated the Worcester Park Athletic Club.

On the suggestion of a member, the words 'founded by ex-Servicemen in 1921' were added, and with this alteration the resolution was carried unanimously.

A set of rules previously drafted, which primarily provided for all ex-Servicemen in the district being members, but permitted others to be elected, was passed, together with rates of subscription.

On the proposition of Mr. Burchell, the members of the existing cricket and football clubs were elected en bloc.

Mr. A. Armitage was appointed President, and the Vice-Presidents elected included Sir G. Rowland Blades M.P., and the Vice-Presidents of the Cricket and Football Clubs.

Other appointments were:- Mr. Burchell, Hon. Treasurer; Mr. Foden, Hon. General Secretary, and Messrs. Hatten and Duncan, Auditors. The committee is to comprise the existing Welfare Committee, viz., Messrs. Burchell, Welsh, Foden, Fairhead, Hughes, Partridge and Bridger with the Captains and Secretaries of the different sports sections.

It was stated that the cricket section hoped to run four teams next summer and that facilities for tennis and bowls would be provided.

Before the meeting closed the Chairman read a letter from the Rev. R. B. Ravenscroft, who, as an ex-Service man, invited the ex-Service men to a special service at St. Philip's Church on the evening of the Sunday before Armistice Day."

W.P.C.C. The A.G.M. of the Cricket Section, which was held on Friday evening the 28th of October, showed the section had had an extremely successful **1921** season both performance wise and financially. In a way, reading between the lines, one gets the feeling that the cricketers felt that they were contributing more than their fair share financially towards the new club. It is interesting to note that they were also handing over their pavilion to the new club, although there is no mention as to whether it was actually physically moved to Skinner's Field.

On November 5th, the 'Comet' reported: *"The Cricket Section - A satisfactory report of the cricket section was submitted at the annual general meeting held in St. Philip's Church-room on Friday last week, Mr. L. S. Hudson presiding.*

Mr. Foden, the Captain, reported that during the past season 22 matches had been played, of which 18 were won, 2 lost and 2 drawn. Mr. F. Blake had been the mainstay in batting and Mr. Brewer in bowling.

The accounts showed a balance in hand of £4 2s. 7d., which was considered gratifying in view of the increased expenses incurred during the season.

Mr. Shrubb, the Secretary, reported that the stock of the section had been valued at about £35, and that with the balance in hand and also the handing over of the Pavilion the section would have contributed no small portion to the new club.

The reports and balance sheet were adopted on the proposition of the Chairman, who commented upon the successful season's work and the good fellowship which had existed, which were good omens for the future.

The rules, as drawn up by a sub-committee, having been approved, Mr. Shrubb expressed regret that he would be unable to continue as Hon. Secretary owing to pressure on his time, but as no nominations for the post were forthcoming, he agreed to continue until the committee appointed a successor.

Mr. J. Phillips and Mr. Griggs were thanked for their services as umpires, and thanks was also tendered to Mr. Watts for the keen interest he had taken in the club for so many years and also for his work as Hon. Treasurer.

The Secretary announced that an Entertainment Committee had been formed, with the object of carrying out social fixtures during the winter months."

Dances and Whist Drives were to become a feature of W.P.A.C. life over the next 20 years as a way of supporting the club, particularly throughout the winter months. In October 1921, Clifford Hughes was appointed the Recreation Secretary, and he certainly hit the ground running. The first recorded event, which was attended by almost a hundred participants, was a whist drive which was held at the local Institute on Thursday evening, October 27th. The event must have been so successful that he organised another whist drive the following week for about seventy players.

At first it seemed as though the two newspaper reports referred to the same event, but although Clifford Hughes was the M. C. for both events, the prize winners were different. In the first whist drive Clifford's brother, Mr. L. Hughes, won the Lady's prize (playing as a lady, which suggests there were fewer ladies than men) whilst in the second drive Miss Holland won that prize. Mr. Cowlard won the men's prize in the first drive, and Mr. Bird won the prize the following week. Miss Chitty provided the refreshments for the first event whilst her father was in charge of catering on the second occasion.

Clifford Hughes (b. 1899) seemed to have been the ideal person to have been elected as the Recreational Secretary, as, apart from being a playing official of both the Football and Cricket clubs, he had also helped to arrange dances and whist drives for both sections. He did not only commit himself to playing cricket and football either. On Wednesday August 31st, 1921, he was recorded in the 'Comet' as playing against the local Worcester Park Ladies Stoolball Club in the final match of the season, when the Ladies were defeated by 39 runs by the Gentlemen.

The local ladies' Stoolball team can be traced back to an article in the 'Comet' of August 17th, 1912, in which, any ladies who might have been interested in joining the club, which had just been formed, were invited to contact Mrs. Shrubb, (the Hon. Sec. of the Worcester Park Stoolball Club), 'Trevar', Lindsay Road. May Shrubb (b. 1885) was the wife of **Edwin Shrubb**[5] (b. 1884), one of the founding fathers of the Athletic Club, who just happened to come from Cowfold in Sussex, a hotbed of stoolball. *"The game is often described in Sussex (where nearly every village has its stoolball club), as the ladies' game of cricket, the rules and method of playing being identical."*

As so many of the men who played against the ladies that day were involved with either the Football or Cricket clubs, it is, in a way, a little surprising that the Athletic Club apparently did not consider creating a Stoolball section to complement the Cricket, Football, Tennis and Bowls sections. They did, after all, shortly thereafter have a quoits section.

For the Ladies, the team was: Miss M. Chitty (capt,), Mrs. Scutts, and Misses K. Phillips, D. Soper, G. Mitchell, E. Chitty, M. Bailey, J. Phillips, G. Roberts, I. Stagg and L. Locke. For the Gentlemen, the team was: A. Chitty (capt.), C. Hughes, W. Bemrose, P. Snook, W. Witts, T. Phillips, F. Williams, L. Hughes, W. Perkins, S. Brown and A. Snook.

In the dance at the Institute, which followed the event, Clifford Hughes was also recorded as having contributed to the music.

W.P.A.C. Executive Committee On October 31ˢᵗ the first ever meeting of the Executive Committee occurred. Their foremost problem was how to transform a badly drained field into a viable sports field. With this aim in mind they formed a powerful Ground Committee with sweeping powers and it was decided to postpone the formation of the bowls and tennis sections until the ground was fit for purpose.

The meeting was reported in the 'Comet' of November 5ᵗʰ under the title of :

'THE ATHLETIC CLUB - Meeting of Executive Committee'

"The first meeting of the Executive Committee of the Club was held on Monday in the church room. Mr. F. G. Williams was elected Chairman for the year. The recommendation from the cricket section that the old ground be retained for next year to cope with the large number of playing members was agreed to.

A Ground Sub-committee, consisting of the Captains of the various sections with Messrs. G. W. Young and F. Blake, was formed to deal with the new ground. This committee was urged to hasten on the preparation of the ground and was given power to act immediately.

The question of a public appeal for funds to drain and re-lay the ground was left to the Chairman, Treasurer and Secretary.

Mr. C. Hughes, Recreation Secretary, reported on the work of his committee and asked for the help of all present towards carrying out the programme of whist drives, dances and socials already arranged.

It was agreed to postpone the question of the formation of tennis and bowls sections until the start had been made on the ground so that prospective members of these sections could see what facilities were to be offered them."

Formal Opening of W.P.A.C. The ground was formally opened on Christmas Eve, Saturday 24th December, 1921, by the Chairman, **Mr. Alfred Armitage**[6] (b. 1867), and was followed by a football match versus Carshalton Athletic. It was reported in the 'Comet' the following week under the heading:

'Worcester Park A.C.'

"This organisation, which is an amalgamation of the sports clubs of the district for the benefit of ex-Servicemen, had its new sports ground formally opened on Saturday afternoon by the President, Mr. A. Armitage. The occasion was marked by the football section meeting Carshalton Athletic in a match and scoring an easy win.

The ground, which is spacious, is conveniently situated, and adjoining Worcester Park railway station, and it is the intention of the committee of management to care for all kinds of sports."

This photograph of the Worcester F.C. team of 1921-22 could possibly have been taken at the opening ceremony of the Athletic Club on Xmas Eve 1921

The named players are: Back Row : **B. Herbert, ? , Ernest Styles**

Centre Row: **Edgar Hayes, Frederick Blake, Clifford Hughes, ? , Wally Harrington**

Front Row: **Charles Taylor, ? , Leslie Carey**

(photo courtesy of David Rymill)

Appendix

Local Figures of Interest in 1921

[1]**Robert Blake Yardley** (b. 1858) had been born, in St. John's Wood, into a wealthy lavender soap and perfume manufacturing family. Following a private education he went to King's College, Cambridge where he obtained his M.A. in 1884. Prior to that he had been admitted to the Inner Temple and had been called to the bar in 1882.

In 1895 he married Margaret Murray Binney, the daughter of Major General William Henry Binney, at Plomesgate in Suffolk. Whilst he had a home in Earls Court, which was more convenient for his work as a barrister, his main home was at 'The Birches', London Road, North Cheam. From 1901 to 1936 he also owned a significant amount of land on the southwest corner of the North Cheam crossroads in the Hemingford Road vicinity, the home of today's 'Yardley Court'. Although he sold much of this land for development, he did give 'Yardley Recreation Ground' to the people in 1929.

Among his many achievements he was a member of the Epsom Rural District Council and served as a member of the Surrey County Council for over twenty years. He was also the Secretary of the Council of the Land Union, Author, President of the Royal Philatelist Society and a Justice of the Peace for Surrey. More importantly he had been a Vice President of Cheam Common Cricket Club and Worcester Park Football Club for many years.

[2]**Philip Burchell** (b. 1878) was one of the most notable characters to appear on the Worcester Park scene with the advent of the War. Philip was the youngest of five children born to a general painter, John Burchell, and his wife, Jane, at Blackmoor, Selbourne, Hampshire. By 1901, he had left the family home and was living in a boarding house in Westminster whilst he was employed as a bank clerk by the Liverpool and Martin's Bank, 43, Charing Cross Road, S.W.1.

By 1905 he was living at 61, Engadine Street, Southfields and on February 18th of that year he married Edith Cowley (b. 1873 in Hackney), at St. Saviour's Church, Hoxton. At some point in the next three years they moved to 2, Ashton Villas, Green Lane, Worcester Park, from where Philip continued to commute upon a daily basis to the bank in Charing Cross.

Although, according to his Army medical records, Philip was quite small in stature, being only 5ft 7ins tall, and weighing only 9 stones, he quickly became a respected pillar of the community. His first mention in the press occurred not on the sport's field, however, but in an article in the 'Comet', entitled 'Presentation by Police', in January 1908, for his bravery in helping a local policeman to arrest a violent burglar.

"An indication of the readiness of the police to recognise any service rendered to them by a civilian was given on Wednesday evening at Malden police-station, when

Mr. Philip Burchell, of Green Lane, Cheam, was made the recipient of a handsome walking stick, suitably inscribed. The presentation, which had been subscribed for by the whole of the officers and men at Malden, was made in acknowledgement of valuable aid rendered to a constable at Cheam.

The ceremony was performed by Supt. Robinson, of the 'V' Division, who briefly related the circumstances of the case. In Green Lane, Cheam, late on the night of December 22nd, P.C. Ernest Sims caught a man who had been fowl-stealing, and who violently resisted him. Fortunately Mr. Burchell arrived upon the scene, and had it not been for his timely assistance it was probable that the policeman would have been seriously assaulted, as the locality was very quiet at that time of night. In addition Mr. Burchell conveyed the stolen fowls to the police station, a distance of 2½ miles. Supt. Robinson personally thanked him for his act, and added that the present was not of great value, but was offered as a mark of appreciation and of the esteem in which all held him.

In reply, Mr. Burchell stated that he felt it his duty to render assistance under such circumstances, adding that he should value the stick very much.

Hearty cheers were then given for the recipient of the gift and for Supt. Robinson."

In 1915 Philip joined the Royal Garrison Artillery as a sergeant and served primarily on the Western Front. On May 2nd, 1917, he was promoted to the rank of Second Lieutenant and, less than six months later, to that of Lieutenant. His war ended in the 31st Ambulance Train Hospital at Etaples that November when he was admitted with bronchitis and emphysema.

After the War, Philip, as Chairman of the Welfare Committee, was one of the prime organisers of the Athletic Club and was to play an extremely important role in the club's success throughout the Twenties as he became the Hon. Treasurer of the parent body and an enthusiastic committee member of both the Tennis and Bowls' sections.

[3]**Frederick Sydney Collett** (b. 1901) was born to Frederick and Kate Mary Collett, at 49, Elliott Road, Lambeth. His father was listed, in 1901, as being a clerk at a booksellers although by 1926 he had graduated to being a merchant.

Frederick Sydney is a bit of a mystery figure as he does not appear on any of the censuses. When he resigned as the Secretary of the football section he probably went to either Canada or the U.S.A. although he appears on none of the passenger manifest lists in the early 1920s. He did, however, appear on an entry document into the States in 1943 when his occupation was listed as being a British Government Official who worked for the Ministry of War Transport. When he died in 1979 he was living in St. Petersburg, Florida, with his second wife, Edith and son, Derek.

Irene, at 'Trevar', 5, Craven Villas, Cheam Common Road. Two years later they moved to a house which they also named 'Trevar' in Lindsay Road where he lived until his death in 1968.

In December 1915, he left his pregnant wife and three children and joined the King's Royal Rifle Corps (22nd Battalion). Six months later, however, he transferred to the Royal Flying Corps, which became the R.A.F. on April 1st 1918. By that time Edwin was serving as a wireless operator in Egypt. His medical records shows that at one point he was hospitalised with P.N.Y.D. on H.M.S. 'Assaye' which was anchored off Alexandria. He was finally demobbed in 1920, and then seems to have devoted much of his energy into helping with the organisation of an Athletic Club for ex-servicemen in Worcester Park.

[6]**Alfred Armitage,** who became the first President of W.P.A.C. in 1921, came from the opposite end of the social spectrum to the majority of Athletic Club members, as his family had been extremely successful woollen merchants in Yorkshire in the late Middle Ages. By the mid-eighteenth century the family had acquired a large estate at Farnley, which is just south of Leeds. The family's fortune was further enhanced in the Industrial Revolution when they exploited the coal and iron found upon the estate, and formed the Farnley Iron Works.

Alfred was born at 'Farnley Hall', on March 17th 1867, the second of four sons of William James Armitage, the Managing Director of the Farnley Iron Company. On his mother's side, Alfred was descended from the Nicholson family of 'Roundhay Mansion', the birthplace of both his mother, Emily, and his uncle, General Sir William Nicholson, later Baron Nicholson.

All four of the Armitage boys were educated firstly at Westminster School in Central London and then at Cambridge University in the middle to late 1880s. Alfred went to Clare College, Cambridge, in 1885, where he obtained a B.A. in 1888, and was ordained as a deacon in 1890.

His brother Philip, who attended Trinity College in 1889, was also ordained as a priest (in 1894), before becoming a missionary in India for several years, whilst another brother, William, studied Law at Emmanuel College and served with distinction as a Major in the 4th Battalion, the York and Lancaster Regiment during the Great War. Alfred's eldest brother, Robert, was the most famous of the siblings for, after studying law at Trinity College, he went on to become a barrister and J.P. in Leeds, besides being the Chairman and Managing Director of Brown and Bayley's Steel Works. In 1905 he became the Lord Mayor of Leeds, whilst in 1906 he was elected as a Liberal M.P. for Leeds Central, a position which he held for sixteen years.

Alfred's first posting as a priest was to a parish in St. Albans in 1891, before becoming the chaplain of West Ham from 1891 to 1897. From 1899 he spent a short time as a member of the Commission in Sierra Leone. By 1902, however, he had returned to England and appeared, in the press, as a parish priest in Guildford. It seems as though it was about this time that he became disenchanted with his religious vocation, for in 1903 he availed himself of the Clerical Disabilities Act and renounced his calling as a priest.

By 1904, therefore, Alfred had made a complete career switch by becoming a Company Director of Brown and Bayley's steelworks, which took over the Farnley Iron Works, alongside his brothers, Robert and the Rev. Philip Armitage.

As he worked in the London Office he settled with his family in Cuddington, and became a Justice of the Peace for Surrey in about 1905, before becoming a J.P. for Somerset, a few years later. By 1909 he had also become the President of the Somerset Automobile Club and a Vice-President of the R.A.C. The Somerset connection is a little strange as the 1911 census showed that Alfred was living at 'Worcester Court', a nineteen roomed house in The Avenue, Cuddington, with his wife, Mary Frances, daughters Emily Frances and Mary Helen, plus six servants, which included a cook, a chauffeur, a parlour maid and a kitchen maid.

This privileged background, however, did not protect Alfred from falling foul of the law. In a case, which today, makes one smile with disbelief, when he was taken to court in Sussex, and fined, for speeding. His misdemeanour which appeared in the 'West Sussex County Times' of 13th December, 1913, probably escaped attention in Worcester Park at the time, but 100 years later one can freely access it on the internet.

"Alfred Armitage, The Court, Worcester Park, Surrey, was summoned for exceeding the speed limit at Cowfold on November 23rd. - P.C. Lambert said the speed was 17 miles 540 yards per hour. When stopped the defendant said the speed according to his speedometer was just over 12 miles per hour."

The article then said that the defendant pleaded not guilty and an argument ensued as to the veracity of only using one stop watch, a method which had been discarded by the Metropolitan Police Force.

The only other smidgeon of information about him is that he married his first wife, the nineteen year-old Kathleen May Battersby, the daughter of the Garrison Sergeant Major at Pontefract Barracks, in 1926. Frederick's occupation was listed as being a 'merchant' and his address was, surprisingly enough, 'Lillie Villas', Worcester Park, the place where he had lodged as an eighteen year old, seven years previously.

No account of the people involved with the foundation of the Athletic club would be complete without mention of the strangely named [4]**Thomas Weeding Weeding**, who, apart from being the club's landlord, proved to be a true friend of the local sportsmen.

Thomas Weeding Baggallay was born in St. Pancras on June 11th 1847, the son of John Baggallay and Emma, the sister of another Thomas Weeding, who was a wealthy landowner in the Malden/Worcester Park/Cheam Common area. By the time of Thomas Weeding's death in 1856 he owned at least 37 small parcels of land locally in the Old Malden area which totalled over 125 acres. One of these fields was Skinner's Field which measured 7 acres. 2 rods and 25 poles. All this land eventually passed into the hands of Thomas Weeding Baggallay who, upon his 21st birthday changed his name by Royal Licence to Thomas Weeding Weeding, hence the strange repetitive name.

Weeding was 6 feet tall, an elegant individual with a commanding presence, who was educated at Marlborough College, where it was noted that he was a quite promising cricketer. In one of the school matches in 1864, for example, he was recorded in the press as hitting a fine, mind-boggling, drive for eight, in an innings of 65.

Upon leaving school in 1865 Thomas played cricket for Upper Tooting and the Quidnuncs, and had shown so much promise that, although only an 18 year old, he was invited to play for Surrey. He made his county debut in August 1865, when he played for Surrey versus Yorkshire and later that month turned out for Surrey versus an England side which was led by W. G. Grace. In October of the same year, he also played in a drawn match for an Eleven of England versus Twenty Two of Carshalton and District at the Alliance ground, Hackbridge.

Under the name of Thomas Baggallay, he was recorded as playing nine first class matches for Surrey, as a wicket-keeper, between 1865 to 1874. His only half century was the 68 runs that he scored, in front of a reported crowd of over 20,000, against the Australian Aboriginal touring team in their first match in England, at the Oval, on May 25th 1868.

Following Marlborough College, Thomas does not appear to have attended university, but trained as a solicitor before entering the service of Surrey County Council, where he eventually became Clerk of the Peace, a post that he held for over 30 years until he retired at the age of 80 in August 1927. In December 1927, he was honoured for his long service by being appointed the Deputy Lieutenant of the County.

For over 30 years Thomas had cycled from his home in Addleston to County Hall upon 'boneshakers' and 'penny-farthings' and was reputed to have covered over 300,000 miles. He kept detailed notes of his journeys, and reckoned that he had done over 40,000 miles upon the penny-farthing before it became too dangerous and he had replaced it with a 'safety' bike.

Apart from being a keen cyclist the shipping manifests show that Thomas was an avid traveller throughout his life. In 1876, he made his first recorded overseas journey when he visited St. Malo to marry his wife Alice Maude Elizabeth Brinkley, after whom Brinkley Road was presumably named. Thereafter the pair were great travellers as the records showed them crossing the Atlantic to Canada, New York, South America and the West Indies on numerous occasions in the first three decades of the twentieth century. The passenger manifests show that he visited Barbados on four occasions between 1924 and 1928.

At the age of 82 he was still an incredibly active person who attributed his good health to the five 'b's: bed (by 9.30 p.m.), bath, bicycle, beef and beer. It was this fitness which, in a way, led to his death, as he died as the result of falling off a chair upon which he was standing, in December 1929.

Although he was a high ranking official for Surrey County Council, as a landowner, Weeding seems to have had more sympathy with the local sportsmen than he did with the local council. Although Epsom Rural District Council had had to threaten him with a compulsory purchase for some of his land, he seemed more than willing to allow the footballers to use Skinner's Field for the 1920/21 season, before agreeing to lease the land to the newly formed Athletic Club for seven years. He not only leased the land to the club but also agreed to help with the cost of drainage. Although he was the landlord of the club, he was also instrumental in the formation of W.P.A.C.

[5]**Edwin Shrubb**, the first Hon. Secretary of W.P.A.C. and the first Match Secretary of the cricket section, must have been quite a positive, go-getting character, who overcame the handicap of a relatively poor background and limited education to rise from being a labourer to become a correspondence and transfer clerk working for an Investment Trust.

Edwin was born on 30th June 1884, the second of eight children, to Caroline and William Shrubb, a coachman and groom, who lived in Cowfold, Sussex. By 1901, however, he had left home and was following in his father's footsteps by working as a groom for a farmer in Chislehurst. His army records show that he was 5ft 7ins tall and weighed in at 140 pounds.

He married his wife, May, the daughter of an American born musician, in Paddington, on the 10th of August 1909, and by 1911, when he made his first appearance for Cheam Common C.C., he was no longer a groom but was by then working as a commercial clerk, and living with his wife, his sister Margaret, and his baby daughter,

"The defendant said that he was a Justice of the Peace for Somersetshire, Chairman of the General Committee of the Royal Automobile Club and Vice-Chairman of the club itself. He had been driving since the year after the Act came into force, and had not been stopped previously. The highest speed his speedometer reached in the control was 12½ miles an hour. He was driving a small 2-seater motor of 10-12 horsepower. He reflected no blame on the constable but knew that accurate timing was difficult."

The fact that Alfred Armitage was a J.P. and held high office in the R.A.C. since about 1906, held no sway with the local magistrate as he was fined 10 shillings with 10s 3d costs.

Apart from his two daughters Alfred also had two sons: Arthur Frank (b. 1895) who joined the Royal Navy as a thirteen year old before eventually rising to the rank of Commander: and Alfred Cecil (b. 1897) who sadly died in an accident on July 22nd 1915, whilst serving as a Second Lieutenant with the 1st Royal West Surrey Regiment in France.

Although Alfred Armitage's sporting experience seemed to have been limited to an occasional game of cricket for Cheam Common, his life experiences of having been a vicar and the director of a large steel works, plus his good social connections, probably made him the ideal person to lead the returning ex-servicemen to a bright new future. It is just a shame that his reign as President of the newly formed Athletic Club only lasted a couple of years as he, and his family, left the area in 1923.

****

The photograph above is of the pavilion in the late 1930s in its current position. It had initially been positioned in the corner of the ground near the 'Huntsman's Hall' in 1925, but was physically carried over a hundred yards by a working party of members one Sunday morning in 1937. The main body of the pavilion was probably the same one that was used by Cheam Common C.C. at their ground almost opposite the 'North End Tavern'. (Photo courtesy of John Fox)

Index

Hamilton, A. 249
Hammond, W. 236-237, 265
Hann, Arthur 121-123, 125
Hanning, James Henry Skrine 72, 79, 109, 128
Harrington, Wally 297
Harrison, Henry 125
Hawke, Lord 262
Hayes, Edgar 297
Hayes, Ernie 51
Haynes, George 145, 275-276
Hawkins, George 157-158, 160, 164, 174, 179-181
Head, Arthur 146, 275-276
Head, Ernest E. 238, 264-265
Head, Francis Lane 238, 241, 264-265
Head, Frederick D. 238, 241, 264-265
Healey, Frederick John 130
Healey, George Edmund 139, 266-267
Heasman, Henry 17
Heather, W. 166-168
Henderson, Robert 195, 219, 241-243
Herbert, B. 297
Highmore, Dorothy Rivers 87
Hilder, Thomas Paine 195-197, 200-201, 204, 206, 219-220
Hillman, Arthur Ernest 156-158, 160-164, 166-168, 170, 174, 176, 180, 185, 285, 288
Hillman, Harry Thomas 127
Hillman, Herbert 127, 131
Hilton, George (b. 1883) 174
Hipwell, Henry 40
Hitchman, William (b. 1813) 41
Holland, Florence Maud 67, 138, 175, 184, 186
Holland, Frederick Charles 67, 138, 148, 184-185, 284, 287-289, 292
Holland, John 67, 138, 144
Holland, John William 67, 138, 144, 147, 175-176, 184-186, 284, 287-289, 291
Holmes, Fred 142
Hook, William (b. 1857) 236-237, 264-265
Hopkins, Joseph William 67, 157-159, 162, 164, 166-167, 169-170, 174, 178, 260, 281-283
Hopkins, William George 69, 157-158, 160-162, 164, 166-168, 178
Hopwood, William James 261
Horne, Henry Warlters 58, 73, 95, 97-99
Hudson, Leonard Stranger 250, 257, 259-261, 268-274, 278, 280, 285-287, 291, 294
Hughes, Clifford 148, 285, 287-288, 290-292, 294-297
Hughes, Leonard 295-296
Hunt, William Holman 21-22, 37

'Hunter's Cottage ' 125, 127
'Huntsman's Hall' 59, 122, 193, 288, 304
Hurles, Edward Dudley 157-159, 173, 179, 183
Hyde, Alfred 122, 150
Johnson, Henry Elliott 60, 72, 86, 92-94, 97, 102, 128
Joscelyne, William 226, 230
Keene, John William 51, 242-243
Kempshall, Henry G. 21
Kempson, Matthew 26
Kent, Thomas 39
Keswick M.P., Henry 146, 256-257
Keswick M.P., William 173, 246
Killick, Alfred 234-235
Killick, William 234-235
Lawford, Herbert Fortesque 74, 96, 104
Lees, Walter Scott 242-243
Legge, R. 238, 264-265
Lewis, Rev. George Bridges 21, 198
Lloyd, Percy 165-168
Lock, A. 268-269, 271
Lock, Thomas 122, 128,
Lock, William 122
Lockwood, John 41, 45, 63, 235
Longman, George Henry 192-193, 195, 211-218
Longman, Henry Kerr 195, 214-217
Lubbock, Arthur 25
Lubbock, Sir John 30
Lubbock, Sir Frederick 25
Lucas, Rev. Herbert Hamilton 234
Luff, Frederick 63
Macey, Joseph 167, 183
Macey, William Francis 166, 183
Madge, Captain Charles Albert 120, 132, 150-152
Madge, Charles Henry 152
Madgwick, Mr. 16-17, 227
Malden Green Farm 154, 175
Manford, Dr. John Stanley 153
'Manor Farm' 60, 120, 150
Marsh, F. 174
Marshall, Alan 203-204, 222
Marshall, Alexander 36
Marshall, Arthur Edward 90
Martin, Henry (b 1811) 19
Martin, Henry (b. 1852) 65, 205, 241
Martin, John 65
Martyn, Orlando Bridgman 113-116
Martyn, William Edward 81, 101-102, 113-117
McKecknie, Cyril 250, 271, 273
Merriman, Hugh Maskelyne 131
Merriman, Septimus 93, 131

Worcester Park. — The Huntsmans Hall.